NIHILISM
IN
POSTMODERNITY

Nihilism in Postmodernity

Lyotard, Baudrillard, Vattimo

Ashley Woodward

The Davies Group, Publishers
Aurora, Colorado

© 2009 by Ashley Woodward. All rights reserved.

No part of the contents of this book may be reproduced, stored in an information retrieval system, or transcribed, in any form or by any means — electronic, digital, mechanical, photocopying, recording, or otherwise — without the express written permission of the publisher, and the holder of copyright. Submit all inquiries and requests to the publisher.: The Davies Group, Publishers, PO Box 440140, Aurora, CO 80044-0140

Library of Congress Cataloging-in-Publication Data

Woodward, Ashley.
  Nihilism in postmodernity : Lyotard, Baudrillard, Vattimo / Ashley Woodward.
    p. cm.
  Includes bibliographical references and index.
  ISBN 978-1-934542-08-8 (alk. paper)
  1. Nihilism (Philosophy) 2. Postmodernism. 3. Lyotard, Jean-François, 1924-1998. 4. Baudrillard, Jean, 1929-2007. 5. Vattimo, Gianni, 1936- I. Title.
  B828.3.W66 2009
  149'.8--dc22
                            2009009651

Cover: Green lines © Elena Klichnikova | Dreamstime.com

Printed in the United States of America
0123456789

Contents

Introduction	1
Nihilism	7
The postmodern	13
Nihilism and the postmodern	19
The economy of *this* writing	22
Overview	25
Chapter 1. The Advent of Nihilism	29
Nietzsche: the devaluation of the highest values	30
Sartre: existentialist nihilism	41
Heidegger: nihilism and metaphysics	54
Chapter 2. Postmodern Nihilism	75
Lyotard: neo-nihilism	75
Baudrillard: the nihilism of transparency	88
Vattimo: positive nihilism	102
Nihilism in postmodern theory	115
Chapter 3. Postmodernity and Nihilism	121
Theories of postmodernity	122
Lyotard: the end of metanarratives	
Baudrillard: hyperreality	
Vattimo: the secularisation of secularisation	
Nihilism at the end of history	159
Chapter 4. Negotiating Nihilism	169
The logic of difference	174
The politics of passivity	183
Postmodern responses to nihilism	188
Lyotard: Dissimulation	
Baudrillard: Seduction	
Vattimo: Verwindung	
Facing the abyss: the problem of contingency	222
Conclusion: the contemporary *mise-en abŷme*	241
Notes	249
Bibliography	293
Index	309

Acknowledgements

This book had its origins in a PhD thesis, and I must acknowledge the invaluable input of my principal supervisor, Aurelia Armstrong, and Associate Supervisors, Michelle Boulous Walker and A.T. Nuyen. I also wish to thank my two examiners, James Williams and David Webb, for their helpful advice and feedback. Thanks are also due to my friends and colleagues at the Melbourne School of Continental Philosophy, both for their general support and intellectual companionship over the years, and for comments on parts of this book. In particular, I wish to thank Jon Roffe, Matt Sharpe, and Jack Reynolds for their continued friendship and support. Thanks to my parents, Frank and Carmen Woodward, for their understanding and support. Finally, special thanks to Anna Szörényi, for everything.

I gratefully acknowledge permission to reprint here some material published in the following journal articles: "Nihilism and the Postmodern in Vattimo's Nietzsche," *Minerva: An Online Journal of Philosophy* 6 (2002): 48-66, http://www.ul.ie/~philos/vol6/nihilism.html; "Was Baudrillard a Nihilist?" *The International Journal of Baudrillard Studies* 5.1 (January 2008), http://www.ubishops.ca/BaudrillardStudies/vol5_1/v5-1-article12-woodward.html; and "The *Verwindung* of Capital: On the Philosophy and Politics of Gianni Vattimo," *Symposium: The Canadian Journal of Continental Philosophy* 13.1 (2009): 73-99.

Today, life is fast. It vaporizes morals. Futility suits the postmodern, for words as well as things. But that doesn't keep us from asking questions: how to live, and why? You're not done living because you chalk it up to artifice.
— Jean-François Lyotard[1]

Nihilism no longer wears the dark, Wagnerian, Spenglerian, fuliginous colours of the end of the century. It no longer comes from a weltanschauung of decadence nor from a metaphysical radicality born of the death of God and of all the consequences that must be taken from this death. Today's nihilism is one of transparency, and it is in some sense more radical, more crucial than in its prior and historical forms, because this transparency, this irresolution is indissolubly that of the system, and that of all the theory that still pretends to analyse it.
— Jean Baudrillard[2]

Nihilism is still developing, and it is impossible to draw any definitive conclusions about it. We can and we must, however, try to understand at what point it stands, in what way it concerns us, and what the choices and attitudes are that it asks us to decide upon.
— Gianni Vattimo[3]

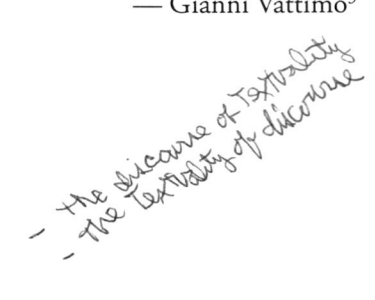

Introduction

The claims that Western civilisation is in decline and that there is a current "crisis of meaning" in contemporary culture are common.[1] These claims are often associated with the following kinds of observations. Life today, it is thought, is more complicated, less certain. The acceleration of cultural and technological changes that the twentieth century has witnessed seems to have left many people confused, unsure about their place in the world and the meaning of their lives. Dominant social institutions such as the Church and the traditional values associated with these institutions, which previously gave orientation to people's lives, seem to have been eroded by these changes. Furthermore, high rates of suicide in the world's most "developed" nations, especially amongst the young, are sometimes taken to suggest that meaning today is more difficult to find than in previous generations.[2] While these kinds of reflections on the contemporary problem of meaning are common, however, they often remain vague, signalling something like a general feeling of unease or disquiet and taking the form of claims that are difficult to clarify or justify. Friedrich Nietzsche and various thinkers following him have attempted to think these problems in a rigorous philosophical manner, using the term "nihilism" to refer to the decline of Western civilization and the difficulty of living a meaningful life in the horizon of this decline. While a contentious and problematic tradition, the discourse of nihilism provides a philosophical framework for thinking through the problem of meaning in the contemporary world that otherwise stands in danger of remaining too amorphous to analyse.

As a philosophical concern, nihilism asks how we are to understand the question of the meaningfulness of existence in the current epoch, and what philosophical positions—ontological, epistemological, ethical, political—this question compels us to decide upon. Towards the end of the nineteenth century, Nietzsche predicted the advent and development of nihilism over the course of the next two centuries.[3] If his prediction was accurate, at the beginning of the twenty-first century we are about half way through this historical process. How are we to understand the status of nihilism as we face it today? This book attempts to engage this question by bringing nihilism into contact with a recent, influential, and wide-ranging theory of the contemporary situation: the discourse of the "postmodern." To paraphrase Jean-François Lyotard in his influential study of the postmodern condition, my working hypothesis is that the status of nihilism is altered as societies enter what is known as the post-industrial age and cultures enter what is known as the postmodern age.[4]

Of course, the view that contemporary culture is afflicted with a crisis or decline is itself nothing new. Within the broad rubric of nihilism thought as the decline of the West in the course of modernisation, we can cite this concern in the writings of Johann Wolfgang von Goethe, Gustave Flaubert, and Charles Baudelaire (among others).[5] If we consider the resonance of this nihilistic theme with religious prophecies of the end of the world as punishment for decadence, we see history scattered with these notions of crisis and decline. However, it is arguably the case that as we have entered the historical epoch referred to as late modernity or postmodernity, changes in both the conditions of culture and the theory that attempts to gauge these changes mean that the nature of nihilism in the contemporary world has also changed. As well as continuities with the past, the contemporary epoch has a specificity that must be thought on its own terms. For nineteenth and early twentieth century thinkers who have taken up the problematic of nihilism, nihilism itself is intricately bound up with modernity understood as a philosophical problem. If modernity has "mutated" into postmodernity, then we should expect that the problem of nihilism has also altered its status. The nature of this changed status, however, has received little exploration, at least in Anglophone literature. Karen L. Carr—one of the few authors to examine the changing status of nihilism in postmodernity—justifies her book, *The Banalization of Nihilism*, as follows:

> Without exception nihilism is portrayed as a monolithic phenomenon which has not changed since its discovery. The present work is an attempt to offer a larger picture of the history of nihilism, showing both that the appraisal of nihilism has changed over the last century, and how it has changed. Thus it seeks to begin to fill an important gap in scholarly reflections on the modern period.[6]

This present work aims to contribute further to the important task of filling the gap that Carr identifies, through a comparative and critical examination of neglected work in this area by prominent "Continental" philosophers.

On the other hand, it might be objected that the discourse of the postmodern was a phenomenon of the nineteen-eighties, widely out of favour today and hence not new *enough* to give any genuine insight into our contemporary situation. While it is true that such perceptions are common in the current academic context, I believe it is instructive to recall a comment Lyotard made in the mid-eighties, to the effect that people would tire of discussing the postmodern before anyone had determined what it means. Arguably, postmodernism was received with the aura of a fad in the nineteen-eighties and early –nineties, and has fallen out of favour for no deeper reason than the weariness with which fads are frequently followed. Moreover, it is becoming increasingly acknowledged that the initial receptions of many Continental philosophers frequently associated with the postmodern misrepresented their thought, often assimilating their views to simplistic versions of epistemic scepticism and metaphysical anti-realism.[7] Indeed, it is often only after the initial burst of enthusiasm for particular ideas that they can be seen in a clearer and more sober light. Against prominent (but by no means totalising) tides of intellectual fashion, then, I assert that postmodern philosophy can both now profitably be reconsidered after its initial up-take and decline in interest in the Anglophone academy, and that it affords depths of insight that not only remain relevant, but have yet to be fully understood or played out. This latter point, as I will show throughout, becomes particularly apparent when the discourse of the postmodern is understood in relation to that of nihilism. Considered in this light, the postmodern appears as a concept designating an epochal shift, a change at the deepest levels of our culture, which canot be subordinated to the fashions of one or two decades.

While several other books have also explored the issue of nihilism in relation to postmodernity,[8] most have done so in a peripheral manner, and none have given significant attention to three major theorists of postmodernity who also deal centrally with the issue of nihilism: Jean-François Lyotard, Jean Baudrillard, and Gianni Vattimo. It is my view that each of these thinkers contributes significantly and in an original way to understanding the postmodern transformation of nihilism, and are ignored to the peril of our understanding of the meaning of nihilism in the current situation. Moreover, each of these thinkers grapples with the problem of how best to mitigate the nihilism of the postmodern situation, and the novel strategies they invent are invaluable for developing a response to meaninglessness appropriate to the new situation in which we find ourselves.

Jean-François Lyotard (1924–1998) was professor of philosophy at the University of Paris VIII, Vincennes, as well as holding appointments at many universities outside France. He was associated with French post-structuralism, and was instrumental in disseminating the idea of the postmodern through his 1979 book *The Postmodern Condition*. Lyotard is best known for his work in this period, while his earlier book *Libidinal Economy* (1974)[9] is usually either ignored entirely or dismissed out of hand as a failed experiment, an example of the excesses of post-May '68 intellectual turmoil (an attitude the later Lyotard himself endorsed). Recently, however, Lyotard scholar James Williams has called for a revaluation of *Libidinal Economy*[10], and here I follow his lead in suggesting that Lyotard's "libidinal" philosophy contributes in important ways to a reconfiguration of nihilism in relation to recent theoretical concerns. In *Libidinal Economy* and associated essays, Lyotard explores the Nietzschen problematic of nihilism through a novel employment of Freudian psychoanalytic theory, a critical analysis of structuralism, semiotics, and Marxism, and stylistic experimentation. While I shall employ Lyotard's later work on the postmodern as an essential reference for our understanding of the current situation, it is the earlier work that provides the best treatment of nihilism and with which I will therefore be primarily concerned.

Jean Baudrillard (1929–2007) taught sociology at the University of Nanterre from 1966 to 1987, and is known internationally for his unique writings on contemporary culture. Like Lyotard, Baudrillard is associated with the post-structuralist strand of French thought and often cited as a key theorist of the postmodern. While Baudrillard's explicit uses of the rhetoric of nihilism are occasional, much of his mature thought may be read in terms of such concerns. His unique contribution to the theorisation of nihilism in postmodernity consists in his focus on the contemporary media- and information-saturated state of culture and society, as well as a keenly reflexive sense of the nihilism of contemporary theory. While the presence of nihilism in Baudrillard's thought is noted by various commentators, he is typically presented as a passive nihilist who offers little of positive value towards responding to the problem of meaninglessness in contemporary life. In the present work I challenge and complexify this reading, showing that Baudrillard's treatment of nihilism is highly ambiguous and suggests positive potentialities that have hitherto been given little recognition.[11]

Gianni Vattimo (1936–) is one of Italy's foremost contemporary philosophers, but is much less well known in the Anglophone world than French post-structuralists such as Lyotard and Baudrillard. Given this, a more extensive introduction to Vattimo is called for. After obtaining a degree in classical studies (the *liceo classico*), Vattimo completed a doctorate at the University of Turin under the supervision of Luigi Pareyson, Italy's foremost existentialist philosopher. He then studied at the University of Heidelberg with Hans-Georg Gadamer and Karl Löwith, and began to gain international recognition with a well-received paper given at the Royaumont colloquium on Heidegger in 1966. Vattimo succeeded Pareyson as Professor of Aesthetics at Turin, and since 1982 has held the position of Professor of Theoretical Philosophy at the same institution. He has been a visiting scholar at numerous universities, including some (such as Stanford) in the Anglophone world. In addition to his reputation as an academic philosopher, Vattimo is popularly known in Italy and Europe for his political activities (he was a member of the European Parliament from 2000 to 2005) and his regular contributions to newspapers such as *La Stampa*.

Vattimo has translated Hans-Georg Gadamer's *Truth and Method* into Italian, and is the leading promoter of philosophical hermeneutics in Italy. He has also devoted several books and numerous essays to the interpretation of Nietzsche and Heidegger, and has brought the theme of nihilism from these thinkers together with hermeneutics and the idea of the postmodern to formulate his own philosophy of "weak thought" (*il pensiero debole*), which has coalesced into a general trend in Italian philosophy (much as Jacques Derrida's deconstruction has on a wider scale). More than any other contemporary philosopher, Vattimo has staked out the connection between nihilism and the postmodern, and argued for a new understanding of nihilism in postmodernity.[12]

My examination of Lyotard's and Baudrillard's treatments of nihilism here seeks to highlight the value and importance of the post-structuralist contribution to this problematic, which has received surprisingly little attention. Furthermore, this examination aims to clarify the connection between post-structuralist thought and nihilism that is frequently alluded to, usually in a predominantly negative way that gestures towards the undermining of theoretical, ethical, and political normativity in post-structuralist discourse. I am concerned to show that it is the problem of nihilism itself that has led certain strands of post-structuralist thought to pursue antifoundational strategies rather than normative positions, and to show how these strategies contribute towards a positive response to nihilism. It is my further hope that this book will contribute to the philosophical literature on nihilism by serving as an introduction to the scene of contemporary Italian philosophy, which is perhaps the most fecund ground of debate concerning the Nietzschean problematic of nihilism in contemporary philosophy. The

Italian scene has received virtually no attention in the Anglophone literature on nihilism despite the important contributions of this tradition. While I restrict my discussion to Vattimo, his work may act as a point of entrance to the wider philosophical debate in Italian philosophy.[13]

As well as contributing to the literature on nihilism by examining it in the light of Continental philosophy and postmodernism, it is my hope that this study will in turn illuminate Continental philosophy and postmodernism through an analysis of nihilism. Nihilism is a problematic that acts as a guiding thread through diverse strands of Continental thought: Nietzsche, Heidegger, existentialism, structuralism, post-structuralism, contemporary Italian philosophy; to a lesser extent Marxist and Hegelian dialectics, psychoanalysis, hermeneutics and Critical Theory. Furthermore, nihilism ties these strands of philosophy, which at times reach points of extreme abstraction and abstruseness, to a very practical concern: how to live, and why? By bringing the concerns expressed in these diverse forms of thought into contact with this practical concern, they are given a philosophical meaning and value that is perhaps at times in danger of being occluded. Furthermore, the often hazy concept of the postmodern may be given sharper focus by examining it through the lens of nihilism. Nihilism is often very loosely associated with the postmodern, with the effect that the postmodern, nihilism, and the relationship between the two concepts remains vague. I am concerned here with bringing these concepts into tighter focus, in the hope that, in illuminating each other, they will shed light on our "current situation."[14]

Most significantly, the three thinkers considered here all offer *responses* to nihilism in postmodernity, and beyond achieving an increased understanding of nihilism in the contemporary world, my aim here is to explore the parameters of how best to respond to the problem of meaninglessness that besets us today. According to the theories examined here, the postmodern situation itself places specific restrictions on our ability to respond to nihilism. Lyotard, Baudrillard, and Vattimo each attempt to calibrate their responses to the problem of meaning according to the particular needs of the current situation. I explore the novel responses to nihilism these postmodern thinkers offer, and assess the value and success of these responses.

This introductory chapter provides an initial clarification of the basic concepts I am concerned with, firstly by giving an outline of the concept of nihilism that indicates its main types and situates it within the philosophical tradition. I then approach the problematic and contested concept of the postmodern, indicating its specific usefulness to this project and clarifying the idea of a postmodern philosophy, as distinct from other cultural expressions of the postmodern sensibility, by outlining several of its distinctive themes. This is followed by a brief history of the association of the concepts of nihilism and the postmodern, which shows that this association is long-standing and far from arbitrary. I then address some of the specific methodological problems that a study of nihilism and the postmodern faces, given that both discourses call into question the representational model of thought and traditional modes of academic writing. Having thus situated the problem under consideration, I provide a brief summary overview of the chapters that follow.

Nihilism

Nihilism is a term that is employed in a variety of ways, often ambiguously, both in philosophy and in wider contexts. The root of the term "nihilism" is the Latin *nihil*, meaning "nothing"; it carries with it the obvious connotations of nothingness and negation, and has been employed in a wide variety of ways to indicate philosophies or ways of thought, belief, or practice that primarily negate or reduce to the point of leaving nothing of value. The specific ways in which the term will be used in this study will become clear in the discussions of particular philosophers' theories of nihilism, but the ambiguity of the term, even when restricted to its philosophical uses, calls for some initial orientation and clarification.

Nihilism, understood very generally as a negative attitude towards life, can be seen as a perennial human problem that is evident in Western thought at least since ancient Greece.[15] As I have already suggested, however, my concern is with the problem of nihilism as it is thought in the European tradition of philosophy since Nietzsche; it is this tradition from which the postmodern theorists of nihilism take their bearings. The source of this tradition can be traced to the first philosophical use of the term "nihilism,"[16] which is usually attributed to Friedrich Heinrich Jacobi's 1799 text, "Open Letter to Fichte."[17] Here, Jacobi accuses Johann Gottlieb Fichte of nihilism in his idealist philosophy. Briefly, Fichtean idealism follows Immanuel Kant's critique of the limits of knowledge, and according to Fichte, we cannot know things in themselves or the ground of the self. All we can know is the ego, which is merely a product of the free power of the imagination.[18] The following passage indicates the profound nihilism Jacobi sees in Fichte's philosophy. Jacobi writes:

> If the highest upon which I can reflect, what I can contemplate, is my empty and pure, naked and mere ego, with its autonomy and freedom: then rational self-contemplation, then rationality is for me a curse—I deplore my existence.[19]

With Jacobi we see the beginnings of the idea that a philosophical position can lead to a mood of despair, and a criticism of this position on that basis. Nihilism, in the tradition that extends from Jacobi, is a concept that suggests that certain philosophical positions or beliefs about the world negate so much that is of value in life that the desirability of living is called into question. Nihilism is a concept that indicates a (dis)connection between abstract philosophical concepts and the practical desire and necessity of living a meaningful life. As a philosophical problematic, it asks us to think about philosophical concepts in a way that is not simply technical or abstract, but that asks about their ramifications on our perceptions of the value and meaningfulness of existence. Moreover, as becomes particularly evident in Nietzsche's treatment of nihilism, nihilistic interpretations of the world are not restricted to the abstract concepts of academic philosophy, but thoroughly permeate human culture. Nihilism asks us to think about what forms of thought and what interpretations of the world are commensurate with a positive valuation of existence, and what forms are detrimental to such a valuation. Moreover, what are the criteria for such judgements? I would argue that even more abstract uses of the term in philosophy—such as the tendency to apply it to any doctrine that denies the existence of something—carries with it these existential ramifications in the critical connotation it has. "Nihilism" is most often an accusation, a criticism, not a neutral description of a doctrine or position.

Briefly summarising the history of the philosophical analysis of nihilism since Jacobi, Japanese philosopher Keiji Nishitani writes that "…the current of nihilism…springs from the decline of Hegelian philosophy and runs through Feuerbach (with a branch off to Kierkegaard), Stirner, and Schopenhauer to Nietzsche and Heidegger."[20] Further early twentieth century philosophers in this tradition include existentialists such as Gabriel Marcel, Karl Jaspers, Jean-Paul Sartre, and Albert Camus, as well as German scholars Ernst Jünger and Karl Löwith. While this lineage, very briefly summarised here, situates my concern with nihilism within the European tradition, I will limit my scope to considerations of nihilism since Nietzsche. Several recent works, as well as classic works such as Löwith's, seek to understand the present meaning of nihilism by illuminating its pre-Nietzschean genealogy.[21] While recognising the importance of this task, it lies outside the scope of my current project. My concern is to bring to light and assess theories of nihilism that appear in the latter part of the twentieth century, all of which take Nietzsche as a primary inspiration. While it is important to indicate the broader historical span within which this tradition of thought is situated, it is not necessary to delve into the pre-Nietzschean history of nihilism in order to appreciate these theories' continuities with, and divergences from, those theories that predominated in the late nineteenth and early twentieth centuries.

It is common for works on nihilism to introduce the concept by means of a typology of the various different meanings that the term can have.[22] Typologies of nihilism that accord with standard philosophical categories are common; we might distinguish epistemological, metaphysical, moral, political, and existential kinds of nihilism. I am predominantly concerned here with existential nihilism, the negation of the value of life. This type of nihilism concerns the problem of the felt meaninglessness of contemporary life with which I began this introduction. Rather than treating existential nihilism as an isolated problem, however, I prefer to characterise it as a *dimension* of nihilism, which I suggest should be understood as a holistic phenomenon. In the European tradition, nihilism is often understood as a multifaceted phenomenon in which one particular type cannot be entirely separated from other types. For Heidegger, to take just one example, existential nihilism is inextricably tied to ontological nihilism, understood in a specific sense (see chapter one below). Furthermore, the theorists of nihilism engaged with in this study often develop their own unique typologies that must be explained along with their rich and complex bodies of work. The necessary distinctions that will allow a sophisticated consideration of nihilism in postmodernity will therefore be developed gradually in the course of this investigation. For these reasons, I will forgo the practise of providing a generic typology of nihilism as an introduction to the concept, and simply indicate that my primary concern is with existential nihilism, allowing that this cannot be thought in isolation from other manifestations and forms of nihilism.

The specification of existential nihilism as my primary interest requires some further clarification, however: the term "existential nihilism" must be distinguished from the term "existential*ist* nihilism." In order to provide the necessary background for understanding the postmodern transformation of nihilism, this study deals in part with theories of nihilism developed within the context of existentialist philosophy, in particular that of Sartre. I shall use the term "existential*ist* nihilism" to refer to these theories. Existentialist nihilism configures nihilism in a particular way, typically in terms of philosophical themes such as individualism and subjectivism. I shall use the term "existent*ial* nihilism" in a broader and more inclusive way, to indicate that kind of nihilism that is concerned with the meaning and value of life or existence. Terms such as "meaning," "value," "life" and "existence," as well as "existential nihilism," remain vague, but this vagueness can be more positively characterised as an "openness" that allows them to be given specificity in different ways by the different philosophical orientations of the writers under consideration. In Vattimo's work, for instance, existence is thought in terms of hermeneutic ontology, where it appears as a play of interpretations. With Lyotard, life is considered in terms of a Freudian-inspired libidinal economy. This deliberate openness of "existential nihilism" is particularly important because the popularity of existentialism in the early-to-middle part of the twentieth century has strongly equated—at least in many people's minds—the possibility of thinking about the meaningfulness of life philosophically with a necessary acceptance of certain existentialist themes, such as freedom of the will or the primacy of the subject. An important part of this project is to show that the ways in which the meaningfulness of life is addressed have changed in line with recent changes in theory, and the possibility of thinking about existential nihilism is not dependent on an existential*ist* framework.

Terms such as "value," "meaning," "significance," and so on, are particularly problematic in the context of a book such as this, because such terms tend to be used in differing, technical ways by the different thinkers discussed. Not only does what counts as existentially meaningful, valuable, or significant differ from thinker to thinker, but these terms themselves are sometimes used negatively, being understood as implicated in nihilism. For example, Heidegger criticises the very notion of "value" as nihilistic, while "significance" etymologically alludes to "signification," which is implicated by Lyotard's and Baudrillard's criticisms of semiotics. However, there appears to be no uncompromised alternative term, and such terms thus remain unavoidable given my concerns here. Unless otherwise specified by context, I will use such terms to indicate that which nihilism denies or negates, or which stands as a positive alternative or response to nihilism. I shall also use the Nietzschean term *life-affirmation* in this regard (a term that might itself be criticised from a Heideggerian perspective).

A final terminological clarification is in order here. While having foregone a detailed typological classification of nihilism, I do wish to introduce a typological distinction between what I shall call "reductive" nihilism and "abyssal" nihilism. As I stipulate these terms, they refer to what I understand as the two main types of existential nihilism, types that may arguably be identified in all the theories of nihilism examined here. This distinction will facilitate interpretation of the various theories of nihilism examined, and be crucial to the assessment of postmodern responses to nihilism with which I conclude this book. Reductive and abyssal nihilism are two "poles" to which nihilism tends. That is, they are two, apparently contrary, ways in which existential meaning seems to be negated. I shall use the term "reductive nihilism" to indicate those forms of nihilism in which meaning is negated through a reduction of some sort. Often, this reduction also involves an abstraction that isolates those elements of a phenomenon that can be rationally schematised or expressed in a theory or discourse. Those elements that cannot be so abstracted are negated, either with respect to their existence, or simply their value. Reductive nihilism is often associated with philosophical reductionism, where phenomena are construed as "nothing but" whatever is expressed in the philosophical theory of those phenomena. For many of the theorists examined below, nihilism follows from reductionism because what gets left out of the reduction is precisely what makes life existentially valuable.

On the other hand, I use the term "abyssal nihilism" to indicate the negation of meaning that takes place when the field of existence becomes too wide and indeterminate, when there are no criteria of evaluation or guidelines for choosing between different possibilities. This form of nihilism is often expressed in accusations of epistemological, moral, or political nihilism, where the theory in question is accused of containing no coherent ground or normative framework for assessing knowledge claims, deciding moral values, or taking politically efficacious action. I choose the term "abyssal" nihilism in reference to the figure of the abyss as it is used in the works of Kierkegaard, Nietzsche, and others, to liken the experience of the inability to choose existential values to the feeling of plunging into a bottomless pit.[23] At times, I also refer to this form of nihilism as *contingency*, a term Sartre sometimes employs. This term expresses the radical absence of any necessity governing the meaning and value of human life; it reflects the non-existence of anything that could ground meaning in a secure foundation, such as God, an objectively meaningful structure of the world, or human nature. In the theories examined here, this form of nihilism is often associated with a delegitimation of traditional structures (both social and theoretical) that previously provided frameworks for meaning and value. This "abyssal" condition of being unable to choose values, beliefs or courses of action negates the value of existence because it undermines the structure and direction that may be taken as minimal conditions for a meaningful life. This abyssal form of nihilism, I suggest, is what critics of postmodern theory often have in mind when they accuse it of being nihilistic – by calling into question the powers of reason, it is claimed, postmodernism undermines the normative framework of modernity and leaves us without the resources for constructing a new normative framework. (In contrast to this understanding of the relationship between nihilism and reason, postmodern theorists themselves often claim that it is the modern hegemony of reason that inculcates a pervasive *reductive* nihilism.)

Despite the fact that the reductive and abyssal forms of nihilism appear to inhabit opposite poles, they may in fact be seen as complimentary, and as developing together in modernity and postmodernity according to a coherent logical unfolding. This complementarity is clearly indicated by Simon Critchley in his following summary of the development of nihilism in modern culture:

> 1. [T]he values of modernity or Enlightenment do not connect with the fabric of moral and social relations, with the stuff of everyday life…The moral values of Enlightenment (…) lack any effectivity, any connection to social praxis.
> 2. However, not only do the moral values of Enlightenment fail to connect with the fabric of moral and social relations, but—worse still—they lead instead to the progressive degradation of those relations through processes that we might call, with Weber, rationalization, with Marx, capitalization, with Adorno and Horkheimer, instrumental rationality, and with Heidegger, the oblivion of Being.[24]

In this passage, Critchley outlines the way in which the reductive processes of abstraction and rationalisation degrade the social relations and structures that provide meaning and value. Reductive nihilism contributes to the development of abyssal nihilism by undermining the frameworks that have traditionally provided the possibility of a meaningful existence. As we shall see in detail below, each of the theorists of nihilism considered here develops the themes of reductive and abyssal nihilism, and the dynamic between them, in their own specific terms.

The postmodern

"Postmodernism" is a highly contested theory of the contemporary. Moreover, as Fredric Jameson notes, the concept of the postmodern 'is not merely contested, it is also internally conflicted and contradictory.'[25] This fact has led some commentators to suggest that the idea of the postmodern itself is hopelessly incoherent.[26] However, this "openness" of the concept, this lack of a settled and secure definition, can also be thought of as an advantage for the attempt to theorise the "current situation." The concept of the postmodern is sufficiently broad to encompass many contemporary trends in academic thought as well as society and the arts: it is a concept that captures diverse aspects of culture within the horizon of a general theory of the contemporary situation. More specifically for my purposes, it allows links to be made between various contemporary discussions of the problem of nihilism, and allows these philosophical discussions to be situated within a wider historical and cultural analysis. Lyotard, Baudrillard, and Vattimo all associate their thought with the analysis of the contemporary epoch as postmodern, and their theories of nihilism may be linked with the specificity of the contemporary situation through the general rubric of the postmodern. The idea of the postmodern thus provides a framework in which to conceptualise the recent transformations the discourse of nihilism has undergone, and to link these transformations with broader cultural trends.

While the general terms employed in the discourse of the postmodern are loose and contested, I shall follow a common practice by using them in the following ways. "Modernity" and "postmodernity" refer to historical epochs. "Modernism" and "postmodernism" refer to the theory and cultural practice associated with these epochs. The terms "the modern" and "the postmodern" refer generally to either or both. The question of the meaning of the *post*modern raises the question of the meaning of the *modern*, itself a notoriously vague concept.[27] Arguably, the concept of the modern acquires coherence in two principal ways. One is by contrast with the ancient, the classical, or the "premodern;" the other is by contrast with the postmodern. The use of the term "modern," Jürgen Habermas tells us, can be dated to the late fifth century, when it characterised the Christian present in opposition to the Roman and pagan past. It was similarly used during the twelfth century and in the late seventeenth century, to distinguish the contemporary age from earlier times.[28] On the other hand, the concept of the modern and of a historical modernity can be differentiated from the postmodern. Theories that posit a relatively recent historical rupture that separates the modern age from the contemporary or postmodern age characterise modernity and the modern in ways that will not necessarily be contiguous with the ways modernists themselves characterised their own age. My prime focus in this study is on the postmodern; I will not attempt a characterisation of that nebulous notion of "the modern" beyond those characterisations that emerge in the specific theories of the postmodern under consideration.

The discourse of postmodernism maintains an ambiguous relation with historical periodisation: a common claim of postmodern theory is that history cannot be neatly compartmentalised into distinct periods, yet at the same time there is a common tendency among theorists of the postmodern to date the end of modernity and the beginning of postmodernity. This ambiguity will be discussed in detail in relation to Vattimo's engagement with Lyotard's theory of postmodernity in chapter three. For the moment, however, we may take a "naïve" approach towards this issue and indicate the historical period to which the term "postmodernity" commonly refers. Although alternative dating systems have been proposed by theorists of the postmodern, a common approach suggests that we make a distinction between the period from the Enlightenment to about 1950—designated "modernity"—and 1950 to the present—designated "postmodernity."[29] Alternative periodisations tend to place the beginning of postmodernity earlier; the period after the end of the Second World War to the present is identified as postmodernity in most theories.[30] The claim is made that social and cultural conditions have changed dramatically enough in recent times to warrant such a distinction.

Alex Callinicos usefully suggests that the postmodern can be broadly understood through the convergence of three distinct cultural trends: the arts, philosophy, and sociology.[31] In each of these trends, the postmodern is thought as breaking with, or proceeding from but transforming in significant ways, themes and practices that are thought of as modern. In the arts, postmodernism refers to styles that are distinguished from the modernist experiments of the early twentieth century avant-gardes, as well as from earlier styles in the history of art. In philosophy, postmodernism has become synonymous with post-structuralism, but also encompasses other forms of philosophy that question central themes of modern philosophy, such as the emancipatory role of reason, the epistemological status of science, or the epistemic centrality of the subject. In sociology, the idea of a postmodern state of society has built upon the concept of the post-industrial, the notion that the primary mode of production in "advanced" societies is no longer industrial, but informational.[32] This transition to a knowledge-based economy is thought to have a profound effect on social organisation and class relationships. Taken together, these three cultural trends suggest that the postmodern signals a broad rethinking of the goals, values, and principles that have animated Western culture since the Enlightenment.

Of the three cultural trends that characterise the postmodern, my focus here is on philosophy. Postmodern philosophy should be understood, however, as one cultural expression of a widespread postmodern sensibility. Manfred Frank writes that postmodern philosophy "…seems to reflect very accurately the current disaffection with government and national politics, as well as a certain weariness with civilization. The sceptical attitude toward rationality is in fact nothing but a particular manifestation of a much more widespread discontent experienced by many in the emotional climate of the whole Western world."[33] As I have indicated above, it is this very pervasiveness of postmodernism across culture that allows the analysis of nihilism in the context of the postmodern to link the discourse of nihilism with a comprehensive theorisation of the contemporary situation. The links between postmodern philosophy and the postmodern moment in other aspects of culture, the arts, and society has already been widely made, and there is no need for me to reproduce those analyses here.[34] I shall focus on philosophical theories of the postmodern, engaging only occasionally with the discourses of other disciplines.[35]

Postmodern philosophy has its own periodisation and its own thematics defining a break with the tradition of modern philosophy. René Descartes is widely regarded as the father of modern philosophy, and the great philosophers of the eighteenth and nineteenth centuries, such as Kant, Hegel and Marx, are characterised as modern. Modernity, in philosophical terms, is characterised as that period extending from the European Enlightenment and that is marked by its ideal, which (simplifying greatly) may be summarised as progress towards social emancipation through the development of reason. Postmodern philosophy takes its direction from critiques of modernity and the modern ideal of progress through reason, particularly those of Nietzsche and Heidegger. Indeed, these two German philosophers might well be considered the "grandfathers" of postmodernism. French post-structuralist philosophy in general has become associated with the postmodern: thinkers as diverse as Lyotard, Baudrillard, Jacques Lacan, Michel Foucault, Gilles Deleuze and Jacques Derrida have been taken under this rubric, and post-structuralism is often characterised as the philosophical branch of postmodernism.

Additionally, thinkers outside of France have taken up similar themes and characterised their own philosophies as postmodern (Vattimo in Italy and Richard Rorty in America are two prominent examples). While the approaches of these thinkers vary widely, it is possible to draw out points of contact through the issues on which they break with various dominant themes of modern philosophy. In these introductory remarks, I wish to signpost five themes that I believe are the most important in characterising postmodern philosophy. These themes allow the particular changes and developments I will chart in the discourse of nihilism to be referred back to the rubric of postmodern philosophy, and thus provide an orienting framework through which the postmodern "transformation" of nihilism may be approached. The five themes that I suggest represent the most significant points of departure from philosophical modernism are the critique of reason, the critique of the subject, anti-humanism, the end of history, and difference.

The critique of reason

Vincent Descombes writes that, "according to the most considerable authorities, for once in agreement—Hegel and Heidegger for example—the pursuit of a truth that has the character of absolute certainty marks the inauguration of modern philosophy."[36] This desire for truth as absolute certainty is the ideal of Enlightenment rationalism, neatly encapsulated by Frank: "'Enlightenment' means to transform anything merely posited, anything merely believed, into objects of secure knowledge."[37] In modern philosophy there is a link between the idea of finding a new, secure foundation for reason and the possibility of social emancipation: if we wipe away the errors of the past and make the world more rational, it is believed, we will alleviate the suffering associated with the human condition, making life both more secure and more free. This modern image of rationality has had its opponents since its inception: it has been argued that the rationalisation of society leads to alienation and social control rather than emancipation, and that the modern emphasis on reason tends to illegitimately devalue emotion, sensation, and all that is deemed to be the "other" of reason.[38] Postmodern philosophy is arguably characterised by a *radicalisation* of this critique of reason in that it rejects the certitude of truth and the foundational character of reason *in toto* (whereas earlier critiques often attempted to find more apodictic truths, more secure foundations). Comparing post-structuralism and weak thought (the two exemplary forms of postmodern philosophy I am interested in here), Giovanna Borradori writes that

> poststructuralist theories in general embody the unequivocal reality that the 'crisis of reason' can no longer be understood in terms of a 'bad truth' for which a 'better truth' can be substituted… 'Weak thought' is similar to French poststructuralism in its opposition to the effort to give the human sciences 'another' or 'alternative' foundation…[39]

The critique of the subject

The postmodern critique of the subject is connected with the radicalisation of the critique of reason in so far as it undermines Descartes's attempt to find a foundation for the certitude of truth in the knowing subject. The self-consciousness of this subject is an indubitable certitude upon which a structure of certain knowledge might safely be erected. Descombes summarises this theme:

> 'Subject' (or 'suppositum') is the name given to a be-ing whose *identity* is sufficiently stable for it to bear, in every sense of the word, (sustain, serve as a foundation for, withstand), change or modification. The subject remains the same, while accidental qualities are altered. Since Descartes, the most subjective of all subjects is the one which is certain of its identity, the *ego* of *ego cogito*. The quality of subjectivity is thus confined to consciousness.[40]

Simply put, the postmodern critique of the subject attempts to undermine the subject's epistemic priority by arguing that it is not transparent to itself (and thus is not the master of meaning and cannot ground the whole of knowledge). Furthermore, postmodern philosophy criticises the common modernist notion that the epistemic subject is transcendent to the world, occupying a neutral position *sub specie aeternitatis*.[41] *Contra* this, it is argued that the subject is itself constituted by its situation in the world, and its perspective is limited by this situation (which constitutes a rejection of the idea that the subject can take a "view from nowhere"[42] and thus have access to universal truths).

Anti-humanism

Postmodern philosophy is associated with certain anti-humanist philosophical currents in twentieth century philosophy. Philosophical humanism takes human being—in whatever way it is defined—as a universal standard for knowledge, and thus as a foundation for reason and truth. The postmodern pathology of humanism asserts that it is simply a secularised form of monotheistic religion: it puts Man in the place vacated by God. Postmodern philosophy rejects the idea that "the human" can act as a stable ground for knowledge in its critique of the view of a generalised conception of the human as a universal subject of history. Rather, the idea of the human is shown to be a historically and culturally contingent one, most famously by Foucault in *The Order of Things*:

> One thing in any case is certain: man is neither the oldest nor the most constant problem that has been posed for human knowledge. Taking a relatively short chronological sample within a restricted geographical area—European culture since the sixteenth century—one can be certain that man is a recent invention within it…If those arrangements were to disappear as they appeared…then one can certainly wager that man would be erased, like a face drawn in sand at the edge of the sea.[43]

The end of history

Arguably, the end of history is *the* most clearly defining thesis of postmodern philosophy. Vattimo writes that "one of the most important points on which the descriptions of the postmodern condition agree—no matter how different they are from other points of view—is the consideration of postmodernity in terms of 'the end of history.'"[44] The postmodern thesis of the end of history is to be radically distinguished from the Hegelian conception of the end of history, in which historical development reaches a logical culmination. The postmodern idea of the end of history is a critique of the idea of history, prominent in modernity and exemplified by Hegelian and Marxist dialectics, in which reason unfolds historically, progressing towards an ever-greater state of enlightenment. The postmodern position is that we can no longer believe in a unilinear and teleological philosophy of history or in the notion of progress through reason. This myth of the philosophy of history has been exploded both by the catastrophic events of the twentieth century that belie the idea of progress and by the collapse of Western historiographical narratives into a multitude of localised stories told from different perspectives and by different cultures.

Difference

The modern images of rationality, the subject, Man, and history are all arguably undergirded by the logical principle of identity, A = A. In modern thought, identity acts as a principle that grounds thought and organises its elements around a central axis. The subject, in being conscious of itself, is self-identical; it is the one thing that maintains its identity without change, and can thus act as a secure ground for knowledge. The idea of humanism operates by identifying common elements amongst different individuals, races, and cultures in order to establish a universal standard. This universal standard only acknowledges a particular set of qualities as legitimately human, disqualifying various individuals, races, cultures, genders, sexualities, and behaviours. The dialectical progress of history operates by synthesising opposites in a higher unity, finding identity where there seemed to be only difference. In these ways, the principle of identity is seen by postmodern philosophers to underlie the modernist conception of reason, which operates principally by establishing identities and excluding differences that might upset the integrity of those identities. Against identity, postmodern philosophy attempts to develop a form of thought that will do justice to difference without subordinating it to a prior identity. Where modern thought thinks difference on the basis of identity (that which is different is that which is non-identical), postmodern thought thinks identity as derivative from a prior difference (identity is a generality about things that in fact differ).[45] The principle of difference underlies postmodern positions on epistemology, ontology, ethics, and politics, enabling a way of thinking that is not dominated by the modern image of reason.

Nihilism and the postmodern

There is a longstanding association between the concepts of the postmodern and of nihilism. Since I am concerned here with elucidating the connection between these concepts, it will be instructive to briefly note the history of this association in order to show that it is far from arbitrary: the discourse of the postmodern has had nihilistic resonances from some of the earliest uses of the term. Given this association, the current link often made between nihilism and the postmodern is more than accidental; in a historical light, the relationship between nihilism and the postmodern appears highly motivated. While the idea of the postmodern achieved prominence in the nineteen-seventies and –eighties, the term originated much earlier.[46] Throughout the twentieth century, various historians, sociologists, and literary critics have employed the idea of the postmodern in ways that resonate strongly with nihilism. Significantly, the first use of the term to designate a historical epoch—Rudolf Pannwitz's 1917 *Die Krisis der europäischen Kultur*[47]—is explicitly informed by Nietzsche's theory of nihilism. Pannwitz characterises the postmodern age as a nihilistic decline of traditional values in Europe. In the late 1940s and early 1950s, the term was again used to distinguish a historical epoch by Arnold Toynbee. For Toynbee, the Modern age ended in 1875, and the contemporary world should be described as post-modern. The post-modern age, according to Toynbee, is characterised by a collapse of the Enlightenment ideals of rationality and progress and by the rise of anarchism and total relativism.[48]

C. Wright Mills's *The Sociological Imagination* (1959)[49] presents the postmodern age as a new Dark Age, characterised by a breakdown of the Enlightenment connection between reason and emancipation. In this new Dark Age, the emancipatory political philosophies of liberalism and Marxism have become defunct. Mills links the process of the rationalisation of society, not with freedom, but with dehumanising bureaucratisation, technological organisation, and a blind drift towards empty conformity. Nihilistic themes are also present in two early essays on cultural postmodernism: Irving Howe's "Mass Society and Post-Modern Fiction" (1959)[50] and Leslie Fiedler's "The New Mutants" (1965).[51] Howe takes a negative stance towards postmodern literature and society, on the grounds that it is characterised by the decline of Enlightenment rationalism, anti-intellectualism, and the loss of faith in social progress through culture. Fiedler announces the death of modernist avant-garde art and the emergence of a new, post-modern art that breaks down the barriers between "high" and "low" art. He associates this art with popular trends in youth counter-culture and the rejection of traditional values such as Protestantism, Victorianism, rationalism and humanism. In the early essay "The New Mutants" Fiedler portrays post-modernism negatively and associates it with nihilism, but in later works he celebrates it as a positive break from stale and repressive modern forms of art and life.

If we understand nihilism in the general sense of a decline of Western culture, then nihilistic themes are clearly evident in the works of Pannwitz, Toynbee, Mills, Howe, and Fiedler. Nihilism is thus closely associated with the postmodern in many of its seminal appearances. The decline of traditional values and the bankruptcy of the Enlightenment ideals of rationality and progress are recurring themes in these early works, and these themes are also prominent in philosophical theories of nihilism and later theories of the postmodern. In many of these early works, postmodernity stands in a lesser relation to modernity; postmodern culture is characterised negatively in terms of a loss of the hopes that infused the modern era with optimism. Many of the theories of the postmodern that popularised the idea in the seventies and eighties are decidedly more positive, but often retain the themes of social disintegration and the dissolution of traditional values. In Ihab Hassan's 1971 "POSTmodernISM: A Paracritical Bibliography"[52] and Charles Jencks' 1977 *The Language of Post-modern Architecture*, postmodernism appears as a new, vibrant alternative to the stale modernist forms of literature and architecture (respectively). Steven Best and Douglas Kellner explain that there are two conflicting matrices of postmodern discourse in the period before it proliferated in the nineteen-eighties, one that casts postmodernity in a negative light, and one that views it positively.[53]

Since the popularisation of postmodernism in the nineteen-eighties, it has often been negatively characterised as a form of nihilism. This characterisation takes two notable forms. Firstly, equations between postmodernism and nihilism are frequently made in passing, with little analysis, as though it were self-evidently true that postmodernism is nihilistic. Secondly, without necessarily using the term "nihilism," many intellectuals have attacked postmodernism for undermining any possibility of coherent theory or normative ethics and politics. As such, postmodernism has effectively been accused of epistemological, metaphysical, ethical, and political nihilism.[54] One obvious and important philosophical approach to the question of nihilism in postmodernity would be to engage these debates. For the most part, however, I shall avoid such engagements, for two reasons. Firstly, as I have already indicated, my primary focus here is on *existential* nihilism, a topic not directly treated by many of the influential attacks on postmodernism. Secondly, many of these attacks on postmodernism fail to seriously engage with the texts of postmodern thinkers, and simply beg the question. Many of the criticisms of postmodernism are made on the basis of assumptions firmly rooted in "modernist" or Enlightenment traditions (Callinicos and Terry Eagleton are Marxists, for example, and Christopher Norris is committed to a form of metaphysical realism). For these thinkers, if postmodernism denies the modernist principles to which they are committed, then it is *ipso facto* nihilistic. These criticisms of postmodernism therefore risk simply begging the question, deciding against the postmodern in advance.[55]

Moreover, even if these analyses are correct in their assessments that postmodernism is epistemologically, metaphysically, ethically, or politically nihilistic, it does not necessarily follow that postmodernism is *existentially* nihilistic. For Nietzsche, from whom the postmodern thinkers examined here all take their bearings, values such as the true, the real, and the good that modernist thinkers accuse postmodernism of undermining are in fact *sources* of existential nihilism: undermining these values may therefore lead to a greater affirmation, rather than negation of, the value and meaning of life. To avoid begging the question in a study of the relationship between postmodernism and existential nihilism, these values must be placed, with Nietzsche, in question. In this study I pursue an "internal" reading of the tradition of nihilism and postmodern theory, avoiding the attempts that have been made to assess postmodernism from the perspectives of other traditions, and interrogating it through the criteria that are established within the tradition itself. While avoiding the problem of question begging, this approach presents its own methodological difficulties.

The economy of *this* writing

The study of nihilism in postmodernity faces particular methodological problems due to the fact that both the discourses of nihilism and of the postmodern call into question many of the conventions of academic practice. The final chapter of Lyotard's *Libidinal Economy* is entitled "The economy of this writing"; in it he explains the unusual style of the book as an attempt to avoid the nihilism of traditional academic theory that the book analyses. The book is a pastiche of styles with a goal he later describes as 'inscribing the passage of intensities directly in the prose itself without any mediation at all,'[56] with the result that some parts of the text read more like an avant-garde novel than a traditional philosophical tract. This problem of style and method is typical of the texts with which I deal in this book; both the discourses of nihilism and the postmodern call into question conventions of academic thought and writing, especially the image of thought as representation.

Baudrillard, for his part, employs a style that is often more poetic than academic, eschewing the usual scholarly apparatus and signalling the renunciation of any claim to representational objectivity. In his paper "The Year 2000 Will Not Take Place" he writes:

> [W]hat I put forward here is nothing other than an exercise in simulation. I am no longer in a position to 'reflect' anything. I can only push hypotheses to their limit, remove them from their critical zone of reference, make them go beyond the point of no-return. I send theory as well into the hyperspace of simulation—where it loses all objective validity, but perhaps gains in coherence, that is to say in real affinity with the system that surrounds us.[57]

The fact that Lyotard and other philosophers who deal with nihilism and the postmodern resort to experimental styles and new methods of inquiry in engaging these issues forces me to reflect on the economy of my own writing and the nature of the methodology I shall pursue here. This demand arises both from the desire to do justice to the theories I am examining (to avoid naïveté), and the desire to contribute in my own way towards a response to the problem of nihilism in postmodernity. As I argue in this book, the increasing reflexivity of the discourse of nihilism is one of the distinctive traits of its postmodernisation, and one risks both failing to do justice to the subject of this study and failing to contribute towards a response to nihilism if one neglects the necessary reflexivity in one's own discourse. Is nihilism to be considered as an objective fact of culture, which this discourse attempts to represent as accurately as possible? Or can my discourse simply represent the discourses of others, bracketing the problem of the relation between those discourses and the cultural reality they purportedly analyse? If neither possibility is adequate, what alternatives are there?

In response to these problems of methodology, I follow several of Vattimo's suggestions and examples. As Vattimo notes, the "current situation" cannot be considered in any simple sense objective; the subject position of the analyst of nihilism is itself within the zone of the nihilism analysed. He writes that

> the ontology of present existence that we are looking for is a theory that both speaks about this existence and belongs to this existence.... In other words, the content of the ontology de l'actualité that we are attempting to construct must be developed by taking into account the meaning of the needs expressed by this very attempt...[58]

The discourse of nihilism in postmodernity is thus both the subject and the object of my study here. It is not simply a matter of producing a secondary text that represents the content of primary texts that themselves represent an objective reality (or rather, which I might assess on the basis of their aspirations to objective representation). Rather, the needs expressed by the discourse of nihilism I am studying *are themselves* part of that nihilism; the philosophical positions and problems that arise from these texts are symptoms of the generalised pathos analysed in the discourse of nihilism. Or, more simply put, the discourse of nihilism is itself a part of the problematic of nihilism. Analysing the discourse of nihilism, then, is analysing nihilism itself, but in a way that cannot pretend to be exhaustive—nihilism has many cultural expressions other than the theory that attempts to analyse it. Furthermore, this means that my own discourse is inevitably part of the postmodern nihilism it attempts to examine—I cannot pretend to take an enunciative position outside of it.

Second, however, the discourse of nihilism—including my own discourse, which is continuous with the textual tradition examined here—cannot avoid staging representations. The nihilistic aspects of culture that are examined in the discourse of nihilism are inevitably treated as objects, separate from the subject of analysis. My own discourse cannot avoid a double representation: firstly it represents the other discourses of nihilism under examination here, and secondly it implicitly endorses the representations made in these discourses. By examining what Lyotard, Baudrillard, and Vattimo say about the conditions of contemporary society and culture, I am unavoidably restaging their own representations. What these two points, taken together, mean is that on the one hand I cannot entirely avoid staging a representation of nihilism, but on the other hand the nature of this staging avoids the most viciously nihilistic and problematic aspects of representational discourse, since it posits no clear distinction between the object of study and the subject that studies. According to the postmodern theorists examined here, the most problematic aspects of representation stem from positing an objective reality that can be known by a transcendent subject. Blurring the distinction between discourse and the "reality" it analyses alleviates the problem of representation somewhat, but leaves the possibility and inevitability of representational effects in discourse intact.

I do not attempt to avoid the problems of representation in discourse stylistically *à la* Lyotard or Baudrillard. For both Lyotard and Baudrillard, such attempts are never entirely successful in any case, but simply remove the viciousness of the problem of representation. Rather, I follow Vattimo's method of the historical analysis of texts, a method that both accepts the unavoidability of representation in discourse, and removes the most problematic aspects of representation by blurring the distinction between "representation" and "reality." I further follow Vattimo's usual method here by reading the texts of philosophy in a comparative and critical way in order to illuminate the "current situation." This does not result in a final, complete, or systematised theory, but a sketch of our current position *vis a vis* nihilism made possible by a comparison of postmodern theorisations of this issue. In gauging the adequacy of the postmodern responses to nihilism, I do not appeal to a pre-theoretical realm that the postmodernists may be judged to have or have not accurately represented. Rather, I assess the postmodern theories with respect to the needs expressed within the discourses of nihilism and the postmodern themselves.

My approach to the question of nihilism in postmodernity is undertaken primarily through a comparative and critical study of Vattimo, Lyotard, and Baudrillard. Furthermore, I seek to characterise the novelty and uniqueness of the postmodern approach to nihilism by comparing it with earlier theorisations of the topic. In this regard I limit my study of earlier theories of nihilism to the three thinkers I believe are most important in defining the problem in the late nineteenth and early twentieth centuries, before the "postmodern turn": Nietzsche, Sartre, and Heidegger. My central focus here is on the characteristic features, advantages, and limitations of the theories of nihilism advanced by the three postmodern thinkers, Lyotard, Baudrillard, and Vattimo. While there are significant differences in their theories of nihilism that must be acknowledged, my concern here is primarily with the *shared* themes that emerge from a comparison of these thinkers in so far as they allow us to recognise a characteristically "postmodern" diagnosis of, and response to, nihilism. Jeff Malpas suggests that comparisons of different philosophers shed new light on the issues that are at stake in their thought through a "fusion of horizons"[59]: my aim is to shed light on the status of nihilism in postmodernity through a comparison of the perspectives on this issue offered by Lyotard, Baudrillard, and Vattimo.

Overview

To conclude this introductory chapter, let me turn, briefly, to a broad examination of the terrain to be explored in this book by giving an overview of the structure and content of the following chapters. Chapter one begins a thematic survey of the development of nihilism, focusing on the main theories of nihilism prior to the "postmodern turn." I examine three major philosophical figures around whom the discourse of nihilism crystallises in the late nineteenth and early twentieth centuries: Nietzsche, Sartre, and Heidegger. In the works of these three thinkers we find the dominant themes of nihilism against which the uniqueness of postmodern theories of nihilism stand out. I resist the temptation to characterise the theories of nihilism advanced by these three thinkers as "modern." Such a characterisation would be reductive to a highly problematic degree, in no small part due to the fact that Nietzsche and Heidegger stand as "grandfathers" of the postmodern. While my intent is to bring to light certain significant recent developments in the theorisation of nihilism that can be thought under the general rubric of the postmodern, these developments do not necessarily constitute a radical break with previous theories of nihilism. Indeed, while Lyotard, Baudrillard, and Vattimo develop nihilism in new ways, all are influenced by Nietzsche and/or Heidegger and there are significant points of continuity in the ways nihilism is understood. In particular, I emphasise the way in which Heidegger's problematisation of the possibility of overcoming nihilism (a possibility that Nietzsche and Sartre both pursue) paves the way for postmodern formulations of, and responses to, nihilism.

Chapter two gives an initial presentation of the three postmodern theories of nihilism that constitute the main focus of this book. I examine the concept of nihilism as it is theorised by Lyotard, Baudrillard, and Vattimo. Lyotard deploys concepts derived from Nietzsche and Freud to analyse representational theory as nihilistic, and rejects "critique" itself as a form of nihilistic theory. He develops a notion of "libidinal economy" in an attempt to side-step critique by releasing feelings and desires rather than setting up an alternative theoretical position. Baudrillard is predominantly understood as a passive nihilist who presents a bleak vision of postmodernity in which there is no more hope for meaning. Against this interpretation, I develop a reading of his work that shows that he not only engages in an astute analysis of nihilism, but is concerned to develop a positive response. Vattimo understands nihilism principally as ontological and epistemological anti-foundationalism, and sees the postmodern as a radicalisation of Nietzsche's and Heidegger's understandings of nihilism. His originality lies in his development of a *positive* understanding of nihilism: he does not see nihilism as a crisis, but primarily as an opportunity for new modes of existence. I conclude this chapter by identifying three points through which a characteristically postmodern approach to nihilism emerges from these diverse theories: they follow the wider theoretical trend known as the linguistic turn, they display a deep reflexivity, recognising the implication in nihilism of the discourse that analyses it, and, most significantly, they abandon the hope that nihilism might be overcome.

While the focus of chapter two is on the philosophical and theoretical aspects of nihilism developed by Lyotard, Baudrillard, and Vattimo, chapter three gives attention to the theories of postmodernity advanced by these thinkers. All three understand postmodernity as significantly marked by nihilism, and emphasise recent changes in technological science and capitalism as decisive for our understanding of the nihilism of the postmodern situation. I develop a picture of the status of nihilism in postmodernity as it emerges from a comparison of these theories, arguing that all three suggest a tension in the way that nihilism manifests in postmodernity. On the one hand, nihilism appears complete in postmodernity; the postmodern condition may be understood as the collapse of the Enlightenment values that Nietzsche identified as the "highest values" of modernity, replacing but holding the same place as the values of religion. This completion suggests a resolution of the problems of nihilism. On the other hand, however, nihilism continues and is perhaps deepened by the recent developments in technoscience and capitalism that characterise postmodernity, and still appears as a problem in postmodernity that requires a response. I argue that this tension is expressed in the postmodern idea of the end of history, an idea that resonates with the postmodern rejection of the possibility of overcoming nihilism.

With the stage now set for the question of how best to respond to nihilism in the current situation, I begin chapter four with a summary of the logical possibilities for such a response, following an analysis given by Simon Critchley. I situate the postmodern responses under consideration here as attempts to respond to nihilism once the hope for its overcoming has been abandoned. Despite the differences between the theoretical approaches taken by Lyotard, Baudrillard, and Vattimo, I argue that it is possible to outline a characteristically postmodern response to nihilism organised around two themes: the "logic of difference" and the "politics of passivity." I turn to Gilles Deleuze's development of a logic of difference in the context of the Nietzschean problematic of overcoming nihilism in order to give rigorous expression to the logic underlying the postmodern responses. The politics of passivity is introduced through further consideration of Heidegger's treatment of the problem of overcoming nihilism. I examine these themes in more detail through concepts and strategies developed by each of the postmodern theorists as responses to nihilism: Lyotard's tactics for releasing affects dissimulated in structures, Baudrillard's deployment of seduction against simulation, and Vattimo's call for a *Verwindung* of metaphysics. Finally, I offer a critical appraisal of the postmodern responses to nihilism. I argue firstly that the responses offered by Vattimo, Lyotard and Baudrillard constitute positive advancements in so far as they deal with the aporia of the attempt to overcome nihilism in a more sophisticated way than Nietzsche, Sartre, and Heidegger. However, I also argue that the postmodern theorisations of nihilism do not deal sufficiently with *abyssal* nihilism, the disorienting feeling that all meanings and values are absolutely contingent, which results from the breakdown in the social traditions and institutions that had previously served to give life structure and direction.

In the conclusion, I return to the general question of the problem of meaninglessness in the contemporary world, and reflect on what this study of nihilism in postmodernity tells us about our current situation. I show how the detailed understanding of the connection between nihilism and the postmodern that emerges from this study clarifies the nature of the contemporary problem of meaning, and sets the parameters for an effective response. I argue that such a response must be a *political* one, and indicate the directions in which this response might be developed. Moreover, I outline the implications of this study for wider debates concerning the postmodern, arguing that it demonstrates that postmodern theory is far more than merely a symptomatic expression of contemporary disaffection as is sometimes supposed. The postmodernists considered here all attempt to respond to nihilism, and, unlike many of their detractors, attempt to calibrate their responses to the demands of the current situation. Ultimately, in undertaking this comparison of postmodern theories of nihilism, my hope is to make a contribution to our understanding of, and potential for responding to, the problem of meaning in the postmodern world. It is to this task I now turn.

Chapter 1
The Advent of Nihilism

What I relate is the history of the next two centuries. I describe what is coming, what can no longer come differently: the advent of nihilism.
—Friedrich Nietzsche[1]

The above words indicate the place Nietzsche holds as both formative thinker and prophet of nihilism in modernity and beyond. He stands at the head of a lineage of philosophers who have confronted nihilism in the twentieth century, from Heidegger and the existentialists through to postmodern thinkers, and his thought acts as a touchstone that gives coherence to the diverse theorizations of nihilism in the Continental tradition. My concern in this chapter is to outline the source of this lineage in Nietzsche's work and its early unfolding in French existentialism—of which I will take Jean-Paul Sartre as representative—and in the thought of Martin Heidegger. These early thinkers of nihilism explore the devaluation of life in modern times, enquiring about the possibility of meaning and value against the backdrop of the historical and cultural situation in which they lived and thought. These theorizations of nihilism, which take place before the "postmodern turn," set the context for the emergence of postmodern theories of nihilism and establish the problems to which later thinkers such as Lyotard, Baudrillard, and Vattimo respond. Outlining the main theories of nihilism in the late nineteenth and early twentieth centuries is therefore essential groundwork if we are to understand the distinctive contributions more recent theorists have made, and how these contributions attempt to deal with what they see as a new situation with regard to nihilism. However, the material covered in this chapter remains background for the focus of this book, and I cannot hope to do full justice to the theories of nihilism, or proposed solutions, offered by these three thinkers.

Nietzsche, Sartre and Heidegger each employ different theoretical frameworks in analyzing nihilism, and offer different solutions to the problem of meaning that modernity poses. While Nietzsche's thought remains central to the discourse of nihilism, subsequent thinkers pose the issue in their own terms, often seriously problematizing both the terms of analysis and the response to nihilism offered by Nietzsche, and by other subsequent thinkers. The history of nihilism appears as a history of increasing problematization, where the adequacy of previous thought on the topic is constantly undermined, and where the possibility of overcoming or effectively responding to nihilism seems increasingly unlikely. In the early history of theorizations of nihilism briefly rehearsed in this chapter, Heidegger is seen to inaugurate this problematization with his critical responses to both Nietzsche and Sartre. Proceeding in a roughly chronological manner, I shall begin with Nietzsche's formulation of and response to the problem of nihilism, followed by a discussion of Sartre's existentialist nihilism, which re-conceives the death of God in an atheistic, humanistic framework, and applies the phenomenological method to the analysis of the problem of existential meaning. I shall then examine Heidegger's confrontation with nihilism, which unfolds in the context of his ontological project. In his engagements with Nietzsche and Sartre, Heidegger alerts us to the danger that the analysis of nihilism might be posed in terms that are themselves implicated in nihilism, and which foreclose the possibility of an effective response. Furthermore, according to Heidegger the attempt to overcome nihilism is itself a nihilistic impulse, and such attempts lead to an aporetic impasse. This chapter thus follows the early history of theorizations of nihilism to an aporetic point, where the possibility of effectively analyzing and overcoming nihilism is severely problematized. It is this scene of aporia that the postmodern theorists of nihilism inherit, and to which they attempt to respond.

Nietzsche: the devaluation of the highest values

What does nihilism mean? That the highest values devaluate themselves. The aim is lacking; "why?" finds no answer.

—Friedrich Nietzsche[2]

While nihilism, understood as the problem of the meaningfulness of life, existed before Nietzsche lived and wrote, with Nietzsche—as Camus puts it—'nihilism becomes conscious for the first time.'[3] Nietzsche provides the first extensive analysis of nihilism, effectively introducing the problem of meaning and value as central for modern thought. In one of his most succinct formulations, Nietzsche defines nihilism as 'the radical repudiation of value, meaning and desirability.'[4] According to Deleuze's interpretation of Nietzsche, *nihil* in the word "nihilism" signifies a value of nil, and 'life takes on a value of nil insofar as it is denied and depreciated.'[5] Nietzsche's theory of nihilism is a critique of modernity as an age in which meaning and value have become problematized; the imminent danger afflicting modernity is the view that "everything lacks meaning."[6] While he is concerned with "social distress,"[7] Nietzsche sees such distress as an effect, the causes of which must be identified as certain values underlying Western thought and culture. According to this analysis, nihilism occurs when all the highest values previously posited become devalued. Nietzsche's theory of nihilism is a diagnosis of this devaluation of the highest values in modernity, and an exploration of the implications this devaluation has on both the social and the individual level. Nietzsche proposes that modernity is in the grip of this process of the devaluation of the highest values, and prognoses the inevitable worsening of this illness. He writes as a prophet of nihilism, declaring that "[t]his future speaks even now in a hundred signs, this destiny announces itself everywhere..."[8] According to Nietzsche the course of this nihilistic process is not inevitable, however, and it in fact represents a chance to revitalize Western culture by renewing the possibility of interpreting life in ways that affirm its value. Nietzsche claims to have confronted the problem of nihilism on the level of the individual, within himself, and worked out a path to its overcoming that might be applied on the level of society. He confesses that he is "the first perfect nihilist of Europe who, however, has even now lived through the whole of nihilism, to the end, leaving it behind, outside himself."[9]

While Nietzsche's discussion of nihilism often takes European culture of the late nineteenth century as its target, thus constituting a critique of modernity, this critique is grounded in a theory that has wider application. Nietzsche's theory of nihilism is elucidated through a typological description of the main ways nihilism manifests in the course of its development. These types of nihilism represent the modes of life-devaluation that particular forms of life and thought effect, and elaborate the "inner logic" at work in the nihilistic process. Alan White suggests that Nietzsche's analysis of nihilism reveals three main types: *religious*, *radical*, and *complete* nihilism.[10] Radical nihilism can be further divided into the subtypes of *active* and *passive* nihilism. The first of these types, religious nihilism, describes the initial constitution of the nihilistic impulse in human culture, which has unfolded through history and resulted in the ailments of European modernity. For

Nietzsche, religious nihilism—and the other types that follow in its wake—originates in a particular interpretation of the world: the *Christian-moral* one. This interpretation has twin origins in the teachings of Plato and Christ, and Nietzsche argues that Platonism and Christianity constitute the prime influences that continue to shape Western thought, and in particular conceptions of meaning and value, in modernity. The Christian-moral interpretation of the world is thus the basis for the "highest values," which Nietzsche believes have begun to devalue themselves, constituting the modern nihilistic crisis.

Nietzsche's analysis of religious nihilism takes the form of a genealogy that traces the origins of the "highest values" back to less-than-noble impulses. This genealogy begins with the problem that existence is marked by suffering. All sentient beings suffer, but human beings are conscious, interpretive creatures who demand that their suffering must have a *meaning*. According to Nietzsche, human beings suffer more from the meaninglessness of suffering than from suffering itself, and it is the inability to find a meaning in suffering that gives rise to the first impulse to negate the value of life.[11] This negation potentially leads to suicide, "the *deed* of nihilism."[12] According to Nietzsche, religious nihilism arises as a way to avoid this outcome; it provides an interpretation of life that gives a meaning to suffering and thus attenuates the devaluation of life. However, it does so in such a way that a fundamentally devalued life is preserved, foreclosing the possibility of fully life-affirmative valuation.

Religious nihilism interprets existence on the basis of three tendencies that Nietzsche calls *ressentiment*, bad conscience, and the ascetic ideal.[13] *Ressentiment* is the resentment against life that arises when a meaning is demanded for suffering and none is found; life is judged to be inadequate and in need of justification and redemption. Bad conscience provides an answer to the question of the meaning of suffering by locating the cause of this suffering in the sufferer him or herself—he or she suffers because he or she is guilty and deserves to suffer. The ascetic ideal provides a sense of meaning and value in conjunction with *ressentiment* and bad conscience by placing value on the denial of the self and the natural world. In order to justify and redeem life, the ascetic ideal sets up categories of valuation *beyond* the world of experience. These categories constitute what Nietzsche calls the "highest values," and these values form the basis of the Christian-moral interpretation of the world.

In a succinct formulation found in *The Will to Power*, Nietzsche identifies the "highest values" according to three categories: aim, unity and truth.[14]

These categories justify and redeem life by interpreting it in such a way that it seems meaningful, yet the categories themselves refer to things that cannot be found in our experience of the world. In Nietzsche's estimation, these categories are imaginative inventions that are projected onto the world in order to give it value, but that place the source of value outside the world. The first posits a *goal* that might be achieved through the process of life, for example: "the 'fulfillment' of some highest ethical canon in all events, the moral world order; or the growth of love and harmony in the intercourse of beings; or the gradual approximation of a state of universal happiness; or even the development toward a state of universal annihilation."[15] The ascetic ideal gives a sense of meaning to life by providing such a goal in the form of the life of self-denial as the highest ideal of human flourishing. The second category, unity, suggests a systematic organization of the world that totalizes all events under the aegis of some supreme form of domination or administration. Conceiving himself as a part of this unity "suffices to give man a deep feeling of standing in the context of, and being dependent on, some whole that is infinitely superior to him, and he sees himself as a mode of the deity."[16] The individual is thus imbued with value and meaning by feeling him or herself to be part of a supreme universal.

The third category, truth, gives a sense of meaning to life by positing a "true world," a transcendent world beyond the immanent world of mere appearance. If the world of experience is judged to lack the qualities that would make it meaningful (that is, qualities that would justify suffering), then these qualities might still be thought to exist in a transcendent, suprasensible realm. This "true world" then becomes the source of value and meaning, which justifies the existence of the "merely apparent" world. This suprasensible world is the central referent of Nietzsche's use of the term "metaphysics," and his polemics concerning metaphysics must be understood in relation to his arguments regarding the life-devaluing effects of religious nihilism. These three categories are typical of religious modes of thinking, and underlie the Christian-moral interpretation of the world. For Nietzsche, all these categories are encapsulated in the figure of the Christian God, the divine legislator of value, the "spider of finality and morality that is supposed to exist behind the great net and web of causality."[17] For Nietzsche, "God" thus functions as a proper name for religious nihilism and the highest values posited hitherto.

While the "highest values" are a means to the preservation of life, protecting against suicide, according to Nietzsche they preserve a sick, impoverished form of life that is incapable of healthful life-affirmation. The

Christian-moral interpretation of the world is a form of nihilism because the "highest values" it sets up are outside of life and in *opposition* to life; the categories of aim, unity, and truth have to be posited beyond life because they cannot be found within it. By implication, such values negate life itself as it is experienced in the "merely apparent" world, and reduce it to the instrumental value of constituting a bridge to the "true world."[18] The Christian-moral interpretation finds this world inadequate in itself, guilty of not having a meaning in itself, and judges that it is in need of a *justification* and a *redemption*. The devaluation of life that this judgment implies finds expression in the ascetic's denial of worldly existence and the forms of gratification that can be found in life, in the name of "higher" ideals. Vincent Descombes succinctly expresses the structure of the religious nihilism constituted by the Christian-moral interpretation of the world, the ascetic ideal, and the "highest values," as follows:

1. An ideal is posited, and then opposed point by point to the reality of the present. [...]
2. This ideal, though itself guilty of not existing, of being no more than an ideal, now permits us to accuse the present of having fallen short of it.[19]

Religious nihilism thus perpetuates the devaluation of life by promoting otherworldly ideals against which life is judged to be lacking. This judgment constitutes a *negation* of the value of life in itself, and a *deferral* of value by placing its source in a world "beyond."

According to Nietzsche, modernity remains thoroughly conditioned by religious and ascetic values, despite the modern attempt to establish thought on a new foundation independent of religion. He argues that philosophy and science remain enmeshed in the ascetic ideal insofar as they are still animated by the ideal of *truth*. Of modern philosophers and scientists, Nietzsche writes that "what *compels* these men to this absolute will to truth, albeit as its unconscious imperative, is the *belief in the ascetic ideal itself*...it is the belief in a *metaphysical* value, the value of *truth in itself*..."[20] Nietzsche's argument is that the idea of truth in itself—or differently expressed, of "facts" free of interpretation—makes the same distinction between the erroneous, merely apparent world, and the "true" world, that the ascetic ideal makes. He argues against the possibility of a presuppositionless science, asserting that there are no "facts" that are not conditioned by interpretation.[21] Insofar as philosophy and science make the distinction between "essence" and "appearance," they are expressions of the ascetic ideal and manifest religious nihilism. On Nietzsche's interpretation, what Christianity and Platonism have in common is the impulse to "otherwordliness" or transcendence, and all forms of thought motivated by this impulse remain nihilistic in the religious sense. Insofar as modern forms of thought still posit transcendent categories (such as "truth"), Nietzsche believes they bear the marks of the Platonic and Christian interpretations of the world. Modernity has not escaped the nihilism of religious thought, merely reformulated it.

Nietzsche's story about nihilism thus far explained concerns the "psychology" of nihilism, that is, the way certain forms of thought of the individual promote certain forms of life for that individual, and vice versa. But Nietzsche's diagnosis also has a "sociological" dimension, which concerns the way the psychology of nihilism takes hold of people collectively and influences an entire culture. He provides a genealogy of the triumph of religious nihilism in Western culture with the aid of a distinction between the psychological types Master and Slave, and the forms of morality associated with each.[22] The Master, Nietzsche's privileged type in this distinction, is a strong type who affirms his or her self, affirms life, and actively creates values. "Master morality" is founded on a primary affirmation of the self as *good*, and a secondary judgment of the other as *bad*. The Slave, on the other hand, is a weak type who cannot affirm life directly, and defines the self in opposition to the Master. Slave morality begins with *ressentiment* against the Master type, whom the Slave blames for his or her weakness and suffering. Slave morality is founded on an initial determination of the Master and Master morality as *evil*, and a subsequent judgment of the self as *good*.[23] In the case of the Slave, *ressentiment* is directed towards the Master type (rather than against existence in general), who is blamed for the Slave's suffering. Motivated by this *ressentiment*, the Slave condemns the life-affirmative, strong traits of Master morality as evil, and elevates the traits of weakness to the level of the good, defining slave morality as the *only* valid morality.

This analysis of Master and Slave moralities takes on a sociological dimension through Nietzsche's argument that Western culture is founded on the triumph of Slave morality over Master morality, of the weak over the strong. The triumph of Slave morality takes place through a weakening of the strong by promoting the belief that strength (Master morality) is evil, and that the strong can freely choose to be weak, thereby imbuing the strong with bad conscience. Nietzsche also calls Slave morality "herd morality," a name that indicates the "leveling" effect he believes this form of morality has on the individuals who comprise a society in which Slave morality takes hold. While Master morality privileges the self-assertion of the individual and his or her personally created values, Slave morality condemns this individualism as evil, favoring selflessness, mildness, and conformity. Nietzsche thus sees "herd morality" as producing a social mediocrity in which individuals only affirm values that are affirmed by the majority, and are not inspired to create their own values. Since Nietzsche views the active creation of values associated with Master morality as the apogee of life-affirmation, the "leveling" associated with Slave morality is a prime component of nihilism. This "slave revolt in morals"[24] takes place in conjunction with the promotion of the ascetic ideal and the "highest values," forming the moral dimension of the Christian-moral interpretation of the world. According to Nietzsche, the belief in transcendent categories and in slave morality are complimentary aspects of religious nihilism, a form of interpretation that preserves an impoverished and degenerate form of life while stifling the possibility of more affirmative life-valuation.

On Nietzsche's interpretation, just as modernity remains conditioned by the "highest values," so too modern European culture remains dominated by herd morality. He argues that the modernist imperative of freedom from religious dogmatism has not undermined Christian morality, as it logically should. Of his contemporaries, he writes, "[t]hey have got rid of the Christian God, and now feel obliged to cling all the more firmly to Christian morality."[25] Moreover, Nietzsche sees modern forms of social organization such as the State, democracy, socialism, capitalism and the bourgeoisie as instantiations of herd morality, in which mediocrity and conformity are privileged over individualism, experimentation, and risk-taking. He identifies modern technological and cultural innovations, such as "[t]he press, the machine, the railway, the telegraph,"[26] as exacerbating the leveling effect of European society. Such innovations increase communication between cultures, and the resulting multicultural consciousness increases leveling by further reducing the possibilities for asserting values, since the majority, which must assent to such values, is more diffuse. For Nietzsche, modern "progress," insofar as it attempts to establish equality and equanimity, is in fact a regress, since it reduces all individuals to the same level, promoting Slave morality and undermining the possibility of Master morality.

While Nietzsche argues that religious nihilism and Slave morality persist in modernity, the crux of his story about the nihilism of modernity is that the modern age is one in which the "highest values" have begun to devaluate themselves. Modernity is thus the historical site of the passage to the next type of nihilism, *radical* nihilism. According to Nietzsche, the Christian-moral worldview, which acts as a preserver of life by giving it a meaningful interpretation, begins to undermine itself in modernity. This self-undermining constitutes a nihilistic crisis because the interpretive categories that had previously bestowed life with meaning and value are withdrawn, producing the imminent danger that the value of life will be reduced to *nil*. According to Nietzsche, the devaluation of the highest values takes place because the Christian-moral value of *truthfulness* has been developed so far that it has turned against the "highest values" themselves, finding them to be untrue. The categories of aim, unity, and truth are seen to be mere fabrications, inventions that have served the purpose of imbuing life with a value it was thought to lack in itself. Summarizing the radical nihilism of modernity, Nietzsche writes:

> What has happened, at bottom? The feeling of valuelessness was reached with the realisation that the overall character of existence may not be interpreted by means of the concept of "aim," the concept of "unity," or the concept of "truth." Existence has no goal or end; any comprehensive unity in the plurality of events is lacking: the character of existence is not "true," is *false*. One simply lacks any reason for convincing oneself that there is a *true* world. Briefly: the categories "aim," "unity," "being" which we used to project some value into the world—we *pull out* again; so the world looks *valueless*.[27]

Nietzsche's thesis that the highest values devaluate themselves in modernity is based on the view that the Enlightenment pursuit of scientific and rational truth has undermined core religious beliefs. Among the most important examples of this undermining for Nietzsche are the Copernican revolution in cosmology, which unsettles the belief that the Earth, and also humanity, is at the centre of (and of central importance in) the universe, and Charles Darwin's development and popularization of the theory of evolution by natural selection, which undermines the theory of a divine creation and thereby the necessity of a creator God. Nietzsche is thus concerned with secularization, which he gives a unique interpretation through his emphasis on the values underlying this process. Nietzsche sees secularization not as a process in which dogmatic belief is replaced by apodictic truth, but as one of the progressive self-undermining of the "highest values," including truth itself. Nietzsche's formulaic expression of the nihilism of modernity, "*God is dead*,"[28] means that the categories that constituted the highest values hitherto posited in Western culture are becoming null and void, undermined by the pursuit of truth in modern thought.

Radical nihilism consists in the devaluation of the highest values, together with the belief that these values constitute the only possible source of value. Life is judged to be without meaning and value, since nothing in *this* world corresponds to the highest values and the modern will to truth will not allow faith in the existence of any *transcendent* world. Of the radical nihilist, Nietzsche writes: "A nihilist is a man who judges of the world as it is that it ought *not* to be, and of the world as it ought to be that it does not exist."[29] According to Nietzsche, modern humanity is so conditioned by thousands of years of belief in the "highest values" that it cannot simply throw off this mode of valuation and posit another. Moreover, the feeling of disappointment that arises with the realization that we have been mistaken all along about the existence of transcendent values may lead to a rejection of belief in any possible value (we have been wrong once, we could be wrong again…).

Radical nihilism manifests as two subtypes with drastically different consequences, as the following fragment in *The Will to Power* indicates.

> Nihilism. It is *ambiguous*:
> A. Nihilism as a sign of increased power of the spirit: as active nihilism.
> B. Nihilism as decline and recession of the power of the spirit: as passive nihilism.[30]

This passage suggests that the primary distinction between these two types of radical nihilism is not one of conceptual content, but the degree of strength or power they exhibit. Both kinds of nihilism involve the radical repudiation of value, meaning, and desirability, but they represent different ways of responding to this repudiation. As with all types of nihilism, these different ways of responding may be manifest on an individual or a social level. Passive nihilism is a despairing resignation in the face of a valueless world. On a sociological level, passive nihilism represents the extreme point of the decadence and social distress of modernity. As a possible destiny of the nihilism germinating in late nineteenth century Europe, passive nihilism indicates that the devaluation of the highest values could potentially lead to a culture dominated by a general pessimism in which meaninglessness is accepted as inevitable. The passive nihilist remains faithful to the "highest values," and concludes that because meaning is impossible by these criteria, it is impossible *absolutely*. Passive nihilism corresponds to a general exhaustion and weariness, a feeling of having had enough of life that could be experienced by a weak individual, or that could take hold of Western culture in its entirety.

Active nihilism, on the other hand, responds to the apparent meaninglessness of existence with a passion to destroy whatever remains of the old values and traditional ways of generating meaning. In reference to this type of nihilism, Nietzsche writes:

> Nihilism does not only contemplate the 'in vain!' nor is it merely the belief that everything deserves to perish: one helps to destroy—This is, if you will, illogical; but the nihilist does not believe that one needs to be logical.[31]

This response to nihilism is an outgrowth of a degree of power not possessed by the passive nihilist; active nihilism is "the condition of strong spirits and wills."[32] For Nietzsche, active nihilism is preferable to passive nihilism, because active nihilism constitutes a movement towards the overcoming of nihilism. This is so because if active nihilism runs its course, it ends in the negation of belief in the "highest values" as necessary sources of value. While the passive nihilist never transcends the belief that the categories posited by the Christian-moral interpretation of the world are the only possible categories of valuation, even though these categories are empty, the active nihilist destroys belief in the necessity of these categories as well. Nietzsche himself engages in such active nihilism through his genealogical critiques of the "highest values." The radical nihilist who pursues this path reaches a point of belief in nothing and an absolute repudiation of value, meaning, and desirability, and this point constitutes the next type of nihilism, *complete* nihilism.

Like radical nihilism, complete nihilism is also ambiguous, indicating both the extreme point of nihilism *and* its overcoming. Complete nihilism wipes away the categories of thought perpetuated by religious nihilism, removing not only belief in the existence of the highest values, but also the belief that transcendent values are necessary for valuation of any kind. For Nietzsche, this freedom from the traditional framework of valuation represents both the anguish of a life in which value and meaning are no longer given by secure, pre-given categories, and the opportunity for new valuations. The ambiguity of this position is well expressed in the following passage.

> *In the horizon of the infinite.*—We have left the land and have embarked. We have burned our bridges behind us—indeed, we have

gone farther and destroyed the land behind us. Now, little ship, look out! Beside you is the ocean: to be sure, it does not always roar, and at times it lies spread out like silk and gold and reveries of graciousness. But hours will come when you will realise that it is infinite and that there is nothing more awesome than infinity. Oh, the poor bird that felt free and now strikes the walls of this cage! Woe, when you feel homesick for the land as if it had offered more *freedom*—and there is no longer any 'land.'[33]

Nietzsche privileges the opportunity that complete nihilism offers, however, for renewing the possibility of the life-affirmative, active creation of values associated with Master morality. The complete nihilist realizes that the value and meaning of life do not necessarily depend on transcendent sources of value, and that other forms of valuation are possible. Nietzsche advocates experimentation and the active creation of values by strong individuals as the way to fill the void left by the destruction of the "highest values." On the sociological level, Nietzsche's story about nihilism suggests that after the two-century long radicalization of nihilism, a post-nihilistic, "postmodern" culture will emerge, invigorated by healthy, life-affirming values. Nietzsche thus privileges the creation of values by strong individuals as the process by which the nihilism of modernity might be ultimately overcome and a strong sense of value and meaning restored. Nietzsche refers to this process of overthrowing the old values, based in transcendent categories, and positing new life-affirmative values, as a "revaluation of all values."

In addition to advocating that individuals create their own values, Nietzsche attempts to develop his own principles for a new valuation of existence through concepts such as the will to power, the eternal return, and the *Übermensch* ("superman" or "overman"). Such categories do not simply name values, they attempt to theorize a new source of values, to explain how valuation is possible without reference to transcendent ideals. In order for these new categories of valuation to be successful, they must avoid the negation of the value of life enacted by the categories associated with religious nihilism. Nietzsche advocates an *affirmation* of life in its totality, including suffering, which will avoid the negation that follows from the religious nihilist's judgment that life is in need of justification. Nietzsche's new valuation must also avoid the positing of transcendent ideals, in all their forms, against which life may be judged negatively. If Nietzsche is to successfully theorize the overcoming of nihilism, then he must also provide an adequate account of how meaning and value are possible in the absence of transcendent criteria. Nietzsche's new principles of valuation and the question of their success in avoiding nihilism will be discussed with reference to Heidegger's confrontation with Nietzsche's thought in the final section of this chapter.

In summary, Nietzsche's theory of nihilism is a critical diagnosis of modernity that identifies a crisis in the underlying values animating Western culture. The crisis facing modernity is that the highest values that imbue life with a sense of meaning are being undermined, and Nietzsche believes that they will eventually be destroyed. Since he believes that these "highest values" are themselves nihilistic, however, he advocates an exacerbation of nihilism to a point where it negates itself. Nihilism may then be overcome by positing new meanings and values through creative acts. Nietzsche's analysis of nihilism applies on both the individual and social levels, and he foresees the deepening of the nihilistic crisis in Western culture and the eventual overcoming of this crisis in the two centuries following his own. In regard to the two main types of nihilism outlined in the introductory chapter, *reductive* and *abyssal* nihilism, Nietzsche can be seen as concerned with both. Religious nihilism and associated concepts such as Slave morality are a form of reductive nihilism, since they restrict the possibilities of life-affirmation and undermine the meaningfulness of life. Nietzsche is also concerned with abyssal nihilism, however, as the absence of meaning in the wake of the delegitimization of the "highest values" (i.e. the death of God). His prescription for a revaluation of all values is an attempt to overcome both types of nihilism. Nietzsche's influential formulation of nihilism is taken up and transformed into existential terms by Sartre, and into ontological terms by Heidegger. Each gives the analysis of the crisis of value and meaning announced by Nietzsche a different emphasis, with repercussions for how this crisis might be resolved. It is to Sartre's reformulation of the nihilistic problematic that I now turn.

Sartre: existentialist nihilism

The being of human reality is suffering…Human reality therefore is by nature an unhappy consciousness with no possibility of surpassing its unhappy state.

—Jean-Paul Sartre[34]

The existentialist confrontation with questions of the meaning and value of life, typified in the thought of Jean-Paul Sartre, gained wide public attention following the Second World War and continues to shape popular understandings of such issues. While Sartre does not make significant use of the term "nihilism," his concern with elaborating Nietzsche's theme of the death of God and the consequences that must be drawn from it place him squarely in the tradition I am concerned with here.[35] Sartre takes up Nietzsche's theme by positioning himself as a radical atheist and arguing that the bourgeoisie have not realized the full consequences of atheism: the loss of belief in God, followed through, necessarily leads to loss of belief in any objective structure that could provide a sense of meaning and value for human life. Sartre defines his philosophy of existentialism as 'nothing else but an attempt to draw the full conclusions from a consistently atheistic position.'[36] He is concerned with the problem of how an individual can live a meaningful, valuable life in the face of an objectively meaningless world, and how he or she can create values without the privilege of a secure foundation. While Sartre's treatment of nihilism develops many of the problems expressed by Nietzsche, his work is distinguished by an emphasis on human reality[37] and the lived experience of the individual, an emphasis partly shaped by his employment of a phenomenological theory of meaning that centralizes consciousness in its account of the production of meaning in the world. Sartre thus contributes a distinctive, and highly influential, chapter to the saga of nihilism in the twentieth century by thinking through meaning and value in a way that places emphasis on the individual, consciousness, and lived experience, construing nihilism as a problem for human reality. These emphases, moreover, constitute some of the main points on which postmodern theories of nihilism have differed in their analyses of the problem.

Sartre plays out the Nietzschean theme of the death of God through the idea of *contingency*, arguing that the objective world and human existence are both radically contingent in the sense of lacking any necessary meaning or value. He argues that the world is meaningless in itself, and only appears meaningful through the human activity of conferring meaning on it. Without a God, there is no exterior guarantor of meaning, and the meaning and value of life are entirely dependent on human beings themselves. Sartre further argues that there is no human nature because there is no God to have a conception of it.[38] Moreover, human beings are unable to found themselves (they are not *ens casua sui*). Because of this, human beings cannot be foundations for their own values—values cannot be determined on the basis of any pre-existing natural human essence, nor on the basis of a consistent and secure self-created essence. The meaning and value of human life thus have no secure foundation or justification, either in a transcendent source or in human nature. Sartre expresses this contingency of human reality in a philosophically rigorous manner through his adoption of a modified form of Husserlian phenomenology. Phenomenology, Sartre argues, shows us that consciousness constitutes the world as meaningful, and that human reality lacks a foundation.

From Edmund Husserl, Sartre takes a significantly modified version of the transcendental reduction (*epochē*).[39] Husserl contrasts the reduction with the "natural attitude," a *prima facie* view of the world that includes an uncritical acceptance of both the "objectivist" view of the world as consisting of external, spatio-temporal facts, and the world of human meanings, values, and conventional beliefs.[40] For Husserl, the reduction "brackets" or "puts out of action" the beliefs accepted uncritically by the natural attitude, and allows consciousness to examine its own structures in abstraction from these beliefs. Sartre rejects the bracketing of the first aspect of the natural attitude, arguing that we cannot bracket the existence of the external world.[41] However, he employs a reduction of the second aspect, that of the world of meanings, values, and significances taken for granted in "everyday" conscious experience. Sartre's reduction reveals the fact that the meaning of the world is constituted by human consciousness, but it also reveals that there are limits to this conscious constitution: when the process of meaning-constitution is in abeyance, the world is perceived as a collection of meaningless objects. In Sartre's terms, the reduction reveals an irreducible residue of "existence." Sartre describes this existence as "brute" or "sheer," indicating the raw and undefined character of the objective world divested of conscious meaning-giving. Furthermore, the limits to meaning-constitution are demonstrated by the fact that for Sartre a *particular* world is revealed to consciousness, and this world has no necessity—there is no reason that the world revealed exists as the world it is, rather than some other world. He writes:

> …phenomenological descriptions can discover, for instance, that the very structure of the transcendental consciousness implies that this consciousness is constitutive *of a world*. But it is evident that they will not teach us that consciousness must be constitutive *of* such a world, that is exactly the one where we are, with its earth, its animals, its men and the story of these men. We are here in the presence of a primary and irreducible fact which presents itself as a contingent and irrational specification of the noematic essence of the *world*.[42]

According to Sartre, the phenomenological method thus reveals that the world is radically contingent, lacking in any reason or necessity in itself, and with no other meaning or value than that conferred on it by human consciousness.

Sartre explores the contingency of the world in his famous philosophical novel *Nausea* (the working title of which was "Memo on Contingency"[43]) in which the protagonist, Antoine Roquentin, undergoes the experience of the reduction. Sartre reveals contingency through Roquentin's feelings of disgust and horror at the recognition that things exist prior to meaning being conferred on them by human structures of significance. According to Sartre, certain moods—such as boredom and "nausea," both of which Roquentin experiences—tend to produce the reduction because they place consciously created structures of significance in abeyance. In the following well-known passage, Roquentin, while contemplating the root of a tree, reflects on the independence of this world of sheer existence from human reasoning, highlighting the absurdity of the world in itself:

> The world of explanations and reasons is not that of existence. A circle is not absurd, it is clearly explicable by the rotation of a segment of a straight line around one of its extremities. But a circle doesn't exist either. That root, on the other hand, existed in so far that I could not explain it. Knotty, inert, nameless, it fascinated me, filled my eyes, repeatedly brought me back to its own existence. It was no use my repeating: 'It is a root'—that didn't work anymore. I saw clearly that you could not pass from its function as a root, as a suction-pump, *to that*, to that hard, compact, sea-lion skin, to that oily, horny, stubborn look. The function explained nothing; it enabled you to understand in general what a root was, but not *that one* at all. That root, with its colour, its shape, its frozen movement, was...beneath all explanation. Each of its qualities escaped from it a little, flowed out of it, half-solidified, almost became a thing; each one was *superfluous in* the root, and the whole stump now gave me the impression of rolling a little outside itself, denying itself, losing itself in a strange excess.[44]

Sartre further argues that contingency does not just apply to the objective world, but to human reality as well. Sartre's argument for the existence of contingency in human reality derives from a further engagement with Husserlian phenomenology: the rejection of the transcendental ego. In Sartre's early essay *The Transcendence of the Ego*,[45] he argues against Husserl's thesis that the ego is a transcendental condition for consciousness, accompanying, and necessary for, all conscious experience. Sartre's argument is that positing such a transcendental ego is superfluous. He notes that it is often thought necessary to posit this ego in order to account for the unity of consciousness and the individuation of separate consciousnesses, but argues that these two features of consciousness can be accounted for by the phenomenological theory of intentionality. According to Sartre, consciousness is unified by the object that it posits, and it limits itself, constituting a "synthetic totality" that isolates itself from other totalities of the same type (other consciousnesses).[46] Sartre further argues that the ego is a "transcendent, external" object of consciousness, a synthetic unity of states, actions, and qualities. It is an object posited by certain conscious acts, but not a permanent accompaniment of all consciousness. The ego arises when consciousness reflects on its past states, acts, and qualities, and synthesizes these elements into a unity. For Sartre, consciousness is an impersonal "Transcendental Field" that acts spontaneously; consciousness is thus the condition for the possibility of the ego, rather than vice versa. The rejection of the transcendental ego means that the spontaneous activity of consciousness has no foundation and is not conditioned or limited by a stable structure. Without the transcendental ego, consciousness 'determines its existence at each instant, without our being able to conceive anything *before* it. Thus each instant of our conscious life reveals to us a creation *ex nihilo*.'[47]

Sartre's phenomenological study of human consciousness thus reveals a radical freedom, which he later expresses in the famous dictum *existence precedes essence*.[48] Human consciousness exists first, surging up spontaneously into the world, and gives itself essence through its actions. The essence consciousness creates for itself is never permanent and does not constrain the freedom of consciousness, however, because consciousness is a transcendence, always going beyond itself. According to Sartre, the realization of this radical freedom at the heart of human reality, revealed by the reduction, produces anguish. Anguish arises with the knowledge that both the world and the ego are contingent; the meaning-conferring activity of consciousness is a necessary condition for a meaningful world and a meaningful sense of self. For Sartre, there is no human nature because there is no prior or exterior determination of human essence by God, and because human being cannot found itself (it is not a self-caused entity, which gives to itself a fixed and permanent essence, and cannot be such because of its self-transcendent nature). Both these forms of contingency mean that the meaning and value of human life has no secure foundation or justification, either in a transcendent source or in human nature. Sartre writes:

> For if indeed existence precedes essence, one will never be able to explain one's action by reference to a given and specific human nature; in other words, there is no determinism—man is free, man *is* freedom. Nor, on the other hand, if God does not exist, are we provided with any values or commands that could legitimise our behaviour.[49]

Sartre develops a phenomenological account of how meaning arises in the world, and how the desire for ultimate meaningfulness in human reality is frustrated, in *Being and Nothingness*. Here, in the major work of his existentialist philosophy, Sartre attempts to develop a phenomenological ontology of human existence, that is, a mapping of the general structures of human existence in so far as they appear to us and constitute reality *for* us.[50] Sartre begins with a basic ontological distinction, derived from his analysis of the intentionality of consciousness: the distinction between *being-in-itself* and *being-for-itself*. While these terms receive a complex elaboration in *Being and Nothingness*, they may briefly be glossed as follows. Being-in-itself is what consciousness is conscious *of*; it includes both matter and the objectified aspects of human reality, such as the ego. Being-in-itself is unconscious being; it is positive, self-consistent, and "is what it is." Being-for-itself is conscious being; it is the conscious dimension of human reality. Sartre conceives of consciousness as nothingness, or more accurately, a nihilating activity. Being-for-itself is negative, it is a "withdrawal" that allows being to relate to itself. As such, Sartre says that being-for-itself is never consistent with itself; it "is what it is not and is not what it is." Being-for-itself transcends being-in-itself, and transcends itself in the sense that it is always going beyond itself, negating its past states. According to Sartre, the interplay between being and nothingness is what constitutes human reality and the world of significance (the *Lebenswelt*, or "life-world"). Through complex modifications of this basic distinction, Sartre attempts to give a description of the fundamental structures of human being and its world. For Sartre, the possibility of meaning, significance, and value is explained by the nihilating activity of consciousness, which introduces distinction into the world, dividing *this* from *not-this* and thus forming the basis of intelligibility. Furthermore, consciousness makes the world meaningful by wrapping it in the for-itself's[51] existential projects (that is, those aims and activities that are significant for the for-itself's life or existence as a whole), a process to which Sartre gives a complex description. This description constitutes a further layer in Sartre's analysis of nihilism, since according to Sartre a consequence of the ontological structure of the for-itself is that its existential projects, and the very project of meaningful human life, is futile.

The explanation of the existential projects of the for-itself begins with a more complex description of the contingency of human reality than is given in Sartre's earlier works. His denial of human nature—in the sense of a fixed, permanent essence, established prior to existence—is explained in the ontological terms of *Being and Nothingness* through the nihilating activity of consciousness that constitutes the for-itself. This nihilation is a nihilation *of the in-itself*. While being-for-itself is negative, and has no positive being, existing only in relation to the in-itself that it negates, being-in-itself is absolute (in the sense of "unrelated") positive being. Being-in-itself has a fixed essence or nature. Consciousness nihilates the in-itself because of the intentionality of consciousness: if consciousness were the same as its object, Sartre reasons, then consciousness would not be *of* the object—it would *be* the object. Thus, consciousness negates the object of consciousness in relation to itself, and negates itself in relation to its object—consciousness *is not* what it is conscious *of*. In Sartre's words, "the for-itself is perpetually determining itself *not to be* the in-itself. This means that it can establish itself only in terms of the in-itself and against the in-itself."[52] Thus, the very being of the for-itself is to negate that which is fixed, permanent, and has an essence, or nature (the in-itself; positive being). The for-itself is, therefore, a *lack of being*.[53]

This lack of being constitutes the fundamental impetus of the for-itself to create existential projects, since all such projects are aimed at overcoming this lack. Further ontological description, which shows the dynamic of the desire to overcome this lack inherent to the ontological structure of the for-itself, takes place via an ontological analysis of *lack, desire*, and *value*.[54] Sartre analyses lack as a trinity comprised of the elements *the lacking, the existing*, and *the lacked*. The lacking is that which is missing; the existing is that which misses the lacking; and the lacked is the totality, which would be restored by a synthesis of the existing and the lacking. According to Sartre, lack can only exist in human reality: only consciousness can conceive of the lacking, and imaginatively project the lacked as a possibility. Furthermore, Sartre insists that human reality itself must be a lack, for only a being that is itself a lack can introduce lack into the world. "Only being which lacks can surpass being towards the lacked."[55] Sartre believes that the existence of *desire* is enough to prove that human reality is a lack. Through desire, the for-itself summons something to itself in order to complete itself. Sartre thus understands desire as the experience of a lack, and reasons that the ontological basis for this experience could only be a lack of being.

The determination of human reality as a lack is fleshed out by specifying the three terms of the trinity that this determination implies. *The existing* is the for-itself. *The lacking*—that which the for-itself lacks—is the self as in-itself. This is because the for-itself founds itself as a negation of the in-itself, as itself being a lack of being (or at least the lack of a certain kind of being, the *positive* being of being-in-itself). Being-for-itself is not a "stable," positive structure that simply differs from the in-itself. Rather, its very essence is the negation of the in-itself, but at the same time it transcends itself *towards* the in-itself. That is, the negation of the in-itself is itself a *lack of being* the in-itself. In this sense, the for-itself *desires* the in-itself; its very constitution is the consciousness of lacking being-in-itself. At the same time, however, it does not desire to simply *become* being-in-itself, for this would mean the dissolution of its transcendence; the for-itself would cease to be by collapsing into the in-itself. Such a collapse would not represent a totality achieved by a synthesis of the existent (the for-itself) and the lacking (the self as in-itself), but rather a dissolution of the existent. What is desired by the for-itself, then, is a totality achieved by a synthesis of the for-itself and the in-itself—an ontological structure Sartre calls the *in-itself-for-itself*. This structure would possess the qualities of both kinds of being: it would have the stable, self-consistent essence of the in-itself, yet also transcend itself as a self for-itself. Simply put, the desire to be being-in-itself-for-itself is the desire to have both *security* and *freedom*. It is the desire to be able to make free choices, and also to be a secure foundation for those choices (in the sense of having a determined, and determining, nature or essence that grounds, limits and directs such choices).

According to Sartre, the achievement of the ontological structure being-in-itself-for-itself is the fundamental desire that animates human reality, and the achievement of this structure is the aim of every individual's existential projects. Sartre goes so far as to identify being-in-itself-for-itself as the ontological structure of *value*. Value understood in this sense is value in general; it is both the supreme value and the origin of all other values. It is that irreducible ontological structure to which all other values may be reduced. Sartre specifies that in relation to any lack, value is not the lacking, but the lacked. Thus, the lacked of human reality is value (or in other words, it is being-in-itself-for-itself). According to Sartre, the for-itself does not exist first and then posit value, but rather, value exists co-extensively with the for-itself; it arises with the uprising of consciousness because this uprising itself constitutes a lack (the lacked of which is value). Sartre moreover identifies being-in-itself-for-itself with *God*, arguing that it expresses our fundamental concept of the necessary being. He writes, '[i]s not God a being who is what he is—in that he is all positivity and the foundation of the world—and at the same time a being who is not what he is and who is what he is not—in that he is a self-consciousness and the necessary foundation of himself?'[56] God may be understood in philosophical terms as the *ens causa sui*, the being that founds itself, and this is what the structure being-in-itself-for-itself expresses. Given this equation of God with being-in-itself-for-itself, Sartre asserts that man is the being whose project is to be God, and even that man fundamentally *is* the desire to be God.

Human reality is thus understood by Sartre as the desire to be God, where "God" is the ultimate value to which all other values may be reduced. According to Sartre, all of the projects that human beings pursue in their lives are at bottom motivated by the desire to be God, and the pursuit of such projects is what introduces meaning into the world. Sartre argues, however, that a profound existential nihilism haunts the ontological constitution of human reality, because the desire to be God cannot be realized on the basis of this constitution. The desire to be God is a futile desire: being-in-itself-for-itself is an impossible structure, because the two terms, being-in-itself and being-for-itself, are fundamentally irreconcilable. The determination of the for-itself is to *not be* the in-itself; the very existence of the for-itself depends on this negation. Sartre summarizes the unhappy consequences of this ontology as follows:

> The being of human reality is suffering because it rises in being as perpetually haunted by a totality which it is without being able to be it, precisely because it could not attain the in-itself without losing itself as for-itself. Human reality therefore is by nature an unhappy consciousness with no possibility of surpassing its unhappy state.[57]

In addition to his arguments that meaning and value are given no foundation in a divine God and in human nature, then, Sartre also argues that the projects through which we attempt to find meaning and value in life are futile. Since all such projects have their basis in the desire to be God, they are all equally futile, and this leads Sartre to a relativism with respect to such projects. He concludes that 'it amounts to the same thing whether one gets drunk alone or is a leader of nations.'[58]

Despite the apparently pessimistic terms of Sartre's analysis, however, he does sketch a path towards a possible overcoming of this existential nihilism. This path was never fully developed in Sartre's writings,[59] but its general direction is discernable. In order to understand Sartre's suggested response, we must follow Thomas W. Busch in distinguishing three forms or levels of consciousness in Sartre's work: *unreflective* (or *pre-reflective*) *consciousness*, *impure* (or *ancillary*) *reflection*, and *pure reflection*. These different levels of consciousness have significance for our relation to, and understanding of, the world. The first two levels, unreflective consciousness and impure reflection, preserve the assumptions of the natural attitude. In the natural attitude, the human orientation toward meanings and values is conditioned by what Sartre calls "the spirit of seriousness," which he describes as follows:

> The spirit of seriousness has two characteristics: it considers values as transcendent givens independent of human subjectivity, and it transfers the quality of 'desirable' from the ontological structure of things to their simple material constitution.[60]

In an *unreflective* state, consciousness is caught up in the world of objects, and attributes meanings and values to the objects themselves. Unreflective consciousness is not conscious of the fact that it constitutes the world as meaningful. *Impure* or *ancillary reflection* is a state of consciousness that reflects on and examines consciousness, but in such a way that the natural attitude's assumptions about the world of objects are maintained. In *Transcendence of the Ego*, for example, impure reflection maintains the illusion that the ego is transcendental to consciousness (rather than *vice versa*).

Sartre's analysis of the desire to be God, like most of his analyses in *Being and Nothingness*, describes a structure of human reality that pertains to the level of the natural attitude, prior to the transcendental reduction.[61] That is, according to Sartre, human beings are motivated by the desire to be God when they are in unreflective or impure reflective states of consciousness. In these states, the desire to be God is a desire that is believed to be attainable because values are thought of in terms of the spirit of seriousness (they are seen as objective, as inhering in external objects and states of affairs). The spirit of seriousness thus gives rise to the illusion that the desire to be God can be fulfilled by fulfilling certain empirical conditions. Sartre understands these unreflective and impure reflective states of consciousness as "fallen"; they are states in which human beings are condemned to strive for an unattainable fulfillment. As such, Sartre's analysis of nihilism is a secularized description of the common religious theme of an original fall from a state of grace, as the following passage from the *Notebooks for an Ethics* makes clear:

> The historical act by which being negates itself into the for-itself is a fall and a memory of Paradise Lost. Myth of the fault in every religion and in folklore…The appearance of the for-itself is properly speaking the irruption of History in the world. The spontaneous movement of the For-itself as a lack (on the plane of the unreflective) is to seek the in-itself-for-itself…[62]

Sartre's apparently pessimistic declaration that human reality is by nature an unhappy consciousness must thus be understood as referring only to this "spontaneous movement of the for-itself" on the unreflective and impure reflective levels of consciousness. He gestures towards a way of overcoming the nihilism inherent in these forms of consciousness, in which life is habitually lived, through the application of the *epochē*, which reveals that meaning and value are creations of consciousness and that the in-itself-for-itself is unattainable.

Sartre's version of the phenomenological reduction is equivalent to the third form of consciousness, pure reflection. This state reveals the constitutive character of consciousness and the contingency of human reality. In *Being and Nothingness* Sartre sketches an "existential psychoanalysis" that would be a therapeutic application of the reduction, freeing the subject of this analysis from his or her assumptions about the meaning and value of life.[63] The goal of existential psychoanalysis, according to Sartre, is to reveal that the reality of human being—on the unreflective level—consists in reaching toward the goal of being God, and to reveal the specific ways in which the subject of the analysis tries to reach this goal. Sartre calls the *specific* project through which the subject of analysis hopes to attain the structure being-in-itself-for-itself the "original project of being." The form of the original project of being is a *choice* about the mode of existence or way of life to be pursued, and such choices always manifest themselves singularly and in the concrete lives of individuals. For example, it may take the form of the choice to be a successful writer, a passionate lover, or a powerful politician—any idealized form of life in which it is hoped that the fusion of freedom and security might be achieved. All the specific existential projects engaged in by individuals are expressions of this original project. It is the purpose of existential psychoanalysis to reveal this original project of being *as* essentially the desire to be God and therefore as *futile*.

Existential psychoanalysis aims to make the one who undergoes this analysis realize the futility of the desire to be God, and so reconcile him or her to the fact of being for-itself, a radically free and ungrounded creator of values. The associated goal of existential psychoanalysis is to lift the spirit of seriousness, thus revealing all value as contingent and a creation of human reality. Sartre suggests that through the reduction and existential psychoanalysis, a new ethics becomes possible in which human reality takes on full responsibility for the *creation* of values that may provide life with meaning. Since Sartre insists on the non-existence of God and human nature, there are no given criteria for the creation of such values. Sartre suggests that in the absence of given criteria, *freedom* itself may be taken as the criterion that guides the creation of values. The ontological freedom of the for-itself thus becomes the basis of the value and meaning that may be created in life, and the measure by which we may judge values. Forms of life that acknowledge ontological freedom are privileged by Sartre (at least implicitly) as more meaningful than those which deny it by continuing to believe in objectively given values.

Sartre expresses the acknowledgement or denial of freedom as a choice between *authenticity* and *bad faith* (*mauvaise foi*), which are two ways of responding to the revelation of freedom that the phenomenological reduction affords. Sartre argues that while becoming aware of our freedom (that is, reflecting on our existence by bracketing the natural attitude) is not an uncommon human experience, it is possible, and quite common, to flee from the anguish that this awareness brings. This flight from anguish, which Sartre calls bad faith, involves deceiving ourselves by insisting that objective values exist or that we have a fixed nature that guides our choices.[64] Sartre's prescription for the overcoming of nihilism therefore consists in an ethic concerning the operations of consciousness, *viz.* performing and accepting the consequences of the phenomenological reduction. Employing quasi-religious language, he suggests that living authentically in full acceptance of the need to create values is only possible after a "radical conversion"[65] to a different "fundamental attitude."[66] This radical conversion to an authentic life is further referred to as a "deliverance," and "salvation,"[67] and described as "a self-recovery of being which was previously corrupted."[68]

Some attempts to formulate the radical conversion to authenticity in collective, inter-subjective terms in the *Notebook for an Ethics* notwithstanding, Sartre's early, "classic" existentialist writings on the whole imply that existential nihilism is a problem that must be overcome by each individual, on their own. His emphases on consciousness as meaning-constituting and the individual's choice to live in bad faith or attempt to achieve authenticity mean that nihilism must be confronted in the personal life of the individual. Sartre's well-known theme of radical freedom means that the individual human being is free to constitute the meaning of his or her own life, unconstrained by any empirical or cultural limitations. While he develops the idea of existential analysis on the Freudian model of analyst/analysand, Sartre suggests that the analyst and the subject of analysis may in fact be the same person.[69] He asserts that "there are many men who have practiced this psychoanalysis on themselves and who have not waited to learn its principles in order to make use of them as a means of deliverance and salvation."[70]

While Sartre's analysis of and prescription for overcoming nihilism centralizes consciousness, his view of consciousness as directly involved in the world (a corollary of views on the intentionality of consciousness and his rejection of the transcendental ego) means that the ethic of authenticity is one of concrete action. He proposes that values are created through concrete acts in the world, through active modes of living rather than merely passive thinking and judging. In a well-known passage, he asserts that 'in this world where I engage myself, my acts cause values to spring up like partridges.'[71] Summing up his position on the meaning and value of life in the wake of the death of God, Sartre writes:

> [T]o say that we invent values means no more nor than this; that there is no sense in life *a priori*. Life is nothing until it is lived; but it is yours to make sense of, and the value of it is nothing else but the sense that you choose.[72]

In summary, nihilism is understood in Sartre's existentialism as the meaninglessness that is drawn as a conclusion from a thoroughgoing atheistic position. Sartre extrapolates the meaning of the Nietzschean "death of God" for human reality, arguing that existence is contingent, ungrounded, and without objective value. Through his emphases on objective meaninglessness and the futility of human life, Sartre appears primarily concerned with the problem posed by the abyssal form of nihilism: how is a valuable life possible in the face of a meaningless world, where there appears to be no source of guidance for determining how our lives should be lived? Like Nietzsche, Sartre proposes an overcoming of nihilism through the free and active creation of values. His phenomenological methodology gives primacy to individual consciousness and lived experience in his analysis of and response to nihilism, and he places a central importance on human beings as the creators of value. Martin Heidegger, while also employing a phenomenological approach, analyses nihilism in terms which differ sharply from Sartre's, and which call into question the validity of the analyses and responses to nihilism offered by both Sartre and Nietzsche.

Heidegger: nihilism and metaphysics

Being itself necessarily remains unthought in metaphysics. Metaphysics is a history in which there is essentially nothing to Being itself: metaphysics as such is nihilism proper.

—Martin Heidegger[73]

Heidegger offers a powerful reworking of the problem of nihilism in the terms of his own highly original thought, and this reworking is pivotal in the movement toward postmodern theorizations of the problem of existential meaning. With Heidegger, the adequacy of the terms in which nihilism is analyzed, and the possibility of its overcoming, become seriously problematized. Like Nietzsche, Heidegger diagnoses modernity as suffering from a breakdown of the structures that traditionally have provided meaning, and traces the cause of this breakdown to fundamental features of the Western cultural and intellectual tradition. Heidegger develops these themes in a unique way, however, by insisting that questions of meaning and significance are fundamentally *ontological* questions, which should be addressed with reference to Being itself, not simply the being of values or of "human reality." Heidegger's engagement with nihilism concerns the actual conditions of culture in Europe (and Germany in particular) of his time, but he attempts to think nihilism in its essence, as a problem concerning Being, a problem which he sees as having a global significance.[74] Indeed, he argues that nihilism remains uncomprehended in the works of Nietzsche and other thinkers who fail to think it in its essential character as the oblivion, or abandonment, of Being.[75]

Throughout his career, Heidegger expressed a concern with the problem of meaning that nihilism represents. In the early 1920s, he centralized the problem of the meaning of human life, which he then referred to as "life," "facticity," and "factical life."[76] The critical confrontation with modernity which his entire philosophy can be seen as enacting, and which arguably goes some way at least to explaining his notorious involvement with National Socialism in the early 1930s, can be understood as concerned with the erosion of meaning in modern culture.[77] Heidegger's explicit engagement with the discourse of nihilism, however, takes place most often through his commentary on Nietzsche, which he began in the mid-1930s concurrently with the "turn" in his thought. In explicating Heidegger's encounter with nihilism, then, I will focus on Heidegger's thought "after the turn," referring to *Being and Time* and earlier writings only insofar as they provide points of reference for situating the later project.

Heidegger's concern with nihilism is perhaps most readily apparent in his critical comments on various aspects of modernity, in particular modern technology and cultural changes associated with the proliferation of this technology. Often such comments are made in the context of popular speeches or lectures, and remain at a relatively superficial level of Heidegger's thought. These comments, however, help to situate Heidegger with other thinkers concerned with nihilism by showing that he shares many of their concerns, and it is thus useful to note these criticisms of modernity before turning to their root cause (according to Heidegger) in ontological conditions. The cultural changes associated with modernization that concern Heidegger include the increasing migration of the populace from rural to urban areas and the widespread exposure to the generalized communication of messages afforded by the mass media. In an address delivered to Schwarzwald peasants, Heidegger explains the plight of many modern Germans as follows:

> Hourly and daily they are chained to radio and television. Week after week the movies carry them off into uncommon, but often merely common, realms of the imagination, and give the illusion of a world that is no world. Picture magazines are everywhere available. All that with which modern techniques of communication stimulate, assail, and drive man—all that is already much closer to man today than his fields around his farmstead, closer than the sky over the earth, closer than the night over day, closer than the conventions and customs of his village, than the tradition of his native world.[78]

From Heidegger's observation of this state of affairs in which the messages of the mass media are more real to people than their traditional customs, he concludes that "the *rootedness*, the *autochthony*, of man is threatened today at its core!"[79]

Heidegger's principal concern expressed here is that in modernity, Western culture has lost a "grounding" which provides the basis for shared concerns, commitments and significance. His assessment of the modern situation is that "there is no longer any goal in and through which all the forces of the historical existence of peoples can cohere and in the direction of which they can develop."[80] Heidegger suggests here that true meaning and significance can only be found in commitment to a goal, and such a commitment requires the existence of a "world," a shared system of understanding in which beings are given particular significances.[81] Such a world of significances has generally been provided by tradition, and traditional beliefs, lifestyles, and cultural practices are precisely what are being undermined by modernization. Heidegger writes that "[a]ccording to our human experience and history, at least as far as I see it, I know that everything essential and everything great originated from the fact that man had a home and was rooted in a tradition."[82] In these "popular" accounts of Heidegger's thought, the central problem of modernity is that modern humanity has lost a sense of meaning that has been provided by tradition. Heidegger's theorization of nihilism is an attempt to account for, and examine the possibilities for overcoming, this loss of meaning. However, his analysis of nihilism in his philosophical works moves far beyond the common understanding of terms such as "home" and "tradition," to considerations of Being.

Heidegger argues that the negative conditions of culture associated with modern technology and mass media have an underlying *essential* determination. He distinguishes between two manifestations of nihilism, using the expression "actual nihilism" to indicate existing cultural conditions and "essential nihilism" to indicate the ontological dimension in which these conditions are grounded.[83] Since for Heidegger essential nihilism is the fundamental cause of actual nihilism, the only hope we have of understanding and effectively responding to the crisis of nihilism is to think it in its essence, that is, in terms of Being. For Heidegger, "essence" does not indicate the unchanging core of a phenomenon as it does in classical metaphysics, but rather the way in which a phenomenon is disclosed, which endures for a time, then passes away.[84] To think a phenomenon in its essence, for the later Heidegger, is thus to think the history of Being out of which that phenomenon arises. An appreciation of Heidegger's understanding of essential nihilism thus requires an acquaintance with the basic concepts of his philosophy, and in particular his thought after the turn which centers around thinking the "history of Being."

As is well-known, Heidegger argues that the meaning of Being has been forgotten, and his entire philosophical project centers around a renewed attempt to think Being. The meaning of Being is a problem because what it means "to be" is one of the most basic philosophical questions we can ask, yet it is a question which does not lend itself to a ready answer. As Aristotle famously noted, there are many ways in which something may be said "to be," and the "leading" meaning of being, which unifies all these ways, is not easy to discern. Heidegger wants to insist on the multiple senses of the verb "to be," and yet insist that they are unified in some way. In addition to these basic problems, according to Heidegger the history of philosophy has clouded our thinking about Being by giving misleading answers to the question of the meaning of Being. It has done this by forgetting what Heidegger sometimes calls "the ontological difference," the difference between Being and beings (or particular entities). Heidegger suggests that there are four basic ways in which the philosophical tradition has tended to answer questions about Being that make the mistake of forgetting the ontological difference:

1. Being is a particular being, often thought as the supreme being, God. (Heidegger sometimes calls this "ontotheology.")
2. Being is an empty universal derived through abstraction from beings. Being is that which all beings have in common.
3. Being is a property that all beings have, along with their other properties.
4. Being is understood by taking one being (often, human being) as a paradigm or standard for all Being.[85]

From his first lectures on Nietzsche (1936–7) on, Heidegger often calls the type of philosophical thinking that forgets the ontological difference "metaphysics" in order to distinguish it from his own attempts to think the question of Being in a more rigorous fashion.

In his first major work *Being and Time* (1927),[86] Heidegger conceives the rethinking of Being as a project of "fundamental ontology," the attempt to find the meaning of Being itself which provides the foundation for all "regional" ontologies (the being of particular entities). This fundamental ontology proceeds methodologically through an analytic of the existential structures of *Dasein* (human being understood as that being for whom being itself is an issue), towards an explication of time as the horizonal, transcendental meaning of Being. However, as is also well-known, the project of fundamental ontology begun in *Being and Time* was aborted before it was completed, and Heidegger's thought underwent a "turn"[87] in the mid-1930s, away from fundamental ontology as a search for the *meaning* of Being and toward "being-historical thinking" (*seynsgeschichtliches Denken*) as a search for the *truth* of Being. While the reasons for this turn are complex, put simply, Heidegger came to believe that the project of fundamental ontology could only thematise Being as time *for Dasein*[88], and could not think Being in itself. This limitation of fundamental ontology is bound up with a conception of the problem of Being as a search for its *meaning*, since Heidegger understands meaning in *Being and Time* as only possible through and in relation to *Dasein*.[89] The turn in his thought sought to think Being itself in terms of its own temporality, or its *history*, as the history of the occurrence of *truth* (understood as disclosure), and as the origin of time-space itself. In short, the turn is a move from the centrality of *Dasein* and its temporality to the centrality of Being and its history. Heidegger's analysis of essential nihilism takes place in the context of this turn, as indicated by the title of one of his central essays on the topic, "Nihilism as Determined by the History of Being."

There is an important sense in which an "adequate" answer to the question of Being was never achieved in Heidegger's thought, since, as we shall see, according to him Being "stays away" in the current epoch, and all our thinking can do is prepare for its return. Moreover, Heidegger's own meditations on Being are complex, sometimes esoteric, and shift significantly through the course of his writings. A brief outline of his views on Being are necessary here in order to allow an appreciation of his approach to nihilism. Such an outline may be made by highlighting some key points on which Heidegger's understanding of Being differs from traditional philosophical understandings. Heidegger thinks through the history of metaphysics in order to show how Being has been understood, and also how these understandings have been forms of misunderstanding—or, more accurately, how in each way Being has disclosed itself, it has progressively kept more of itself hidden. Heidegger attempts to think the "hidden" side of Being, and thus indicate what Being might be beyond its metaphysical determination. In what follows I will indicate some of the salient points of Heidegger's "more originary" thinking of Being. However, this brief outline will unavoidably remain partial and approximate.

For Heidegger, Being is that which *discloses* entities, or makes them present. Being itself, however, should not be understood as a particular being, or as anything that is itself present. The tendency to understand Being as presence is, for Heidegger, characteristic of the metaphysical tradition. This tendency was established in Ancient Greek philosophy, and especially the philosophy of Aristotle. Aristotle identified *ousia* (essence, or what it means "to be") with *parousia* (presence), thus claiming that what it means to be, is to be present. However, Heidegger argues, the idea of presence implies temporality, and this is a deeper meaning of Being which metaphysics itself cannot think.[90] For Heidegger, Being is a processual, temporal, event-like occurrence in which particular beings are revealed, disclosed, or "come to presence." Drawing on the Ancient Greek concept of nature as *phusis*, Heidegger understands Being as an "emerging power" which brings particular beings to light and stabilizes this disclosure of beings for a time, but does not make them permanently present.[91] On this account, Being is a dynamic process that discloses beings in different ways at different times. Being thus has a history, which is the history of these changing disclosures. Heidegger identifies stages in this history, in which a particular way of disclosure predominates for a time, which he calls "epochs" (*Epochen*). However, he also identifies trans-epochal regularities or tendencies in the history of Being, which he refers to as "destining," or "sending" (*Geschick*).

Significantly, Heidegger conceives of the disclosure of Being as also implying a necessary dimension of *concealing*. As Michael Inwood explains, this double process of revealing and concealing operates on two levels. On one level, particular beings are revealed, but never fully. In our encountering of particular beings, their being is unconcealed or disclosed to us "partially and case by case."[92] On a "higher" level, beings as a whole are disclosed in what Heidegger at times calls a "world" or the "open." On this level, Being conceals itself insofar as not all of reality, or all of its possibilities, are revealed in a particular disclosure of Being.[93] Heidegger likens Being in its self-concealing aspect on this level to a chasm, abyss, or open space, which allows beings which are revealed to stand out, but which itself falls away, remaining hidden. In different epochs of the history of Being, not only are different aspects of reality revealed, but Being itself can remain concealed to varying degrees. As is well-known, Heidegger associates the double process of disclosure and concealing with an understanding of truth as *aletheia*, which he takes to be more primordial than truth as correspondence.[94] Thus, Heidegger's turn to the history of Being also marks a shift to a concern with the *truth* of Being (and no longer its meaning), in so far as the different ways Being has disclosed and concealed itself historically may be understood as occurrences of truth.

According to Heidegger, Being discloses beings in a way which is *event*-like. For him, Being is not something static; it cannot be correctly thought as an eternal essence, a universal, or a transcendental structure.[95] In

Contributions to Philosophy, Heidegger develops the term *Ereignis*[96] as an attempt to think Being itself, free from the metaphysical perspective that only thinks Being in relation to beings.[97] For Heidegger, then, Being itself is *Ereignis*[98]—"event" or "occurrence"—rather than stable structure or enduring presence. The sense of "event" to which *Ereignis* alludes is not simply a local occurrence, but an epochal disclosure which reveals the totality of beings in a world. Moreover, *Ereignis* cannot be understood as an event which occurs to a being within a given space and time; rather, it is what gives, founds, or discloses the very time-space in which beings appear.[99]

Events of Being disclose beings *as* particular kinds of beings. In showing up as particular kinds of beings, beings have certain significances, and relate to each other in ways which themselves have significance. All beings, including human beings, are disclosed by Being in this way, and the network of significant relations between things includes relations between persons, and between persons and their environment. The event of Being is thus what founds social roles and hierarchies, the sense individuals have of their place in their community and the world, and the meaningful life projects which might be pursued within the world. Thus, for Heidegger, the disclosive power of Being is what lies at the origin of the "lifeworld," the world of significances which gives coherence to lived human existence.

In Heidegger's statements such as those from the *Discourse on Thinking* quoted earlier, it appears as though tradition is what gives coherence to these networks of significant relations and allows their persistence over time. Tradition thus indicates a "rootedness" in a disclosure of beings, which constitutes a world for a community, providing the members of that community with a sense of meaning and significance. Heidegger's concern with the loss of rootedness or autochthony in modern Western society is thus expresses itself as a concern with the breakdown of traditional communities and the networks of meaning and significance they embodied. On Heidegger's view, it would seem that a minimal degree of coherence in a community, provided by rootedness in tradition, is a prerequisite for a sense of meaning. However, it is essential to understand that for Heidegger, all beings and their significance have their origin in Being. That is, it is that which discloses beings—and our relation to it—which is the issue at stake for Heidegger, rather than any particular tradition or way of life grounded in such a disclosure. Moreover, for him Being itself is more originary than distinctions such as individual and community, or tradition and progress. Tradition and community are not the *origin* of significance, and Heidegger thus disavows any anthropological reading of his philosophy which would locate his analysis at the sociological level. That is, the breakdown of traditions and rural communities is for Heidegger only a symptom of nihilism, not its origin. Thus, while denouncements of modernization such as the ones from the *Discourse on Thinking* can make Heidegger appear to be a romantic traditionalist, he does not believe we can overcome nihilism by simply returning to traditional ways of life. Because for him the essence of nihilism lies with Being itself, issues of existential meaning can only legitimately be confronted through "being-historical-thinking."

As is well known, Heidegger's critique of modernity and analysis of nihilism is bound up with a critique of technology. This critique, however, is itself a form of being-historical-thinking: it is a critique of the *essence* of technology, rather than of technology itself. Heidegger understands the essence of modern technology as the culmination of metaphysics in the current age, insofar as it constitutes a way of disclosing beings in which Being itself is covered over and forgotten. For Heidegger, the essence of technology is a way of revealing beings that predates the developments of modern science and the proliferation of actual technological artifacts. The essence of modern technology is closely tied to the subjectivism that characterizes modern philosophy. For Heidegger, the categories of subject and object are not universal and necessary givens, but particular, contingent ways that beings are revealed. Heidegger gives an analysis of the subject as "that-which-lies-before, which, as ground, gathers everything onto itself."[100] The subject is the privileged centre of the world which acts as a ground or foundation for knowledge, while everything else in the world has the character of objectness. Objectness is understood as "whatever stands-over-against,"[101] or that which appears to the subject as a contingent object on the ground of its own subjectivity. Heidegger moreover argues that the *will* is an extension of subjectivism and thus a part of the metaphysical worldview that contributes to the essence of technology. On Heidegger's account, the will presupposes a willing subject which sets itself up before the world of objects and sees the world as consisting of objects for its manipulation and control. Understood in conjunction with modern philosophy, which privileges the subject, the will appears at bottom as a will to dominate the world. The division of the world into subject and object thus gives the subject a priority that is ethical as well as epistemological, in the sense that the world appears to the subject as a series of objects for its use and disposal. Objects are not seen to have any meaning or worth in themselves, but have worth only insofar as they are used as means to meet the ends of knowing and willing subjects.

On Heidegger's interpretation, the essence of technology is a crystallization and apotheosis of the worldview set up by subjectivism and the will. He names the essence of technology *Ge-stell*, a term commonly translated as "enframing."[102] As this translation suggests, the essence of technology consists in the setting up of a fixed framework or perspective through which beings are disclosed, which predetermines the way they are disclosed. Heidegger calls the way beings are disclosed in the technological enframing *Bestand*, which may be variously translated as standing reserve, stock, resource, or raw material. Through the perspective of *Ge-stell*, beings are revealed as potential energy that may be stored and put to use according to the calculations and plans of willing subjects. Modern technology is thus understood, in its essence or its relation to Being, as a means to the willing subject's domination of the objective world. However, Heidegger argues that the essence of modern technology extends beyond this determination because *Ge-stell* is a way of disclosing beings, which has a hegemonic tendency. *Bestand* is a disclosure of beings in which the qualities of subject and object disappear: beings are "ordered" or placed in a series in which the elements are interchangeable; there is no longer a hierarchical relation between objective beings and a subject which acts as their ground. Because *Ge-stell* tends towards hegemony, *all* beings are susceptible to being disclosed as *Bestand*, including human beings who were previously disclosed as the willing subjects that manipulated the object-world.[103]

Heidegger argues that the essence of modern technology is the zenith of metaphysics because *Ge-stell* is the way of disclosing beings in which Being itself is most completely covered over and forgotten. *Ge-stell* is an especially narrow way of disclosing beings that maximises the degree of concealment in the process of disclosure on both levels identified earlier. First, in relation to particular beings, through *Ge-stell* any particular being is revealed as *Bestand*, and nothing but *Bestand*. As all beings are disclosed as raw materials awaiting use, this disclosure covers over the particularity and uniqueness of beings, the fact that they appear in a *particular* way, and that they hide other potentialities of disclosure. As Heidegger phrases this, *Ge-stell* does not let beings: *be*. Rather, it seizes beings and determines their way of being narrowly. That is, *Ge-stell* conceals a particularly large range of potential other ways of being disclosed that any particular being will have. Second, in relation to the disclosure of beings as a whole, *Ge-stell* discloses all beings in fundamentally the same way: as *Bestand*. Moreover, this disclosure covers over disclosure itself in a profound way, since beings are determined in their pure presence, as fully accessible to calculative rationality and fully disposable according to whatever task they are turned to. In other words, *Ge-stell* conceals the totality of Beings *as* disclosed, and thus conceals Being itself, because it presents the world as consisting of beings which are simply present, which contain no mystery, no side of their being which remains hidden, and which would be in no need of disclosure.

Heidegger's understanding of the metaphysical nature of philosophy and of modern technology is decisive for his determination of the nature of essential nihilism. He determines this essential meaning by isolating the root of the word nihilism, *nihil*—meaning "nothing"—and thinking it in terms of Being. Heidegger's answer to the question, "What is happening to Being, such that actual nihilism is the case?" is answered with the assertion that '*Nothing* is happening to Being.'[104] By this he does not mean that nothing at all is happening to Being, but rather that Being itself is *becoming* nothing. With this move Heidegger identifies the problem of nihilism announced by Nietzsche with the forgetting of Being in metaphysics, interpreting the nothingness of Being as the way in which Being remains unthought—and hence is effectively reduced to nothing—in metaphysical thinking. For Heidegger, like Nietzsche, the history of Western thought and culture can be understood as a slow decline into a nihilistic state, the crisis-point of which is reached in modernity. Heidegger's analysis differs from Nietzsche's, however, in that he gives the meaning of nihilism a primarily ontological determination: nihilism as determined by the history of Being is the waning of Being in accord with the waxing of metaphysics, reaching its culmination in the world of modern technological enframing. Heidegger thus names the essence of nihilism by identifying it as metaphysics, writing that "*metaphysics as such is nihilism proper.*"[105]

Heidegger further argues that the concealing of Being in metaphysics is a *double* concealing, and that this double concealing constitutes the full essence of nihilism. Metaphysics doubly conceals, or doubly forgets Being because not only is Being forgotten, but the forgetting of Being itself is forgotten. In philosophy, metaphysics gives an answer to the question of Being by providing a theory about beings, obscuring the question of Being itself by passing off an inadequate answer as adequate. In modern technology, beings are disclosed in such a way that there appears to be no more to them than their appearance as *Bestand*, obscuring the necessity of a power of disclosure which discloses them as such, and which might disclose them in other ways. Heidegger employs the terminological couplet authentic/inauthentic to distinguish the two senses of the forgetting of Being in the essence of nihilism: *authentic nihilism* designates the concealing of Being in metaphysics, and *inauthentic nihilism* designates the concealing of this concealing.[106] In this context, the term "authentic" (*eigentlich*) indicates the holding-fast of a thing to its essence, whereas "inauthentic" (*uneigentlich*) indicates the deviation of a thing from its essence. In the case of nihilism, authentic nihilism indicates the concealing of Being as the essence of nihilism, but Heidegger notes that this authenticity is not itself something authentic, since it consists in a concealing of the essence of Being. Inauthentic nihilism, on the other hand, consists in a deviation of nihilism from its own essence, since it conceals the very concealing of Being. However, Heidegger states that it is the unity of authentic and inauthentic nihilism—the concealing of Being and the concealing of this concealing—which must be understood as the full essence of nihilism, and which is expressed in the culmination of metaphysics in modernity.[107]

Heidegger's meditation on the essence of nihilism may be related back to the problem of actual nihilism *via* the importance he gives to the conception of a "world," as the totality of beings in networks of significance, for the establishment of meaning. Heidegger argues that in the era of modern technology the rootedness and autochthony of cultures is being eroded because the disclosure of beings as *Bestand* does not allow for the significant relations that are required for meaningful human life. While *Ge-stell* constitutes a world by disclosing beings, it discloses them in such a way that they do not constitute or connect with meaningful human purposes and activities. This is because beings, as resources or "standing reserve," reveal nothing about the nature of the world such that certain ends or purposes might appear significant. Simply put, *Ge-stell* discloses a world of means, without ends. Resources tell us nothing about the purposes to which they might meaningfully be put. More pointedly, *Ge-stell* undermines the meaning of human life by reducing human beings themselves to the status of resources; interchangeable items held on hand for use, without purposes or ends of their own.

In this way, Heidegger's analysis of nihilism in the essence of modern technology constitutes a form of *reductive* nihilism, since it decreases the possibilities for a meaningful sense of existence by reducing the perspective in which existence is revealed to one which doesn't effectively establish meaning for human life. Heidegger's argument here rests on the supposition that the world of modern technology, calculation, and planning is ultimately without purpose, despite the apparent purposefulness of industry and the many practical applications of technological devices. The disclosure of beings as *Bestand*, in becoming hegemonic, coincides with an autonomy of modern technology in which resources are employed instrumentally without significant thought to overall aims or purposes. The world that modern technology reveals is thus one in which human beings no longer have a home; the sense of significance and purpose has been eroded by the technological disclosure of beings and this same disclosure prevents further disclosive events of Being which might restore a more meaningful world. In this sense, Heidegger's analysis of nihilism also contains an *abyssal* dimension, since direction and purpose evaporate in the perspective of *Ge-stell*.

We have now seen in outline Heidegger's analysis of nihilism. How does he propose we respond to this problem? Heidegger's reflections on the possibility of overcoming nihilism may be approached by first noting his engagements with Nietzsche and Sartre and his rejection of the kinds of responses to nihilism offered by these philosophers.[108] In the context of Heidegger's construal of nihilism, some of the concepts central to Nietzsche's and Sartre's analyses of and responses to nihilism appear implicated in the problem of nihilism itself, and hence cannot be seen to herald an effective way out. On Heidegger's account, both Nietzsche's and Sartre's philosophies are metaphysical, and their analyses of and responses to nihilism are founded on metaphysical categories such as the subject, the will, and value. Heidegger argues that despite Nietzsche's and Sartre's attempts to overturn the metaphysical tradition, both of their philosophies reflect traditional metaphysical categories and thus remain rooted in the tradition of thought which obscures Being itself.

Nietzsche attempts to overturn the metaphysics associated with Platonism and the Christian-moral interpretation of the world by replacing belief in a suprasensory world with an affirmation of the world as will to power. The will to power is an interpretation of the world as a flux of forces, consisting entirely of quanta of force that expand outwards, increasing their outward expansion relative to other such quanta of force. Nietzsche's view of the world as will to power is a vision of a dynamic, chaotic interplay of forces in which becoming, rather than Being, is the ontological principle, and seemingly fixed identities are only relative stabilizations of different forces in flux.[109] The will to power is an immanent ontology, which promises to overcome the "two world" ontologies Nietzsche associates with religious nihilism: it eschews belief in any transcendent, "true" world, and affirms *this* world. While the will to power might be an effective alternative to nihilism as Nietzsche understands it, however, Heidegger argues that it is not effective against nihilism understood as metaphysics as such. According to Heidegger, Nietzsche's ontology of the will to power is complemented by his doctrine of the eternal returning of the same (*die ewige Wiederkunft*). The eternal returning of the same is a cyclical view of time which posits that in a cosmos of finite space and infinite time, the same arrangements of matter will recur an infinite number of times. This means that every event will recur, exactly the same, infinitely.[110] On Heidegger's interpretation, the will to power and the eternal returning of the same conform to the traditional metaphysical categories of essence (*essentia*) and existence (*existentia*): will to power is the essence of what is, and the eternal returning of the same is the way this essence is actualized.[111] For Heidegger, these metaphysical terms are not originary enough: Being discloses beings in terms of these categories, but we need to think beyond them to think Being itself. Nietzsche's attempt to overcome metaphysics is therefore unsuccessful according to Heidegger's reckoning, since he does no more than set up a new metaphysics in place of the Christian-Platonic metaphysics he has deposed.[112]

Heidegger gives an even more critical analysis of Nietzsche's reflections on nihilism in arguing that the concept of *value* which underlies these reflections is implicated in nihilism. Indeed, he argues that Nietzsche holds a special place in the history of Western philosophy as that thinker in whose thought nihilism is consummated, precisely because Nietzsche thinks Being as value. Heidegger supports this interpretation by giving an analysis of the will to power as a metaphysics of value, and arguing that this metaphysics is the answer Nietzsche gives to the question of Being. Heidegger interprets Nietzsche's understanding of value with reference to aphorism 710 of *The Will to Power*: "The point of view of 'value' is the point of view constituting the *preservation-enhancement conditions* with respect to complex forms of relative duration of life within becoming."[113] According to this aphorism, value is a point of view, and Heidegger understands this in both the sense of that which is viewed in a certain perspective and of that which does the viewing. As the latter, value implies a point which directs the gaze towards something and posits it according to an aim. As the former, value is the positing of a view according to this aim. As such, values are not things in themselves, but only points of view posited by and dependent upon that which views.[114]

Heidegger further interprets this aphorism as identifying value with the will to power through the terms "life" and "becoming." As previously noted, Nietzsche's theory of the will to power is an ontology and metaphysics of becoming, and the world itself is nothing but will to power. On Heidegger's interpretation, the 'complex forms of relative duration of life within becoming' are "dominating centres" or "ruling configurations" shaped within the will to power. Art, the state, religion, science, and society are forms of these ruling configurations, and these configurations attempt to preserve and enhance themselves.[115] According to Nietzsche's aphorism, values are the conditions posited by the will to power in order to preserve and enhance itself. On Heidegger's interpretation then, '[t]he will to power is the ground of the necessity of value-positing and of the origin of the possibility of value judgement.'[116] Moreover, since the will to power is itself nothing but a dynamic interplay of forces for preservation-enhancement, values appear as the fundamental condition of the will to power itself.[117] Given the identification of the will to power with Being, Heidegger thus interprets Nietzsche's thought as implying that Being itself is value.

Heidegger's argument for the association of value with nihilism derives from that aspect of value which implies a point from which the viewing of values takes place. He associates this point with the subject of modern philosophy, and argues that all value-positing is a subjectivising.[118] Heidegger argues that while values purport to impart worth to what is valued, they in fact detract from such worth by making this worth dependent on, and relative to, a value-positing subject. That which is valued is implicitly judged as having no worth in itself, independently of the subject's valuation of it. Heidegger writes:

> [P]recisely through the characterization of something as "a value" what is so valued is robbed of its worth. That is to say, by the assessment of something as a value what is valued is admitted only as an object for man's estimation.[119]

That which is given value by a subject can just as easily have that value taken away, and value is thus a very weak way of conceiving the worth or meaningfulness of a thing. Heidegger's critical stance towards value-thinking can also be understood as owing a debt to his phenomenological heritage: for him, true meaning and significance must be imbedded in the unified whole of a background network of significances, which constitutes a "world." Values, as objects of intentional consciousness, are abstracted from such networks of significance, and as such do not form part of a meaningful contextual whole. Instead, they may be chosen or rejected by subjects as mere objects of conscious attention, rather than forming part of the background conditions for choice which give such choices meaning and significance. Arguably, it is only the type of meaning or significance that constitutes such background conditions that has true significance, and which can motivate real commitment and serious concern. Heidegger expresses this weakness of value in his comment that "[n]o one dies for mere values."[120] He concludes that "thinking in values is the greatest blasphemy against Being,"[121] since it reduces it to contingent positing by a subject. He views Nietzsche as the consummate nihilist because, while believing he has thought Being in the most exalted manner (i.e. as a value), he has devalued Being to the greatest degree and covered over the question of Being most completely. Since Nietzsche's entire thinking about nihilism takes place in terms of values, on Heidegger's view he is thoroughly embroiled in nihilism itself, with no hope of overcoming it.

Heidegger's portrait of Nietzsche as the consummate nihilist is completed by linking Nietzsche's thought with the metaphysics of modern technology. This link is made *via* the subjectivising tendency that Heidegger notes in the will to power, which in turn corresponds with the disclosure of beings as objects to be manipulated and controlled by willing and evaluating subjects. Heidegger interprets Nietzsche's project of a revaluation of all values as consisting essentially in establishing a new source of valuation, a change that involves a move from the suprasensory world as the source of value to the will to power as this source. For Heidegger, this move is analogous to the attempt of modern philosophy to establish subjectivity as the seat of certainty in preference to external sources of justification, such as religion: in human subjectivity the value-positing activity of the will to power becomes conscious of itself, and thus establishes itself as the ground of valuation. This subject then posits beings as objects to manipulate for the end of its own preservation and enhancement. As such, Heidegger sees Nietzsche's metaphysics of the will to power as manifesting a will to the domination of the earth, the very will which enframes beings as *Bestand* and inaugurates the culmination of nihilism in modern technology. On this account, Nietzsche's analysis of and response to nihilism is thus not only an impasse, but a recapitulation and deepening of the tendencies in the history of metaphysics which have led to the nihilistic crisis of modernity.

Heidegger's criticisms of Sartre are comparatively brief, and may be treated briefly here since they encompass some of the same points on which he critiques Nietzsche. Heidegger gives an analysis of Sartre's phenomenological ontology which picks out the same fundamental points as his discussion of Nietzsche's ontology, and which focuses on Sartre's slogan "existence precedes essence" (*existentia* precedes *essentia*). Sartre's formula is a reversal of the traditional metaphysical doctrine that essence precedes existence. Heidegger argues that, like Nietzsche, Sartre does not succeed in overcoming what is decisive about metaphysics, *viz.* its obscuring of Being, because he does not enquire into the origin of the categories of essence and existence. For Heidegger, Being must be questioned at a more fundamental level and understood as that which discloses the categories of essence and existence. A reversal of a metaphysical statement, such as the one Sartre performs, remains a metaphysical statement because it still accepts the categories of metaphysics. According to Heidegger, with the slogan of existentialism, "existence preceeds essence," Sartre "stays with metaphysics in oblivion of the truth of Being."[122] Insofar as Nietzsche and Sartre both retain traditional metaphysical categories as the philosophical ground for their analyses of nihilism, from Heidegger's perspective these analyses will reproduce the fundamental traits of nihilism as metaphysics and will not enable a move beyond nihilism. In both these cases, then, Heidegger argues that a reversal of metaphysical categories is not enough to overcome metaphysics and thereby overcome nihilism.

Insofar as Sartre's theorization of nihilism is also heavily dependent on values, his thought is also subject to the same judgment as we have seen him give to Nietzsche on this count. Sartre's proposal to overcome nihilism through the free creation of values is seen, from a Heideggerian perspective, as nothing other than a deeper entanglement in the problem of nihilism. Heidegger's final criticism of Sartre's existentialism is that it is a humanism, as the title of Sartre's popular lecture itself asserts. He takes issue with Sartre's statement, "we are precisely in a situation where there are only human beings."[123] In the context of his own philosophy, Heidegger asserts that this should say instead, "we are precisely in a situation where principally there is Being."[124] The difference between Sartre and Heidegger here can be understood in terms of their respective understandings of the origin of meaning in the world: for Sartre, the world is meaningless in itself, and is only imbued with meaning through the meaning-conferring activities of conscious human beings. For Heidegger, although human beings (as *Dasein*) have an essential role to play in the revelation of meaning, Being takes priority since Being is that which *gives* meaning to human beings. From Heidegger's perspective, Sartre's central focus on consciousness and human reality reproduces the subjectivism of modern metaphysics. In supposing that meaning issues entirely from human consciousness, Sartre's theory of meaning remains blind to the way Being gives the meaning of beings. Heidegger criticizes humanism in general as a metaphysical conception of what it means to be human, which decides the answer to this question in advance of "essential" considerations. Humanism takes a particular disclosure of the human being as universal and necessary, and is unable to think the essence of human beings in their special relation to Being.[125] The humanistic character of Sartre's existentialism is therefore a contributing factor to its remaining metaphysical and its consequent failure as a solution to nihilism.

Heidegger's own response to nihilism seeks to avoid the aporiae that he sees in Nietzsche's and Sartre's responses. This response hinges on the insight that the metaphysical way of disclosing beings is not simply a mistake made by human beings, but is given by Being itself. This follows from Heidegger's understanding of the necessary interplay between Being and human being (*Dasein*) in the process of the disclosure of beings: while *Ge-stell* consists of a reification of the way human beings interpret beings, this way of disclosing beings is itself given by Being. This follows from Heidegger's account of meaning, in which all disclosure of beings is necessarily given by Being, but Being itself may be concealed in such disclosure. According to Heidegger, nihilism is therefore the history of Being itself, and cannot be conceived of as simply a human mistake. Nihilism, as the oblivion of Being, is Being in its *self*-concealing, or as Heidegger phrases it, in its "default."

This determination of nihilism is most clearly evident in Heidegger's response to Ernst Jünger on the topic,[126] where he argues against the adequacy of representing nihilism as a line between two historical epochs, which humanity must cross in order to proceed with a meaningful history. On Jünger's account (as Heidegger construes it), it is as if human beings currently occupy the side of the line designated by "nihilism," but may cross the line to (re)join Being on the other side. For Heidegger this image is inadequate because it separates both nihilism and Being from human beings, treating the former terms as objects and the latter as subjects. On this objectification of nihilism, Heidegger writes:

> People have tended to represent the 'oblivion of Being' as though, to say it by way of an image, Being were the umbrella that has been left sitting somewhere through the forgetfulness of some philosophy professor.[127]

This way of thinking nihilism is not conducive to an overcoming of nihilism because it reproduces the metaphysical thinking that divides beings into subjects and objects. As such, it cannot think nihilism in its essence, that is, with regard to what is going on with Being prior to the disclosure of beings in terms of subjects and objects. Heidegger prefers the image of nihilism as a *zone* in which nihilism, Being, and human beings are co-present. This image more closely approximates Heidegger's understanding of nihilism as Being itself in its default, and human beings as implicated in nihilism because nihilism concerns the way Being discloses beings to human beings, and human beings to themselves.

This understanding of nihilism as Being itself in its default has decisive implications for the attempt to overcome nihilism. If the essence of nihilism consists in Being's self-withdrawal, then any attempt by human beings to overcome nihilism will not be sufficient in itself. Indeed, such attempts appear counterproductive. Heidegger writes:

> To want to assail the default of Being itself directly would mean not heeding Being itself as Being. The overcoming of nihilism willed in such a way would simply be a more dismal relapse into the inauthenticity of its essence, which distorts all authenticity.[128]

In other words, to attempt to overcome nihilism directly would only deepen nihilism since it would result in an even greater distancing of human being from Being (in its default). Moreover, from Heidegger's perspective, the effort to overcome nihilism through an act of the will remains within the purview of the subjectivism which dreams of technological mastery of the world. Together with the supposition that the thinking of nihilism as something that might be overcome maintains the metaphysics of the subject/object distinction, these points converge into a powerful argument that the attempt to overcome nihilism is deeply aporetic.

Heidegger is by no means resigned to a passive acceptance of nihilism, however, and argues that although nihilism cannot be overcome directly, an appropriate form of thinking can prepare the way for a turning in Being which may establish a new foundation for existential meaningfulness. He maintains that in withdrawing or concealing itself, Being holds itself as a "promise" of itself, a promise which at this point in the history of Being remains a "mystery." The content of this mystery, insofar as we are able to think it in a preparatory fashion, is a post-metaphysical understanding of Being which may allow a new foundation for a meaningful world of genuine concerns and significances. For Heidegger, thinking which prepares for a turning of Being away from nihilism must itself turn towards nihilism, into a closer thinking of its essence. In this way, thinking draws closer to Being itself. In the terms established in the essay "Nihilism as Determined by the History of Being," preparatory thinking involves a move from metaphysical thought, in which the inauthentic essence of nihilism holds sway and the oblivion of Being itself is forgotten, to a form of thought which tries to think Being in its oblivion.[129]

Such preparatory thinking involves a "destruction"[130] of the categories of metaphysics and of the technological framework of *Ge-stell*, towards the ideal of encountering beings as Being gives them.[131] From the mid-1930s, and particularly in the *Contributions to Philosophy*, Heidegger attributes the history of Being with two "beginnings" (or, more accurately, a single beginning with a double aspect). The "first beginning" is the one we are most familiar with: it is the history of Western metaphysics since the birth of Ancient Greek philosophy. On Heidegger's account, the history of Being since the "first beginning" has been the history of nihilism, that is, of the forgetting of being. The "other beginning," however, is what preparatory thinking prepares for; it is in some sense the overcoming of nihilism. Preparatory thinking, however, does not proceed via a radical break from metaphysical thought; this would only be to flee further from Being in its default. Such thinking, rather, "repeats" the "first beginning," running through the history of metaphysics again from a different perspective, attempting to free Being from the metaphysical determination of this history. As Miguel de Beistegui points out, there is a sense in which linear time and historicity are metaphysical determinations which themselves arise from the "first beginning," and the attempt to think the "other beginning" thus ought to frees us from the linear view of history which places this other beginning within the clearly marked category "the future."[132] The thinking of the first and the other beginning is thus deeply ambiguous with respect to temporality: on one hand the other beginning is a repetition of the first beginning, so in a sense this thinking turns to the past; on the other, it prepares for what is to come, and in that sense turns to the future. Ultimately however, the thinking of the other beginning should free us from thinking temporality as linear, and thus displace the categories of future and past themselves. Despite this ambiguity, there remains an important sense in which Heidegger's thinking prepares for something that is "not yet," a turning in Being away from nihilism and towards the fullness of its essence as *Ereignis*. Heidegger's being-historical thinking thus attempts to move beyond the inauthentic nihilism of metaphysics to the authenticity of Being in its oblivion in modernity, the age of consummate nihilism, indicating, in some sense, the possibility of a new epoch to come. This form of thought is indeed what Heidegger attempts in his own later writing. Such thinking remains preparatory, however, and Heidegger does not presume to have accomplished an overcoming of nihilism. Any such an overcoming must ultimately proceed from Being itself. Gregory Bruce Smith provides an evocative summary of Heidegger's position:

> [W]hen Heidegger stands in his solitude peering into the dark, mysterious core of reality, he seems—unlike Nietzsche, who openly says that the Dionysian [i.e. the overcoming of nihilism] must be willed—actually to be waiting for a silent call to course through his or some future thinker's being.[133]

The advent of nihilism, announced by Nietzsche and developed by two of the most prominent European philosophers of the twentieth century, gives philosophical expression to the concern that life in the modern world is in danger of losing its meaningfulness. All three thinkers examined in this chapter are concerned with actual feelings of meaninglessness experienced by individuals, and Nietzsche and Heidegger are further concerned with empirical signs of social degeneration, but all believe that these problems of meaning require analysis at a deeper level. For both Nietzsche and Heidegger, nihilism is understood as the historical declination of Western culture that reaches a crisis point in modernity. Nietzsche analyses this declination in terms of the values underlying Western culture, while Heidegger analyses it according to the history of Being. For Sartre, nihilism is the problem of meaninglessness that confronts the individual in his or her own life, whether on the unreflective and impure reflective levels of consciousness where true meaning is futile, or on the pure reflective level, which brings the realization that there are no objectively guaranteed values or guidelines for living a meaningful life. Sartre interprets nihilism with the aid of the phenomenological method, understanding it in terms of universal structures that constitute human reality rather than as a historically determined phenomenon.

Both Nietzsche and Sartre see the possibility of overcoming nihilism through the active creation of values. The philosophical analysis of the advent of nihilism in the late nineteenth and early twentieth centuries draws to a close, however, with Heidegger's rejection of this active attempt to overcome nihilism and his preference for preparatory thinking. It is certainly the case that if one does not accept Heidegger's arguments for the priority of the question of Being, then his critical reactions to Nietzsche and Sartre will not appear entirely convincing. Indeed, subsequent scholars have raised serious objections to Heidegger's reading of Nietzsche in particular.[134] Nevertheless, Heidegger's critiques of metaphysics, subjectivism, and humanism have been enormously influential on the theorists of nihilism in the postmodern age, even those who do not accept Heidegger's central project. The aporia to which these critiques lead us with respect to the overcoming of nihilism functions as the decisive point of departure for theorizations of nihilism after the postmodern turn.

Chapter 2
Postmodern Nihilism

To reiterate the hypothesis guiding this book, the postmodern turn in theory and culture announced in the later part of the twentieth century coincides with a decisive shift in the way nihilism comes to be understood by theorists associated with this turn. In this chapter, I turn to this new mutation in the history of nihilism that may be found in the works of three of the most significant postmodern theorists of nihilism, Lyotard, Baudrillard, and Vattimo. This chapter offers an initial overview of each thinker's theory of nihilism, focusing on the way nihilism is characterized by each, and the theoretical terms in which this analysis takes place. Just as Sartre's and Heidegger's analyses of nihilism are shaped by their interpretations of phenomenology, the theories of nihilism offered by the postmodern thinkers under consideration here are each shaped by a leading philosophical theory of meaning: Lyotard and Baudrillard each develop forms of post-structuralism, and Vattimo works with his own version of hermeneutic ontology. As we shall see, these theories of meaning give a particular shape to theories of postmodern nihilism, with implications for how nihilism is to be understood and for the possibilities of a response to the problem it constitutes. This shift in theoretical emphasis moves the discourse of nihilism away from the familiar existentialist terms in which problems concerning the meaningfulness of life are still often popularly understood. This examination of the problem of nihilism as it is understood by these three postmodern thinkers thus shows how the problem itself continues to be engaged after the postmodern turn in theory, gaining new meaning and significance in new areas of application.

Lyotard: neo-nihilism

…nihilism has worsened. Vast vision of a West destined to deepen its lack. [1]
Semiotics is nihilism. Religious science *par excellence*.[2]
—Jean-François Lyotard

Nihilism is one of the central concerns running throughout Jean-François Lyotard's work, although this theme is rarely the subject of commentary.[3] It appears as an explicit concern in his late works on André Malraux, and as a theme in his "middle" works surrounding *The Postmodern Condition* and *The Differend*.[4] Lyotard's most sustained treatment of the problem of nihilism occurs, however, in his early "libidinal" philosophy, developed in *Libidinal Economy* and various essays from the same period.[5] Lyotard develops an account of what he calls in one essay "neo-nihilism,"[6] a development of Nietzschean themes through the theoretical frameworks of Freudian psychoanalysis, post-Marxian politics, semiotics, and structuralism. Lyotard's libidinal philosophy is less well known than his later work on the postmodern and the differend and has been less well received. Even Lyotard himself repudiated *Libidinal Economy*, calling it 'my evil book, the book of evilness that everyone writing and thinking is tempted to do...a piece of shamelessness, immodesty, and provocation.'[7] Lyotard's key criticism of this work is that it ignores the issue of justice, a central concern in his later thought. While the set of problems concerning justice and the set of problems concerning nihilism may overlap, however, they are separate sets. Despite Lyotard's retrospective condemnation, then, his libidinal philosophy may be approached as a legitimate and powerful treatment of the problems associated with nihilism. Recently, Lyotard scholar James Williams has called for a re-evaluation of *Libidinal Economy*.[8] Following Williams' lead, I shall present this book as one of the most significant contributions to the discourse of nihilism in the post-Nietzschean tradition. In this work, Lyotard reformulates the inquiry into the problem of nihilism while beginning to develop new modes of thought that he later terms postmodern, rejecting dominant themes of modern philosophy and experimenting with new theoretical directions.

Lyotard's commentators often mark a disparity between the libidinal and postmodern phases of his work, and express a preference for one over the other.[9] In this study, however, I will focus on the continuities between the earlier and later periods in order to show how he develops a theory of nihilism that complements a theory of the postmodern condition. Following Williams' argument that the libidinal philosophy is a more effective counter to nihilism than the later philosophy of the differend,[10] I shall focus on *Libidinal Economy* in my discussion of the problem of and response to nihilism in general theoretical terms, but integrate this discussion with *The Postmodern Condition* in chapter three in order to situate nihilism in Lyotard's theory of the contemporary scene. In short, I wish to focus on the libidinal philosophy as the more thorough theorisation of and response to nihilism, but include the work on the postmodern condition as a complementary description of the state of society in which nihilism is a stake.

It is common to characterize Lyotard's diverse *oeuvre* as dominated by a concern to negotiate the relationship between events and attempts to represent those events.[11] The events with which Lyotard is concerned are singular, unpredictable occurrences that always exceed the representations that attempt to capture them, and that often compete for the status of definitive interpretation of the particular event to which they lay claim. Moreover, the event in Lyotard's sense is also disruptive of pre-existing representational frameworks that attempt to fix our understanding of reality according to rational convention. Lyotard's work can therefore be seen as a critique of reason as representational thought and a defence of the subtleties of life of which only faculties and methods more sensitive than representational thought can make us aware. Lyotard explores this theme of event and representation throughout many registers, focusing particularly on the realms of art, politics, and philosophy. It is this theme that gives shape to Lyotard's treatment of nihilism: simply put, he understands nihilism as the tendency of representational structures to become hegemonic and stifle the emergence of events, thus reducing life to the sterility of rationally explicable structures. Lyotard's confrontation with the problem of nihilism, thus understood, consists in the difficult task of negotiating representation while recognizing that this mode of thought cannot simply be avoided and replaced with a purely "life-affirmative" alternative.

Lyotard's concern with the event and representation is situated in the trends of French philosophy through his critiques of both phenomenology and structuralism, and his development of a theory of meaning that can be characterized as post-structuralist. As Peter Dews notes,[12] Lyotard's critique of representation emerges as early as his first book, *Phenomenology*,[13] where he argues that phenomenology is a self-contradictory philosophical method because it attempts to capture, in language, our pre-linguistic experience of the world. Rather than side with those post-phenomenological thinkers who focus on the primacy of language,[14] however, Lyotard sides with the pre-linguistic object of experience, arguing that the deficiency that the contradictory nature of phenomenology reveals is with language itself. In his first major work, *Discours, figure*,[15] Lyotard develops this problematic through a complex engagement with both phenomenology and structuralism, arguing the deficiencies of both theories of meaning. It is with *Libidinal Economy*, however, that this concern with representation is explicitly connected with the Nietzschean theme of nihilism. Here, Lyotard focuses on structuralism, semiotics, and Marxism, which constituted the most prominent trends in representational theory in the French scene of the early nineteen-seventies. Lyotard's concern with Marxism, and with political structures of representation in general, will be given some consideration in the following chapter in the context of Lyotard's theory of the postmodern state of society. For now, I shall concentrate on the nihilism of representation in structuralism, semiotics, and traditional academic theory in general, as Lyotard develops these themes in his libidinal philosophy.

Lyotard argues that representational thought is a form of religious nihilism, in Nietzsche's sense, because it places the meaning of events in a transcendent position. The meaning of that which is represented therefore occupies the same position as the "highest values" of the Christian-moral interpretation of the world. This characterization of representational thought as religious nihilism is developed through Lyotard's analysis of rational theory in general and structuralism and semiotics in particular. He analyses theory by drawing an analogy with the structure of a theatre, the words "theory" and "theatre" sharing an etymological root in the Greek word *theasthai*, meaning to look at, contemplate, or behold. The architectural set-up of the theatre allows Lyotard to describe the religious nihilism of theory, and of representational thought in general, by indicating the essential divisions, exclusions, or limits that theatrical representation presupposes.[16] The most important of such distinctions is that of the theatre walls, which separate the interior of the theatre from the exterior. Theatrical representations are what take place on stage, inside the theatre. Such representations purport to be *of* that which is exterior to the theatre, and the structure of meaning set up by theatrical representation is therefore one of transcendence: that which is represented inside the theatre is justified or given meaning by that which is transcendent to, outside, and excluded from, the theatre's interior.

In ascribing a rational meaning or sense to an event, representational theory "hollows out" the event, giving it a theatrical structure and dividing an "interior" representation from an "exterior" meaning. This exteriorized meaning is absent from the representation itself, just as for Nietzsche the "highest values" are placed in a position transcendent to the world. Representational thought is thus an analogue to religious nihilism insofar as it subordinates meaning to a basic lack or absence; the meaning of the representation is never present in the representation itself.[17] The religious nihilism of representation is perhaps most evident in the representational metaphysics of Platonism, where the phenomenal or immanent world is taken to be a representation of the world of the Forms, a transcendent world that gives meaning to the immanent world, thereby denying the immanent world value in itself. Representation indicates a transcendent source of meaning, excluded from the here-and-now (the interior of the theatre). Considered representationally, events have no meaning in themselves, but only insofar as they are taken as signs for something else, for an absent, deferred sense. Representation thus subordinates meaning to a lack or absence (the exterior of the theatre), which Lyotard calls the "great Zero." This Zero is the dominant figure of nihilism in Lyotard's libidinal philosophy.

More detail is given to Lyotard's analysis of representational thought as religious nihilism through his focus on semiotics as a particular representational theory of meaning. Provocatively, Lyotard writes that '[s]emiotics is nihilism. Religious science *par excellence*.'[18] He proceeds in his analysis by firstly highlighting the following characteristics of semiotics:

1. The "thing" which semiotic theory represents may always be treated as a sign.
2. The sign is something which replaces something for someone.
3. This sign is thought within a network of signs, which is a system of communication.
4. The sign itself is a message, an element in a code, and may be decoded to reveal the information it carries.
5. There is a sender of the message (sign, thing) and an addressee who receives and decodes it.[19]

On the basis of this summary, Lyotard argues that in semiotic theory the "thing" that acts as a sign—its "material" element—loses significance in itself and is reduced to the status of a *substitute* for the information that the addressee is supposed to receive. In other words, in treating the "thing" as a sign, in making it stand for something else, an absent meaning, semioticians devalue the material "thing" itself. Lyotard addresses himself to the semioticians: "See what you have done: the material is immediately annihilated. Where there is a message, there is no material."[20] Paul Ricoeur expresses this annihilative function of the sign concisely: "The linguistic sign can *stand for* something only if it is *not* the thing. In this respect, the sign possesses a specific negativity."[21]

According to Lyotard, this semiotic substitution and negation may take place in two ways, according to two different theories of signification. According to the first theory, the sign itself may replace what it signifies (or, in other words, the message may replace the information[22]). On this view, the sign—the material that has been coded to form a message—acts as a replacement or substitute for the signification, information, or *meaning* that it bears (the sense yielded once the message is decoded). Lyotard identifies this understanding of the sign with "the Platonism of the theory of Ideas," because "the sign at the same time screens and calls up what it announces and conceals."[23] That is, the material thing acts as a sign for a particular signified (concept) in the same way that for Plato material things are imperfect representations of Ideas. By implication—following Nietzsche's critique of Platonism—the thing that acts as a sign is devalued in relation to what it signifies.

The second possibility is that, since the meaning of signs is given in a network of signs that constitutes the system of communication, there is *nothing but* signs. On this theory of the sign, signs refer only to each other, and we never have anything but references: "signification is always deferred, meaning is never present in flesh and blood."[24] Lyotard associates this theory of signification with Saussurean linguistics, noting the link between the endless deferral of signification and the view that each sign gets its meaning by virtue of its difference from other signs.[25] Thus, the search for what a sign signifies leads to an endless quest, with each sign referring us to another sign for its meaning. Moreover, Lyotard implicates Freud and Jacques Lacan in this theory of signification through the idea that beneath this system of endless signification is "the image of a great signifier, forever completely absent,"[26] which guarantees both the process of signification and the impossibility of ever arriving at a fully-present meaning. This theory of the sign also constitutes a kind of religious nihilism, according to Lyotard, since we never reach the meaning that signs signify.[27] Semiotics thus displays "the despair of lost-postponed meaning."[28] According to Lyotard, then, both of these ways in which the semiotic sign may be understood are nihilistic. His verdict is that

> the sign is enmeshed in nihilism, nihilism proceeds by signs; to continue to remain in semiotic thought is to languish in religious melancholy and to subordinate every intense emotion to a lack and every force to a finitude.[29]

Since the sign is the basic unit of meaning employed by structuralist theories, Lyotard's analysis of semiotics also implicates structuralism within religious nihilism. However, Lyotard has a more complex story to tell about structures, a story that is inseparable from his own, post-structuralist, theory of meaning that is developed in *Libidinal Economy* and related essays. Briefly put, Lyotard's concern with structuralism is that it treats the meaning of a thing as given by its place in the structure in which it appears; the thing is taken as a sign in a network of signs, and the meaning of each sign is deferred throughout the structure. As with semiotics and other forms of representational thought, the thing itself is devalued by conferring on it a rational sense or meaning that is absent and deferred. Like other post-structuralist thinkers—such as Deleuze, Derrida, and, as we shall see shortly, Baudrillard—Lyotard develops a theory of meaning that retains the idea that meaning manifests through a structure of signs, but modifies the structuralist theory with the addition of a "plastic force" that is both the genetic element of, and disruptive to, static structures. Lyotard argues that "there is a dimension of *force* that escapes the logic of the signifier,"[30] and representational theories of meaning such as structuralism and semiotics are incomplete because they do not take this dimension of force into account. In Lyotard's libidinal philosophy, this plastic force takes the form of a modified version of the Freudian libido. In Freud's work, the libido is the positive, energetic and processual aspect of desire, contrasted with the understanding of desire as wish (*Wunsch*), the negative desire for what is absent.[31] The libido becomes, for Lyotard, a "theoretical fiction" that can express the force of the event, allowing reference to what exceeds representational structures without reducing the event to a wholly representational description. This is possible, according to Lyotard, firstly because the libido expresses the feelings and desires that are typically excluded from (and thus exceed) rational, representational thought, and secondly because of the non-representational status Freud gives to his own theory by positing it as a theoretical fiction.

Using Freud, Lyotard develops a nuanced response to representational nihilism with his "libidinal economy," which is a description of the various relationships between libidinal events or intensities and the structures that channel and exploit their energy. Lyotard describes the events the libido gives rise to as libidinal intensities or affects, which are understood as material forces of desire. An affect might be a sound, a color, a smile or a caress: anything that may have a quanta of libidinal energy attached to it, or that has an ability to "move," to produce feelings and desires. Lyotard emphasizes the "plastic" or mobile aspect of the libido, describing it metaphorically in terms of speed and heat, in contrast to the cold, static qualities of structures.

Insofar as it is possible to conceive the libido in itself, it is the free-flowing intensity of desire, unbound by limits or structures. Just as Freud posits the libido as the source of the conscious mind, which is formed by filtering and structuring unconscious libidinal impulses, Lyotard describes libidinal energies as giving rise to structures in a very general sense of the term (i.e. in the sense employed by structuralist theorists, who identify structures in numerous areas of life and thought). Lyotard describes the channeling of libidinal energies into structures as taking place through figures and *dispositifs* (libidinal dispositions or "set-ups"). These figures and dispositions structure desires into more or less well-ordered wholes, and constitute, from a libidinal point of view, the structures analyzed by structuralist theoreticians. According to Lyotard,

> what is essential to a structure, when it is approached in economic terms, is that its fixity or consistency, which allows spatio-temporal maintenance of identical denominations between a this and a not-this, work on pulsional movement as would dams, sluices and channels.[32]

Thus every structure posited by structuralists can be understood in libidinal economic terms as a relative stabilization of libidinal energies, that is, as a channeling and limiting of desire. These structures, considered as figures and *dispositifs*, are themselves stabilizations of libidinal energy, which channel further energy into specific conduits, stabilizing it along the lines of convention the figure or *dispositif* has established.

Libidinal energy not only forms structures, but also disrupts and transforms them. In the context of the libidinal economy, an event is understood as the occurrence of an excess of desire that cannot be efficiently dammed and channeled by existing structures. Such events take place on different scales and in many different registers, in accord with the multitude of phenomena that may be understood as structures: in cinema, an event might consist of a particularly striking scene, the meaning of which cannot be reduced to the narrative structure of the film[33]; in the political arena, upheavals such as May '68, which emerge unpredictably to disrupt the existing social system, may be understood as events.[34] Moreover, such events give rise to competing, or what Lyotard calls "incompossible,"[35] structures that attempt to represent, or in other ways exploit the energy of, these events. For example, the same event is often claimed by competing political factions to support their own ideology. The tension between these incompossible *dispositifs* is itself a source of libidinal energy, sometimes giving rise to events that cannot be contained within the existing *dispositifs*, forcing them to change or giving rise to new figures and dispositions. In sum, Lyotard's libidinal economy is a description of the relations between structures, understood as *dispositifs*, and force, understood as libidinal energy, which attempts to account for meaning in multiple registers. Unlike structuralism, which tends to give a static, synchronic account of meaning, Lyotard's post-structuralist theory attempts to account for the genesis of meaning and changes in meaning through structures by pointing to the generative and disruptive forces of desire operative in meaningful systems. While Lyotard accepts that meaning is constituted through structures of signification, he argues that these structures are themselves constituted by desires, and may be disrupted and changed by desires, which always exceed the structures that exploit them.

Considered economically, nihilism is understood as the decrease in the intensity of desires or affects. Lyotard tacitly associates life and its healthful affirmation with intense feeling and novel differences that stimulate change in structures and systems. Structures effectively dampen the intensity of the libidinal energies they channel, thus tending towards nihilism and the devaluation of intensely felt, affirmed life. Lyotard's description of the libidinal economy gives a deeper dimension to his analysis of the nihilism of representational thought, and extends this analysis to wider systems and structures (the political dimensions of which will be given further consideration in the following two chapters). Lyotard understands representation as a particularly nihilistic *dispositif*, that is, a libidinal set-up that dampens libidinal intensity to a significant extent. The theatre that he uses to explain the religious nihilism of representation is a figure that disposes of libidinal energy in such a way as to regulate and disintensify desire by channeling it towards an absent ideal (the meaning or sense of the thing represented). In libidinal terms, the exclusion, which the theatrical set-up imposes between the exterior and interior of the theatre, places the object of desire outside, and represents it inside, on stage, as absent. The theatre, which must be understood as the general structure of representation, disintensifies desire by regulating it in a structure of absence and deferral, in which that which is desired is never present.

The "great Zero," as Lyotard calls the absent and transcendent position of the theatrical structure, performs the same hegemonic function that "God" (as the name for the highest values) performs in the context of the Christian-moral interpretation of the world. That is, the Zero is constituted as the *only* thing worthy of desire, and subordinates all libidinal intensities and affects to it. This hegemonic function can be understood as a kind of filtering:

that which is placed outside the theatre of representation, the great Zero, filters desires so that what takes place on stage, in the interior, is reduced to a representation of the Zero itself. In more prosaic terms, the rationalizing function of representational thought filters feelings and desires so that only a selected and reduced form of these desires gets represented, suppressing surplus libidinal energies. Lyotard's concern with the Great zero of theatricality and representation is therefore not just that such structures dampen libidinal intensity, but that they condition a wide field of energetic phenomena, attempting to regulate all energy in a stabilizing and stabilized way. Again, an analogy can be drawn with Nietzsche's analysis of religious nihilism in the Christian-moral interpretation of the world: just as this interpretation attempts to control all aspects of life, Lyotard sees representational set-ups as dominating the modern world, threatening to subordinate all phenomena to rational meaning and regulation. In this way, we can see Lyotard's theorization of the great Zero and representation as a form of reductive nihilism, which reduces the intensities of libidinal energies by filtering and dampening them within hegemonic structures.

Lyotard's engagement with nihilism can be understood as a continuation of the Nietzschean critique of religion, transferring the analysis to new registers by engaging recent theories of meaning such as structuralism and semiotics. In the first few pages of *Libidinal Economy* he announces this task: "So we rebegin the critique of religion, so we rebegin the destruction of piety, we still seek atheism..."[36] However, Lyotard quickly makes the important move, already announced in several essays preceding the book, of renouncing critique as a position implicated in the very nihilism it would denounce. Drawing on both Marx and Nietzsche, Lyotard argues that the position of critique remains conditioned by the object that it critiques, and is incapable of escaping the theoretical terms set by that object. In Marx, an awareness of this problem is manifest in his criticisms of Feuerbach's atheism, which retains the place occupied by religion.[37] Lyotard is also aware of the Nietzschean problem, highlighted by Heidegger, of negation and *ressentiment* as constitutive of nihilism. Critique, in its negative function, is a reactive formation that manifests and is conditioned by *ressentiment*, and is therefore incapable of the healthful affirmation of life that both Nietzsche and Lyotard seek.[38] Lyotard sees critique as a trap, writing that, "[t]his trap consists quite simply in responding to the demand of the vanquished theory, and this demand is: put something in my place. The important thing is this place, however, not the contents of the theory. It is the place of theory that must be vanquished."[39]

In the case of Lyotard's own work, a particular danger of the critical position is that critique remains representational, and therefore nihilistic. Lyotard's challenge is thus to analyse and respond to nihilism whilst avoiding the trap that critique represents. He writes, "the *critique* of religion which we rebegin is no longer a critique at all, no longer remains in the *sphere* (that is to say, note, the theatrical volume) of what it critiques, since critique rests in turn on the force of lack, and that *critique is still religion*."[40]

Eschewing critique, the task Lyotard sets for himself is to analyze and respond to nihilism in such a way that he does not simply condemn nihilism in a reactive fashion, and does not set up an alternative in the same position vacated by the nihilism criticized. His employment of the Freudian libido is aimed at meeting precisely these needs. This is accomplished, firstly, by proposing an alternative to the nihilism of representational theory in the deployment of libidinal intensities, that is, material desires and affects, rather than in an alternative representational theory. Secondly, however, Lyotard avoids the further danger of setting up desire in a wholly privileged position, which would involve him in critique and *ressentiment* by making his work a simplistic kind of anti-theory, against the rational and representational. Such a move would devalue the representational modes of thought, and structures in general, which are a pervasive aspect of contemporary existence, in the name of a "pure" desire that would take the form of an impossible (absent, transcendent) ideal. This danger is avoided by blurring the borders between desire and representation, or libido and structure; structure is affirmed as a libidinal disposition rather than being criticized and condemned outright. Lyotard is acutely aware of the problem of the return of nihilism through setting up a new privileged term, writing that "[w]e do not speak as the liberators of desire,"[41] and "it is in no way a matter of determining a new domain, another field, a *beyond representation* which would be immune to the effects of theatricality, not at all, we are well aware that you are waiting for us to do this, to be so 'stupid.'"[42]

Lyotard invents the concept of "dissimulation"[43] to explain the relationship between affirmative libidinal energies and nihilistic structures in such a way that there is no rigid distinction between the two, thus allowing him to avoid a critical position. We have already seen the basic dynamic of this relationship in his description of the libidinal economy, where libidinal energies are channeled by figures and dispositions into more or less stable structures. The concept of dissimulation indicates the fact that structures are themselves libidinal dispositions, that is, particular formations of desire. Moreover, structures hide (dissimulate) the energy they contain by appearing static, but this energy is itself never entirely stable: structures may be disrupted by the influx of new energies or by the release of the energy they contain. The libidinal economy thus allows Lyotard to avoid critique by understanding all structures as libidinal formations, meaning that no structure is purely and simply condemned as nihilistic. Every structure is a manifestation of desire, and is therefore accorded a degree of value from the perspective of the libidinal economist. Lyotard applies this judgment even to the great Zero, the central figure of nihilism in the libidinal philosophy. He writes:

> We do not even have to say: this great Zero, what crap! After all, it is a figure of desire, and from what position could we assume to deny it this quality? In what other, no less terrorist Zero? *One cannot assume a position* on the twisted, shock-ridden, electrified labyrinthine band. One's got to get this into one's head: the instantiation of intensities on an original Nothing, on an Equilibrium, and the folding back of complete parts onto the libidinal Moebian band, in the form of a theatrical volume, does not proceed from an error, from an illusion, from malice, from a counter-principle, but again from desire. One must realise that representing [*la mise on representation*] is desire...[44]

The idea of dissimulation is further elaborated by the insistence that libidinal intensities, or events, can only manifest through structures: there is no pure libidinal energy, which would be without form or content; rather, libidinal energy is only known through its effects in and on structures.[45] Lyotard thus avoids producing a set of binary terms in which one is privileged and the other devalued. The libidinal philosophy nevertheless supplies criteria for evaluation,[46] since structures differ in the way they deal with libidinal intensities. Lyotard privileges as life-affirming those structures that best allow for the emergence of events, defined as intense desires or libidinal energies. While the great Zero is not denounced outright, it is accorded the status of a problem that needs combating because of the "terroristic" way it regulates libidinal energies, hegemonically collecting all desires and dampening their intensity through a mechanism of lack and deferral. Rather than a binary opposition, then, Lyotard's libidinal economy provides a sliding scale of evaluation, with the nihilism of the great Zero and rigid representational structures at one end, and a freer flow of intensities in and through structures at the other end.

Lyotard is aware that his own discourse is implicated in the problem of nihilism, insofar as the analysis of nihilism remains necessarily representational and theoretical. For Lyotard, theory constitutes a structure that attempts to capture events in networks of signification, thus dampening their force. He paints a picture of the theorist as Medusa, whose desire is to perfectly immobilize her prey.[47] Lyotard accepts the necessity of presenting his ideas in theoretical, representational structures, but applies the principle of dissimulation to theory by affirming that these structures are themselves constructs of desire, and may be disrupted by desire. *Libidinal Economy* is an unconventional, experimental book, written in a variety of juxtaposed styles, shifting in a seemingly haphazard manner between conventional theoretical argument and more avant-garde modes of writing. This unusual combination of styles may be understood as Lyotard's attempt to enact dissimulation in the text, letting desire play within structures more flexible and open than traditional philosophical genres allows.[48] Such techniques do not seek to avoid representational and hence nihilistic effects, but to circumvent the hegemony of such effects by releasing life-affirmative desires in and through the structures of theoretical discourse.

Lyotard's response to nihilism, then, is not a simple "overcoming," or the postulation of an absolute and distinct alternative to nihilism. For Lyotard, nihilism cannot be overcome, because the very attempt to do so involves one in critique and hence reintroduces the nihilistic position. The terroristic function of the great Zero can be ameliorated, however, through the principle of dissimulation, that affirms as immanent and present the desire that the great Zero, the theatre, and representation defer and thrust into transcendence. Lyotard writes:

> Let us be content to recognise in dissimulation all that we have been seeking, difference within identity, the chance event within the foresight of composition, passion within reason—between each, so absolutely foreign to each other, the strictest unity: dissimulation.[49]

Dissimulation is a concept that allows Lyotard to advocate the release and flow of libidinal intensities in and through structures, increasing the occurrence of events in dispositions that tend to dampen or deny them. The specific concepts and strategies Lyotard develops towards a libidinal response to nihilism, particularly in the spheres of politics and theory, will be given consideration in the following two chapters.

Lyotard's philosophy of libidinal economy takes up the Nietzschean problematic of nihilism in a way that develops it in new directions. In translating Nietzschean religious nihilism into the register of discursive meaning, analyzed through structuralism and semiotics, Lyotard moves away from phenomenological models of meaning such as that employed by Sartre, and allows nihilism to be understood in terms of extra-subjective structures. An implication of Lyotard's shift to a post-structuralist theory of meaning is that nihilism is no longer understood as a problem for individual consciousness, but as one that saturates cultural structures of meaning and must be met in this register. Lyotard's originality as a theorist of nihilism lies in his understanding of the problem as situated within those structures of meaning that dominate contemporary life and thought, dampening the desires and affects that are essential to a healthful expression of life. Nihilism is developed through a somewhat different post-structuralist theory of meaning in the works of Jean Baudrillard, to whom we now turn.

Baudrillard: the nihilism of transparency

I am a nihilist.

If it is nihilistic to be obsessed by the mode of disappearance, and no longer by the mode of production, then I am a nihilist.

—Jean Baudrillard[50]

Jean Baudrillard is an original and controversial thinker whose work is frequently associated with both postmodernity and nihilism. Like Lyotard, Baudrillard develops an analysis of nihilism in new, post-structuralist terms, in synchrony with a theory of the contemporary situation as postmodern. Baudrillard's relationship to nihilism is a problematic one, since his own position is frequently characterized as nihilistic.[51] Typically, Baudrillard is portrayed as a thinker who has abandoned all effective criteria for critical analysis and judgment, and whose own theory simply reflects the hopelessness and uncertainty that he sees in the current state of society. Moreover, those scholars who have paid some sustained attention to Baudrillard's relation to nihilism in the Nietzschean tradition have predominantly interpreted him as a passive nihilist, content to dwell on the disappearance of meaning without a sustained attempt to offer an alternative to the nihilism of postmodern culture, or to transcend it towards a Nietzschean affirmation of life.[52] Without denying the pessimistic tone of much of Baudrillard's writing, I wish to show that his relation to the problem of nihilism is more nuanced and complex than is commonly believed. Baudrillard is a thinker who often vacillates, especially concerning the effectiveness of theory to respond to the nihilism of the contemporary social system. I will demonstrate, however, that his work is marked by a consistent attempt to find just such a theoretical response.

Before considering Baudrillard's theory of nihilism, it is pertinent to make some preliminary comments on the difficult task of interpreting, evaluating and employing Baudrillard's thought. Baudrillard is a highly original thinker who uses a confusing array of unusual terminology and develops a strange "logic" that is at times difficult to follow, and perhaps difficult to accept. His thought is elusive; he rarely provides definitions or thorough theorizations of his terms, and close study of his work still tends to leave one with the feeling of remaining on the edge of understanding. One effect of this difficulty is that Baudrillard's commentators often do not agree on the meaning of his work. This means that, more than is the case with any of the other theorists I am examining here, a choice must be made as to the line of interpretation I wish to take on Baudrillard's thought.

The commentator I shall take the most significant cue from in my own interpretation of Baudrillard is Rex Butler, who, of all Baudrillard scholars, makes the most rigorous attempt to read and criticize Baudrillard on his own terms. Many of Baudrillard's commentators are working in the tradition of (post-)Marxism and Critical Theory,[53] and they tend to read and assess Baudrillard on their own terms, rather than on his terms. That is, they employ what Butler correctly identifies as a question-begging structure in their approach, assuming the validity of their own intellectual tradition, in relation to which they find Baudrillard lacking. Butler successfully avoids this problem by following carefully following and explicating the internal logic of Baudrillard's own thought.[54]

Butler, however, concentrates almost exclusively on the way Baudrillard's logic operates, on the *form* of his thought, referring to its *content* primarily by way of example. On Butler's interpretation, it seems that Baudrillard really has only one idea. In order to counter this tendency, the interpretation I develop here also takes direction from the work of those interpreters who pay attention to the nuances of the changing content of Baudrillard's work, such as Gary Genosko, who reads Baudrillard through the semiotic and linguistic theory that informs his work, and Mike Gane, who insists—unlike many commentators—that we should pay more attention to the shifts in his position.[55] I intend to attempt a balanced approach here, paying serious attention to the content of Baudrillard's texts—what he writes about nihilism and the postmodern situation—but also being attentive to the logic Baudrillard employs.

Baudrillard's explicit use of the rhetoric of nihilism is occasional, his most extended statement on the topic being the short essay "On Nihilism."[56] Here, he announces that nihilism has entered a new phase:

> Nihilism no longer wears the dark, Wagnerian, Spenglerian, fuliginous colours of the end of the century. It no longer comes from a weltanschauung of decadence nor from a metaphysical radicality born of the death of God and of all the consequences that must be taken from this death.[57]

Although short, the essay is dense, employing a wide range of concepts from Baudrillard's other writings. The effect is to explicitly link Baudrillard's wider works, on topics such as simulation and seduction, to the Nietzschean problematic of nihilism, and to make the intelligibility of the essay itself dependent on a knowledge of the main themes in Baudrillard's thought in general. Rather than give a concise reading of this essay, then, I shall explicate Baudrillard's theory of nihilism through the concepts expressed in his wider works, referring to "On Nihilism" where appropriate. Since this essay also contributes to a theory of postmodernity, aspects of it will be left for consideration in the following chapter.

Baudrillard's diverse *oeuvre* is given coherence by his suggestion that it can be envisaged as a double spiral comprising two related sets of terms, where his work both theorizes and follows the movement from one set of terms to the other. Baudrillard writes that 'this double spiral moves from *The System of Objects* to *Fatal Strategies*: a spiral swerving towards a sphere of the sign, the simulacrum and simulation, a spiral of the reversibility of all signs in the shadow of seduction and death.'[58] This spiral allows us to characterize Baudrillard's work as a continually evolving attempt to think the nihilism of the contemporary situation (one set of terms) and a possible response to this nihilism (the other set of terms), as well as the complex relation between the two. On the nihilistic side, Baudrillard's terms of analysis include the system of objects, consumer society, the code, political economy, production, simulation, the hyperreal and the transfinite. On the other side, Baudrillard's alternatives to nihilism include symbolic exchange, death, the anagram, seduction, the fatal, the vital illusion, and impossible exchange. In insisting that this spiral is double, Baudrillard indicates the difficult concept of *reversibility*, that is one of the factors that make his works so dizzying and hard to pin down. Neither set of terms is stable, and all terms are always susceptible to reversal into their opposites. Simulation may always become seduction, and vice versa. Furthermore, reversibility is itself reversible, and functions as *both* the underlying principle of the nihilism of simulation and its related terms, and as the principle of the affirmative alternative to this nihilism. As we shall see, the only consistent difference between Baudrillard's nihilistic and affirmative terms are that the nihilistic terms deny this reversibility, whereas the affirmative terms embrace it.

Baudrillard's early works apply semiological and structuralist principles to a critique of consumer culture within a broadly Marxian framework. These works employ a semiological[59] methodology to critically analyze the capitalist system, characterizing it as dominated by a "code" that regulates social meanings according to commodity exchange. On this theory, commodities have a "sign value" that confers significations of social status on consumers through the act of consumption.[60] Baudrillard later argues, however, that Saussure's "semio-linguistic" theory of meaning on which semiology is predicated is complicit with the capitalist system, and an analysis of the system on the basis of this theory of meaning cannot, therefore, provide the basis for a preferable alternative. Baudrillard first seeks an alternative to the system of capitalist political economy—which he understands as a complex of commodity exchange and the semio-linguistic structure of meaning—in the concept of "symbolic exchange." This concept refers to the form of exchange he believes existed in pre-capitalist societies.[61] Baudrillard takes from Marcel Mauss the idea that gift-giving in "primitive" societies takes place in a network of cultural symbols, and founds the social bond itself in an economy of symbolic exchange.

Unlike capitalist political economy, which abstracts objects from their cultural meaning and subjects them to a specific (and therefore non-ambiguous) law of value, symbolic exchange is ambiguous, reversible, and constitutes a challenge in the form of the obligatory counter-gift. That is, the economy of symbolic exchange involves the circulation of ambiguous cultural meanings according to the reciprocal giving of gifts; this process involves reversible meanings because counter-gifts respond to gifts and change the social relations between the giver and receiver. For Baudrillard, societies based on these principles of ambiguity and reversibility are richer in "existential" meaning (although Baudrillard himself does not use this term) than capitalist societies, since they allow socially meaningful exchanges and interactions that are eroded by the abstraction of capitalist exchange. Like Lyotard, Baudrillard gives an analysis of nihilism in terms of the semiological and structuralist theory of meaning, taking this theory as an accurate account of the way sign systems, dominant in modern capitalist societies, are reductive of more existentially satisfying forms of meaning. However, Baudrillard's analysis of semio-linguistics, and the consequences he draws from this analysis, differ markedly from Lyotard's.

Baudrillard's clearest analysis of the nihilism of semio-linguistics is to be found in the essays collected in *For A Critique of the Political Economy of the Sign*.[62] One of these essays, "Towards A Critique of the Political Economy of the Sign," also gives a formal analysis of the "logic" of the Saussurean sign that underpins Baudrillard's later concept of simulation, the key concept through which nihilism is to be understood in much of his work. Baudrillard argues that the critique of the system of political economy must include a critique of the sign, and he employs a deconstructive method inspired by Jacques Derrida to enact this critique. This critique is undertaken on the level of the structure of the sign; he argues that the sign is formally equivalent to the structure of the commodity: *'the logic of the commodity and of political economy is at the very heart of the sign.'*[63] The homology between the commodity and the sign is drawn between the component parts of each, as identified by Marx and Saussure, and formally represented as follows:

$$\frac{EcEV}{UV} = \frac{Sr}{Sd}$$

Baudrillard argues that economic exchange value (EcEV) and the signifier (Sr) are both *forms* (or reductive formalizations) that impose themselves upon use value (UV) and the signified (Sd), which are *contents*. In these binary oppositions, the term that represents the content is given a kind of metaphysical and moral privilege; use value and the signified are respectively the utility and meaning that act as both origin and end for the systems of exchange and signification. As such, Baudrillard sees the content-term functioning as an *alibi* for the form-term. While the content-term is given a certain privilege, the form-term actually has dominance in the opposition, since it imposes itself on the content, determining its expression. According to Baudrillard, use value is simply the alibi that allows commodities to be exchanged, and the signified is nothing more than the alibi that allows signs to be exchanged. In each case, a formalistic reductionism is operative, a rationalization that does violence to ambivalent and nuanced meanings. In effect, Baudrillard is applying Marx's well-known argument that in the commodity the use value of objects is reduced to exchange value, to the dimension of language, where meanings are reduced by the formal requirements of signification.

Baudrillard extends this idea that the signified acts as an alibi for the signifier by considering Emile Benveniste's revision of Saussure, which consists in his addition of the *referent* to the structure of the sign. According to Baudrillard's analysis, Benveniste attempts to reduce the arbitrariness of the signifier/signified relationship by shifting this arbitrariness to the relationship between the sign and the referent (the "thing" in the world that it refers to). This move gives a stronger "motivation" for the relationship between a particular signifier and a particular signified, making the relationship between words and concepts less arbitrary and conventional than Saussure supposed. According to Baudrillard, however, the referent then becomes the alibi for the sign, and the relationship between sign and referent exactly mirrors the relationship between signifier and signified in the Saussurean schema: the referent is the supposed content of the world (or of our phenomenal perception of the world), and the sign is the form imposed upon this content. Baudrillard further argues that the semiological schema is an *idealist* one, in that it always considers the "content" of signification as a concept or idea, rather than a material referent existing concretely in the world. Baudrillard unpacks this claim by insisting that the referent in Benveniste's schema is not a thing in the world, but at best is a perception or idea of such a thing. As evidence for this claim, he quotes a semiologist who admits as much:

> The referent is not truly reality…it is the image we make of reality. It is a signified determined by an intention carried toward things (!) and not considered in its simple relation to the Sr, as is usual in linguistics. From the Sd-concept, I pass to the referent as a concrete approach to the world…[64]

What interests Baudrillard here is the way that, as soon as the referent is theorized as a part of the sign (a special kind of signified), reality or "the thing" appears behind it once again (he emphasizes this point by his addition of the bracketed exclamation mark in the above quotation). While the sign is itself an idealist schema, it is predicated on the non-idealist notion that there is a material, independently existing "reality" to which it refers. Baudrillard's point is to show that the signifier maintains a position of dominance in the sign, but is always in need of a term that acts as an alibi. This alibi must have an arbitrary relationship to the signifier, and appear to transcend it, but Baudrillard argues that the signifier can never really be transcended—the idealist schema of semiology can never reach the world. He writes that

> in a kind of flight in advance, the referent is drained of its reality, becomes again a simulacrum, behind which, however, the tangible object immediately re-emerges. Thus, the articulation of the sign can gear down in infinite regress, while continually reinventing the real as its beyond and its consecration. At bottom, the sign is haunted by the nostalgia of transcending its own convention, its arbitrariness; in a way, it is obsessed with the idea of *total motivation*. Thus it alludes to the real as its beyond and its abolition. But it can't "jump outside its own shadow": for it is the sign itself that produces and reproduces this real, which is only its *horizon*—not its transcendence. Reality is the phantasm by means of which the sign is indefinitely preserved from the symbolic deconstruction which haunts it.[65]

Baudrillard's argument is that the semio-linguistic theory of meaning cannot claim to capture a pre-existing reality, because it can only ever project the idea of reality as the horizon of its transcendence. It projects "the real" as the alibi of its signifying-rationalizing function. Baudrillard's conclusion in this paper—which is decisive for his subsequent thought, and especially for the notion of simulation—is that the deconstruction of the sign can never take place in the name of the referent or "the real," since these categories are the very alibis that found the order of signification. Such a deconstruction will rather be a matter of showing, as Baudrillard has attempted to do, that the real is an alibi of the signifier, that it is projected from the order of signification. This constitutes a deconstruction of the semio-linguistic theory of meaning because it shows that the sign cannot ground its signifying function in the way it purports to. The arbitrary relation between the signifier and the alibi-term that attempts to ground it must remain arbitrary; every attempt to fully motivate this relationship— that is, to ground the relationship between the signifier and the alibi— shows up another alibi as the sign's shadow.

Baudrillard's analysis of the sign is in many respects similar to Lyotard's analysis of the nihilism of semiotics: both view the theory of the sign as reductive of richer, more ambiguous forms of meaning, and both criticize it for placing the locus of meaning—that which the signifier signifies—in an exterior position, unreachable from within signification itself. However, Baudrillard draws out the implications of this critique of the sign in a direction uniquely his own, in the theory of simulation. This theory, for which Baudrillard is most well known, forms the hub of his theory of nihilism. The deconstruction of the sign Baudrillard undertakes in *For a Critique of the Political Economy of the Sign* is the formal, structural basis for this theory of simulation, which is developed in *Symbolic Exchange and Death*, *Simulacra and Simulation*, and other later works.[66] According to Baudrillard, simulation is the fate of representation in the contemporary state of culture. Simulation occurs when a model or representation precedes the "real thing" it purports to be a model or representation of; simulations produce this "real" themselves rather than modeling a pre-existing reality. This analysis of representation follows the idealism of the semio-linguistic sign that Baudrillard has analyzed, insofar as it produces its referent as the horizon of its transcendence, and cannot ever really transcend this horizon. The referent, or some other term designating "the real," remains nothing more than the shadow cast by the sign. Baudrillard writes that 'to simulate is to feign to have what one hasn't'[67]: the sign and simulation feign to establish a relationship with the real, to capture the real in their signifying function while maintaining this real as an external, independent, pre-existing reality. Simulations are in fact copies without originals, however, since they precede and produce the so-called original, which merely acts as an alibi to support the simulation.

According to Rex Butler—as I have suggested, one of Baudrillard's most astute commentators—all of Baudrillard's work may be seen as an exploration of "the paradox of representation," and this paradox further explains the underlying logical structure of simulation. Butler identifies the origin of this paradox in Plato's *Cratylus*:

> *Socrates*: Let us suppose the existence of two objects: one of them shall be Cratylus and the other the image of Cratylus, and we will suppose, further, that some god makes not only a representation such as a painter would make of your outward form and colour, but also creates an inward organisation like yours, having the same warmth and softness; and into this infuses motion and soul and mind, such as you have, and in a word copies all your qualities, and places them by you in another form. Would you say that this was Cratylus and the image of Cratylus, or that there were two Cratyluses?
>
> *Cratylus*: I should say that there were two Cratyluses.[68]

According to Butler, this paradox means that the more a copy resembles an original, the less it resembles it. If a copy resembles an original *exactly* it is no longer a copy, but another original. A copy that is too good is paradoxically a bad copy, and by the same reasoning a bad copy might be a good copy. The essential point of this paradox is that the copy and the original need a space, a gap, or a difference between them, in order to be distinguished as copy and original. Representation and reality, a model and its original, function in the same paradoxical way. Furthermore—and here we see the logic of simulation begin to operate—because the representational system can only function on the basis of a distance between representation and the real, once the gap has closed and it has lost contact with the real, it has to *produce its own* real in order to continue to function. This real is not the (pre-existing) real that the model attempts to represent, but what Baudrillard calls the *hyperreal*—the *more real than real*.

The goal of representation is to eradicate all imperfection—to close the gap between itself and the real, to produce a perfect model. But once this has occurred, there is no longer any "outside," any limit to the system, to which it can refer. In a perfect system of representation, the real does not exist. So in order to keep functioning as a meaningful system—that is, in order to have an "outside" to which it can refer, it produces this "outside" from within itself. Models no longer represent reality, but *produce* their own *hyperreality*. It is this implication of the paradox of representation that we have seen operating in Baudrillard's analysis of the idealism of the sign: each attempt by semiologists to remove the arbitrariness of the sign is in effect an attempt to perfect its representational accuracy, to enclose the referent in the sign itself. But each time this occurs (such as with the theorization of the referent as a kind of signified), a new "outside" reality springs up, a distance between the sign and the real that reinstates a certain arbitrariness in its signifying function. This "outside" is only produced by the sign itself, but the very idea of an outside is essential to its functioning. Baudrillard sums up the relationship between representation and simulation as follows:

> Representation stems from the principle of the equivalence of the sign and of the real (even if this equivalence is utopian, it is a fundamental axiom). Simulation, on the contrary, stems from the utopia of the principle of equivalence, *from the radical negation of the sign as value*, from the sign as the reversion and death sentence of every reference.[69]

Baudrillard draws out nihilistic implications from simulation, which he sees as continuing and exacerbating the reductive nihilism of the political economy of the sign. Simulation is the new stage of nihilism that Baudrillard announces in the essay "On Nihilism." He writes:

> Today's nihilism is one of transparency, and it is in some sense more radical, more crucial than in its prior and historical forms, because this transparency, this irresolution is indissolubly that of the system, and that of all the theory that still pretends to analyse it. When God died, there was still Nietzsche to say so—the great nihilist before the Eternal and the cadaver of the Eternal. But before the simulated transparency of all things, before the simulacrum of the materialist or idealist realisation of the world in hyperreality (God is not dead, he has become hyperreal), there is no longer a theoretical or critical God to recognise his own.[70]

The transparency Baudrillard associates with contemporary nihilism is the loss of the distance between representation and the real that comes with simulation. Baudrillard argues that when simulations no longer refer to an independent real, there is a confusion between models and their referents, which results in a kind of generalized epistemological nihilism. Theories float free from any reference in the real: each theory produces its own "real," and there is thus no independent reference by which one theory may be judged better or worse than another. Simulation therefore leads to a relativism of theory and the impossibility of knowledge.

As well as a collapse of the difference between representation and the real, Baudrillard argues that simulation is accompanied by the collapse of the difference between all the binary oppositions that structuralist theories of meaning posit as the basis of intelligibility.[71] Following Roman Jacobson's argument that the most basic differences in language are binary oppositions, many structuralists understand the basic differences in all structures as such oppositions. Baudrillard also follows this tendency, understanding these oppositions as an integral part of the semio-linguistic order of meaning that dominates contemporary capitalist societies. The real itself functions as the distance between such oppositions, the "third term" that mediates between them and allows judgments to be made about the relative veracity of theses and antitheses, or the relative application of one term or its opposite to the field under consideration. With the disappearance of this referential term, the distance between binary oppositions effectively collapses, causing them to bleed into each other and liquidate stable structures of meaning.

Baudrillard analyses this breakdown of binary oppositions in terms of the critical concept of the "imaginary." For Baudrillard, this term indicates that "other" against which the self is defined, or that which is excluded by a system in its self-definition. Each term in a binary opposition functions as the imaginary of the other term: man is the imaginary of woman and vice versa, the Third World is the imaginary of the First World and vice versa, and so on.[72] According to Baudrillard, simulated systems that have lost their reference in the real hide this loss by producing an imaginary, an opposite. This imaginary maintains the illusion that a reference in the "real" still operates by upholding the binary oppositions that require and imply this reference. Baudrillard calls this "the strategy of the real" or "the strategy of deterrence." Two celebrated examples of this strategy, from the essay "The Precession of Simulacra," are Disneyland and Watergate.[73] Baudrillard sees Disneyland as the imaginary of America, which maintains the distinction between the real and the simulated or hyperreal. Disneyland is posited by America as a simulated world in contrast to the "reality" of the rest of America, a strategy that, according to Baudrillard, hides the fact that the rest of America has passed into simulation. Similarly, Watergate was construed as a scandal by the American media to hide the fact that there is no scandal in politics anymore: the distinction between the scandalous and non-scandalous has broken down, but the belief in this distinction is perpetuated by the projection of Watergate as an imaginary "other" to quotidian politics. In each case, the projected imaginary maintains the illusion that the binary oppositions on which the system is founded are still operative, and the reference to the "real" that grounds these oppositions still functions.

Baudrillard refers to the breakdown of clear distinctions between binary oppositions as "reversibility." In simulation, systems become reversible, all hypotheses are equally plausible, and counter-hypotheses function to support their opposites and the system of simulation in general. Counter-hypotheses act as the imaginaries of hypotheses, and simply support a simulated system of imaginary oppositions where neither term has any purchase in the real. Baudrillard writes that "it is always a question of proving the real through the imaginary, proving truth through scandal, proving the law through transgression, proving work through striking, proving the system through crisis, and capital through revolution..."[74] The loss of reference and the reversibility of binary oppositions is thoroughly nihilistic because in this simulated state nothing is really at stake: the stakes the system predicates itself on are illusory. The reversibility of simulation explains Baudrillard's view that today's nihilism is in a way more crucial than its past forms, in that all opposition to the nihilistic system can be absorbed by the system itself: any opposition to the system maintains the fiction that critical distinctions are still operative and founded in a "real." Furthermore, Baudrillard is aware that his own discourse is subject to this problem: the discourse of the analysis of nihilism cannot pretend to an exterior position of enunciation, and is itself embroiled in nihilism. Baudrillard's work here enacts a reflexivity of the discourse of nihilism itself that recalls Heidegger's problematization of analyzing and responding to nihilism, but which constitutes a deepening of the aporetic implications of this problem in that Baudrillard, unlike Heidegger, often seems to hold little hope that nihilism will ever be overcome. It is for this reason that Baudrillard is often understood as a passive nihilist, and he suggests just such a passive stance in the following passage from the essay "On Nihilism":

> Melancholia is the brutal disaffection that characterizes our saturated systems. Once the hope of balancing good and evil, true and false, indeed of confronting some values of the same order, once the more general hope of a relation of forces and a stake has vanished. Everywhere, always, the system is too strong: hegemonic.[75]

By Baudrillard's own admission, he is a nihilist insofar as he is obsessed by the mode of the disappearance of meaning that characterizes contemporary culture.[76] However, it is essential to understand that the form of meaning Baudrillard sees simulation as eroding is the semio-linguistic one, which structures intelligibility on the basis of clear distinctions. This is precisely the form of meaning that Baudrillard has analyzed as complicit with capitalism, and which he sees as nihilistic in that it is reductive of the richness of symbolic meaning. Simulation is therefore radically ambivalent: on the one hand, it strengthens the modern capitalist, rationalist order, giving this system total hegemony in the power to incorporate all oppositions; on the other hand, simulation is itself a partial deconstruction of the system of meaning on which this order is founded. Baudrillard understands simulation as predicated on representation, which functions as its alibi, but which it in fact undermines. Simulation is therefore both an exacerbation of, and a deconstruction of, semio-linguistic meaning, depending on the perspective from which it is seen. Simulation passes itself off as representation, and Baudrillard's analysis might be understood as a kind of ideology critique that exposes the way simulation operates. According to Baudrillard, once you realize you are in simulation, you're no longer there.

Baudrillard can here be compared with Nietzsche: he sees nihilism as the self-destruction of the "highest values" of modernity, understood as the semio-linguistic form of meaning, but he also sees this form of meaning that is being destroyed as nihilistic, just as Nietzsche understands the "highest values" as expressions of religious nihilism. Like Nietzsche, Baudrillard's analysis of the nihilistic system is an attempt to push the nihilistic tendencies of this system to an extreme point, in the hope that the system will collapse. In this sense, Baudrillard displays traits of the active nihilist. He sometimes conceives of his work as a kind of theoretical terrorism; his gambit is that the closer systems of simulation approach perfection (the closer the gap or distance comes to being completely eradicated), the closer the system is to collapse. This stance is one Baudrillard also suggests in "On Nihilism":

> The more hegemonic the system, the more the imagination is struck by the smallest of its reversals…If being a nihilist, is carrying, to the unbearable limit of hegemonic systems, this radical trait of derision and violence, this challenge that the system is summoned to answer through its own death, then I am a terrorist and a nihilist in theory as the others are with their weapons. Theoretical violence, not truth, is the only resource left us.[77]

While Baudrillard often vacillates between active and passive forms of nihilism, it is clear that in all his mature works he avoids the notion of a straightforward overcoming of nihilism.[78] Indeed, his arguments that the analysis of nihilism remains within the purview of nihilism, and that any opposition to simulation acts to bolster it, decide against the possibility of such an overcoming. Rather, Baudrillard develops a position in which the nihilism of simulation and its life-affirmative "other" are seen as the reverse sides of the same process.

Baudrillard's conceptualization of nihilism and its alternative can be seen in the relationship between simulation and his concept of "seduction." This concept of seduction is a complex idea that operates in registers beyond its usual, sexual meaning, and which is posited as an affirmative "other" to simulation. Seduction, and the other "affirmative" terms of Baudrillard's thought, are given the following analysis by Butler in terms of the paradox of representation: "if simulation attempts to cross the distance between the original and the copy that allows their resemblance, seduction is both the distance that allows this resemblance and the distance that arises when this space is crossed."[79] Seduction is therefore the gap, the distance, the *nothingness* that the sign or the simulated system attempts to abolish, but which allows the system to operate. Hence the ambiguity and reversibility of this term: it is both what allows simulation, and is thus complicit with it, and what simulation attempts to abolish, and is thus potentially subversive of it.

In this theory of the complicity between simulation and seduction, Baudrillard develops a post-structuralist theory of meaning, which complements the stasis of representational structures, understood as simulations, with the dynamic force of seduction. For Baudrillard, the complex concept of seduction is both productive and disruptive of simulation. Like Lyotard, Baudrillard attempts to exploit the principle of seduction contained within simulation rather than overcome the nihilism of simulation by moving beyond it and leaving it behind. This principle of seduction will be given more consideration in chapter four; what it is necessary to note in the present context is that like symbolic exchange, seduction is a form of meaning that operates according to ambiguity and reversibility. While simulation predicates itself on the semio-linguistic theory of meaning, which relies on clear distinctions and non-reversible binary oppositions, seduction functions according to the very ambiguity and reversibility that undermine the semio-linguistic order. This is why Baudrillard writes, at the end of "On Nihilism," where he seems to have given up hope of overcoming the destruction of meaning: "This is where seduction begins."[80] Seduction is therefore a principle by which Baudrillard attempts to effectively respond to the nihilism of the current situation without positing a restoration of dominant modernist modes of meaning or a definitive overcoming of nihilism.

In summary, Baudrillard is an original thinker who explicitly theorizes that nihilism has entered a new phase, and analyses this new phase in terms of semiological and structuralist theories of meaning. He analyses the way semio-linguistic meaning self-deconstructs in the contemporary state of society, the stable oppositions on which such meaning depends becoming reversible and deepening nihilism from the perspective of this semiological theory of meaning. However, Baudrillard holds that the ambiguous meanings that rational meaning reduces cannot be destroyed entirely, and he develops critical articulations of this mode of meaning (such as symbolic exchange and seduction), which he sees as more "existentially" meaningful than rational meaning. Reversibility is a fundamental principle of this mode of meaning; while it signals a deepening of nihilism from a rational, semiolinguistic perspective, Baudrillard also privileges it as the basis of a richer, more ambiguous kind of meaning. The principle of reversibility, therefore, is itself reversible: it can indicate both the collapse of structures of meaning predicated on stable oppositions, and the recuperation of more ambiguous modes of meaning. Baudrillard's project can be seen as similar to Nietzsche's in that his analysis of nihilism is also an exacerbation of it, which seeks to complete the self-deconstruction of modern, rationalist meaning and replace them with a more fundamental and existentially richer meaning. Baudrillard cashes out this project in various ways, however, and seems undecided whether reversibility means that the nihilism of simulation is unassailable, since every opposition to the system acts to support it, or fated to a decisive reversion into a more life-affirmative form of meaning that accepts this very reversibility as its fundamental principle. This vacillation concerning reversibility, and the reversibility of reversibility, accounts for the varying prognoses of nihilism at different points in Baudrillard's texts.

Vattimo: positive nihilism

What is happening to us in regard to nihilism, today, is this: we begin to be, or to be able to be, accomplished nihilists…an accomplished nihilism is today our only chance…

—Gianni Vattimo[81]

No contemporary philosopher has contributed more to the theorization of nihilism in postmodernity than Gianni Vattimo. Vattimo is one of the few thinkers to deal explicitly and extensively with the connection between postmodernism and nihilism, and he develops this connection as a central point for understanding the current situation of thought and culture. Like Lyotard and Baudrillard, Vattimo develops his analysis of nihilism in new theoretical terms, but through a far more direct engagement with Nietzsche, Heidegger, and the history of the discourse of nihilism. The most unique contribution Vattimo makes to the discourse of nihilism consists in a *positive revaluation* of nihilism; in his thought, nihilism is no longer posed as a problem that must be solved but as a solution to the problems of modernity, which becomes possible as we enter postmodernity. For this philosopher, the nihilism characteristic of postmodernity must not be thought of as "a hellish negation of all that is human," but as our only chance for social emancipation.[82]

Vattimo thus ceases to use the term "nihilism" to designate the problem of existential meaning. Instead, he uses it primarily to designate ontological and epistemological antifoundationalism, the views that there is no permanent, objective structure to reality, and that there are no objective and certain truths. However, Vattimo engages directly with the problematic established by Nietzsche and continued in various fashions by the other thinkers thus far considered. Following Heidegger, Vattimo refers to the set of problems designated "nihilism" by other thinkers as "metaphysics." Moreover, while they are not always made the explicit focus of his analysis, Vattimo indicates that his philosophical concerns "contribute to a rethinking of the existential problems of late modern society."[83] Vattimo's work therefore contributes, in a new and unique way, to an analysis of the problems that have been under consideration throughout.[84]

Vattimo insists that his thought cannot be separated from the context of the Italian tradition of philosophy in which it developed,[85] and since this tradition is not well known in the Anglophone academy a brief introduction is required in order to appropriately situate Vattimo's work. Italian philosophy contributes in original and significant ways to many of the most central debates in Continental philosophy, and displays many continuities with other European philosophical traditions of thought. After the fall of the Fascist regime, Italian intellectuals attempted to find a new and more secure foundation for reason in reaction to what was perceived as the irrationality of Fascism. This emphasis on rationality manifested in intellectual trends such as Gramscian Marxism, structuralism, and semiotics. By the early seventies, however, the rise of post-structuralism in France made its presence felt in the Italian intellectual scene, and the possibility and desirability of rational foundationalism was called into question.

Through his work on Heidegger and Nietzsche—both primary reference points for post-structuralism—Vattimo emerged as one of the key players in the debate concerning the limits of reason and the foundational aspirations of thought. The meaning of nihilism and the problem of metaphysics are key elements in this debate: on one side thinkers such as Vattimo and Pier Aldo Rovatti advocate a "weak thought" that emphasises antifoundationalism and the impossibility of a decisive overcoming of metaphysics; on the other, certain philosophers argue for a regrounding of thought that will overcome nihilism, a prime example of which is Emanuele Severino's call for a return to Parmenides.[86] Vattimo's and Rovatti's edited volume *Il pensiero debole*[87] [*Weak Thought*] sparked the high point of this heated debate in the early 1980s. The contemporary Italian philosophical scene is arguably further characterized by the attempt to deal with modernization in a social context where traditionalism and provincialism still hold sway, and in which the isolationism of the Fascist years has left its mark.[88] Vattimo's twin concern with nihilism and the postmodern, then, can be seen as a response to the particularities of the Italian situation, while nevertheless having a much wider field of application.[89]

Vattimo's thought is an original and apparently syncretic amalgam of Nietzsche, Heidegger, hermeneutics, and postmodernism. The coherence of this eclectic mix is given in Marta Frascati-Lochhead's characterization of Vattimo's work as a conversation-in-progress between Nietzsche and Heidegger, in which the voices of those who have addressed the questions raised by these two thinkers are also heard.[90] Vattimo's central project may be described as a hermeneutic ontology that attempts to be an *ontologie de l'actualité*,[91] a philosophical description of our "current situation." He works through interpretations of texts in the recent history of Western philosophy, especially those of Nietzsche and Heidegger and those writers who have engaged their problematics, in order to develop an interpretation of the meaning of Being at this point in history. For Vattimo, this amounts to a determination of the meaning of nihilism in postmodernity. Vattimo believes that Nietzsche and Heidegger are the two thinkers who have done most to change the way we view thought today, and any understanding of our current situation must proceed through a hermeneutic engagement with their works. Vattimo's own unique perspective on nihilism is largely determined by the way this engagement of his proceeds; he reads Nietzsche and Heidegger together, bringing out their substantial similarities and using each as a corrective to the other, to develop a theory of the meaning of nihilism in terms of both the death of God and the era of the oblivion of Being.

Vattimo's interpretation of Nietzsche and Heidegger proceeds on the basis of a "betrayal" of Heidegger's reading of Nietzsche, but a betrayal that is made in order to be true to what Vattimo believes is the spirit of Heidegger's philosophy—a spirit that is far closer to Nietzsche than Heidegger was willing to admit.[92] For Vattimo, Heidegger clarifies Nietzsche by emphasizing the philosophical, ontological implications of his thought, while Nietzsche clarifies Heidegger by presenting nihilism as the key to the ontology of the contemporary situation. Summing up these points, Vattimo writes:

If Heidegger confers meaning on Nietzsche by demonstrating that the will to power is "the destiny of being" (and not a pure play of forces unmasked through a critique of ideology), Nietzsche gives meaning to Heidegger by clarifying that the destiny of being (thought unmetaphysically) is nihilism.[93]

Vattimo reads both Nietzsche and Heidegger as antifoundational thinkers, and argues that the nihilism theorized by both thinkers must be understood in a "positive" sense as an answer to the problems of metaphysical foundationalism that each diagnose. Nietzsche and Heidegger are linked by this attempt to think beyond metaphysics, and according to Vattimo the meaning of nihilism today takes shape through the legacy of these attempts.

Breaking with Heidegger's reading of Nietzsche, Vattimo situates a preferable reading *between* Heidegger's interpretation and that given by Wilhelm Dilthey.[94] While Heidegger interprets Nietzsche alongside Aristotle, as an ontological philosopher, Dilthey interprets him primarily as a cultural critic and "philosopher of life."[95] For both interpreters Nietzsche stands at the end of metaphysics, but for different reasons. Heidegger, as is well known, focuses almost exclusively on Nietzsche's *Nachlass* in order to present him as the last of the metaphysicians, whereas Dilthey is primarily concerned with Nietzsche's earlier essays and aphoristic writings in which he critically engages with history and culture. Vattimo uses Dilthey's emphasis as a corrective to Heidegger's, suggesting that Nietzsche's historical consciousness and cultural criticism show that he is not trying to present a "new foundation" for thought, or a new metaphysical system. In his own interpretation of Nietzsche, Vattimo focuses particularly on the "middle period" of Nietzsche's works,[96] from the second of the *Untimely Meditations* to *The Gay Science*.[97] Vattimo's concern is to show that Nietzsche develops a "deconstruction" of metaphysics[98] through his critique of culture, religion, and philosophy; a deconstruction that rules out the possibility of instituting a new foundation for thought. This reading is deployed against Heidegger's attempt to read Nietzsche as a metaphysical thinker; for Vattimo, Nietzsche, like Heidegger, must be thought of as a thinker at the end of metaphysics who is struggling to find a way beyond it.

Vattimo focuses on the method of "chemical" decomposition of moral, religious, and aesthetic ideas and feelings that Nietzsche announces in *Human, All-Too-Human*.[99] This idea of philosophy as chemistry is a precursor to Nietzsche's later genealogical method, and, as Vattimo understands it, a deconstruction of metaphysics. Philosophy as chemical decomposition seeks to show how even the most exalted moral, religious and aesthetic ideals are derived from base feelings and motivations, and this method directs itself explicitly against a philosophy of origins or foundations. Instead of a secure origin, source, or foundation underlying our religious, philosophical, and cultural beliefs and practices, Nietzsche attempts to show that such origins are in fact ignoble and our beliefs about the purity and goodness of such ideals and practices are thus errors. However—and this is the decisive point for Vattimo's reading of Nietzsche—such errors cannot be corrected with recourse to alternative truths, and ignoble origins cannot be supplanted by pure foundations. This is because, in the process of "chemical decomposition," the notions of truth and of a foundation for thought are themselves decomposed, reduced to the mere desire for security or power.[100]

Furthermore, according to Vattimo the idea of a foundation for thought that would secure true knowledge depends on the idea that it is possible to know things in themselves, but this possibility is also undermined by Nietzsche through his argument that "knowledge" of a thing is the result of a series of metaphoric transformations that take place between the thing and our understanding of it.[101] These arguments against truth and foundation cited by Vattimo are early versions of Nietzsche's understanding of nihilism as the process in which the "highest values" devalue themselves. Vattimo thus reads Nietzsche as an anti-foundational thinker, a reading that is supported by a number of aphorisms in *Human, All-Too-Human*. Firstly, Vattimo makes much of the phrase "the philosophy of morning" that occurs in the last section of the book.[102] Here, Nietzsche tells in an allegorical fashion of the difficulties of living without a final goal or foundation, but also of the joys that accompany it. Vattimo interprets this "philosophy of morning" as containing no other content than the errors of metaphysics, but seen in the light of a different attitude. One who has "overcome" metaphysics by reaching the end of the process of chemical decomposition does not seek new foundations, but sees the essence of reality as a "tissue of erring."[103]

Nietzsche's rejection of a new foundation for thought that would supplant the errors of metaphysics is clearly expressed in another aphorism from *Human, All Too Human*:

> *A few rungs back down.*—One, certainly very high level of culture has been reached when a man emerges from superstitious and religious notions and fears and no longer believes in the choir invisible, for

> example, or in original sin, and no longer speaks of the salvation of souls; if he is at this level of liberation he still has, with the greatest exertion of his mind, to overcome metaphysics. *Then*, however, a *retrograde step* is required: he has to grasp the historical justification that resides in such ideas, likewise the psychological; he has to recognise that they are most responsible for the advancement of mankind and that without such a retrograde step he will deprive himself of the best that mankind has hitherto produced.—With regard to philosophical metaphysics, I see more and more who have reached the negative goal (that all positive metaphysics is an error), but still only a few who are climbing back down a few rungs; for one may well want to peer over the topmost rung of the ladder, but one should not want to stand on it. The most enlightened only get as far as freeing themselves from metaphysics and then looking back down it: whereas here too, as in the hippodrome, it is necessary to round the bend once you have reached the end of the straight.[104]

Here Nietzsche emphasizes the necessity of in some sense remaining within metaphysics once the errors of metaphysical thought have been seen. The ladder of metaphysics doesn't lead to a higher plane; Nietzsche even tells us that we cannot stand on the top rung. He leaves us with the untranscendable necessity of viewing life, history and culture through the lens of metaphysical error.

Vattimo links this analysis with Nietzsche's later works through antifoundational interpretations of the dictum "God is dead" and of "accomplished" or "complete" nihilism. Vattimo interprets the pronouncement "God is dead" to mean that there is no objective structure to the world; it is not an atheistic position because this would imply that there *is* an objective structure to the world, one in which God does not exist.[105] The death of God is not an objective "fact"; it is the historical event of the abolition of the belief in grounds, foundations, origins, and ends, the "highest values" of the Western religious and philosophical traditions that Nietzsche collectively terms "metaphysics." For Vattimo, the death of God means the advent of nihilism, where nihilism is understood ontologically and epistemologically as the lack of an objective structure of the world and an absence of objective facts. This is a common interpretation of Nietzsche's thought; what is noteworthy about Vattimo's interpretation is that he asserts that the death of God, understood as nihilism, is a condition that cannot be transcended.

While many Nietzsche commentators understand him as asserting the necessity of creating new gods or new values after the completion of nihilism, in a way that suggests a decisive and permanent *overcoming* of nihilism, Vattimo does not believe that this is a legitimate move within the bounds of Nietzsche's thought. By highlighting the earlier works in which Nietzsche rejects the possibility of a new foundation for thought, Vattimo argues that nihilism cannot be thought in terms of an overcoming, since such an overcoming implies just such a new foundation. Instead, Vattimo argues that the stage of nihilism that Nietzsche calls *complete* or *accomplished* nihilism must be understood precisely as the condition in which the belief in foundations, including the possibility of a new foundation, is entirely dissolved. The meaning of Nietzsche's story of nihilism, for Vattimo, is that metaphysics, understood as foundational thought, is "overcome" in accomplished nihilism. Vattimo understands accomplished nihilism as ontological and epistemological anti-foundationalism, as expressed in Nietzsche's assertions that there is no "true world"[106] and that there are no facts, only interpretations.[107] Vattimo thus gives Nietzsche's nihilism a decisively *positive* meaning, asserting that accomplished nihilism is the only way to deal with the impasse of the attempt to overcome metaphysics.

Just as Vattimo reads Nietzsche against Heidegger's interpretation, he also reads Heidegger against Heidegger's own intentions. As with his interpretation of Nietzsche, Vattimo's concern is to show that Heidegger may be read as an anti-foundational, nihilistic thinker. This reading requires a certain "distortion" of Heidegger, in which some aspects of his texts are emphasized and turned against other aspects in an attempt to show that he did not always fully understand the implications of his own thought. Situating his own interpretation in the field of Heidegger scholarship, Vattimo suggests that readings of this German philosopher can be divided into a "right" and a "left"camp.[108] The "right" interpretation focuses on Heidegger's suggestions that overcoming nihilism and metaphysics requires a return to a grounding for thought and meaning through a renewed and more authentic relationship of man and Being. On this reading, nihilism will be overcome through a return of Being, which has been obscured and cast into oblivion through the history of metaphysics. The "left" interpretation, however, which Vattimo advocates, focuses rather on the suggestions in Heidegger's texts that any return to a grounding or foundation will be simply a reinstatement of metaphysics, because one of the mistakes of metaphysics is to think Being as ground—in the sense of stable structure or enduring presence.[109] Summarizing this interpretive distinction, Vattimo writes:

> Right, in the case of Heidegger, denotes an interpretation of his overcoming of metaphysics as an effort, in spite of everything, somehow to prepare a 'return of Being,' perhaps in the form of an apophasic, negative, mystical ontology; left denotes the reading that I propose of the history of Being as the story of a 'long goodbye,' of an interminable weakening of Being. In this case, the overcoming of Being is understood only as a recollection of the oblivion of Being, never as making Being present again, not even as a term that always lies beyond every formulation.[110]

In an argument similar to that employed in his interpretation of Nietzsche, Vattimo asserts that the terms of Heidegger's own thought do not allow a consistent and coherent notion of a "return" or a "remembering" of Being in such a way that this would overcome nihilism and institute a new foundation for thought. Vattimo's argument depends on Heidegger's notion of Being as event, in which Being always "stays away" or conceals itself in the process of bringing beings (entities) to presence. Vattimo emphasizes this aspect of Heidegger's understanding of Being as the event of unconcealment, and argues that this understanding is inconsistent with any idea that Being might itself be grasped as something present. He writes that "[t]he forgetting of Being that is characteristic of metaphysics…cannot be understood in contrast to a 'remembering of Being' which would grasp it as present."[111] On the basis of this argument, Vattimo gives a new interpretation of Heidegger's work on nihilism, arguing that the oblivion of Being is itself consistent with the notion of Being as event. Rather than understanding nihilism as a forgetting of Being that needs to be overcome, Vattimo understands ontological nihilism as consistent with Heidegger's own thesis about Being, in which it is "nothing" in the sense of being no "thing" that might be made present. Vattimo's argument for this nihilistic understanding of Being is further justified with reference to the ontological difference that is so important to Heidegger:

> Ultimately, the issue of the difference between Being and beings, called the ontological difference, leads much further than even Heidegger expected. This difference means first of all that Being *is* not. Entities are what can be said to be. Being, on the other hand, *befalls* or occurs. We truly distinguish Being from beings only when we conceive of it

as historical-cultural happening, as the instituting and transforming of those horizons in which entities time and again become accessible to man, and man to himself.[112]

Vattimo's interpretation of Heidegger as an anti-foundational thinker is given further weight by reading his work in the light of Gadamer's appropriations of it. Heidegger and Gadamer are the two founding fathers of hermeneutic ontology, and Vattimo situates his own understanding of this approach to philosophy between the two German thinkers. Hermeneutic ontology, Vattimo writes, predicates itself on a necessary link between Being and language, but the nature of this link varies for the different thinkers.[113] Heidegger focuses on Being with some supplementary indications of the important place language has in ontology; Gadamer is primarily concerned with language but indicates its ontological dimension. Vattimo attempts to clarify the link between Being and language by reading the two thinkers together, giving Being a linguistic determination that contributes to his conception of a nihilistic ontology. This "clarification" of Heidegger depends on what is itself a radical interpretation of Gadamer, framed around his famous phrase "Being that can be understood is language."[114] Vattimo argues that the usual interpretation of this phrase, that Being exceeds language but language is that part of Being that is intelligible to human beings, is incorrect. Instead, Vattimo argues for a radical identification of Being and language, such that Being is nothing more than the transmission of linguistic messages through history. Such messages in no way form a static text, the meaning of which is objectively given; rather, the meanings of these linguistic messages must be constantly interpreted anew, and this process of the reception and interpretation of messages is what constitutes the ontological "openings" in which beings are revealed. This interpretation makes sense of Gadamer's insistence that with each interpretation, both the subject and object of interpretation are changed; for Vattimo this means that there is no objectively given structure to Being, objectivity being dissolved in the fluidity of interpretations.[115]

Vattimo applies this reading of Being to Heidegger's work in what is self-consciously an "urbanisation"[116] or a "demystification," a removal from Heidegger's thought of those aspects that tend towards the esoteric and mystical. Referring to the understanding of Being made available by Heidegger, Vattimo writes that

> [a]ll we can say about Being at this point is that it consists in transmission, in forwarding or destiny: *Ueber-lieferung* and *Ge-schick*. The

world plays itself out in horizons constructed by a series of echoes, linguistic responses, and messages coming from the past and from others (others alongside us as well as other cultures)....Being never really *is* but sends itself, is on the way, it trans-mits itself.[117]

The nihilistic implications of this understanding of Being are suggested in this passage: understood as the transmission of linguistic messages that open interpretive horizons, Being is not something that could ever be thought as spatially or temporally present; rather, Being is always an echo from the past that makes the present possible. From the perspective of metaphysics, which only thinks beings in terms of presence, Being is really "nothing." Being cannot be thought of as an objective, ahistorical structure, but only as a series of historical events through which language establishes cultural horizons.

An important implication of this understanding of Being as historical event is that this theory of Being itself cannot be understood metaphysically, that is, as an objective and ahistorical structure of the world. In order to be consistent, Vattimo must and does insist that this interpretation of Being is itself an event of Being, and is given to human beings by Being. As Heidegger emphasizes, human beings cannot make judgments about Being as if they were in some exterior relation to it. We cannot simply develop theories about Being that might be "true" or "untrue" on the basis of some objective criterion, since according to Heidegger and Vattimo truth itself is a disclosive opening of Being.[118] For Vattimo, this also means that the history of metaphysics cannot simply be considered a history of erroneous understandings of Being on the part of human beings; as Heidegger emphasizes, the forgetting of Being in metaphysics is itself given by Being. For Vattimo, the most salient aspect of Heidegger's understanding of metaphysics is that it conceives of Being as a stable structure or enduring presence that serves as a *foundation* or ground for beings. In contrast to these "strong" qualities of stability and foundation attributed to Being throughout much of the history of philosophy, Vattimo refers to the current understanding of Being as event as a "weakening" of Being. For Vattimo, the history of Being should be thought of as an "ontology of decline" that culminates in the current situation, in which there is very little of Being left (in the "strong" metaphysical sense of Being as objective structure or ground).[119]

Despite the above qualification concerning metaphysics, Vattimo remains critical of metaphysical thinking, associating it with reduction and violence. In arguing this point, he gestures towards Theodor W. Adorno's association of metaphysics with the society of total organization that erodes the freedoms of individuals and Emmanuel Levinas's critique of metaphysics as doing ethical violence in the reduction of the other to the same, as well as Nietzsche's assertion that metaphysics is an attempt to gain control by force and Heidegger's understanding of metaphysics as the basis of the technological domination of the world.[120] Vattimo argues for a specific understanding of the relationship between metaphysics and violence, however, by defining violence from a hermeneutic perspective as "the peremptory affirmation by an authority which forbids further interrogation, breaks down dialogue, and imposes silence."[121] In this sense, metaphysics may be thought of as violent because it manifests a suppressive authority in the form of a foundation: metaphysical thought limits the free play of dialogue and interpretation by silencing those voices that are not appropriately related to the foundation that metaphysics appeals to as an arbiter of legitimacy. The violence of metaphysics is thus a process of reduction, which limits the range of interpretations that are allowed currency. Furthermore, Vattimo suggests that metaphysics, in positing eternal structures of existence, is reductive in the sense that it delegitimizes or devalues those aspects of life that are bound up with growth, change, and mortality.[122] While Vattimo positively revalues the term "nihilism," then, the concerns with a reductive devaluation of the richness of existence that other theorists express with this term are present in Vattimo's thought, but expressed by the term "metaphysics."

In addition to being motivated by a refusal of new foundations, Vattimo's revaluation of nihilism can be understood as a critical opposition to the violence of metaphysical thinking. In a passage that summarizes the key move in his interpretation of Heidegger, as well as his own thought more generally, Vattimo writes:

> The overcoming of metaphysics can be realised only in the degree to which, as Heidegger writes of Nietzschean nihilism, "nothing is left of being as such." *The overcoming of metaphysics is not the overturning of the metaphysical oblivion of being; it is this very oblivion (nihilism) taken to its extreme consequences.*[123]

According to Vattimo, the nihilistic oblivion of Being overturns metaphysics when taken to its extreme consequences precisely because the metaphysical notions of objectivity and foundation are dissolved in this oblivion. Thus Vattimo draws the parallel between Nietzsche's accomplished or complete nihilism and the nihilistic destiny of Being in Heidegger: both involve pushing nihilistic tendencies to their *n*th degree, and both problematize the possibility of a new foundation. According to Vattimo, it is precisely the thought of Nietzsche and Heidegger that has done the most work to dissolve the metaphysical conception of Being as permanent presence and foundation. Nietzsche and Heidegger are thus proper names for the event of Being that has given Being itself as "weakened," and inaugurated a new era in which nihilism gains a positive determination.

Since Vattimo rejects the possibility of overcoming on the grounds that it implies a new foundation, and thus metaphysical thought, he cannot posit nihilism as a new form of Being and thought that leaves metaphysics outside and behind. Rather, he writes that "[f]or Heidegger, as for Nietzsche, thought has no other 'object' (if we may even still use this term) than the errancy of metaphysics, recollected in an attitude which is neither a critical overcoming nor an acceptance that recovers and prolongs it."[124] From Heidegger, Vattimo appropriates the concepts of *An-Denken* and *Verwindung* to explain the relationship between metaphysics and nihilism in the form of thought made possible by the "weakening" of Being. The term *An-Denken* implies a remembering or a recollection of the traditions passed on through history in such a way that they are not simply taken as static givens, but interpreted anew according to present circumstances. Because, for Vattimo, Being is understood as the historical transmission of such messages, and the history of Being is the history of metaphysics, then the current configuration of Being remains conditioned by the metaphysical thought of the past (albeit in a weakened form).

For Vattimo, Heidegger's rarely-used term *Verwindung* defines the way these metaphysical messages should be interpreted in the age of accomplished nihilism. This term suggests an alternative to overcoming (the German term for which is *Überwindung*), an alternative Heidegger himself suggests in a number of places.[125] Vattimo notes the difficulty of translating this term, and indicates a number of meanings, all of which must be taken into account to understand Heidegger's intent. Firstly, Vattimo notes, Heidegger himself told some French translators of his works that *Verwindung* indicates a going-beyond that is both an acceptance and a deepening. Vattimo further indicates two important shades of meaning this term can have in German: it can mean convalescence, to be cured of an illness while still bearing the traces of it, and it can mean "distortion," from *winden*, which means "to twist." The meaning of *Verwindung* as convalescence also has the connotation of "resignation"; one can be *verwunden* to a loss or pain.[126] Taken together, these meanings suggest that when Heidegger speaks of *Verwindung* in relation to metaphysics, he is suggesting a twisting-free from metaphysics through a resignation to it. While this seems a paradoxical notion, Vattimo interprets the *Verwindung* of metaphysics as an acceptance of the necessity to think in metaphysical terms, but bereft of their *most* metaphysical aspect—that is, without reference to Being as permanent foundation.[127]

The *Verwindung* of metaphysics means to think in reference to the "opening" of Being we find ourselves in, rather than in reference to any foundation that can serve as a ground for permanent and apodictic truth. Since this kind of thinking is much less ambitious and less certain than the deductive logic appropriate to periods when Being was "strong," Vattimo calls it *weak thought* (*il pensiero debole*). The Italian term *sfondamento*, which Vattimo uses to indicate the anti-foundational nature of weak thought, further clarifies what it means for metaphysics to be subjected to a *Verwindung*. David Webb, the translator of Vattimo's *Beyond Interpretation*, explains that this term is derived from the root *fondamento*, meaning "foundation," and that the related term *sfondare* means to break through or knock the bottom out of something.[128] Vattimo's weak thought thus aims to interpret the metaphysical thought that still constitutes our horizons, bereft of the foundations to which it has historically laid claim. Weak thought is thus oriented towards the history of philosophy, and the interpretation of texts in this history, but in such a way that new understandings of metaphysical concepts are created by reading them with a view towards elaborating the meaning of our current situation. Vattimo enacts weak thought in his own writings by staging a play of interpretations between thinkers that deliberately "distorts" their ideas by reading them against each other, just as he does in the cases of Nietzsche and Heidegger. Weak thought makes no appeal to a transcendent foundation or point of reference that would secure the certainty of knowledge, but takes the criteria of interpretation to be given within the play of interpretations itself by the power of arguments to convince us that one interpretation is preferable to another. Vattimo therefore understands his own arguments concerning Nietzsche, Heidegger, and the contemporary meaning of nihilism as lacking any appeal to objective validity, resting only on their rhetorical persuasiveness. It is in this sense that weak thought is to be understood as "weak," but this weakness coincides with a rigorous practice of interpretation.

With Vattimo, we see a new understanding of nihilism emerge through just such a rigorous interpretation of the texts of Nietzsche and Heidegger. He takes from these thinkers the lesson that we cannot step outside the metaphysical tradition, but must work within it in a *Verwindend* relation to it. This means that "negative" nihilism, understood as metaphysics, cannot be directly overcome. Vattimo's idea of a positive (complete or accomplished) nihilism is a result of this recognition, and can be understood as a solution to an apparently insoluble situation with respect to the problem of overcoming metaphysics. As such, Vattimo takes up and responds to the aporia of overcoming nihilism identified by Heidegger, but argues—against Heidegger—that Nietzsche had already shown the way to negotiate this aporia. Insofar as nihilism dissolves foundational thought, the most violent aspect of metaphysics, it can be seen as opening up a new field of possibility, where thought and life will relinquish the nostalgic desire to hold fast to foundations. Seeking out and taking advantage of these new possibilities, Vattimo believes, is our sole opportunity for social emancipation in the current situation. Since Vattimo understands metaphysics as having existential implications, impacting on the meaning and value of life by reducing its possibilities, his positive nihilism may also be understood as a response to the existential nihilism that is my primary concern here. The new possibilities for existence, and Vattimo's strategies for responding to nihilism, will be explored in the following chapters.

Nihilism in postmodern theory

We have thrown off that old existential garb…Who cares about freedom, bad faith and authenticity today?

—Jean Baudrillard[129]

The above quotation from Baudrillard reflects a widespread feeling that the discourse of existentialism, which strongly shaped the understanding of nihilism (including the reception of Nietzsche's and Heidegger's concerns) in the early part of the twentieth century, is an outmoded form of thought. This feeling is borne out in the changes of theoretical focus evident in the postmodern theories of nihilism examined above. Writing after the deposition of existentialism and phenomenology by structuralism, and concurrent with the "postmodern turn," Lyotard and Baudrillard develop post-structuralist positions that criticize the earlier dominant theories. Vattimo, also following this postmodern turn, breaks with earlier theoretical perspectives by developing an understanding of hermeneutic ontology that is deployed against metaphysics. Although Vattimo draws heavily on Nietzsche and Heidegger, he develops their thought in original ways, sometimes consciously betraying the letter of their texts. While Lyotard, Baudrillard, and Vattimo adopt different theoretical perspectives, some salient points shared by all three allow us to identify a general shift in theoretical perspective from earlier understandings of nihilism. Since there is also much continuity with earlier thinkers, especially Nietzsche and Heidegger, it is not possible to draw a simple schematic distinction that would allow us to clearly divide the later group of thinkers from the earlier group. Nevertheless, the postmodern thinkers bring new emphases and draw aspects of the earlier thinkers' works into new light, allowing us to identify a number of points that indicate the novelty of the postmodern perspective. These points—some of the implications of which will be drawn out more fully in the following chapters—are as follows.

The linguistic turn

As we have seen, the analyses of nihilism in the European tradition of philosophy under examination here have typically been shaped by various leading theories of meaning. Sartre, for example, applies a phenomenological understanding of meaning to existential concerns, and Lyotard and Baudrillard both frame their concerns with nihilism in the terms of their post-structuralist stance. This suggests that no clear distinction is made by these thinkers between the theoretical framework appropriate for the examination of existential meaning, and the framework applied to semantic meaning and intelligibility in general. It is therefore possible to see the changes in the theoretical terms in which nihilism is analyzed as following wider trends in philosophy and theory; the postmodern theories reject phenomenology and existentialism and frame themselves in terms of post-structuralism (often understood as the theoretical dimension of postmodernism in the Anglophone world) and hermeneutic ontology. Moreover, both the post-structuralism of Lyotard and Baudrillard and Vattimo's hermeneutic ontology can be understood as coinciding with the widespread "linguistic turn" that is often posited as characterizing mid to late twentieth century philosophy.

Lyotard, Baudrillard, and Vattimo can thus be seen as turning away from some of the terms central to earlier theories of nihilism. The turn in French thought from existentialism and phenomenology to structuralism and post-structuralism is popularly characterized as a turn away from the centrality of the subject, and this is in fact how Lyotard and Baudrillard understand their opposition to Sartrean existentialism.[130] Vattimo, too, understands existentialism as elevating the subject to a privileged position, and rejects it on the basis of the arguments problematizing this elevation proffered by Nietzsche and Heidegger.[131] In the case of Sartre, however, such opposition arguably rests on an inaccurate characterization of his philosophy,[132] and it would be more accurate to characterize the difference between Sartre and the postmodernists in terms of individual consciousness (which for Sartre cannot be reduced to the subject, "traditionally" understood as self-identical) versus the field of language, extra-individual structures, and events, as the central locus of meaning. For Sartre, meaning is constituted by the meaning-conferring activity of consciousness; when this activity is in abeyance, the world appears absurd. As exemplified by Roquentin's experiences in *Nausea*, the experience of nihilism and the attempt to overcome this problem are largely an individual affair. Moreover, if we understand individual conscious experience as the theory of meaning from which the postmodernists depart, we can also understand them as breaking with the individualist tendencies in Nietzsche's work (those tendencies that allow him to be characterized as an existentialist thinker). While Nietzsche understands nihilism as a broad cultural and historical process, he also understands it as a problem that can be lived through and overcome by an individual thinker.

In contrast to this theorization of nihilism in terms of consciousness and the individual, post-structuralism and hermeneutic ontology both focus on language or discourse, broadly understood as extra-individual networks of semantic meaningfulness, as the locus of meaning. Structuralism and semiotics interpret social institutions and artifacts as meaning-bearing structures composed of signs that, like language on Ferdinand de Saussure's model, determine meaning according to the relationships between the elements of the structure. Structuralism and semiotics are thus attempts to extend the linguistic theory of meaning to all dimensions of intelligibility. Post-structuralists such as Lyotard and Baudrillard critique this model as overly-rationalist, asserting that a more ambiguous dimension of meaning—often expressed as *force* or *event*—both makes structures of meaning possible and disrupts established structures. As such, these post-structuralists should be understood as a responding to, and going beyond, the linguistic turn. Nevertheless, they still assert the importance of this structural dimension of meaning, positing a preferable model of meaning in terms of the dynamic interplay of structure and event rather than individual consciousness *á la* Sartre.

Hermeneutic ontology, as understood by Vattimo, takes language as the model of all meaning; it approaches Being as a text that is both something to be interpreted, and that sets the bounds of interpretation. Vattimo also posits an ontological interplay between structure and event, albeit in very different terms. For Vattimo, metaphysics, which posits Being as a static structure, is being *Verwindend* by Being as event, which consists in the historical transmission of messages that constitute the cultural horizons in which meanings are established. For Lyotard, Baudrillard, and Vattimo, the forms of meaning associated with static structures (semiotics and structuralism for the poststructuralists; metaphysics for the Italian philosopher) are criticized as the locus of existential nihilism. These new theories of meaning in which nihilism starts to be analyzed after the "linguistic turn" thus allow nihilism to be identified in the structures of language itself (the semiotic sign, for Lyotard and Baudrillard) and in wider social structures and institutions, thus constituting a new understanding of nihilism, beyond the familiar existentialist problematic of the anguished individual. An implication of this shift in focus, to be explored in the following chapters, is that the problem of nihilism becomes one to be engaged on a political, rather than individual, level.

Reflexivity

In what can be seen as a consequence of the linguistic turn in the analysis of nihilism, with Lyotard, Baudrillard, and Vattimo this analysis becomes increasingly reflexive. If language itself is the locus of nihilism, then the analysis of nihilism, which takes place through language, is also subject to the dangers of nihilism. This reflexivity in the discourse of nihilism is an extension of the problems identified by Heidegger, who makes it clear that nihilism does not confront us like an object, but is part of the ontological "opening" in which we think, speak, and write.[133] Of the three postmodern thinkers considered here, Baudrillard announces most clearly that the discourse that attempts to analyze nihilism is implicated in nihilism, and may in fact exacerbate it. He writes:

> Analysis is itself perhaps the decisive element of the immense process of the freezing over of meaning. The surplus of meaning that theories bring, their competition at the level of meaning is completely secondary in relation to their coalition in the glacial and four-tiered operation of dissection and transparency. One must be conscious that, no matter how the analysis proceeds, it proceeds toward the freezing over of meaning, it assists in the precession of simulacra and of indifferent forms. The desert grows.[134]

For Baudrillard, the analysis of nihilism, insofar as it seeks to be an accurate representation of nihilism, falls into and exacerbates the hyperreal simulation he sees as the fate of representation. Moreover, if this analysis continues to use traditional academic styles and concepts it remains enmeshed in the semio-linguistic order of meaning, which abstracts from the ambiguity and reversibility of concrete social interactions and reproduces the logic of capitalist political economy, again implicating itself in a nihilistic devaluation of existential meaning.

Lyotard also displays a deep reflexivity in his analysis of nihilism through his recognition that semantic meaning is necessarily theatrical and representational, thus nihilistic in his terms, and he does not pretend that his own discourse is free from the operations of the "great Zero." Lyotard argues that there is no pure, affirmative region beyond representation, and accepts the necessity that his own discourse, insofar as it does attempt to convey an understanding of nihilism through relatively well-defined concepts, remains representational and nihilistic. Vattimo follows suit by emphasizing that the linguistic transmissions from the cultural past that constitute the present epoch of Being are largely the messages of metaphysics. He recognizes that his own analysis of "negative" nihilism, which he calls metaphysics, must necessarily continue to be framed in terms of the metaphysical concepts handed down through the history of philosophy. Each of these thinkers is thus acutely aware that their own position, as an analyst of nihilism, cannot aim at an external vantage point and is implicated within the horizon of the problem that the analysis itself diagnoses.

Against overcoming

The key theme that distinguishes all of the postmodern theorists of nihilism considered here from the theorists considered in the previous chapter is their unanimous rejection of the possibility of a definitive overcoming of nihilism. Nietzsche, Sartre, and Heidegger each in their own way understand nihilism as a problem with a horizon that might be transcended: Nietzsche believes he has left nihilism beneath and behind himself; Sartre points to a "radical conversion" that will save us from meaninglessness; and Heidegger, although problematizing the notion of overcoming nihilism, still hopes for a turning in Being that will bring about a new, non-nihilistic epoch. In the terms of their own very different theoretical frameworks, Lyotard, Baudrillard, and Vattimo each advance arguments against the possibility of overcoming nihilism. Lyotard argues against the possibility of any system free of nihilistic effects, asserting that the affirmation of any such system necessarily implies a critical position that opposes and devalues that which it excludes, reproducing the pattern of nihilistic thought. Baudrillard's opposition to the overcoming of nihilism may be understood as following from his argument that attempts to oppose or transgress the system of simulation simply support this system by becoming its imaginary. Moreover, Baudrillard's mature thought rejects a "real" exterior to simulation to which appeal might be made in positing the possibility of a future free of simulation. Since Baudrillard argues that the real is a category that acts as an alibi for simulated systems, propping them up, he has no legitimate recourse to any alternative system opposed to simulation.[135] Vattimo, reading Nietzsche and Heidegger against the letter of their texts in an attempt to formulate their thought more rigorously, problematizes the possibility of overcoming the negative nihilism of metaphysics by linking such an overcoming with foundational thought, itself constitutive of metaphysics.

In their own ways, each of the postmodern theorists of nihilism considered here accentuate the aporetic nature of the attempt to overcome nihilism identified by Heidegger. While Heidegger still hopes for an eventual overcoming of the nihilistic crisis besetting modernity, the postmodernists reject such an overcoming outright. In the next chapter we will see how this rejection of the possibility of overcoming nihilism is linked with postmodernity through the idea of the end of history. Despite the aporiae and problematizations involved with overcoming nihilism, however, each of these postmodern thinkers understands nihilism as a problem that must be engaged, and each develops new theoretical concepts in the attempt to effectively respond to this problem. These postmodern strategies for responding to nihilism, which are proffered beyond any hope for a definitive overcoming, will be given detailed consideration in chapter four.

Chapter 3
Postmodernity and Nihilism

Up to this point, we have examined the theories of nihilism developed by Lyotard, Baudrillard, and Vattimo largely in abstraction from the theories of postmodernity that inform their understandings of nihilism. This chapter focuses on these theorizations of postmodernity, linking the theories of contemporary society offered by these thinkers with their understandings of nihilism. In their own ways, each of the theorists examined here suggest that postmodernity means that we are in a new situation with regard to nihilism. By examining the similarities and differences between the ideas of these three postmodernists, I shall be concerned to illuminate the nature of this new situation. In the introductory chapter, we saw how the idea of postmodernity has developed in close relation to the theme of nihilism, and how early theorists of postmodernity tended either to condemn this new stage of culture as one of meaninglessness and decadence, or celebrate it as a liberation from the various limitations and failings of modernity. In each of the theories of postmodernity examined below, a mixture of these perspectives is evident, and I shall argue that a tension between the affirmative and negative perspectives is constitutive of the meaning of nihilism in postmodernity. Of course, the theorization of the postmodern condition is a much-contested field, and the three theories under examination here cannot be considered exhaustive. The theories of postmodernity developed by Lyotard and Baudrillard, however (along with that of Frederic Jameson) are generally considered to be the most influential, and constitute a good representation of this field. Moreover, the very breadth and diversity of the field of postmodern theory means that, in connecting nihilism with postmodernity, the three thinkers considered here situate the philosophical thought of nihilism in a wide cultural and theoretical context, allowing us to think the problem of meaning within a broad range of contemporary conditions of existence.

In the first section of this chapter I outline the theories of postmodernity offered by Lyotard, Baudrillard, and Vattimo, concentrating on the way nihilism is connected to these theories and on the new conditions of technological science and capitalism that are prominent aspects of the postmodern scene for all three. In the second section, I offer an analysis of the meaning of the current status of nihilism that emerges from these theories of postmodernity in terms of a tension they all exhibit: on the one hand, announcing the completion of nihilism (in the Nietzschean sense of reaching a point where meaninglessness is attenuated and new forms of meaning become possible), on the other, admitting that it is not yet complete (the nihilism that afflicted modernity prevails). Furthermore, I examine the way that the idea of the end of history connects with the postmodern rejection of a decisive overcoming of nihilism, thus foreclosing the possibility of this line of response to the problem of existential meaning in the current situation. The stage will then be set for examining, in chapter four, the possibilities for responding to nihilism that remain open to these theorists of the postmodern scene.

Theories of postmodernity

Lyotard: the end of metanarratives

Lyotard famously engages, and is in large part responsible for disseminating, the "discourse of the postmodern" through his 1979 work *The Postmodern Condition*.[1] He dramatically alters the jargon and tone of his work in *The Postmodern Condition* and subsequent works such as *The Differend*.[2] Freud and Marx are replaced by Wittgenstein and Kant as central reference points, and the emotionally charged style of *Libidinal Economy* is replaced by a cool, detached mode of writing. The difference in content in the later works is marked by a shift to language as the primary subject of analysis, and a foregrounding of the problem of justice. Nevertheless, many continuities remain between the "libidinal" and "postmodern" phases of Lyotard's work, and in each the concern for the event and the limits of representation are recurring themes.[3] His description of society as entering a postmodern condition bears many similarities with his earlier description of society as a libidinal economic system, particularly in the way that the negotiations between structures and events take place.[4] Moreover, although we do not again see an engagement with nihilism as extensive as that in *Libidinal Economy*, Lyotard retains this theme as an ongoing concern. My intent here is to present Lyotard's theory of postmodernity as largely congruous with his libidinal work, and as linking his libidinal encounter with nihilism with the wider discourse of the postmodern. Such a link allows us to see how his earlier work on nihilism bears upon the status of nihilism in postmodernity.

In *The Postmodern Condition* and various essays from the 1980s,[5] Lyotard develops a theory of the most developed contemporary societies that characterizes them as having broken from the goals and aspirations that characterized modernity. Lyotard attempts various formulations of the idea of the postmodern—in terms of art, literature, and time, as well as society[6]—but the formulation of central interest here is the explicitly social and historical one contained in *The Postmodern Condition*. This text explains postmodernity as a new stage in history with a complex relation to modernity, in which the development of new technologies in conjunction with the global development of capitalism parallels changes in the status of knowledge. It is in relation to these broad social changes that Lyotard develops a theory of postmodernity that allows for comparison with Nietzsche's theory of nihilism. Lyotard explicitly makes such a comparison, and this readily allows us to examine whether the advent of postmodernity also signals a change for the status of nihilism.

Lyotard's description of the postmodern condition is historically and socially specified as the state of culture that exists in post-industrial societies[7] after World War Two.[8] For Lyotard, the postmodern should be understood as an end to the widespread acceptance of "metanarratives" as providing legitimation for social institutions and practices. Famously, he defines the postmodern as "incredulity toward metanarratives."[9] These metanarratives or grand narratives (*metarécits* or *grand récits*) are philosophies of history that attempt to organize all events and social projects around a projected goal, and give meaning and legitimation to these events and projects according to that goal. According to Lyotard, modernity is marked by metanarratives that take the Enlightenment ideals of the increase in knowledge and social emancipation as their goal, but that appeal to divergent philosophies of history in order to legitimate this goal. Lyotard lists what he takes to be the most significant metanarratives of modernity as follows:

> ...the Christian narrative of the redemption of original sin through love; the *Aufklärer* narrative of emancipation from ignorance and servitude through knowledge and egalitarianism; the speculative narrative of the realisation of the universal Idea through the dialectic of the concrete; the Marxist narrative of emancipation from exploitation and alienation through the socialisation of work; and the capitalist

narrative of emancipation from poverty through techno-industrial development.[10]

Lyotard argues that the modernist metanarratives all appeal to a philosophy of history that is a secularized form of the Christian eschatological narrative. This narrative tells of a subject affected by a lack that will be redeemed at the end of time. According to Lyotard, modern metanarratives secularize this narrative, but retain its overall form by positing a basic lack or division that will be healed or resolved at a future time. He writes that

> ...modernity maintains this temporal device, that of a "grand narrative," as one says, which *promises* at the end to reconcile the subject with itself and the overcoming of its separation. Although secularized, the Enlightenment narrative, Romanticist or speculative dialectics, and the Marxist narrative deploy the same historicity as Christianity, because they conserve the eschatological principle.[11]

On the basis of this eschatological interpretation, we can see Lyotard's concept of the metanarrative as a modernist form of religious nihilism, where belief in a "true world" is transposed to belief in a future utopia. In proposing a homology between Nietzsche's story of nihilism and the delegitimation of metanarratives, Lyotard is intimating the functional similarity between metanarratives and God. Both categories collect and attempt to explain a wide field of phenomena with respect to a transcendent source of value; where for Nietzsche the name "God" signifies the metaphysical idea of a "true world" beyond the world of appearance, the metanarratives of modernity posit a *future* legitimation for current events. Metanarratives can thus be seen as secularized transcendent categories of value and meaning, which, like God, confer value and meaning on human life. This form of value and meaning is impoverished, however, since it defers the full attainment of value to a future time.

In postmodernity, Lyotard claims, the metanarratives of legitimation that marked modernity have lost their plausibility, or become "delegitimated." Lyotard identifies at least three causes of this process of delegitimation. First, he points to certain historical events of the twentieth century that he believes problematize each of the major metanarratives of modernity. Lyotard lists these events:

> *All that is real is rational, all that is rational is real*: "Auschwitz" refutes the speculative doctrine. At least this crime, which is real, is not

rational. *All that is proletarian is communist, all that is communist is proletarian*: "Berlin 1953", "Budapest 1956", "Czechoslovakia 1968", Poland 1980" (to name but a few) refute the doctrine of historical materialism: the workers rise up against the Party. *All that is democratic is by the people and for the people, and vice versa*: "May 1968" refutes the doctrine of parliamentary liberalism. Everyday society brings the representative institution to a halt. *Everything that promotes the free flow of supply and demand is good for general prosperity, and vice versa*: the "crises of 1911 and 1929" refute the doctrine of economic liberalism, and the "crisis of 1974-1979" refutes the post-Keynesian modification of that doctrine.[12]

Taken together, Lyotard contends, these events signal the failure of modernity as a philosophically plausible conception of contemporary history.

In pointing to such events, Lyotard is appealing to what he hopes will be a shared sense that they cannot be captured adequately in the metanarratives that claim to be able to represent *all* historical events. These singular events thus act as dehiscences that radically interrupt and problematize the totalization of history that such metanarratives attempt. For Lyotard, "Auschwitz" acts as a privileged proper name that signifies the untenability of any universal history, especially any teleological and progressive history. Metanarratives such as Hegelianism and Marxism attempt to make sense of history as constituted by events that all contribute towards a future good, but Lyotard insists that events such as the Holocaust cannot be incorporated into such a narrative: any attempt to redeem this event in a philosophy of history ignores the monstrous injustice of the event itself. It is in relation to this particular form of argument for the delegitimation of metanarratives—i.e. the appeal to historical events—that one of the most common objections to Lyotard's theory of postmodernity is most keenly felt. This objection charges Lyotard with performative contradiction, arguing that he is himself presenting a metanarrative *of* the end of metanarratives, with reference to an objective and collective meaning of historical events of the very kind he is attempting to problematize.[13] This is an important objection to Lyotard's theory of postmodernity, and I shall give it consideration in the context of Vattimo's engagement with the same problem later in this chapter.

Second, Lyotard claims that the metanarratives of modernity contain the seeds of their own delegitimation within them. It is on this point that he compares the delegitimation process to the story of nihilism told by Nietzsche.[14]

As we have seen, Nietzsche presents nihilism as a process in which *"the highest values devaluate themselves,"*[15] where these "highest values" are circumscribed by the Christian-moral interpretation of the world. In this second way of explaining the delegitimation process, Lyotard applies Nietzsche's logic of "self-decomposition" to the values driving the metanarratives of modernity. In his discussion of this self-delegitimation in *The Postmodern Condition*, he focuses on what he indicates are the two dominant narratives of legitimation deriving from the *Aufklärung* and animating modernity: the speculative narrative and the emancipatory narrative. Using a strategy that is characteristic of this phase of Lyotard's work, he tries to show that the seeds of delegitimation are contained within each of these narratives by translating them into a philosophy of language inspired by Wittgenstein, speech-act theory, and other theories of language in the Analytic tradition of philosophy. In general, his strategy is to show that metanarratives consist of two or more language games,[16] which are incommensurable; metanarratives are therefore internally inconsistent and fail to legitimate knowledge in the way they purport to.

Lyotard's analysis of the speculative narrative points to a gulf between the narrative that legitimates knowledge and the statements of knowledge itself. This gulf is clearest with respect to scientific knowledge, since according to Lyotard's analysis narrative knowledge and scientific knowledge are radically different kinds of language games. The speculative narrative, exemplified by Hegel, requires that knowledge be legitimated by a second-level discourse higher than the level of positive science. At the level of positive science, denotative statements bear on certain referents (describing states of affairs in the world), but these statements need to be cited in a second-level discourse of legitimation in order to be considered knowledge. Science thus needs legitimation, but the discourse that legitimates it cannot itself be scientific (that is, this second-level discourse cannot be limited to denotative statements bearing on empirical referents). By the criteria of the legitimation of science (i.e. that all knowledge be restricted to denotative statements), however, the discourse of legitimation itself must be considered unscientific, and perhaps superstitious or ideological. On the other hand, by the criteria of legitimation—the necessity of grounding scientific statements in a second-level discourse—science itself cannot be considered knowledge. What we have here, according to Lyotard, is a delegitimation of knowledge driven by the need for legitimation itself. According to Lyotard, 'this is exactly what Nietzsche is doing, though with a different terminology, when he shows that "European nihilism" resulted from the truth requirement of science being turned back against itself.'[17]

Lyotard also identifies the seeds of delegitimation in the narrative of emancipation. This narrative grounds the legitimation of science and truth in "the autonomy of interlocutors involved in ethical, social, and political praxis."[18] The problem here, Lyotard indicates, is the divide between the denotative statements with cognitive value proper to science, and the prescriptive statements with practical value proper to the sphere of ethical, social, and political praxis. Denotative statements and prescriptive statements belong to two autonomous sets of rules defining different kinds of relevance, and therefore, competence.[19] Lyotard is here reiterating David Hume's famous "is/ought gap": prescriptions of what *ought* to be the case cannot be unproblematically derived from descriptions of what *is* the case.[20] Lyotard sees this as a division between theory and praxis that undermines any claim of science to be able to ground praxis, or indeed to ground any other, non-scientific form of knowledge. As a language game with its own specific rules, science is on a par with other language games; it cannot have the status of a second-level discourse or metanarrative. This gap between denotative and prescriptive statements means that science cannot act as a basis or guiding narrative for social praxis, and, in turn, science cannot legitimate itself with reference to such praxis. The modernist metanarrative of emancipation is thus undermined because it is premised on the relation and mutual development of scientific knowledge and social emancipation, a relation Lyotard's analysis disallows.

Third, delegitimation has occurred because science and political economy have become increasingly autonomous, gaining their legitimacy from a criterion of "performativity" and thus no longer requiring recourse to metanarrative legitimation. According to Lyotard, in modernity science gained its legitimation from metanarratives of progress and emancipation. However, in the Industrial Revolution the spheres of science, technology, and economics were bound together through the application of machine technology to industry, and this produced a change in the form of legitimation appropriate to each of these areas. Science and technology become coupled in "technoscience," in which science does not investigate nature for the sake of knowledge, but for the sake of technological innovation. Technoscience and capital were discovered to have a reciprocal relationship: just as wealth contributes to the development of technoscience, so too does technoscience contribute to wealth. Lyotard explains: "A technical apparatus requires an investment; but since it optimizes the efficiency of the task to which it is applied, it also optimizes the surplus-value derived from this improved performance."[21] Science, technology, and capital thus became intimately entwined, giving rise, Lyotard argues, to a new criterion of legitimation. This criterion is one of optimum performance, efficiency, or what Lyotard calls *performativity*; it consists of the simple rule: minimum input, maximum output. According to Lyotard, this criterion of performativity has increasingly come to legitimate science, technology, and economics, rather than any metanarrative about goals or aims.[22] While the complex of technoscience and capital began to form in the Industrial Revolution, it is only recently that the criterion of performativity has dominated over and replaced metanarrative legitimation, contributing to the advent of the postmodern condition.

Moreover, Lyotard points to a shift in technological innovation since the end of the Second World War, claiming that the new technologies developed in this period place an increasing emphasis on language.[23] That is, new technologies are largely concerned with communication and with the codification and transmission of information.[24] It is here that Lyotard's analysis of the postmodern condition draws on the theories of post-industrial society offered by Daniel Bell, Alain Touraine, and others, for whom the primary means of production are no longer industrial, but informational. For Lyotard, the impact of new technologies on language also effects changes in the nature of society, since social relationships are mediated by communication. He argues that

> [t]he important fact is this: in handling language, the new technologies directly handle the social bond, being-together. They make it more independent of traditional regulation by institutions, and more directly affected by knowledge, technology, and the marketplace. Confidence in the establishment and in the representatives of the institution (notables, parties, syndicates, ideologies, etc.) declines. The values that are associated with the institutions also decline.[25]

This decline in established social institutions and values that Lyotard believes is associated with the rise of new, language-based technologies deepens the link between his theory of postmodernity and the discourse of nihilism. Echoing Heidegger's concern that new media and technologies attack the autochthony of cultures, Lyotard writes that "[c]urrent technology, that specific mode of tele-graphy, writing at a distance, removes the close contexts of which rooted cultures are woven."[26] For Lyotard, postmodernity should be understood as a state of society characterized by a fragmentation and pluralization of language games, and the forms of life they express, which can no longer be unified by metanarratives or established social institutions, traditions, and values. Moreover, Lyotard claims that "[t]he social subject itself seems to dissolve in this dissemination of language games."[27] The self exists in a complex and mobile web of language games, as a "nodal point" in specific communication circuits. The self is a "post" through which messages pass, and which has a degree of control over those messages.[28] For Lyotard, then, the unity of the self as well as the community is fragmented by the communication and information based nature of post-industrial societies.

Lyotard thus presents postmodernity as a fragmented and pluralized state of society, an understanding of the postmodern condition that is now very familiar. While Lyotard acknowledges that it is possible to see this fragmentation of society in a pessimistic light, as the failure of the hopes of modernity, he chooses to view the situation more positively. Since on Lyotard's reading modernist metanarratives are secularized forms of the Christian eschatological narrative, and therefore nihilistic in a religious sense, the end of metanarratives signals the end of this form of religious nihilism. Moreover, Lyotard's motivation for this positive view of postmodernity is political: he sees metanarratives of legitimation as linked, in principle, to injustice and "tyranny." Lyotard explains this through an analysis of the pragmatics of the narrative of emancipation: the model of linguistic communication characteristic of modernity, Lyotard tells us, is one that involves the first, second, and third persons (I/you/he or she). The subject of history in the ideology of emancipation is a "we," a community of speakers made up of first and second persons (I/you). The movement of emancipation involves the process of the third person (he/she, or perhaps "them") being brought into the community of speakers and situated as a first or second person (I or you). This is a kind of tyranny, according to Lyotard, because meaning is always controlled by the first person. While the third person is invited into the community of speakers, s/he is always under threat of expulsion if s/he does not speak "correctly." Modernist metanarratives, then, are theories of universal history that have a homogenizing effect and work to emancipate only by erasing differences.[29] While the linguistic analysis Lyotard gives may not appear *prima facie* to hold high political stakes, the kind of "silencing" and erasure of differences he has in mind include genocidal actions such as the Holocaust. The positive import Lyotard gives to the decline of metanarratives and fragmentation of society in postmodernity therefore has a weighty political imperative: it is a concern for justice.

Lyotard's theory of postmodernity bears both strong continuities and strong discontinuities with the story of nihilism told by Nietzsche, Heidegger, and others. While Lyotard identifies his story of the advent of postmodernity with Nietzsche's story of the advent of nihilism, we can understand Lyotard as positing a stage further along in the development of nihilism than the one Nietzsche claims to diagnose in his own time. This "advance" Lyotard posits consists in the breakdown of the metanarratives of modernity, which we might understand as the secularized forms of God. As we have seen, Nietzsche argues that many of the so-called advances of modernity merely repeated the logic of religious nihilism by positing transcendent categories of aim, unity, and truth that bestow meaning upon the world. The meaning of postmodernity, for Lyotard, is that these secular categories have significantly broken down, a condition that Nietzsche predicted. In this sense, we may understand Lyotard's theory of postmodernity as positing that we have moved further towards the "completion" of nihilism. However, unlike Nietzsche, Heidegger, and other earlier theorists of nihilism, Lyotard does not understand the social fragmentation and loss of tradition as a crisis of meaning that must in some manner be overcome. Rather, he posits this state as one that removes certain conditions that contributed to injustices perpetrated in modernity.

While Lyotard does not recognize social fragmentation as necessarily nihilistic, he does identify persisting nihilistic trends in postmodernity. These trends are associated with the very complex of technoscience and capital that contributed to the advent of postmodernity, and consist in the *reductive* effects of the criterion of performativity. While metanarratives are no longer capable of unifying diverse language games, the criterion of performativity attempts to perform this unification, bringing with it the same tyranny as metanarratives. This criterion attempts to exclude as illegitimate any move in any language game that does not contribute to the overall efficiency of the game itself, however it is defined. The effect of the criterion of performativity is a reduction of differences that takes place in both theory (knowledge) and social praxis. According to the performativity criterion, society is seen as a system that must aim for efficient functioning, and this efficiency is a kind of tyranny that threatens to exclude inefficient elements. Highlighting the criterion of performativity operative in capital, Lyotard writes that

> there are several incommensurable genres of discourse in play in society, none of which can transcribe all the others; and nonetheless one of them at least—capital, bureaucracy—imposes its rules on the others. This oppression is the only radical one, the one that forbids its victims to bear witness against it.[30]

The criterion of performativity acts as a form of *reductive nihilism*, filtering differences and reducing the forms of life (language games) that are considered legitimate. There is thus a tension in Lyotard's account of postmodernity and the nature of nihilism in this account. On one hand, with the end of metanarratives nihilism is theorized in such a way that we appear to be close to its completion. On the other hand, the phenomena of technoscience and capital that have contributed to the delegitimation of metanarratives develop and deepen nihilism in their own way through the reduction of the performativity criterion.

This tension concerning nihilism is more clearly expressed in the libidinal philosophy, a comparison with which is in order to show how the libidinal treatment of nihilism resonates with Lyotard's theory of the postmodern condition. The functional equivalent of metanarratives in the libidinal philosophy is the great Zero; both are analogous forms of religious nihilism, and both terms express transcendent categories that collect and filter events, whether these events are understood libidinally or linguistically (in the postmodern philosophy, events are understood as phrases or linguistic occurrences, and their exploitation by structures is understood in terms of language games). In the libidinal philosophy, Lyotard expresses an idea similar to that of the delegitimation of metanarratives through the analysis of capitalism as a force that liquidates both archaic or pre-modern forms, and the forms through which capitalism itself has developed in modernity.[31] As with the end of metanarratives, Lyotard celebrates this widespread liquidation, asserting that '[t]he dissolution of forms and individuals in the consumer society must be *affirmed*.'[32] For Lyotard, this dissolution is a process that overcomes the barriers and limits imposed on the potential investment of libidinal energies by the great Zero as it operates in traditional social, political, and theoretical representational structures.

In Nietzschean terms, capitalism acts as a deepening of nihilism, an active nihilism that destroys religious nihilism. Lyotard privileges this process of active nihilism, asserting that it must be affirmed, because the breakdown of traditional social forms allows a greater circulation of libidinal intensity, and hence affirmation of life, in the system. Lyotard thus gives a positive value to capitalism, arguing that it is a good economic system from a libidinal point of view since it promotes the production and circulation of intensities. According to Lyotard, capitalism positively encourages the emergence of intensities through seeking out new intense energies to exploit and circulating them within the system, and through its tendency to confer value on everything (through the process Marx referred to as commodity fetishism). For example, the music industry in a capitalist economy seeks out new musical forms in foreign countries and in emerging subcultures, commodifying them and distributing them throughout the capitalist system. This process introduces new energy to the system and enables new encounters with intensive events (in this case, the novelty of new musical forms).

On the other hand, however, Lyotard asserts that capitalism is itself a form of nihilism. He writes that

> Kapital is at once depression, nihilism and the culmination of theology....it plunges humanity into the theology of atheism, immerses it in the theology of a-theology, in the belief in (the death of) God. It reintroduces nothing, but itself rests upon the law of value, that is on the equality of the parties involved in any metamorphosis...[33]

Lyotard explains that although capitalism dissolves the traditional limitations placed on libidinal investment, capitalism itself rests upon an axiom that in turn limits the intensity of libidinal events. This axiom is the law of value that accords commodities a price in relation to the universal standard of money.[34] For Lyotard, the intensity of libidinal energy consists in its *difference* in potential, its ability to metamorphose or displace elements of the system in which it occurs, and the *singularity* that constitutes it as an event. In subsuming libidinal energies under the law of value, and regulating them within a system of exchange, capitalism effectively dampens the intensities it exploits. Lyotard argues that capitalism

> functions by ignoring the inequality of force and resorbing its potential of disturbance, creation and mutation. Because of the principle governing energetic connection, the capitalist system privileges repetition without profound difference, duplication, commutation or replication, and reversibility.[35]

The tendency of capitalism to exploit new intensities therefore comes at the expense of the tendency to annul the very intensities sought through their translation into exchange value. The conferring of exchange value tends to take on absolute importance within the capitalist system, and risks hegemonically annulling the singularity of all intensities within that system. In relation to the example of the music industry above, the circulation of new musical intensities may also dampen those intensities, as they take on a value in the system of general economic exchange. Thus, capitalism itself appears as a kind of nihilistic zero,[36] threatening to take the place of the religious nihilism it has displaced. Summing up the effect of this dampening of intensity through the law of value, Lyotard likens the capitalist system to a society functioning on Valium.[37]

In both the postmodern and libidinal phases of his work, Lyotard tells a story about nihilism that displays a tension between the dissolution of old nihilistic forms, and the rise of a new nihilism ("neo-nihilism") in the form of the very forces that brought about the dissolution of those old forms. These forces are analyzed as the reductive tendencies inherent in technoscience and capitalism, manifest through the criterion of performativity and the commodity law of value. For Lyotard, the dissolution of traditional forms of meaning and value does not constitute a nihilistic crisis; he celebrates this form of nihilism alternately as allowing a greater possibility for justice and a greater circulation of life-affirming libidinal energy. In both analyses, the dissolution of traditional forms allows a freer expression of events in relation to the structures that have traditionally exploited them and suppressed their expression. In this respect, Lyotard understands postmodernity as a state of society in which nihilism nears completion, and understands this completion in a positive manner. On the other hand, however, Lyotard sees nihilism, in the form of technoscience and capital, as a very real problem in postmodernity, that threatens to take the place evacuated by metanarratives and the traditional religious forms of the great Zero.

Baudrillard: hyperreality

Baudrillard is widely regarded as one of the most important theorists of postmodernity, despite the fact that his use of the term "postmodern" is rare, and he has disavowed association with the wider discourse of postmodernism.[38] I am in agreement with Nicholas Zurbrugg when he writes that "Jean Baudrillard's disclaimer 'I have nothing to do with postmodernism' is rich with irony. Considered in terms of his general arguments and assertions, Baudrillard has *everything* to do with postmodernism."[39] For cultural critics such as Arthur Kroker and Douglas Kellner, as well as Zurbrugg, Baudrillard's work is central to the discourse of postmodernity; he is understood as the first "hi-tech" theorist who both examines the social implications of new technologies (holograms, virtual reality, etc.) and employs concepts from recent scientific innovations (chaos theory, non-Euclidean geometries) to up-date the analytical terms of social theory. As such, he is perceived as a central theorist of recent cultural change whose works must be engaged for any adequate understanding of the "postmodern scene."[40] In this section I shall examine those arguments and assertions of Baudrillard's that contribute to a vision of contemporary society that marks a break with dominant modernist conceptions, and that may be interpreted as a theory of postmodernity. Significantly, Baudrillard's genealogy of nihilism in the essay "On Nihilism" makes use of the modernity/postmodernity distinction,[41] and his pronouncement that we are in a new stage with respect to nihilism links this stage to a postmodern state of society and culture. Baudrillard's theory of nihilism, introduced in the previous chapter, attains its full meaning only in relation to his theory of postmodern society. I shall draw out this relation by firstly examining the genealogy of nihilism Baudrillard proposes, and then by linking this with his wider theories concerning the current state of society and culture.

In the essay "On Nihilism" Baudrillard provides a brief genealogy of the successive stages of nihilism, which he associates with various historical periods. The first two stages of nihilism may be schematized as follows:

1. The destruction of *appearances*. Romanticism and the Enlightenment. An aesthetic form of nihilism (dandyism).

2. The destruction of *meaning*. Surrealism, dada, the absurd, political nihilism. A political, historical and metaphysical form of nihilism (terrorism).[42]

Baudrillard identifies the first stage of nihilism with the nineteenth century and modernity. The second stage is identified with the twentieth century and postmodernity, but this century also includes a third, current stage, which differs from the second stage. Baudrillard does not clearly name the second and third stages in the twentieth century, but following the conventional interpretation established by Zurbrugg, Kroker, and others I will take the third stage—the stage we are in now—as Baudrillard's theorization of postmodernity proper.

On Baudrillard's account the nihilism of modernity concerns the destruction of appearances and the consequent "disenchantment" of the world, a process that took place through the Enlightenment project of the pervasive development and application of reason through theory and interpretation. Interpretation, in Baudrillard's characterization[43], seeks truth behind appearances: it employs models that suggest that there is a "deep structure" to things, a hidden depth that might be illuminated. This form of theory is sometimes labeled "the hermeneutics of suspicion," and is associated with theoretical frameworks such as Marxism and psychoanalysis.[44] History, psychoanalysis, representation, dialectical reason, "depth models," criticism and interpretation are all examples of the kind of rational theory that Baudrillard believes stems from the Enlightenment aim to rationalize all of reality, and which, for Baudrillard, characterizes modernity. On this account, modern theory seeks to establish the true *meaning* of all things, behind or beyond their surface appearances. Baudrillard therefore sees modernity as the destruction of appearances by the establishment of meaning, where meaning is understood as the deployment of theories that posit a "true" reality behind appearances. He writes, "[t]he true revolution of the nineteenth century, of modernity, is the radical destruction of appearances, the disenchantment of the world and its abandonment to the violence of interpretation and of history."[45]

Baudrillard describes a second nihilistic revolution that is a destructive reaction to the pervasive rational meaning established in the nineteenth century, a reaction expressed through artistic and philosophical denials of the *existential* meaningfulness of modernist reason, such as Dada and existentialist anguish. Baudrillard also locates Nietzschean nihilism in this category, and by extension all nihilisms that are concerned with the destruction of existential meaning by rational meaning, figurally expressed by the death of God. As Baudrillard puts it, "[h]e who strikes with meaning is killed by meaning."[46] For Baudrillard, this second phase of nihilism is a dark drama in which stakes are still clearly marked and nihilism itself retains a certain nostalgic meaningfulness, exemplified by the romantic affectation of the angst-ridden individual. According to Baudrillard, however, we are now in a new stage, which he calls *the nihilism of transparency*. He asserts that

> [w]e are in a new, and without doubt insoluble, position in relation to prior forms of nihilism…These two forms of nihilism no longer concern us except in part, or not at all. The nihilism of transparency is no longer either aesthetic or political, no longer borrows from either the extermination of appearances, nor from extinguishing the embers of meaning, nor from the last nuances of an apocalypse.[47]

According to Baudrillard, this new stage of nihilism consists in the fact that the process of the self-destruction of meaning is complete. The current stage of nihilism is one in which the rational structures of meaning developed in modernity overextend themselves into simulation and hyperreality, leading to all the nihilistic consequences detailed in the examination of Baudrillard's work in the previous chapter. In effect, meaning destroys itself (in Baudrillard's words, meaning "freezes-over") through a process of excrescence, that is, through a hypertelic extension beyond its own ends. It is this hypertelos of meaning that Baudrillard analyses in the order of representation through the concept of simulation. For Baudrillard, nihilism is no longer dark—where darkness represents the failure of the light of reason to penetrate the deepest mysteries of existence—but over-lit, leaving nothing concealed. Baudrillard accordingly describes today's nihilism as one of transparency, since no secret depths remain in any corner of the postmodern world. The mood of this nihilism of transparency, Baudrillard asserts, is not one of anguish or existential panic, but of melancholic fascination with the disappearance of meaning.

Baudrillard's genealogy of nihilism is clearly influenced by Nietzsche and in its general contours is very close to that developed by Lyotard. For Baudrillard, as for both Nietzsche and Lyotard, nihilism consists in an auto-destruction of the highest values of modernity. Baudrillard understands these values as the depth-models of meaning and theories of the real that have attempted to represent the world, and that have rendered themselves meaningless by becoming hyperreal or simulated. Baudrillard's analysis of the depth models of meaning is thus necessarily linked with his earlier analyses of the semio-linguistic order of meaning and the fate of representation in simulation. When Baudrillard uses the term "meaning" in the context of his discussions of modernity and postmodernity, he has in mind a modernist form of meaning which seeks to found itself on a theory of the real; this notion of the real underlies the semio-linguistic sign, depth models such as Marxism and psychoanalysis, and the image of thought as representation in general. When Baudrillard posits the destruction of meaning by meaning, all of these registers—united by the category of the real—must be taken into account as characteristic aspects of modernist thought and culture. For Baudrillard, modernity can be understood most essentially as that era of Western culture in which the theory of the real, as that which lies behind appearances and which might be fully explicated by the correct use of reason, is dominant. As in Nietzsche's formulation of nihilism as the process in which the highest values devaluate themselves (the will to truth reveals truth itself to be untrue), Baudrillard understands nihilism as the destruction of meaning by the very attempt to make the world meaningful; the destruction of the real through the very attempt to realize the world.[48]

The brief genealogy presented in the essay "On Nihilism" is filled out by Baudrillard's wider writings on the current state of society and culture, and we must turn to these writings for a more adequate picture of Baudrillard's understanding of the meaning of nihilism in postmodernity. Baudrillard's most influential work of contemporary social theory is the short book *In the Shadow of the Silent Majorities*.[49] His theorizations of the social, the masses, and the media presented in this work are central to the vision of postmodern culture for which he has become known. In this work Baudrillard extends his unique logic of the hypertelos of meaning to the realm of the social, proposing the concept of "the masses" as the only appropriate way to think "the social" after the implosion of modernist categories of meaning:

> Beyond meaning, there is fascination, which results from the neutralization and implosion of meaning. Beyond the horizon of the social, there are the masses, which result from the neutralization and implosion of the social.[50]

In this analysis, "the social" groups together all those understandings of society and socialization that construe social reality in terms of the modernist projects of rationalization and emancipation. The social indicates the notion of an *advancement* in the general state of the human population through projects and institutions such as "urbanization, concentration, production, work, medicine, education, social security, insurance, etc."[51] Moreover, for Baudrillard the concept of the social also includes within its rubric the methodological assumptions that contribute to rationalization and socialization. Such assumptions include the belief that social reality can be more or less accurately mapped by the methods and theoretical models of traditional sociology: surveys, case studies, statistical analysis, and so on. Baudrillard's argument in *In the Shadow* is that the social, in both these respects, is no longer a tenable category.

Baudrillard contends that the social is radically problematised by what he calls "the masses," and his argument here links with both his genealogy of nihilism and his theory of simulation.[52] Baudrillard insists that the social must be understood as a process of socialization that requires an unsocialized percentage of the population to justify its project. This unsocialized part of the population is what Baudrillard terms "the masses": they are the poor, the unemployed, the sick, the criminal, the insane, the "underclasses." He then effectively argues that the relationship between the social and the masses follows the same dynamic as the relationship between representation and the real, or between the sign and its referent. The masses are that remainder left over from the process of socialization; they are the residues of humanity that the social attempts properly to socialize in order to complete itself. This process of socialization takes place through institutions such as the social work industry and health care organizations, and is coordinated by disciplines such as sociology that attempt to represent and understand "the masses." Baudrillard argues, however, that the paradox of representation that constitutes simulation is operative in contemporary social reality: the attempts to represent the masses have over-extended themselves, resulting in an implosion of the categories upholding the social.

Baudrillard argues that "[t]he social exists on the double basis of the production of remainders and their eradication."[53] Like the semiological sign, which attempts to fully encompass its referent yet requires an external referent as an alibi, the social attempts to eradicate the masses by socialising them, yet requires them as a remainder, limit, or "other" in order to function *as* the social. This is the case because the masses act as that gap or distance between the representational architecture of the social and the real that it supposedly represents, and that it requires in order to function as representation. Rex Butler explains:

> On the one hand, that is, it is the masses—the resistance or difference of the masses—which allow that infinite extension of the social whereby the social is realised, becomes equivalent to the real. And, on the other hand, it is also the masses—the resistance or difference of the masses—which ensure that the social is never realised or becomes real because this is only possible due to the masses…[54]

Baudrillard argues that—like other representational structures he analyses—the social has extended itself too far, and fallen into simulation. The modern process of socialization has become more and more effective, more and more accurate in both its representation and socialization of "the masses." According to Baudrillard's analysis, however, the result is not a rational socialization nearing completion, but a growth of the masses to the point where Baudrillard asserts that the social itself has imploded into the masses (that is, the two categories have lost the distance between them). The masses have become the hyperrreal *product* of the social; they cannot truly be said to exist prior to the social, but are produced through the very process of socialization. Baudrillard characterizes the masses as that part of the social that resists representation, or about which knowledge can never be complete. While the process of socialization has become more and more sophisticated, the representation of society more and more accurate, the process is always incomplete. As Butler writes, "in the idea that the masses constitute our image of society through polls, questionnaires, and surveys, we get the feeling that they are a little *too* typical, a little *too* much themselves, fulfill our expectations about them a little *too* perfectly. We get the impression that there is something we are not getting at in the very match between question and answer."[55] Baudrillard therefore proposes that the masses are both hyperconformist with respect to sociological representations of them, and that absolutely nothing can be said about them. In terms of the paradox of representation, the masses are the hyperreal that is both produced by the representational model (and are thus hyperconformist to it), and that exceeds this model (since the gap between representation and reality must be preserved).

Baudrillard extends his analysis of the masses along the same lines on which we saw the paradox of representation extended in the previous chapter, where simulation spells the end of the stable categories and distinctions that constituted meaning in modernity. For Baudrillard, the masses are not only the hyperreal limit of the social, but in a sense mean the end of the social. Read as a theory of postmodernity, Baudrillard's theory of the masses means that the modernist dream of social enlightenment and emancipation is no longer tenable, and we must approach an understanding of postmodern society in a way completely different to that of modernist sociology. What Baudrillard emphasizes most strongly is the collapse of the traditional categories of the social into the undifferentiated masses, asserting that nothing can really be known about contemporary social reality. He writes that

> it is impossible to manipulate the masses in any determinate way, or to understand them in terms of elements, relations, structures and wholes. All manipulation plunges, gets sucked into the mass, absorbed, distorted, reversibilised.[56]

Baudrillard likens the masses to a black hole; they absorb all attempts to understand them and give up no information.[57] Understood as that necessary limit to the social, the masses in principle defy representation. Furthermore, however, the fact that the social and the masses form a system of simulation means that the social, with all its attempts to map "the real" of society, has lost touch with any external referent or "real." As hyperreal, the masses do not constitute an external limit to the social, but an internal limit, produced by the social itself.[58] As discussed in the previous chapter, this loss of reference to an external real means that the oppositions on which modern theories of meaning typically rest implode or become reversible, because there is no external criterion against which to judge the correct application of one term or the other of the opposition. Baudrillard argues that the social implodes in the masses, meaning that the representational frameworks characteristic of the social can no longer maintain their distinct oppositions and categories because there are no longer external criteria for application. Is society dominated or emancipated? Is socialization progressing or regressing? Without a referent in the real, such categories become inapplicable, imploding into each other and erasing all the critical distinctions of social theory. For Baudrillard "the masses" therefore also names the fate of the social in the current situation, where '[n]o analysis would know how to contain this diffuse, decentered, Brownian, molecular reality: the notion of object vanishes just as "matter," in the ultimate analysis, vanishes on the horizon of microphysics.'[59]

Baudrillard's theory of postmodernity as a state of society characterized by the implosion of meaning is given further depth through his analysis of the part that recent developments in technology—in particular, information technology employed by the mass media—and capitalism have played in this implosion. An analysis of the role of the media in this process is given in the third essay collected in *In the Shadow*, "The Implosion of Meaning in the Media," where Baudrillard writes that

> the media do not bring about socialization, but just the opposite: the implosion of the social in the masses. And this is only the macroscopic extension of the *implosion of meaning* at the microscopic level of the sign.[60]

As this passage suggests, Baudrillard reads the media and information technology as forms of representation, to be analyzed in an analogous manner to that of the representational function of the sign. Baudrillard carries out this analysis by finding an analogue to the microscopic formalism of the sign at the macroscopic level of the media in Marshall McLuhan's dictum "The medium is the message."[61] He argues that in the circulation of information through the mass media, the form that information takes is constituted by the medium through which it is sent—television, radio, and so on. Baudrillard then argues that the media of information distribution reduce its message in the same way that (as he has argued) the formal dimensions of the sign (the signifier) reduce its content (the signified or referent).

Baudrillard posits an hypothesis of extreme reduction in relation to the media, contending that the circulation of information through the mass media is directly destructive of meaning and signification, and that the more mediatized information proliferates, the greater the implosion of meaning.

For Baudrillard, it is the very *exchangeability* of information that makes it destructive of meaning, since on his account meaning requires a degree of nonreversible stability of reference in order to function. This argument is further fleshed out in the essay "The Ecstasy of Communication," where Baudrillard compares the messages transmitted by information technology to the commodity form of the object as analysed by Marx.[62] For Marx, the commodity form consists in the reduction of the object to its exchange value, so that it may be circulated freely in a system of economic exchange. The commodity is abstract, formal, and light in opposition to the weight, opacity, and substance of the object.[63] Baudrillard contends that the commodity form is the first great medium of the modern world, since it allows objects to "communicate" through their reduction to a common "language" (that of exchange value). On Marx's analysis, however, the commodity form reduces and negates the use value of the object. By Baudrillard's analogy, this is the first case of the destruction of the content or message by the form (or medium) that allows it to be communicated. Just as the content of the commodity is reduced to the formal dimension of its exchange value, Baudrillard argues that the message of all mediatized information is the formal dimension of information technology (the medium) itself—it is this formal dimension that is primarily propagated through the media, overshadowing the content of the message. Baudrillard thus argues that twentieth century developments in the media have contributed to the second nihilistic revolution, the destruction of meaning by meaning, and led to our current nihilistic state, since the media is intended as a development and expansion of the communication of meaning.

Baudrillard's theory of postmodernity is in an important way further constituted by the complex theorizations of recent mutations in capitalism that he has offered in numerous works. The full range of Baudrillard's engagement with capitalism is beyond the scope of this study. However, a brief overview of the stages of capitalism as analyzed by Baudrillard, and their accompanying cultural conditions, may be gleaned from *Symbolic Exchange and Death*.[64] Such an overview will contribute to an appreciation for the place of political economy in Baudrillard's theorization of postmodernity. Baudrillard posits a revolution in capitalism between the nineteenth and twentieth centuries, which he broadly describes as a shift from the commodity law of value (as Marx analyzed it) to what he calls the "structural" law of value. In this shift from the nineteenth to the twentieth century (which Baudrillard names *the structural revolution of value*), capitalism becomes dominated by a form of logical organization that he calls "the code." Following Marx, Baudrillard suggests that the nineteenth century was dominated by the commodity law of value, in which production was the primary mode of the social, and exchange value was the primary form of value. On Baudrillard's interpretation the commodity law of value forms a determinate system of dialectical oppositions, and non-economic values (use value, desires, needs, "human" values) are negated through an annexation to exchange value. This annexation is a form of nihilistic reduction at work in nineteenth century capitalism, where all values (including any values that might be held to make life existentially meaningful) are reduced to exchange value.

With the structural revolution of value in the twentieth century, the code comes to replace exchange value as the logically privileged mode of operation in the capitalist system. According to Baudrillard, contemporary capitalism is marked by the fact that it is not objects as *commodities* that are consumed, but objects as *signs*. Objects signify that which is desirable, such as social status, concepts, values, or lifestyles, and it is these significations that are consumed through the purchase of objects. He suggests that in contemporary capitalism the system of commodities forms a system of signs that allows it to be conceptualized as a structure, analogous to other signifying structures analyzed by structuralists.[65] "The code" that Baudrillard posits as central to contemporary capitalism is the method of organization of this system of signs. In general terms, a code is a system of rules for the combination of stable sets of terms into messages.[66] The code is a structure that is not a language because it does not have a syntax, but also because its terms act as *signals* rather than manipulable linguistic units. That is, the code sends a message, but is not itself open to a reciprocal receiving of messages. As such, it operates in society as a system of structural domination. In Gary Genosko's words, "The code *terrorizes* the process of communication by fixing the two poles of sender and receiver and by privileging the sender."[67] Furthermore, Baudrillard has it, the code is characterized by the interchangability or commutability of its terms, and this interchangability takes precedence over the principle of equivalence that is the privileged logic of exchange value.

The code induces an even more nihilistic dimension to capitalism than that of exchange value, and it is this stage of capitalism that, according to Baudrillard, accompanies the current nihilism of transparency. While the commodity law of value reduces everything to an equivalence in exchange value, the system is still ordered in a determinate way through dialectical oppositions. This means that there are terms radically opposed to each other in a system of political economy, and thus that there are real political stakes: one term may be privileged over or set against another in relations of domination and resistance. The whole system of political economy as Marx analyzed it contains terms that are opposed to the capitalist system (such as non-alienated labour) and from which a critique may be derived. The code, however, negates the stability of all oppositions. The code is a system in which every term is substitutable for every other term, and all oppositions become reversible. The structural ordering of value 'leads to fluid and aleatory combinations that neutralize by *connection*, not by *annexation*, whatever resists or escapes them.'[68] Baudrillard furthermore argues that the whole system of the circulation of commodities, first made possible through the equivalence of exchange value, becomes a system of floating signifiers that no longer primarily refer to anything as such, except the code itself. The code contributes to and accompanies the era of hyperreality and simulation, since the signs deployed by the structural revolution of value no longer refer to the real. The code takes priority, and since anything can be codified (commodified, reduced to its sign value), the actual terms in the system no longer matter. Everything is substitutable and reversible. There are no longer dialectical oppositions, and nothing is any longer at stake. The code is therefore a completely hegemonic system of nihilistic reduction suffusing contemporary capitalism, reducing everything to the nihilistic, indifferent play of hyperreal simulation.

Baudrillard's theory of the structural revolution of value indicates how recent developments in political economy have contributed to the current state of culture as one of postmodern simulation, and hence, nihilism. This theory further bears out Baudrillard's hypothesis of the destruction of meaning by meaning, since capitalism may be understood as part of the modernist project to "socialize" the world through the advancement of economic prosperity, and it is this very advancement that has undermined social meaning through the excessive abstraction of the code. Baudrillard's theorisation of a postmodern society is extended further by new analytical concepts employed in *The Transparency of Evil*[69] and other texts of the nineteen-nineties, and these new terms deepen and clarify Baudrillard's vision of contemporary nihilism. In these later works Baudrillard introduces the idea of a new stage of value, beyond the structural revolution, and uses the concept of the "transfinite" to further characterize the generalized implosion of categories and erasure of distinctions that characterized modern thought and modern societies. Announcing the end of modernity in *The Transparency of Evil*, Baudrillard writes:

> The glorious march of modernity has not led to the transformation of all values, as we once dreamed it would, but instead to a dispersal and involution of value whose upshot for us is total confusion—the impossibility of apprehending any determining principle, whether of an aesthetic, a sexual, or a political kind.[70]

This generalized confusion of values and categories is now presented as according with a "fractal," "viral," or "radiant" stage of value, in which there is no longer any rule of equivalence regulating exchange, but a haphazard proliferation of value in which terms are exchanged in all directions. In this stage of culture, Baudrillard suggests, value spreads by a metonymic function of contagion: one term takes on another term's qualities and becomes exchangeable with it purely through contact, through the mere chance of being adjacent to it. The effect of this stage of value, according to Baudrillard's analysis, is a general contagion of culture in which traditional categories and discreet cultural spheres lose their consistency and specificity. Baudrillard argues that modernity has destroyed itself through the liberation, in every sphere of culture, from traditional boundaries. The concept of the "transfinite" expresses the way that each sphere of culture has undergone this liberation, extending itself beyond its own bounds and blurring its borders with all other cultural spheres. Like simulation, transfinite systems are hypertelic; they extend beyond their own ends.[71] Baudrillard likens this liberation and hypertelic extension of spheres of culture to a vast orgy:

> The orgy in question was the moment when modernity exploded on us, the moment of liberation in every sphere. Political liberation, sexual liberation, liberation of the forces of production, liberation of the forces of destruction, women's liberation, children's liberation, liberation of unconscious drives, liberation of art.[72]

The effect of this orgy of liberation is that the distinctions between cultural spheres breaks down, and each sphere becomes totalizing in itself: sexual liberation has made *everything* sexual, political liberation has made *everything* political, the liberation of the aesthetic has made *everything* aesthetic, etc. This transfinitude of systems means that a total exchange between every term of the system becomes possible, and that every system is totalizing, leaving nothing outside of it (nothing that is not political, nothing that is not sexual, etc.) This totalization, however, also results in the greatest degree of generalization, so that each category loses its distinctness and bleeds into (or implodes with) all others. The transfinite is an extension of the nihilism of the hyperreal; in transfinite systems all oppositions and all references disappear entirely, and the possibility of all valuations and critical judgments also disappear. In this current state of culture, Baudrillard writes, "…it is as impossible to make estimations between beautiful and ugly, true and false, or good and evil, as it is simultaneously to calculate a particle's speed and position."[73]

With his emphasis on the destruction of modern categories of valuation as a collapse of meaning, Baudrillard has more in common with Nietzsche and Heidegger than with Lyotard. Like Lyotard, however, Baudrillard argues that postmodernity is characterized by the end of history, a notion that is given a typically paradoxical treatment in his work. Baudrillard understands the modernist conception of history in a linear fashion, as "a succession of non-meaningless facts, each engendering the other by cause and effect."[74] Like Lyotard, he also understands the modernist notion of history as teleological, following the Christian model of eschatology in which the goal of history will be achieved at the end of time with the Last Judgment.[75] Baudrillard theorizes the end of the linear time of modernity in such a way that the possibility of history actually reaching an end is disallowed. The end of history in postmodernity cannot be thought of as an event within history or at the end of a continuous historical line, since these are the very concepts problematized by the postmodern idea of the end of history. Instead, Baudrillard suggests the model of an asymptote (a line that continually approaches a curve but doesn't meet it at a finite distance) to describe the dynamic of history in postmodernity.[76] On this model, history is continually ending, but this process of ending never itself reaches an end. In the essay "The Year 2000 Will Not Take Place,"[77] Baudrillard suggests three "plausible hypotheses" that might explain how history has ended, and which link the concept of the end of history with his analyses of the masses and of the media. Firstly, he makes an analogy with the velocity a body needs to escape the gravitational force of a mass. He suggests that the acceleration of human culture has brought us to a velocity at which we escape the mass of the real and of history. History has disappeared not because things no longer happen, no longer change, but because they change too fast, because events are dispersed and diffused so quickly that they do not seem to cause any other events. According to this hypothesis, history can only take place within a certain horizon of change, and the speeding-up of events has accelerated us beyond this horizon. This hypothesis of the end of history is linked with Baudrillard's analysis of the implosion of meaning in the media, through the proposition that the instant diffusion of events through the media causes historical time to accelerate: '[e]ach fact, each political, historical, cultural act is endowed, by its power of media diffusion, with a kinetic energy that flings it out of its own space forever, and propels it into hyperspace where it loses all meaning, since it can never return.'[78]

Baudrillard's second "plausible hypothesis" is an analogy exactly the opposite of his first, and draws on his analysis of the masses. He suggests that time has decelerated in proportion with the mass of culture—the "masses" of the social body. This mass has increased to the point where time—and hence history—has decelerated to stasis. In the "mass" of the masses, Baudrillard is invoking what he calls their *inertia*—their overwhelming indifference to all attempts to represent or socialize them. History might, therefore, be said to end through the resistance of the masses to the modernist project of socialization. This inertia of the masses is again linked by Baudrillard with the excessive proliferation of mediatized information. Of this mass of information exchange, Baudrillard says, '[i]t is the cold star of the social, and around this mass history cools, it slows down, events succeed each other and vanish in indifference.'[79] Now the description of the end of history is reversed—it is the real and history that cannot find their escape velocity. All events are devoured by the rapacious indifference of the masses. The two hypotheses of acceleration and inertia are thus paradoxically complementary, and arrive at the same point: the end of history. In sum, Baudrillard proposes that the implosive, nihilistic forces of the media and the masses invalidate the unity of social reality that allowed the conception of linear history in modernity. For Baudrillard, the end of history in postmodernity means that there are no longer any events of historical import, since there is no longer a background history against which such events can be registered.[80]

Baudrillard gives us an image of postmodernity in which the implosion of the categories of modernity, brought about by recent shifts in capital, developments in mass media information technology, and pervasive cultural liberation, results in a static historical situation in which events of historical magnitude no longer take place. The mood of contemporary culture, on Baudrillard's analysis, is neatly summarized in the following statement from one of his interviews:

> Postmodernity is neither optimistic nor pessimistic. It is a game with the vestiges of what has been destroyed. This is why we are 'post-': history has stopped, one is in a kind of post-history which is without

meaning. One would not be able to find any meaning in it. So, we must move in it, as though it were a kind of circular gravity. We can no longer be said to progress. So it is a 'moving' situation...postmodernity is the attempt—perhaps it's desperate, I don't know - to reach a point where one can live with what is left. It is more a survival among the remnants than anything else. (Laughter.)[81]

This passage reiterates the melancholic nihilism that is a consistent theme in Baudrillard's works. As with Lyotard, however, there is a tension in Baudrillard's account of the nihilism of postmodernity. As we have seen, Baudrillard understands the nihilism of postmodernity as the completion of the destruction of meaning by meaning and the constitution of a cultural state of hyperreality or transfinitude in which the meaningful categories of modernity no longer operate. Beyond this, however, Baudrillard frequently hints at the possibility of what he calls a "poetic reversal" of the nihilism of postmodernity that would signal the final collapse of modernist conceptions of meaning and a restitution of the more existentially fulfilling forms of meaning based on principles of reversibility, ambiguity, and challenge.[82] Baudrillard associates this form of meaning with the appearances destroyed by semio-linguistic and depth-model forms of meaning in modernity. At the end of the essay "On Nihilism" he posits the immortality of appearances, intimating their possible resurrection. The possibility of this "poetic reversal" of nihilism into a more existentially meaningful state of culture is explored through many registers in Baudrillard's work, and is expressed by terms such as symbolic exchange, death, the anagram, seduction, and the vital illusion. The concept of seduction will be considered in the final chapter in the context of a detailed examination of Baudrillard's positive response to the nihilism of postmodernity. In the present context, however, I wish to indicate briefly how this possibility of a poetic reversal introduces a tension into Baudrillard's theorization of nihilism in postmodernity through the concept of "impossible exchange."

Impossible exchange can arguably be understood as Baudrillard's critical alternative to the transfinite; this possibility is developed most clearly in the relatively recent collection of theoretical essays, *Impossible Exchange*.[83] As many commentators have noted, with *Fatal Strategies*[84] Baudrillard's work takes a decisive turn towards metaphysical speculation, and *Impossible Exchange* is perhaps the apogee of such speculation. He begins the title essay with a number of metaphysical propositions:

> Everything starts from impossible exchange.
>
> There is no equivalent of the world.... No equivalent, no double, no representation, no mirror. Any mirror whatsoever would still be part of the world.
>
> Since the world is a totality, there is nothing outside it with which it can be exchanged.[85]

The impossible exchangeability that Baudrillard here asserts of the world he also asserts is the case with any totalizing system: since there is nothing outside of it, there is nothing with which it can be exchanged. This totality of systems accords with the transfinite expansion of cultural spheres that he examines in his earlier works.[86] Implicitly harking back to the semio-linguistic theory of meaning, which posits that meaning functions according to the exchange of signs, Baudrillard argues that such systems are meaningless. He writes: "Literally, they have no meaning outside themselves and cannot be exchanged for anything."[87] In this context Baudrillard gives a new definition of nihilism, relating it directly to the lack of meaning and value stemming from the transfinitude of systems and their impossible exchange: "The true formula of contemporary nihilism lies here, rather than in any philosophical or moral considerations: it is the nihilism of value itself...Here and now, the whole edifice of value is exchangeable for Nothing."[88]

This "Nothing," however, can in one sense be understood as the gap or distance between representation and the real, which is indicated by Baudrillard's previous "positive" terms, such as seduction. Simulation and the transfinite are those principles that try to eradicate the Nothing with pure positivity, to leave nothing outside themselves. The Nothing, for Baudrillard, indicates both that there is nothing left outside simulated and transfinite systems—hence a kind of nihilism of value—*and* that outside simulation, Nothing *is* left. Baudrillard is here enacting a kind of poetic reversal that hinges on the double meaning of "Nothing" as both substantive term and as quantifier. He continues this poetic reversal by valorizing the Nothing itself, asserting that "The Nothing is the only ground—or background—against which we can apprehend existence...In this sense, things only exist *ex nihilo*. Things only ever exist out of nothing."[89] Baudrillard insists here, and elsewhere in his later works, that the system of simulation and transfinitude tries to eradicate the nothing through sheer positivity, but that the nothing inevitably continues as a "substratum" beneath Something. Again, we see the familiar themes of simulation: the sign tries to be a full positivity, but cannot help casting the shadow of its transcendence.

Baudrillard's similarity to Heidegger in this later work is striking. While Baudrillard names another source for his concept of the Nothing,[90] his use of this concept is reminiscent of Heidegger's own play on the ambiguity of "Nothing" in "What is Metaphysics?"[91], and his insistence on the necessity of concealment in the process of ontological unconcealment. Baudrillard marks this connection himself with occasional references to Heidegger, particularly with regard to the concept of *Ge-stell* as the ontological dimension of technology, and to the "secret" and the "stellar course of the mystery,"[92] terms that Heidegger uses to indicate that Being keeps itself in secret promise, and cannot be entirely lost no matter how far nihilism extends. For Baudrillard, today's nihilism is one of an "overlit" world, where the light of reason has penetrated into every dark corner. Yet there is a sense in which light cannot help but cast shadows, and Baudrillard insists on the continuity of the Nothing beneath the total realization of the world, the attempt to turn everything into Something. Baudrillard's most positive suggestion is that the nihilistic world of technology, hyperreality and simulation will reach a point at which it will be reversed into a re-enchanted, more existentially meaningful world of seduction and mystery. This may take place through the eradication of the reality principle on which the whole edifice of simulation is predicated, a principle that is destroyed through the development of simulation and transfinitude to an extreme degree. The tension in Baudrillard's analysis of the nihilism of postmodernity thus reflects the undecidability we saw in the previous chapter: on the one hand, he suggests that postmodernity is suffused with a nihilism that cannot be transcended, since all critical oppositions and philosophies of history have been annulled. On the other hand, he suggests the possibility that the system might be pushed even further, to the point of a poetic reversion that will finally eradicate the imploded categories of modernist systems of meaning and restore a more "enchanted" order of meaning that takes reversibility as its principle. This undecidability concerning these two hypotheses is maintained as a tension throughout all Baudrillard's mature works, and is a defining feature of his understanding of nihilism in postmodernity.

Vattimo: the secularisation of secularisation

Of the three thinkers considered here, it is Vattimo's theory of postmodernity that is developed most explicitly and extensively in relation to the contemporary meaning of nihilism. With Vattimo's work we see many of the same themes and issues that preoccupy Lyotard and Baudrillard in their meditations on the contemporary situation, but with Vattimo the connection between the idea of postmodernity and the theme of nihilism issuing from Nietzsche and Heidegger is foregrounded. Vattimo directly draws on and engages Lyotard's theory of postmodernity as the end of metanarratives, and like both Lyotard and Baudrillard he thinks the meaning of postmodernity in relation to recent developments in science and technology, capitalism, and mass media. The unique elements of Vattimo's theory of postmodernity, however, are his emphasis on secularization as constitutive of postmodernity, and the hermeneutic-ontological character of his analysis. To understand the meaning of the current situation as postmodern, for Vattimo, means to provide an interpretation of the meaning of Being at the end of modernity. Employing Nietzschean terminology, Vattimo argues that the advent of postmodernity coincides with nihilism reaching its "accomplished" or "complete" stage.

Vattimo understands the process of secularization begun in modernity and reaching a decisive point in postmodernity as paralleling the decline of Being. This process is one in which foundations gradually dissolve, and Vattimo associates the end of modernity with the process of *self-dissolution*, or internal deconstruction, identified by Nietzsche and Heidegger. Vattimo defines modernity as that era in which the modern, or the new (the *novum*), is itself a value. On his interpretation, this value derives from the innovations in artistic culture at the end of the fifteenth century, when the cult of the artistic genius as a creator of the original first came to prominence, and is linked with the Enlightenment idea of history as progress towards emancipation.[93] The idea of the new in modernity is linked with the idea of foundation because Enlightenment thought conceives of itself as wiping away all the errors of history and arriving at a point in history that is simultaneously new *and* a return to that mythic "pure" origin before the errors of myth and religion arose. The modern idea of the new is thus paradoxically a nostalgia for a lost origin that might be regained, a *tabula rasa* of culture and thought that will act as a firm foundation on which true knowledge and just societies might be built.[94]

In accord with the analyses given by Lyotard and Baudrillard, Vattimo declares that the teleological history that characterizes modernity is a secularized form of the Judeo-Christian soteriology and eschatology in which salvation lies at the end of time. It is, of course, typical to understand modernity in terms of secularization—as the rejection of the authority of religion and the embrace of reason as a new foundation. Vattimo's novelty consists in his suggestion that we must also understand the end of modernity and the advent of *post*modernity as a result of the secularization process. The end of modernity occurs when the new is no longer a value, and when the modernist conception of history is no longer tenable. Postmodernity thus constitutes "the end of history." For Vattimo, these events have in fact occurred, and necessitate an understanding of our current situation as postmodern. Vattimo identifies a number of complementary themes that have played themselves out in recent history and that constitute a self-dissolution of modernity, an end of modernity brought about by the very progression and realization of modern values. This self-dissolution of modernity constitutes secularization taken to its logical extreme, where the process beginnning with the dissolution of religious and mythic foundations ends up dissolving foundations *in toto*. Vattimo describes the end point of this process as *the secularization of secularization*, indicating that in postmodernity the process of secularization that marked modernity turns against and undermines its own foundations.

In agreement with Lyotard and Baudrillard, Vattimo understands the ideal of progress that characterizes modernity as resting upon a *teleological* and *unilinear* view of history. That is, if we posit a goal—such as the Enlightenment goal of emancipation—towards which mankind may be said to progress, we see all of history in terms of this goal. We have only *one* view of history, and this view is constructed as a *line* along which society moves through time, towards this goal. Vattimo identifies at least four themes that help to explain why history has ended in postmodernity. First, in the nineteenth and twentieth centuries theory has exposed the unilinear view of history as *ideological*. That is, it is a selectively biased view of history that clearly serves the political purposes of a limited group of people at the expense of others. Vattimo claims that philosophers of history and historiographers alike have come to recognize that the unilinear view of history that supports modern progress only represents the history of European Man.[95] He writes that "the idea of a progressive temporal process, and even of such a thing as history, belongs to a culture of masters. As a linear unity history is actually only the history of those in power, of the victors. It is constituted at the cost of excluding, first in practice and then in recollection, an array of possibilities, values, and images."[96] Against this, contemporary historiographers assert that there are multiple histories that may be told from multiple perspectives, and to assert one history as dominant or totalizing is to do violence to the others. This dissolution of unilinear and teleological history may thus be seen as a result of developments in the study of history.

Second, the breakdown of a unilinear view of history has been precipitated by concrete events, especially the end of European imperialism and colonialism. The stories of subjugated peoples have begun to be told widely, making us keenly aware both that there *are* alternative histories and that the ideology of progress is deeply implicated in severe injustices (i.e. the European domination, exploitation, and extermination of "inferior" or "primitive" peoples). The expansion of the liberal political currents underlying modernity can be seen as contributing to the willingness of Westerners to listen to these dissenting voices, and realize the limitations of a Eurocentric viewpoint. Third, for Vattimo the meaning of postmodernity is linked to the fact that we live in a society of generalized communication, or mass media. In opposition to Adorno and Horkheimer's prediction that mass media would lead to a fully homogenized society,[97] Vattimo claims that the most obvious effect of this media explosion is the proliferation of a multitude of alternative points of view. More and more subcultures are allowed to "have their say." History has ended not only for the theoretical and practical reasons outlined above, but because the mass media has made us aware of the untenability of a unilinear history. The information technology that suffuses contemporary society can of course be seen as a result of the Enlightenment faith in science and technology to improve the conditions of existence, and Vattimo suggests that it can also be seen as a realization of Hegel's dream of Absolute Spirit becoming fully conscious to itself, in which events coincide with knowledge of those events. Instead of rendering society fully transparent, however, Vattimo argues that the proliferation of communication in fact fragments and distorts the possibility of any unified vision of reality because the messages that are transmitted cannot be unified.[98] Moreover, the proliferation of conflicting messages in the media reveals such messages as having a *mythic* character, which undermines the understanding of reality as an objective structure to which true statements might correspond, and thus by implication undermines the notion of history as the objective development of this structure.[99]

Fourth, Vattimo draws on the work of Arnold Gehlen to show that history has ended and we are living in an era of "post-history" precisely because progress itself has become routine.[100] In contemporary Western society, dominated as it is by capitalism and technology, constant innovation is required simply in order to preserve our current way of life. The idea of the new becomes devalued through its pervasiveness and perennial nature; the *novum* is demoted from its place in an emancipatory teleology where it signifies constant progress to a necessary feature of a stable economy, preserving the capitalist way of life. This paradox of the loss of the sense of the new through a proliferation of innovation may be summarized with the popular expression, "the more things change, the more they stay the same." These four points all contribute to what Vattimo calls the secularization of secularization, that is, the secularization of the ideal of progress, which amounts to the end of modernity and the beginning of postmodernity. Summing up this process, Vattimo writes:

> For Christianity, history appears as the history of salvation; it then becomes the search for a worldly condition of perfection, before turning, little by little, into the history of progress. But the ideal of progress is finally revealed to be a hollow one, since its ultimate value is to create conditions in which further progress is possible in a guise that is always new. By depriving progress of a final destination, secularisation dissolves the very notion of progress itself, as happens in nineteenth- and twentieth-century culture.[101]

Vattimo situates the end of history, understood in the above manner, as central to the meaning of postmodernity. This conception of postmodernity is given further depth by his engagement with the paradox that arises from the consideration of postmodernity as a philosophy of history. This paradox, indicated by Fredric Jameson's characterization of the postmodern as 'an attempt to think the present historically in an age that has forgotten how to think historically in the first place,'[102] is a point on which Lyotard's interpretation of postmodernity has often been criticized. As indicated above, critics of Lyotard accuse him of presenting postmodernity, the age of the end of metanarratives, *as* a historical metanarrative, thus catching his own discourse in a vicious performative contradiction. Vattimo engages explicitly with Lyotard in his own discussion of this problematic aspect of postmodern theory.[103] Vattimo endorses Lyotard's notion of postmodernity as the end of metanarratives, linking this idea with the decline of Being. He criticizes Lyotard, however, for not being reflexive enough about the paradox he has apparently caught himself in, effectively providing a metanarrative of the end of metanarratives. Vattimo cites Lyotard's reference to actual historical events (such as the Holocaust) as "proof" of the delegitimation of history as evidence of this lack of reflexivity, arguing that such citation can only be seen as an attempt to legitimate the theory of the end of history by *appealing to* history. Rather than reject Lyotard's theory on this basis as others have done, however, Vattimo suggests a more reflexive way in which this paradox might be negotiated. Unsurprisingly, Vattimo here has recourse to Nietzsche and Heidegger and the conceptual tools he has discerned and refined from his engagement with their theories of nihilism.

Summarising his solution to the problem of historicity, Vattimo writes that "postmodernity is the epoch that has a relation of *Verwindung* (in all senses of the word) to modernity."[104] Vattimo believes that the problem of understanding the meaning of postmodernity follows the same logical contours as the problem of overcoming metaphysics. That is, the relation of postmodernity to modernity is the same as that of post-metaphysical thinking to metaphysics, which, as we have already seen, Vattimo argues must be one of *Verwindung*. Like metaphysics, modernity cannot be overcome outright because of its internal logic. This, in fact, is precisely what the paradox of postmodernity shows: a new epoch cannot be thought "after" modernity without relying on some of the central concepts that define modernity itself (such as unilinear history). Vattimo further points out that we cannot think postmodernity as an *overcoming* of modernity, since overcoming is itself definitive of modernity, linked to the ideas of the new and the innovative, and suggesting progress towards a goal (overcoming the old by inventing the new; progressing further along the line of history towards our future destination).[105] Vattimo's "solution" to the paradox of postmodernity is a reflexive acceptance of the necessity of this paradox, since he maintains that postmodernity no more breaks entirely with modernity than weak thought does with metaphysics. We are obliged to use the "fiction" of history in order to theorize our current situation, even if the meaning of that very situation calls into question this notion of history. Vattimo's own theory of nihilism in postmodernity, he concedes, is a *metarécit* of the history of Being, but one with no more content than the decline of this Being and the dissolution of the *metarécits* themselves.[106] Vattimo's ultimate gain over Lyotard, then, is really nothing more than a certain reflexivity, but one that arguably gives more rigour and coherence to a form of thought that is inherently paradoxical, and that assuages the criticism of naïve performative contradiction in the discourse of postmodernity.[107]

In addition to the above arguments, which explain the meaning of postmodernity in terms of secularization and the end of history, Vattimo contributes to the theorization of postmodernity through his ontological reflections on technological science and (to a lesser degree) capitalism. For Vattimo, technoscience and capitalism are both decisive expressions of the decline of Being, and his analyses of these give further color to his understanding of postmodernity as the age of accomplished nihilism. As we have seen, Heidegger identifies the essence of technology (*Ge-stell*) as the highest point of metaphysics, and as such, the fullest realization of the oblivion of Being. As is well known, however, there is a tantalizing ambiguity in Heidegger's analysis of technology, and Vattimo exploits this ambiguity in order to develop his own positive interpretation of ontological nihilism. The text that interests Vattimo most is not the famous "The Question Concerning Technology," but the less well-known first essay of *Identity and Difference*.[108] Here, Vattimo interprets Heidegger to be making a tentative suggestion that he makes nowhere else—the suggestion that *Ge-stell* itself dissolves metaphysics and enables a more authentic understanding and experience of Being. Heidegger writes:

> What we experience in the frame [*Ge-stell*] as the constellation of Being and man through the modern world of technology is a prelude to what is called the event of appropriation [*Ereignis*]. This event, however, does not necessarily persist in its prelude. For in the event of appropriation the possibility arises that it may overcome the mere dominance of the frame to turn it into a more original appropriating. Such a transformation of the frame into the event of appropriation, by virtue of that event, would bring the appropriate recovery—appropriate, hence never to be produced by man alone—of the world of technology from its domination back to servitude in the realm by which man reaches more truly into the event of appropriation.[109]

Here Heidegger writes of the authentic relation of man and Being in terms of the "event of appropriation," or *Ereignis*, and indicates that *Ge-stell* may act as a prelude to *Ereignis*. Heidegger tells us that 'In *Ge-stell*, we glimpse a first, oppressing flash of *Ereignis*.'[110] Most significant for Vattimo's interpretation of this text is the following passage:

> The event of appropriation [*Ereignis*] is that realm, vibrating within itself, through which man and Being reach each other in their nature, achieve their active nature by losing those qualities with which metaphysics has endowed them.[111]

According to Vattimo, Heidegger is here suggesting that the essence of technology enables a dissolution of metaphysical characteristics, the most prominent of which is the division between subject and object. *Ge-stell* is thus simultaneously the accomplishment of metaphysics and the beginning of the dissolution of metaphysics. This ambiguity is explained by Vattimo as follows. On the one hand, *Ge-stell* manifests the most obvious characteristics of technology, such as planning, calculation, and total organization. This is the metaphysical aspect of *Ge-stell*, since it reduces Being to a manipulable objectivity. On the other hand, Heidegger stresses the character of *Ge-stell* as an "urging," or a "provocation," which demands that beings be revealed in a certain way (i.e. as *Bestand*, standing-reserve). This urging persists beyond all bounds, and takes up human being into the standing-reserve. It is at this point that metaphysical characteristics begin to break down, since the subject/object distinction (between human being and the beings (s)he manipulates) loses coherence. According to Vattimo, this aspect of *Ge-stell* constitutes a shaking, instability, or transitiveness in which we glimpse the first flash of the *Ereignis*. On Vattimo's reading, this means that it is in *Ge-stell* and *Bestand* that the *unfoundational* character of Being is revealed—Being is really nothing (i.e. it is not an entity, and may not be understood as either subject or object).[112] The revelation of the unfoundational character of Being frees Being from its metaphysical interpretation in terms of the subject/object distinction, and clears the way for a more authentic relation between Being and human being.

Vattimo elaborates on the nihilism of modern technology, and extends his analysis of contemporary nihilism into the dimension of political economy, by drawing a link between the different concepts of *value* in Heidegger and Marx. He suggests that both Nietzsche's formulation of nihilism in terms of the death of God, and Heidegger's formulation of it as the oblivion of Being, can be interpreted in the terms of Marx's analysis of the dissolution of use value in exchange value. Vattimo writes, "When read in the light of Nietzsche, Heidegger, and the accomplishment of nihilism... [the death of God] can be understood in terms of the generalization of exchange value in our society: it is that same occurrence that appeared to Marx to be still definable strictly in the moralistic terms of 'generalized prostitution' and the desacralization of what is human."[113] Vattimo asserts that to think Heidegger's notion of value rigorously is to think it as exchange value.[114] His "rigorous" interpretation of Heidegger's notion of value as exchange value, I suggest (although Vattimo does not quite make this explicit), depends upon the analogy that can be made between exchange value and the "orderedness" of the standing reserve (*Bestand*). Heidegger's notion of value, which he develops most explicitly in relation to the metaphysics of objectness grounded in subjectivity, might be extended to exchange value by applying it to the highest expression of the nihilism of metaphysics in the essence of technology, the standing reserve.

In the standing reserve, objectness is dissolved precisely because beings become elements in an ordered system, in which the only value they have—arguably—is exchange value. Vattimo writes:

> If we follow the main thread supplied by the nexus nihilism / value, we may say that—in Nietzsche's and Heidegger's sense of the term—nihilism is the consumption of use-value in exchange-value. Nihilism does not mean that Being is in the power of the subject; rather, it means that Being is completely dissolved in the discoursing of value, in the indefinite transformations of universal equivalence.[115]

This means that the subject no longer acts as a ground for beings as objects; instead, what can be said to *be* is now only what has value in the system of exchange value. This furthermore suggests that beings no longer have a ground or foundation at all, an idea that supports Heidegger's assertion that the standing reserve is the highest point of nihilism if we understand nihilism in the sense of groundlessness or foundationlessness. By the same token, this homology between exchange value and the standing reserve links Marx's analysis of capitalism to the nihilistic destiny of Being in contemporary society. In substantial agreement with Lyotard, Vattimo understands the generalized exchange propagated in the capitalist system as eroding metaphysical concepts such as use value or non-alienated labour, those concepts that Marx attempted to use as a foundation for a critique of the capitalist system and the basis for an alternative system. Vattimo positively revalues this exacerbation of the nihilism of capitalist exchange value, and sees the expansion of capitalism as a defining feature of postmodernity insofar as it contributes to the erosion of metaphysical categories of valuation.

These ontological analyses of technology and capital contribute further to Vattimo's analysis of nihilism in the current situation. Technology and capitalism, however, are typically identified as characteristic features of modernity, and we can understand their significance for Vattimo's conception of postmodernity only by relating them back to his analysis of secularization. Technology and capital can be determined as marks of postmodernity only at that point where their nihilistic tendencies achieve zenith, and both the tendency to see them as part of historical progress *and* the tendency to recognize their nihilism and hope to overcome it through a new foundation (apparent in both Marx and Heidegger) are dissolved. Simply put, for Vattimo, technology and capital are distinctive of postmodernity only insofar as their nihilistic potential is realised in "accomplished" or "complete" nihilism.

Vattimo's theory of nihilism in postmodernity appears as a celebration of the very social fragmentation and groundlessness identified as an existential problem by Nietzsche, Heidegger, and Baudrillard. For him, "nihilism is no more than the world of the multicultural Babel in which we are actually living."[116] Vattimo is close to Lyotard in positively valuing postmodern fragmentation as politically desirable; both associate such fragmentation with a reduction of the violence and injustice that accompany more cohesive forms of social organization. Vattimo does not depart from Heidegger's analysis of social and cultural meaning in terms of a collective *ethos*, given by Being, which reveals beings in a network of meaningful relations. However, in accord with his understanding of the nihilistic destiny of Being, Vattimo understands the erosion of the collective *ethos* of communities and cultures as given by Being, and therefore itself constituting an *ethos*.[117] In Vattimo's terms, postmodernity is the age in which there is very little of Being left, where Being is understood as networks of meaningful relations given as objective structures of the world. The thread of meaningful interpretation left to us, and with which we must understand the contemporary nature of social ontology, is the decline of Being itself. Vattimo argues that being faithful to this decline is our only chance for social emancipation in the current situation.[118] The dreams of social emancipation through progress and the completion of knowledge being no longer tenable, Vattimo understands the nihilistic destiny of Being as offering a new possibility of achieving such emancipation in the form of society conceived of as a play of conflicting interpretations, where all interlocutors must be considered equal. On Vattimo's understanding this state of society is an ideal democracy.[119] The conflict of interpretations is prevented from being merely a conflict of forces—where a stronger force prevails over weaker forces—by the guiding thread of nihilism as the history of Being: being faithful to such a history entails adherence to the principle of the reduction of violence. This principle means that all interlocutors should be given equal right to speech.[120] By this line of reasoning, Vattimo ties nihilism as the ontology of the current situation with the ideals of equality and democracy, and this allows him to affirm contemporary nihilism as a form of social emancipation.

Despite Vattimo's announcement of the completion of nihilism in postmodernity, and his assertion of the contemporary state of Western culture as a "heterotopia"[121] of conflicting interpretations, there is nevertheless a tension in his theory of nihilism in postmodernity not unlike the tension in the works of Lyotard and Baudrillard. This tension consists in the fact that Vattimo recognizes the contemporary prevalence of metaphysical thought and the continued existence of social institutions predicated on foundational suppositions and threatening violence (i.e. the exclusion of voices from the dialogic constitution of reality). Neither the current state of theory nor culture is fully "heterotopian" in the manner that Vattimo sometimes suggests; instead, his philosophy of weak thought is charged with the positive task of subjecting metaphysics to the *Verwindung* that will allow this heterotopia to be actualized. In the theoretical sphere, this is evident through Vattimo's many critical confrontations with thinkers whom he believes remain metaphysical in their orientation, such as Emmanuele Severino, Deleuze, and Derrida.[122] In the social and political sphere, Vattimo identifies the twin targets of a contemporary nihilistic politics as the rise of new fundamentalisms and the pervasiveness of capitalist "supermarket culture."[123] Fundamentalism is a clear target of weak thought and a nihilistically-oriented politics because of its foundational, and hence potentially violent, aspirations.[124] The issue of capitalism is more complex: on the one hand, as we have seen, Vattimo celebrates the secularizing effects of generalized exchange value. On the other hand, however, he acknowledges the potential violence of contemporary capitalist culture. Vattimo concedes that the contemporary capitalist supermarket culture has the same anti-foundational traits as a nihilistic society of the play of interpretations, but argues that it lacks the reduction of violence given by the nihilistic history of Being. Instead, contemporary capitalism glorifies competition and an ideology of development at any cost: "The supermarket culture is a pluralism without nihilistic orientation which ignores the guiding thread of the reduction of violence."[125] Weak thought is therefore conceived of by Vattimo as a positive task that must "commit itself to the reduction and dissolution of violence"[126] and thereby bring about the completion of nihilism in postmodernity.

Nihilism at the end of history

Everyone remains aware of the arbitrariness, the artificial character of time and history. And we are never fooled by those who call on us to hope.
—Jean Baudrillard[127]

Despite their differences, a more or less unified story about the status of nihilism in postmodernity emerges from a comparison of the three theories of nihilism considered above. This convergence of themes should not be surprising, since each thinker draws on the genealogy of nihilism developed by Nietzsche and employs it to interpret the current meaning of the nihilist problematic. On Nietzsche's analysis, nihilism remained incomplete in his own age, in part because the modern categories of valuation repeated the logic of religious nihilism. Lyotard, Baudrillard, and Vattimo each characterize this perpetuation of religious nihilism in modernity in terms of the modernist conception of history, which follows the form of the Christian doctrine of eschatology. The dynamic of this perpetuation is neatly encapsulated by Julian Young in the following passage, with specific reference to the modernist theories of history proposed by Hegel and Marx:

> [Hegel and Marx] do not abandon the true world. Rather, they relocate it, transport it from a supposed *other* world into the future of *this* world. The history of the (one and only) world is pictured as moving according to inexorably progressive, "dialectical" laws towards a final utopia the arrival of which will bring history to an end. The old distinction between nature and super-nature is reinterpreted as a distinction between present and future.[128]

Lyotard, Baudrillard, and Vattimo each posit that in postmodernity nihilism is nearing or has reached its completion, where this completion is understood as the collapse of the metanarratives of history that took the place and function of the religious God in modernity. This completion of nihilism in postmodernity is indicated by Lyotard in the incredulity toward metanarratives, by Baudrillard in his thesis of the completion of the destruction of meaning by meaning in hyperreality, and by Vattimo in the secularization of secularization and the oblivion of Being. The story that these thinkers tell reveals a close conceptual link between the meaning of contemporary nihilism and the meaning of postmodernity: both indicate the end of modernity, where modernity is understood as constituted by the Enlightenment aspiration to achieve social emancipation through the development of reason and knowledge. Since modernist metanarratives retain religious nihilism's tendency to absent and defer the source of value, placing it in a future utopia rather than a "true world," and can thus be seen to perpetuate the "highest values" of Western culture, the loss of credulity towards these metanarratives can be seen as the final collapse of these values.

In some sense, then, the completion of nihilism in postmodernity suggests the resolution of problematic tensions that constituted modernity according to Nietzsche's theory of nihilism. While they tell a similar story concerning the completion of nihilism in postmodernity, however, the postmodernists considered here are divided on the issue of the sense in which this completion is to be understood, and how it ought to be received. On the one hand, both Lyotard and Vattimo celebrate the end of modernist conceptions of meaning, asserting that metanarratives are tyrannical and that a more emancipated society is possible in their wake. On the other hand, while Baudrillard fundamentally agrees that modernist forms of meaning are tyrannically reductive, he focuses much of his analysis of the contemporary situation on the negative effects of the disappearance of meaning in postmodernity. Following Nietzsche more closely on this point than either Lyotard or Vattimo, Baudrillard sees the essential role that modernist conceptions of meaning played in maintaining a vital sense of life: just as religious nihilism provides an interpretation that gives meaning to existence, so do modernist categories of meaning, despite the fact that they are destructive of existentially richer forms of meaning. Baudrillard therefore follows Nietzsche and Heidegger in recognizing the collapse of the highest values of modernity as having serious negative existential repercussions, since this collapse deprives contemporary existence of a meaning-giving interpretation.

These differences raise the question of whether nihilism, understood as an existential problem of the meaningfulness of life, appears to have changed its status according to the theories of postmodernity considered above. Typically, proponents of a pessimistic view of postmodernity imply that the nihilism that affected modernity has been radicalized or deepened in postmodernity.[129] This view may be understood along the same lines as Baudrillard's analysis—the collapse of modernist metanarratives removes the structures of meaning and value, which replaced mythical and religious conceptions of the world, leaving the postmodern world without any framework providing meaning and value. On this view, the crisis of nihilism, which threatened modernity, appears to have become more urgent in postmodernity.

Karen L. Carr argues, however, that nihilism in postmodernity is not accompanied by a deepening sense of crisis, but rather by a widespread passive acceptance of meaninglessness. She calls this change a "banalization" of nihilism, writing that

> ...there is a sense in which the *angst*-ridden reflections from the first half of this century sound dated, almost comical in their intensity and self-seriousness. One might infer from this that the dangers of nihilism, so vividly painted by Nietzsche, have passed, that the crisis has been resolved, that human reason has resumed its progressive investigation into the true and the good. Yet what in fact has happened in the last two decades is a recasting of the problem of nihilism into a framework so different from that shared by Nietzsche and his unwitting successors that the work of these earlier thinkers is in danger of becoming unintelligible.[130]

For many thinkers of the latter half of the twentieth century, Carr argues, nihilism becomes 'a relatively innocuous characterization of the radically interpretive character of human life.'[131] While Carr names Jacques Derrida and Richard Rorty as exemplars of this banalized understanding of nihilism, we might also characterize Lyotard and especially Vattimo in this way. This apparent contrast between the radicalization and banalization of nihilism is not necessarily contradictory however, since a deepening of nihilism might be accompanied by the loss of the very sense of crisis in the face of growing meaninglessness. This is, in fact, Carr's thesis. The possibility then appears that Lyotard's and Vattimo's disregard of a deepening of existential nihilism brought about by the collapse of modernist metanarratives is itself symptomatic of this deepened nihilism. This question concerning the postmodernists' reception of and response to nihilism in postmodernity will be given further consideration in the following chapter.

While nihilism in postmodernity appears as a completed form of nihilism due to the collapse of modernist metanarratives, each of the thinkers considered above maintains a tension or irresolution in their theory of postmodern nihilism that seems to belie this notion of completion. For Lyotard, the criterion of performativity deployed in technological science and capitalism, as well as the prevalence of representational theories such as structuralism and semiotics, repeat the logic of religious nihilism and sustain the problems of modernity in postmodernity. For Baudrillard, an undecidability persists between the nihilism of hyperreality and the possibility of a "poetic reversal," leaving the status of nihilism in postmodernity uncertain. In Vattimo's account, the traits of "negative" nihilism persist in the prevalence of metaphysics in philosophy, all kinds of fundamentalism, and capitalist "supermarket culture."

Postmodernity and Nihilism 163

This tension in the works of all three is perhaps explained by the "untimely" nature of their thought, a nature admitted by each of the postmodernists in question.[132] Vattimo phrases his announcements of the completion of nihilism as the *beginning* of a completion, the dawning of a new age of Being, the consequences of which we have barely yet begun to fathom: "What is happening to us in regard to nihilism, today, is this: we begin to be, or to be able to be, accomplished nihilists…an accomplished nihilism is today our only chance…"[133] In *The Postmodern Condition*, Lyotard writes at one point, "This 'Atomization' of the social into flexible networks of language games may seem far removed from the modern reality, which is depicted, on the contrary, as afflicted with bureaucratic paralysis."[134] The incredulity towards metanarratives that he announces, as well as the attendant fragmentation of social reality into language games, might be taken as strong tendencies towards which Lyotard gestures, rather than merely a description of the current state of the most technologically advanced societies. The admission of untimeliness is most strikingly made, however, by Baudrillard:

> Today, the world has become real beyond our wildest expectations. The real and the rational have been overturned by their very realisation. Such a proposition may seem paradoxical when we look at all the traces of the unfinished nature of the world, the traces of penury and poverty, such that one might think it had barely begun to evolve towards a more real, more rational state. But we have to leap ahead of ourselves: this systematic practicalisation of the world has gone very quickly, the system actualising all the utopian potential and substituting the radicalism of its operation for the radicalism of thought… What we must do is think this unconditional realisation of the world, which is at the same time its unconditional simulacrum.[135]

The theories of nihilism under consideration here, understood in this sense of thought "leaping ahead," are selective interpretations; they focus on certain trends and aspects of contemporary society in order to bring particular formations and suggested possibilities into focus. In each case, these thinkers present and attempt to think through the implications of certain possibilities that are emerging in the current situation, but which yet cannot be said to totalize the field of contemporary experience. These interpretations of nihilism in postmodernity are therefore arguments for how the current situation *ought* to be understood, as propaedeutic to a full actualization of such a situation. Vattimo neatly encapsulates this point in writing that "[p]ostmodern is both a normative ideal and a descriptive, or at least interpretive, notion."[136]

The untimely nature of these theories of nihilism in postmodernity perhaps suggests that the tensions they embody might be resolved historically, that is, through a *future* completion of the process of nihilism. Such a "future completion" would push the postmodern tendencies diagnosed by postmodern theorists to the full actualization of a postmodern society, the full implementation of the postmodern as a normative ideal that would finally resolve the malaise of modernity. The task of thought for each of these thinkers might thus appear as completing the nihilistic process of the destruction of modernity, only the cusp of which has been reached in the current situation. In Lyotard's terms, this would mean undermining the potential hegemony of performativity and inaugurating a postmodern society of fragmented language games where no powers attempt to force a common measure upon heterogenous games. For Baudrillard, this would mean fully undermining the notion of the real so that postmodern hyperreality undergoes a poetic reversion into an enchanted, more meaningful state. For Vattimo, this would mean extending the *Verwindung* of metaphysics so that the last traces of foundational thought are eradicated, and the full emancipatory potential of a nihilistic society is realized.

The imperative postmodern theme of the end of history, however, emerges to interrupt the utopic character of these reflections. If we conceptualize the nihilism of postmodernity in teleological terms, what is to distinguish this from a modernist conception of history, a conception in distinction to which the idea of postmodernity is developed? Arguably, earlier conceptions of nihilism, such as those of Nietzsche and Heidegger, retained this resemblance to modernist history and therefore also to Christian eschatology, conceiving history as unilinear and teleological, where a lost state of grace might be regained in a future utopia. Lyotard suggests such an association between nihilism and modernity, as well the potentially problematic status of the idea of postmodernity in this regard, in the following passage:

> Is this the sense in which we are not modern? Incommensurability, heterogeneity, the differend, the persistence of proper names, the absence of a supreme tribunal? Or, on the other hand, is this the continuation of romanticism, the nostalgia that accompanies the retreat of..., etc? Nihilism? A well-executed work of mourning for Being? And the hope that is born with it? Which is still the hope of redemption? With

all of this still remaining inscribed within the thought of a redemptive future? Could it be that "we" are no longer telling ourselves anything? Are "we" not telling, whether bitterly or gladly, the great narrative of the end of great narratives? For thought to remain modern, doesn't it suffice that it think in terms of the end of some history?[137]

As Lyotard here suggests, the "classical" narratives of nihilism share a common form with modernist metanarratives. This is evident in the works of Nietzsche and Heidegger, both of whom were motivated by hopes that a better social form might be instituted after the ills of modern nihilism had been cured. While both are careful to reject the simple nostalgia for a lost form of meaning that might be restored, they nevertheless hope for the inauguration of a new sense of meaning in a "new beginning."[138] In this sense, their critiques of modernity might be interpreted as narratives of a redemptive future on the same model as modernist metanarratives. Sartre's theory of nihilism, incidentally, might similarly be seen as a secularized version of religious nihilism, as his concept of "radical conversion" suggests. For Sartre, who employs explicitly religious language in this regard, nihilism is understood as a historical "fall" from a "Lost Paradise" into the pre-reflective and impure reflective states of consciousness that constitute human reality as a lack (the impossible desire to be God).[139] Sartre's hope is that this lack might be appeased through a correct work of phenomenological reduction, enabling a radical conversion beyond which meaning again becomes possible.

The postmodern theme of the end of history can be understood as motivated precisely by the attempt to resist the repetition of these modernist and religious gestures. If *postmodern* nihilism has a distinctive meaning, I would argue, it is tied to the rejection of any notion of critical overcoming, and of historical process, since such conceptions are recognized to be residual forms of religious nihilism (nostalgia for the lost object of desire, whether located in a metaphysically transcendent "true world" or temporally transcendent, future utopia). Postmodern theories of nihilism attempt to divest the remnants of religious nihilism from the theory of nihilism itself, just as the theories of postmodernity attempt to divest the remnants of the modernist theory of history from contemporary conceptions of culture. In proposing the end of history in postmodernity, postmodern theories of nihilism also render null and void the model of nihilism as a historical process that will result in a utopian age in which affirmation will reign unhindered by negative, nihilistic tendencies. If "history has ended," then we cannot hope for an overcoming of nihilism through historical process. The postmodernist conception of the end of history must therefore be added to the other arguments against the possibility of overcoming nihilism that we have seen. The postmodern view of history disallows a resolution, according to the idea of theory as "untimely," of the tension between the announcement of the completion of nihilism and the recognition of the persistence of nihilism in postmodernity. Rather, in the light of the end of history a new tension appears between the desire to critically confront the nihilism of postmodernity (a desire manifest in the works of all three postmodern thinkers considered here), and the disallowal of the hope that nihilism might be overcome or in some way resolved at a future time.

This problem of postmodern historicity is well expressed in the claim, made by both Lyotard and Baudrillard, that the mood appropriate to the postmodern scene is melancholia.[140] This mood should not be understood essentially as one of pessimism, but rather as a rejection of and attempt to move beyond nostalgia and mourning, both of which are bound too closely to modernist sensibilities. Nostalgia—from the Greek *nostos*, meaning "to return home"—suggests the modernist and religious desire to be reunited with a lost object. Mourning, on the other hand, implies a process of healing through which the pain of a loss is eventually annulled, and the mourner arrives at a state of restoration. As Lyotard suggests in the passage quoted above, the Heideggarian project of a well-executed work of mourning for Being brings with it the hope of a redemptive future. From the perspectives of Lyotard and Baudrillard, postmodernity cannot therefore be understood in terms of nostalgia or mourning, neither for the dreams and aspirations of modernity, nor for any deeper form of meaning that modernity destroyed. Rather, both thinkers suggest that melancholia, a pensive sadness that acknowledges loss but does not hope for a restoration, is the mood appropriate to postmodernity. Baudrillard writes:

> Nostalgia had beauty because it retained within it the presentiment of what has taken place and could take place again…Whereas, with mourning, things come to an end and therefore enjoy a possibility of returning, with melancholia we are not even left with the presentiment of an end or of a return… [141]

In Freud's classic treatment "Mourning and Melancholia,"[142] on which Lyotard and Baudrillard implicitly draw, a successful work of mourning consists in withdrawing cathexis (libidinal investment) from a lost object of love and cathecting a new object. Melancholy, on the other hand, "consists in the threatened libidinal cathexis at length abandoning the object, only, however, to draw back to the place in the ego from which it had proceeded. So by taking flight into the ego love escapes extinction."[143] Applying these psychoanalytic terms to postmodernity, we may understand the postmodern situation as one in which the dream of the Enlightenment constitutes a lost object, but this dream cannot be replaced with a new one. Employing different terminology, Vattimo echoes this diagnosis of postmodernity as affected by a mood of melancholy in his understanding of the contemporary meaning of Being as one of a "long goodbye"[144] without hope of return or restitution, and in his formulation of postmodernity as a *Verwindung* of modernity (a "recovery" from modernity that bears inevitable traces of the modern). Such a mood is fitting in light of the aporia constituted by the convergent themes of nihilism and the end of history in the postmodern situation. While Vattimo, Lyotard, and Baudrillard are all acutely aware of this aporia into which the attempt to definitively overcome nihilism is drawn, however, they are still committed to finding new forms of resistance to the nihilism that marks postmodernity.

Chapter 4
Negotiating Nihilism

Given the aporiae into which the problem of nihilism and its overcoming seems driven, what might count as a response to nihilism?....What form(s) of imaginative resistance is (are) still possible, both [sic.] philosophically, aesthetically, and politically?

—Simon Critchley[1]

The vision of postmodernity that emerges from the works of Lyotard, Baudrillard, and Vattimo is one of a world in which nihilism persists as a problem to be critically confronted, despite an abandonment of the hope for its definitive overcoming. Each of these thinkers develops new forms of resistance to nihilism that negotiate the aporiae to which attempts to overcome it lead. While these forms of resistance differ significantly, they nevertheless display shared themes that allow us to understand them as particular instances of a common, distinctively postmodern, approach. This approach is usefully contextualized by Simon Critchley's consideration of the various possibilities open for a response to the problem of nihilism, which may be summarized as follows.[2]

1. Refusing the problem through a return to religion or metaphysics.
2. Rejecting nihilism as a pseudo-problem with a fallacious view of history.
3. Passive nihilism; the acceptance of meaninglessness.
4. Active nihilism; destruction aimed at overcoming.
5. Overcoming *the desire to overcome* nihilism.

This typology illuminates the postmodern responses to nihilism I wish to examine here by throwing them into relief against other possible responses, and by showing the compelling nature of the postmodern response once the other possibilities have been rejected as untenable in the current situation.

The first possibility may be thought of as a rejection of the values of the Enlightenment and modernity and a return to premodern, "traditional" values, either in the form of religion or some premodern form of metaphysical philosophy. In religious terms, this response accords with religious fundamentalism of any creed, and the rejection of philosophy in favor of a nonrational faith. Critchley suggests that in philosophical terms, this means continuing as a pre-nihilist metaphysician, a position that may or may not be based on a critical encounter with philosophical modernity.[3] Such a position responds to the nihilism of the breakdown of the "highest values" in modernity and postmodernity by denying the validity of the intellectual and cultural currents that have brought about this breakdown. In effect, it is the attempt to reject the legacy of modernity and return to premodern forms of thought, belief, and valuation. This response to nihilism is exemplified by Pope John-Paul II's call for philosophy to turn away from the nihilism of postmodernism and back to the metaphysical search for the truth.[4] In the light of Nietzsche's thought, however, such a response to the nihilism of modernity and postmodernity appears as a preservation or reinstitution of religious nihilism, with its faith in transcendent categories of valuation and consequent devaluation of life. As followers of Nietzsche, none of the postmodern thinkers considered here would consider this a desirable option for responding to the nihilism of postmodernity.

The second response to nihilism rejects the validity of the various theories of nihilism as based on a fallacious philosophy of history. Critchley relates this view to the "hateful cheerfulness" of philosophers who claim to have no particular metaphysical commitments and not to be bothered by not having any.[5] What Critchley seems to have in mind here are certain tendencies within the analytic tradition of philosophy that emphasise this tradition's positivistic influences, its commitment to ordinary language, and skepticism towards philosophies of history. Arguably, this approach fails to engage seriously with the question of how meaning in life is to be found, and fails to consider how thought interacts with social and cultural realities. Furthermore, this approach, while claiming to have no metaphysical convictions, in many respects remains thoroughly metaphysical (and hence nihilistic) in the Heideggerian sense. The metaphysical nature of this approach is evident in the rejection of the cultural and historical conditionedness of thought and the faith in positive science and transcendent rationality with which "historical" thinking is replaced. This second approach, then, remains unknowingly mired in nihilism despite its intentions, and appears no more tenable than the first approach.[6]

The third alternative is what Nietzsche calls passive nihilism. This amounts to accepting the meaninglessness of life, whether as a perennial condition of absurdity, or as the result of the prevailing historical and cultural conditions underlying contemporary Western society. In either case, the passive nihilist does not believe nihilism can effectively be challenged, or simply doesn't have the will to do so. This position is defeatist, and needless to say, contributes nothing towards a constructive response to nihilism in postmodernity. Despite their awareness of the difficulties of confronting nihilism, none of the postmodernists considered here (not even Baudrillard, despite claims to the contrary) succumbs to passive nihilism.

The fourth possibility in Critchley's typology is the attempt to willfully overcome nihilism through what Nietzsche calls *active* nihilism. This is the attempt to take the destructiveness of nihilism to its limit, to follow the logic of nihilism to its end, exacerbating nihilism in the hope of destroying it by its own hand. Critchley places in this category all attempts to create a better social order through total revolution, whether consisting in a violent overthrow of existing powers or the pervasive revolution of everyday life. He includes here

> [...] the romantic and neo-romantic transformation of modernity through the production of a great work of art, Marxist revolution, fascist revolution, Ernst Jünger's total mobilization, apocalyptic Heideggarianism (there are other Heideggarianisms), the neo-Nietzschean obliteration of 'Man', or that unsubtle blend of Fichtean spontaneity and Fourieresque utopianism that one finds in the Situationist International and its various progeny: terrorism, angry brigades, punk and libidino-cyber revolution.[7]

This fourth response, then, may be broadly defined as any attempt to overcome nihilism completely, in the sense of leaving it outside, beneath, and behind one's self and one's world. It looks forward to a future, non-nihilistic utopia.

It is this fourth option of responding to nihilism by attempting to actively overcome it that we have seen repeatedly rejected by the postmodernists. According to arguments advanced by Lyotard, Baudrillard, and Vattimo, as well as by Heidegger before them, the attempt to overcome nihilism carries with it that which is constitutive of nihilism; through this attempt, nihilism is therefore only preserved and perhaps deepened. Critchley likewise rejects this possible response on several counts. First, he suggests that the nature of the contemporary world makes the success of any revolution that seeks to overcome all the problems of nihilism unlikely. Second, Critchley believes that such a revolution would be undesirable because of the enormous social costs (a position with that many postmodernists, such as Lyotard and Vattimo, agree). Moreover, he suggests that there is something altogether too *reactive* (in the Nietzschean sense) in this intense desire to overcome nihilism, and that the subtleties of the problem are missed in this "gung-ho" approach.[8] In *Very Little…Almost Nothing*, Critchley engages with Heidegger and Adorno to draw out these subtleties, and to show the aporia that the very idea of overcoming nihilism is drawn into—an aporia we have already seen illustrated in various ways.

Heidegger sums up the difficulty in overcoming nihilism well in the famous phrase, '[n]o one can jump over his own shadow.'[9] Our very being is so embroiled in nihilism that it seems the more strenuously we twist and turn in the attempt to escape nihilism, the more agitated the shadow of nihilism itself becomes. A more subtle approach, then, is called for. Critchley's approach is to suggest the fifth response in his typology: overcoming *the desire to overcome* nihilism. This approach does not renounce the need to resist nihilism, but attempts to develop such resistance in new ways. Critchley outlines his approach as follows:

> With this fifth response, it is not a question of overcoming nihilism in an act of the will or joyful destruction, because such an act would only imprison us all the more firmly in the very nihilistic logic we are trying to leave behind. Rather than overcoming nihilism, it is a question of *delineating* it. What will be at stake is a liminal experience, a deconstructive experience of the limit—deconstruction *as* an experience of the limit—that separates the inside from the outside of nihilism and which forbids us both the gesture of transgression and restoration.[10]

Critchley explores this fifth response to nihilism through an extended meditation on death, largely through the lens of literature. While the postmodern thinkers I am considering here pursue a different path, their responses to the problem of nihilism can all arguably be characterised as species of this fifth genus of response. In their own ways, Lyotard, Baudrillard, and Vattimo each attempt to overcome the desire to overcome nihilism, while developing the new forms of imaginative resistance Critchley calls for.[11]

While the postmodernists considered here offer differing responses to nihilism, these differing approaches respond to a shared concern that recognizes, in the postmodern situation, the paradoxical demand of acknowledging the impossibility of overcoming nihilism and the necessity of responding to this persistent problem. These varied responses compliment and contrast with each other in such a way as to allow a rich appreciation of the postmodern approach to the problems nihilism presents. Critchley's following characterization of the fifth alternative neatly summarizes this postmodern approach to responding to nihilism:

> On such a view, neither philosophy, nor art, nor politics alone can be relied upon to redeem the world, but the task of thinking consists in a historical confrontation with nihilism that does not give up on the demand that things might be otherwise.[12]

This chapter draws out these postmodern responses to nihilism, examining the ways in which they attempt to meet the problems outlined in the previous chapter, and seeking to establish the degree of their success. In responding to nihilism, Lyotard, Baudrillard, and Vattimo each develop concepts that are designed to fulfill two tasks: first, to avoid the aporia involved in the attempt to overcome nihilism, and second, to critically engage with the particular problems of nihilism they have identified in postmodernity. In examining these concepts, I will focus my analysis around two themes that can be identified in all three of the postmodern thinkers under consideration here: the "logic of difference" and the "politics of passivity."[13]

The "logic of difference" explains the way that certain concepts developed by the postmodernists avoid the impasse to which the attempt to overcome nihilism leads. At the same time, these concepts allow judgments about nihilism to be made without resorting to oppositional distinctions, thus enabling a non-nihilistic form of critique. This critique allows the identification of, and response to, the nihilistic traits of postmodernity without becoming caught in the aporia of oppositional negation, and hence falling back into nihilism. The strategies of "passive politics," or "affirmative weakness," that these thinkers develop may be thought of as existential politics or ethics, which are offered as alternatives to the projects of overcoming nihilism through political revolutions or through individual value-creation. In this sense, these strategies are answers to the existential problem of how to live a meaningful or valuable life in the wake of the death of God, and within the constraints imposed by the postmodern situation. The first two sections of this chapter examine the general contours of the logic of difference and the politics of passivity, respectively. The third section examines the ways in which this logic and this politics are manifest in the responses to nihilism of each of the three postmodernists under consideration, preparing the way for an assessment, in the final section, of the degree of success these responses achieve.

The logic of difference

The arguments we have seen advanced for the inevitable failure of the attempt to overcome nihilism may all be seen as invoking the ineluctability of the logic of *negation* and *opposition*. Seen in this way, the acceptance of a particular logical perspective is what makes the prospect of effectively responding to nihilism appear hopeless. This apparent ineluctability of the logic of negation at the heart of nihilism is the reason that so many of Nietzsche's commentators have found his attempt to overcome nihilism untenable.[14] A number of scholars have argued, however, that Gilles Deleuze has successfully shown how the aporia implied by the logic of negation might be avoided by a logic of "difference" that he finds in Nietzsche's thought.[15] This logic is expressed in Deleuze's 1962 work, *Nietzsche and Philosophy*,[16] which had a profound impact on the development of French post-structuralism. I wish to argue that this concept of difference is the "enabling factor" in the postmodern responses to nihilism; this logic shows a way of taking a stance against nihilism that avoids the aporia associated with overcoming and the logic of negation. The postmodernists considered here do not explicitly reference Deleuze on this topic, nor do they follow Deleuze in positing the possibility of an overcoming of nihilism (an issue I shall take up further below). Nevertheless, Deleuze's treatment of the logic of difference provides a lucid explanation of the dynamic evident in the thought of these postmodernists, and shows how such a dynamic is directly related to the problem of nihilism. A digression on Deleuze and the logic of difference, then, will lay important groundwork for the later discussion of the responses to nihilism developed by Lyotard, Baudrillard, and Vattimo.

The role of negation in the failure of the attempt to overcome nihilism has its *locus classicus* in Heidegger's reading of Nietzsche. The arguments concerning specific aspects of Nietzsche's thought that we saw in chapter one can all be understood as resting on his argument about negation. Simply stated, the argument runs as follows: negation is itself constitutive of nihilism; the attempt to overcome nihilism is an act of negation; therefore, nihilism is preserved in the attempted overcoming. On Heidegger's reading, Nietzsche fails to overcome nihilism because he simply inverts or reverses Platonism (the philosophical form of religious nihilism), and this inversion preserves the logic of negation, which is constitutive of nihilism itself.

In Heidegger's own ontological terms, metaphysics is nihilism because it negates—or forgets - Being. By inverting Plato and affirming becoming instead of being, Heidegger believes, Nietzsche preserves the oppositional structure constitutive of religious nihilism. For Heidegger, Nietzsche's will to power (as a philosophical account of becoming) is just as much a metaphysical thesis as Plato's supersensible world, and functions in the same way to obscure or negate Being. Of Nietzsche's attempt to overcome nihilism, Heidegger writes:

> [A]s a mere countermovement it necessarily remains, as does everything "anti," held fast in the essence of that over against which it moves. Nietzsche's countermovement against metaphysics is, as a mere turning upside down of metaphysics, an inextricable entanglement in metaphysics...[17]

Heidegger may be understood to be arguing that it is the oppositional structure itself that preserves nihilism; it is the *form* of these terms and their relation, rather than their content, which is constitutive of nihilism.[18] As Heidegger writes with reference to Sartre, "the reversal of a metaphysical statement remains a metaphysical statement."[19]

The role of negation in the constitution of nihilism can be further explained with reference to the structure of Nietzsche's concept of religious nihilism. Religious nihilism is understood as the setting up of transcendent categories of value (unity, truth, goal) that are opposed to the immanent world of experience, and which consequently negate the value of *this* world with reference to the projected ideal of the *true* world. The negation or devaluation of life results from this oppositional structure. Howard Caygill expresses this point well:

> In the inaugural moment of nihilism, identified by Nietzsche with Platonism and later its popular form Christianity, the spatio-temporal world is negated when compared with the "highest values" or ideas. The transcendent ideas of the good, the true and the beautiful negate and so diminish any good, true or beautiful acts or works that we may accomplish under finite conditions.[20]

In an attempt to overcome negation and the nihilism implied by it, Nietzsche aspires to a kind of thinking that would have no recourse to negation, but consist in a *pure affirmation*.[21] This idea of pure affirmation, however, is mired in difficulties: how is a purely affirmative form of thought possible? As many commentators have pointed out,[22] the idea seems to be incoherent because *any affirmation implies a negation*. In the philosophical tradition, this problem has its source in Benedict de Spinoza's famous principle, '[all] determination is negation' (*ominis determinatio est negatio*).[23] According to this principle, it is the properties or features of the concept or thing determined that imply a negation, because properties are thought to be only determined negatively, in contrast to other properties that they *are not*. The affirmation of anything determinate appears to necessarily imply a negation; the attempt to escape nihilism through affirmation and the positing of new, life-affirmative values thus inevitably reinstitutes nihilism. Caygill argues that Nietzsche's attempts to escape nihilism fail for this reason:

> Every revaluation of values demands a devaluation or negation of existing values, and this negation prepares the revaluation to serve as a vector for the propagation and survival of nihilism.[24]

The problem Caygill identifies is that the new values affirmed are inevitably set up as "higher values," taking on the form and function of the values they have deposed: the new values become impossible ideals that negate the value of actual existence. Caygill expresses the problem as one of "figuring negation," that is, giving what is affirmed figural form, and thus properties, which imply negation. The positing of new values gives affirmation such figural or determinate form, thus reinstating the opposition between "higher" and "lower" values that is constitutive of nihilism. According to Caygill, even Nietzsche's concept of "life," in so far as it evokes determinate biological properties, succumbs to this reinstitution of negation, and hence nihilism.[25] Furthermore, it may seem that if pure affirmation *were* logically possible, it would mean that everything Nietzsche has diagnosed as nihilistic—every reactive and impoverished form of life—would also be affirmed. The logic of negation thus seems to involve the attempt to overcome nihilism in a double bind: either pure affirmation is impossible (because affirmation is determination and determination is negation), or if it is possible, then nihilism itself is affirmed. Either way, the attempt to overcome nihilism fails.[26]

As I have already suggested, the logic of negation is closely tied to the logic of opposition: it is the oppositional relation of two terms that allows a hierarchical organization in which one term is privileged and affirmed, and the other negated. In *Nietzsche and Philosophy*, Deleuze develops this affinity of opposition and negation in his interpretive strategy of pitting Nietzsche against Hegel: Hegel identifies opposition as a highly developed form of negation,[27] and Deleuze thereby associates opposition with the negation underlying nihilism. In an opposition, a concept or thing does not negate *all* things that are not it, but a *particular* thing (its opposite). For example, "north" and "south" are polar opposites: they are determined not by the negation of other things in general, but are mutually determined by the negation of each other.[28] Oppositional thought is thus founded on negativity, and this negativity is associated by Deleuze with the devaluation and reactivity of nihilism.

In Deleuze's study of Nietzsche and other works (especially *Difference and Repetition*[29]) the logic of *difference* is offered as an alternative to negation and opposition, an alternative that arguably enables the possibility of a pure affirmation that avoids oppositional negation.[30] While Hegel understands difference as implying negation and opposition, Deleuze (following Nietzsche) sees oppositions as "roughly cut" from a prior and more-subtle field of differences. For Deleuze, difference should be understood in terms of continuous variations that are prior to the establishment of identities and oppositions.[31] This understanding of difference is explained by Deleuze as involving a "unilateral distinction." As distinct from an opposition in which both terms are distinguished from each other, in a unilateral distinction the distinction only functions for one of the terms. Deleuze explains:

> [T]he distinguished opposes something which cannot distinguish itself from it but continues to espouse that which divorces it. Difference is this state in which determination takes the form of unilateral distinction.[32]

Unilateral distinction is thus a form of determination that is not negation, since that from which the determined is distinguished "continues to espouse that which divorces it," and is not negated by this "divorce."

To illustrate unilateral distinction, Deleuze suggests the example of Socrates and the Sophists: Socrates distinguishes himself from the Sophists, but they consider him to be one of them.[33] Judith Norman suggests the example of a one-way mirror: from one side, both sides can be seen (and in this sense, they are not distinguished), from the other, one side cannot be seen (they are distinguished).[34] Unilateral distinction allows for an asymmetrical relation in which the relation appears differently depending on the perspective of the term from which it is seen: it may be seen as an opposition from the perspective of one term, but as a difference from the perspective of the other term.

The role of the unilateral distinction in Nietzsche's treatment of nihilism is demonstrated by Deleuze's analysis of the figures of the "noble" and the "slave."[35] These figures and their relation indicate the relation between nihilism and its affirmative alternative: the "mode of existence" of negation, reaction, and opposition is represented in Nietzsche's works through the figure of the slave, as contrasted with the master or noble as affirmer of life. Nietzsche indicates the fundamental difference between these types as follows:

> While all noble morality grows from a triumphant affirmation of itself, slave morality from the outset says no to an 'outside', to an 'other', to a 'non-self'....with the aristocratic mode of evaluation: this acts and grows spontaneously, it only seeks out its antithesis in order to affirm itself more thankfully and more joyfully. Its negative concept, 'low,' 'common,' 'bad,' is only a derived, pale contrast to its positive basic concept which is thoroughly steeped in life and passion—'we the noble, we the good, we the beautiful, we the happy ones!'[36]

The slave derives his identity and value from an initial negative judgment about "the other" to whom he then contrasts himself. Deleuze explains the logic of this position with the following syllogism:

> Let us suppose that we have a lamb who is a logician. The syllogism of the bleating lamb is formulated as follows: birds of prey are evil (that is, the birds of prey are all the evil ones, the evil ones are birds of prey); but I am the opposite of a bird of prey; therefore I am good.[37]

On Deleuze's interpretation, the slave (or in this example, the lamb) views his relationship to the noble (the bird of prey) as one of negation and opposition: the slave negates the noble (he is condemned as evil), and then opposes himself to the noble (therefore I am good). The noble views his relation to the slave, however, as one of difference, rather than opposition. In contrast to his self-affirmation, the slave appears as a weak and pathetic type, but he does not oppose himself to the slave in such a way that a negative relation of exclusive disjunction is imposed. The relationship between Nietzsche's slave and noble can therefore be seen as one of unilateral distinction, and the logic of difference illustrated by the noble can be seen to enable a purely affirmative form of thought that circumvents the oppositional logic of Spinoza's principle. Considered with respect to the logic of difference, affirmation does not imply negation, and the return of nihilism no longer appears inevitable.

Establishing the possibility of pure affirmation still leaves Nietzsche and Deleuze with the second problem: total affirmation would appear to affirm nihilism, thus ensuring its persistence. Moreover, a purely affirmative thought bereft of all negation would appear to disable any form of critical, or even selective, thought. How can nihilism be critically confronted on the basis of an affirmative and differential logic? Nietzsche recognizes the problem of only saying "Yes" and portrays it in the character of the Yea-saying Ass in *Thus Spoke Zarathustra*, who is unable to say "No."[38] This Ass says "Yes" to everything, including the old values that are associated with negativity and nihilism. Clearly Nietzsche does not want this, and Deleuze suggests a way out of the problem by arguing that affirmation must contain within itself the possibility of negation in order to enable critical and selective thought.[39] He develops this possibility by asserting that negation and affirmation themselves are terms that are subject to a unilateral distinction. He writes:

> Negation is *opposed* to affirmation but affirmation *differs* from negation. We cannot think of affirmation as "being opposed" to negation: this would be to place the negative within it. Opposition is not only the relation of negation with affirmation but the essence of the negative as such.[40]

Deleuze thus argues that from the perspective of affirmation, negation is not necessarily opposed or excluded. He furthermore argues that there are two forms of both affirmation and negation, forms that are again derived from the "noble" and "slave" of Nietzsche's genealogy. While the negation that issues from the slave is oppositional, creating and perpetuating nihilism, the negation that issues from the noble is of another type. Deleuze explains this other type as follows:

> Negation, like the ripples in a pond, is the effect of an affirmation which is too strong or too different.... Nietzsche opposes the Yes *and* No of the Ass to the Yes *and* No of Dionysus-Zarathustra: the point of view of the slave who draws from 'No' the phantom of an affirmation, and the point of view of the 'master' who draws from 'Yes' a consequence of negation and destruction; the point of view of the conservers of old values and that of the creators of new values.[41]

Deleuze thus argues that the slave negates first, and this negation gives rise to an affirmation. This relation of affirmation and negation is an oppositional one, and is dominated by negation. The affirmation and negation of the noble, however, have a differential relation, and the two terms are dominated by affirmation. For Deleuze, only the affirmation and negation of the slave have the oppositional structure that gives rise to and perpetuates nihilism. The affirmation and negation of the noble, on the other hand, enables the possibility of critical and selective thought without succumbing to nihilistic forms of negation: nihilism may be negated without being opposed (thus avoiding the *essence* of negation, which for Deleuze resides in opposition). Deleuze explains this possibility by arguing that the negation that issues from affirmation only negates that which opposes affirmation—that is, it only negates nihilism. Nihilism is negated by pure affirmation simply because it attempts to oppose what is affirmed. Opposition therefore remains entirely on the side of the slave, who is negated by the noble only because he attempts to oppose the noble, whose affirmation is too strong for the slave to bear.

Norman argues that the logic of difference allows Deleuze to successfully posit the possibility of a definitive overcoming of nihilism, where other interpreters believe this is an impossibility.[42] Deleuze himself announces this overcoming, writing that "the long story of nihilism has a conclusion: the full stop where negation turns back on reactive forces themselves."[43] Despite the fact that the logic of difference circumvents the logic of negation, however, I would argue that this does not in itself license a definitive overcoming of nihilism. Deleuze's positing of the overcoming of nihilism arguably rests on further concepts, in particular his interpretation of Nietzsche's concept of the "eternal return" (*die ewige Wiederkunft*) as selective being. An extended analysis of Deleuze's thought would be required to establish the cogency of this point, but a brief summary must suffice in order to show how the logic of difference may be employed by the postmodern thinkers under consideration here freed from the orbit of the desire to overcome nihilism.

On Deleuze's understanding, what nihilism denies or negates is difference. He interprets the eternal return as a metaphysical theory of Being as selective: what returns is not the same, but rather what remains the same in the eternal return is the production of difference. Deleuze argues, however, that not everything returns: nihilism, that which denies difference, is destroyed by Being itself, which for Deleuze is the continual movement and change of becoming. Throughout his work, Deleuze constructs a complex metaphysical system that establishes becoming, rather than a static conception of Being, as the fundamental nature of reality. This metaphysical principle of becoming is what grounds the affirmation of difference in the very nature of things, and dooms the denial of difference to futility and destruction. Arguably, then, it is only the addition of this metaphysical principle to Deleuze's conceptual system that allows him to envisage an overcoming of nihilism.[44]

While forms of the logic of difference may be identified in the thought of Lyotard, Baudrillard, and Vattimo, these three postmodern thinkers do not follow Deleuze in positing an overcoming of nihilism. Significantly, all of these thinkers explicitly criticize Deleuze for his metaphysics of difference, and we may see this *metaphysics*—rather than the *logic* of difference—as the basis for the claim that nihilism can be overcome. To take one example of these criticisms as representative, Lyotard argues that the ethics Deleuze derives from his metaphysics of difference reinstitutes an oppositional logic.[45] In *Libidinal Economy*, he expresses this point in the form of a self-interrogation:

> —So you thereby challenge Spinozist or Nietzschean ethics, which separate movements of being-more from those of being-less, of action and reaction?—Yes, let us dread to see the reappearance of a whole morality or politics under the cover of these dichotomies, their sages, their militants, their tribunals and their prisons.[46]

This passage, which is unmistakably directed at Deleuze, accuses him of perpetuating the logic of opposition (dichotomy) through the ethics derived from his interpretation of the eternal return as selecting active forces and eliminating reactive forces. The privileging of active forces over reactive, it seems to Lyotard, implies a morality or politics of oppression. We may fill out Lyotard's argument here, beyond the letter of his text, by suggesting that the act of basing a judgment such as the superiority of active forces on a metaphysical principle—effectively inscribing such a superiority in the order of being, or "naturalising" it—is a small step away from licensing the oppression and perhaps destruction of all those forms of life deemed "reactive." In other words, it seems to return the negative and oppositional to the side of the supposedly "noble," who no longer simply affirms, but is licensed to actively negate. From a Lyotardian perspective (and the arguments offered by Baudrillard and Vattimo could, I would argue, be cashed out in similar terms) Deleuze's dream of the overcoming of nihilism depends on a metaphysical principle that seems to reintroduce oppositional negation and the potential for violence associated with metaphysical thought.[47]

The postmodern thinkers under consideration here may be understood to employ the logic of difference as a conceptual tool that allows a principled response to nihilism, a response that circumvents the disabling aporia suggested by the logic of negation. However, they do not believe that it licenses the possibility of a definitive overcoming of nihilism. The positing of such an overcoming, it seems, simply reintroduces an oppositional relation, and hence nihilism. The postmodernists examined here employ forms of the logic of difference precisely in order to respond to nihilism whilst avoiding the oppositional negation involved in the attempt to overcome it. The logic of difference developed by Deleuze nevertheless gives a lucid explanation of the way that the affirmative concepts developed by the postmodernists function: differentially, not oppositionally. The three postmodern thinkers considered here all develop concepts that may be seen as involving a unilateral distinction: one side of a conceptual couplet is oppositional, the other differential. The differential term of the couplet allows an affirmative response to nihilism: it posits an alternative that is not oppositional, and thus avoids oppositional negation.

Moreover, Deleuze's logic of difference allows us to see how the avoidance of oppositional negation does not automatically lead to the collapse of all criteria for valuation. Bereft of its metaphysical dimension, the secondary, non-oppositional negation that Deleuze posits may be interpreted as having a purely epistemological value: it enables principled judgments to be made concerning nihilism, but does not constitute a "metaphysical destruction" of nihilism. Lyotard, Baudrillard, and Vattimo each provide theories that mirror this secondary negation by providing non-oppositional criteria for making judgments concerning nihilism. For these thinkers, the nihilistic and non-nihilistic are never absolutely distinguished from one another, and there is no possibility of a simple opposition of life-affirmation to nihilism. However, the concepts these thinkers develop provide criteria for making judgments concerning the *degree* to which phenomena affirm or deny life. Such criteria provide a "yes" *and* a "no," and are thus able to avoid the second danger of pure affirmation, the danger that nihilism itself will be unreservedly affirmed, and hence conserved. The logic of difference employed by these thinkers thus manages to avoid an oppositional negation of nihilism, whilst also avoiding an affirmation of that which is nihilistic. This differential logic will be fleshed out below in a discussion of key concepts that each of the postmodernists employ in responding to nihilism: Lyotard's "dissimulation," Baudrillard's "seduction," and Vattimo's "*Verwindung*."

The politics of passivity

The logic of difference explains, on an abstract level, how the postmodernists under consideration here are able to pursue a response to nihilism concomitant with an overcoming of the desire to overcome nihilism. The question remains, however, of what the concrete, practical dimension of these responses involves. How is it possible to act in the world in a way that will effectively respond to the meaninglessness of life in postmodernity? I wish to argue that on the basis of the differing but complementary perspectives offered by Lyotard, Baudrillard, and Vattimo, the dimension of this practical response must be understood to be *political*, and the acts appropriate to such a response must, in a specific sense, be understood as *passive*. The practical dimension to the postmodern response to nihilism may therefore be glossed as a "politics of passivity."

The political nature of postmodern responses to nihilism may be approached by reconsidering the turn of postmodern theorists away from the understanding of nihilism as principally an individual problem of the self to an understanding of it as a problem manifest in wider structures of meaning. For Sartre, and to a lesser extent for Nietzsche, nihilism is a problem that might be engaged through the personal transformation of one's own consciousness, beliefs, and values. This approach mirrors those of other existentialist philosophers such as Søren Kierkegaard and Gabriel Marcel, and is well-summarized by Keiji Nishitani when he writes: "[I]f nihilism is anything, it is first of all a problem of the self…When the problem of nihilism is posed apart from the self, or as a problem of society in general, it loses the special genuineness that distinguishes it from other problems."[48]

As we have seen, Heidegger's critique of subjectivity and the rise of structuralism turned the analysis of nihilism away from the self and towards language, following the "linguistic turn" characteristic of much twentieth century philosophy. This turn must be considered from the perspective of the role that language plays in structuralism, post-structuralism, and hermeneutic ontology: for all of these approaches, language is not merely a system of symbols that subjects use to communicate their intentions, but a system that is constitutive of subjects and their world. Language is thus understood as a network of meaning that embraces the world and constitutes human culture, social institutions, and human subjectivity. For the postmodern theorists, nihilism is then understood as a problem constituted by and suffusing language understood in this sense, and the problems of semantic meaning and of existential meaning are therefore treated as associated problems.

The implication of this linguistic turn in the theory of nihilism, I wish to argue, is that the engagement of the problem of meaninglessness can no longer be considered an individual matter, but must be understood as a *political* problem. If the postmodern theories of nihilism understand the social subject and his or her experience as constituted by extra-subjective forces, forces that are linguistic in the broad sense outlined above, then the feelings of existential meaninglessness experienced by subjects (at the extreme, the feeling that life is not worth living) also have their origin in these forces, and must be confronted on this level. Nihilism thus becomes a political problem insofar as "the political" may be understood as the arena of the play of meanings that are the expressions of language through social institutions and discourses. The relationship between language and politics is emphasized by Lyotard's theory of postmodernity, in which society is envisaged as a play of competing language games. Vattimo suggests a similar vision, in which social ontology is composed of competing interpretations transmitted as linguistic messages, with the interference patterns of these messages establishing the horizons of our world. Baudrillard emphasizes the relationship between language and politics in somewhat different terms, arguing that the semio-linguistic theory of meaning is homologous to the capitalist system, and reproduces this system through the perpetuation of a reductive model of meaning. Whether understood as a play of competing language games or a system of structural domination, however, the postmodern view of language conceives linguistic messages as forms of power. If language constitutes social ontology, then it is plausible to understand those language games that dominate, or have more power than others, as playing a greater constitutive role. The nature of social reality will therefore be constituted according to which language games dominate, and the field of language may be understood as a political realm of power relations and struggles in which the stakes are the very constitution of ourselves and our world.

Understood as a problem of language, nihilism reproduces itself through the linguistic utterances of individuals, institutions, and discourses. Nihilism is transmitted from the past through culture and contributes to the constitution of social ontology. The postmodern approach to responding to nihilism seeks to confront it throughout the networks of language in order to produce changes in social ontology. This may be seen as a political task insofar as it engages on the level of the extra-individual or "the social" (political in the sense of the *polis*, of "being-together"), and insofar as it involves engagement in a power struggle between competing uses of language (discourses). The question now arises, what *kind* of politics—what kind of *political action*—constitutes an appropriate response to nihilism in postmodernity? As we have seen, the postmodern stance is associated with an abandonment of the revolutionary and utopian political projects of modernity, an abandonment that accords with a rejection of the possibility of overcoming nihilism. What hopes are left to a postmodern politics in the face of a nihilism that cannot be overcome? Caygill suggests a direction in which the answer to this question might lie when he writes: "If the revaluation of values is unable to escape the radical nihilist predicament the question posed to the future changes from revaluation to that of how to live with nihilism."[49]

Lyotard, Baudrillard, and Vattimo develop the political dimensions of their thought along significantly different paths. For Lyotard and Baudrillard, the move away from the attempt to overcome nihilism has as its political corollary a move away from the "macropolitics" of governments and institutions towards a "micropolitics" of particular practices and actions. For these postmodernists, the rejection of the hope of overcoming nihilism is also a rejection of the hope of solving the contemporary problem of meaninglessness through changing current social and political formations. The French thinkers' orientation towards micropolitics is well indicated by Lyotard's attempt to formulate an idea of the political appropriate to his libidinal philosophy. This philosophy is political

> [...] in a sense that is neither institutional (Parliament, elections, parties, and so on) nor even "Marxist" (class struggle, the proletariat, the Party, and so on)—a sense obviously much too close to the first one. It is political in a sense that is "not yet" determined and that perhaps will remain, must always remain, to be determined.
>
> This politics would not concern the determination of institutions—that is, the rules of organisation—but the determination of a space for the play of libidinal intensities, affects, and passions. There is nothing *utopic* about it in the current sense of the term. Rather, it is what the world seeks blindly today through practises or experiences of all kinds, whose sole common trait is that they are held to be frivolous.[50]

Vattimo, on the other hand, has frequently and actively engaged in politics as traditionally understood, and attempts to draw implications for public policy and the structures and institutions of government from his philosophy of postmodern nihilism. He thus continues to engage on a macropolitical level, arguing that certain forms of the political organization of society are more compatible with his vision of postmodernity than others. He is a social democrat, and holds that socialism and democracy are the forms of political organization most compatible with (positive) nihilism, hermeneutics, and the reduction of violence. Despite these divergences concerning the political level at which these different postmodernists engage, they are united by the common theme of *passivity* as the principle guiding their political prescriptions.

The link between passivity and the task of responding to nihilism may be approached *via* a reconsideration of Heidegger's problematization of active willing with respect to the issue of overcoming nihilism. As we saw in chapter one, Heidegger questions the attempt to overcome nihilism through both collective political movements and the individual activity of the creation of new values. Heidegger problematizes political action, a problematization that stems from his assertion that nihilism is given by Being itself and can only be revoked by Being. Any attempt by human beings to actively overcome nihilism, Heidegger writes, amounts to a deeper entrenchment in nihilism itself:

> To *want* to overcome nihilism...and to *overcome* it would mean that man of himself advance against Being itself in its default.... To want to assail the default of Being directly would mean not heeding Being itself as Being. The overcoming of nihilism willed in such a way would simply be a more dismal relapse into the inauthenticity of its essence, which distorts all authenticity.[51]

This critique of willed action decides against the possibility of overcoming nihilism through the collective actions of political parties and movements, insofar as these attempt to directly change the nature of the world through an active implementation of willed goals. Moreover, Heidegger argues that the active willing implied by the attempt to overcome nihilism is implicated with the modern *subjectivism* he associates with nihilism. This subjectivism understands the world as objects to be manipulated by willing subjects, covering over the essential relation of Being and human being. For Heidegger, the individual activity of value creation advocated by Nietzsche and Sartre is a species of active willing that implies this metaphysical relation of the subject to the world. In actively creating or choosing values, the subject stands in relation to the world as one who imposes its will and measures the value of the world against its needs, rather than standing in openness to Being. For

Heidegger, then, neither political activity (as traditionally conceived) nor the individual revaluation of values can be effective responses to nihilism.

Lyotard, Baudrillard, and Vattimo all implicitly accept Heidegger's argument with respect to the problematization of action and the will, and develop similar arguments in their own philosophical terms. In different ways, each of the postmodernists under consideration here embraces a form of *passivity* as a strategy with which to circumvent the aporia of active overcoming. Paradoxically, this notion of political passivity is not intended as a form of quietism, but rather as a particular kind of action, or engagement with the world. This is the specific, if ambiguous, sense in which the passivity of postmodern politics is to be understood. This ambiguity is expressed in Lyotard's term "active passivity" and in a term coined by Gary Genosko, "affirmative weakness."[52] These terms both recall and call into question the traditional Western associations between activity and strength, and between passivity and weakness. Lyotard, Baudrillard, and Vattimo each employ the rhetoric of "weakness" as a counter to Western metaphysics, arguing that there is a particular potency to be found in "weak" or passive stances and strategies that have been ignored by the Western tradition. It is the exploitation of such potency that governs the postmodern responses to nihilism. For my purposes here, Genosko's term "affirmative weakness" usefully carries the connotation that such weak or passive strategies enable the affirmation of life in the face of nihilism, as an alternative to the active, wilful attempt at overcoming.

As a way of responding to nihilism, the politics of passivity attempts to negotiate nihilism without hoping to overcome it. That is, passive political acts are aimed at mitigating nihilism and creating conditions in which life may be experienced as meaningful through the employment of "weak" strategies. Such strategies have an affinity with the logic of difference discussed above, and can be understood as the practical correlate of such a logic: while the active attempt at overcoming *opposes* nihilism, the passive politics of affirmative weakness seeks to affirm forces of life that *differ* from nihilism. This means that nihilism is not confronted directly and destroyed, but its power is weakened through the affirmation and strengthening of those aspects of life and thought that nihilistic forces threaten to reduce to nothing. The postmodern response to nihilism is thus an attempt to live with nihilism, but also to resist its totalizing tendencies, affirming life to a maximal degree. Thus far we have examined the general contours of the logic of difference and the politics of passivity. In the following section, I will examine Lyotard, Baudrillard, and Vattimo in turn, showing how the logic of difference and the politics of passivity operate in their thought, and outlining how these principles allow each to respond to the various manifestations of nihilism in postmodernity that they identify.

Postmodern responses to nihilism

The activity of life is like a power of falsehood, of duping, dissimulating, dazzling and seducing.

—Gilles Deleuze[53]

Lyotard: Dissimulation

We have already seen the general trajectory of Lyotard's response to nihilism through the discussion of his avoidance of (oppositional) critique and employment of the concept of dissimulation. In this section, I will explain how dissimulation functions according to a logic of difference, and outline the strategies Lyotard develops for putting dissimulation to work. These strategies, I will show, enact a form of the politics of passivity outlined above. To reiterate, Lyotard understands nihilism as the dampening of intense feelings and desires and hence the devaluation of life through representational structures. He understands such structures on the model of Nietzsche's analysis of religious nihilism, that is, as mechanisms of absence and deferral. Lyotard's response to nihilism is to privilege the Freudian libido as an energetic force of life-affirmation. In effect, this means affirming the material, bodily dimension of desire and affect as healthful and essential aspects of existence, aspects that representational thought reduces and devalues. He understands libidinal energies as events that are unpredictable and uncontrollable, and implies that remaining open to the occurrence of such events is an essential part of a meaningful life. His response to nihilism exploits the dissimulatory relationship he posits between libidinal energy and the representational structures that channel and hide it.

Lyotard's privileging of the libido and the principle of dissimulation can be understood in terms of the logic of difference as a circumvention of the nihilistic logic of opposition. Like Deleuze, Lyotard associates opposition and the negation it implies with nihilism. In Lyotard's thought, negation is expressed as the great Zero that divides two opposed terms. In the context of representation, these opposed terms are the representational structure and that which is represented. The oppositional relation of these terms implies the negation of that which is represented by the representational structure, and hence the absence, transcendence, and continual deferral of the represented "thing." Opposition and negation thus operate as the motors of nihilism in Lyotard's analysis. Moreover, he understands oppositional negation as underlying conceptual thought and rational theory: according with the structuralist model he follows, Lyotard understands conceptual thought as instituting distinctions and giving meaning according to oppositional relations. As such, conceptual thought minimally implies an opposition between two terms, "this" and "not-this." Lyotard calls the logical operator of this opposition "the bar of disjunction." We may see this bar of disjunction as the bar between signifier and signified in the body of the sign, and as both the law of excluded middle and the law of noncontradiction in Aristotelian logic. Lyotard thus understands opposition and the negation it implies as the fundamental unit of nihilism. Based on this opposition, intensely felt libidinal energies are annulled through conceptual and representational thought. Lyotard writes:

> The operator of disintensification is exclusion: either this, or not this. Not both. The disjunctive bar. Every concept is therefore concomitant with negation, exteriorization. It is this exteriorization of the not-this that will give rise to theatricalization...[54]

Having associated conceptualization with nihilism, and defined the concept according to opposition and negation, the challenge Lyotard sets for himself is to find a form of affirmation that will not simply negate or be opposed to the regime of the concept. These problems of negation and opposition explain his recourse to Freudian libidinal themes. Lyotard understands oppositional negation in Freudian terms as operating in the secondary processes of consciousness, which are associated with conceptual thought and the logical function of negation. In the operations of the libido in the primary processes of the unconscious, however, he finds the possibility of an affirmation that is not dependent upon negation. As Geoffery Bennington has noted,[55] Lyotard's use of Freud turns on several revisions and changes of emphasis. First, Lyotard notes that desire has two meanings in Freud's work, and asserts the primacy of desire as *libido* or force over desire as wish (*Wunsch*). The latter, founded in lack and implying representation (what is desired is lacked and represented in the form of a wish), is a form of negation that Lyotard associates with nihilism and seeks to avoid.[56] Lyotard understands libido, however, as a purely affirmative force, which he associates with Nietzsche's will to power.[57] This interpretation rests on Freud's claim in his 1915 paper "The Unconscious" that the unconscious knows no negation:

> There are in this system [the unconscious] no negation, no doubt, no degrees of certainty: all this is only introduced by the work of the censorship between the *Ucs.* [unconscious] and the *Pcs.* [preconscious]. Negation is a substitute, at a higher level, for repression. In the *Ucs.* there are only contents, cathected with greater or lesser strength.[58]

Freud asserts that the unconscious is characterized by a mobility of libidinal investments (cathexes[59]) in which investment may be displaced wholly from one idea to another, or an idea may appropriate the investment of several other ideas. Freud refers to these operations as *displacement* and *condensation*, and characterizes them together as the *primary psychical processes* of the unconscious.[60]

Lyotard takes this description of the primary processes as evidence for the pure positivity of the libido. In these unconscious processes, desires are displaced and condensed in such a way that no negation, lack, or absence is implied:

> The slow or lightning-quick displacement of investments is precisely positivity insofar as it escapes the rules of language and is without reason. What is positive in this sense is what is beyond regulated deviations, gaps or borders, or hierarchies.[61]

In the unconscious operations of the libido, Lyotard finds a principle that contravenes Spinoza's *Ominis determinatio est negatio*, precisely because a thing can be affirmed (in libidinal terms, invested) without implying the negation of another thing. For Lyotard, the libido exists in a space that remains undivided by the bar of disjunction.

Lyotard needs a further move, however, since to stop at this point would still imply a bar of disjunction, this time between the unconscious regime of the libido and the conscious regime of concepts and representation.[62] This move is given through a further revision of the Freudian theory of desire, this time in relation to the two "drives" or "pulsional principles," Eros and the death drive (Thanatos). Lyotard argues that the two drives are not separate, but twin aspects of desire as libido. As such, the libido is split between two "regimes," which handle desire differently in the way that it works in and on structures and systems. Eros regulates desire in such a way as to contribute to the order and stability of the system. The death drive, on the other hand, acts as a "deregulating" force of desire that tends towards the disorder and instability of systems.

In the essays collected in *Des Dispositifs pulsionnels*, Lyotard tends to follow Freud's description of the respective functions of the two regimes. According to Freud, Eros is the principle of life, self-preservation, sexuality, a structuring force that works "to combine organic substances into ever larger unities"; "the preserver of all things"; "which seeks to force together and hold together the portions of living substance."[63] The death drive, on the other hand, is the principle of death, dissolution, the unbinding of libidinal energy, the desire to return to an original, inorganic (or un*organ*ized) state. Following this designation of Eros as a binding, structuring force and the death drive as an unbinding, destructuring force, Lyotard characterizes Eros as that movement of desire that gives rise to, and stabilizes, structures (including representational structures).[64] The death drive, on the other hand, is paradoxically privileged as a force of life-affirmation because it destabilizes structures and thus undermines representational, and hence nihilistic, systems.[65] This dichotomy between binding and unbinding energies allows Lyotard, in some of these early essays, to posit the possibility of an eventual dissolution of nihilistic structures such as the capitalist system through the raising of libidinal energies to a sufficient degree of intensity (at which point they can no longer be contained by the systems that attempt to regulate them). As such, this early theory of desire licenses the hope for revolution through excess, suggesting a "pure" affirmative region delimited by the death drive.[66]

By the time of writing *Libidinal Economy*, however, Lyotard has become sensitive to the problem that this privileging of the death drive implies the inevitable preservation of nihilism: it sets up an *opposition* between force and structure, where force is exclusively valued to the detriment of structure. In *Libidinal Economy*, Lyotard solves this problem by further revising the Freudian theory of the drives, problematizing their respective functions:

> [B]ound wholes can be congenial to life (organisms, statutes, institutions, memories of all kinds) as to death (neuroses and psychoses, paranoiac confinements, lethal stable disorders of organic functions)... [and] unbinding is as much for the relief of bodies—orgasm and the relief of semen, drunkenness and the blurting out of words, the dance and loosening of the muscles—as for their destruction...[67]

This confusion of the functions of the drives means that Eros and the death drive cannot be simply identified with the binding and unbinding of energy, that is, with the respective creation and dissolution of structures. Rather, Lyotard asserts that *both* Eros and the death drive—the ordering and disordering principles—can be associated with the functions of binding and unbinding energy. That is, either binding or unbinding libidinal energy can contribute to the well-regulated order of a structure, and either binding or unbinding energy can deregulate and destabilize a structure.

The problem that this confusion of functions overcomes is the ability to ascribe distinct *properties* to the death drive (i.e. those properties that relate to the unbinding or discharge of energy, and are manifest, for example, as particular symptoms of patients undergoing psychoanalysis). Given Spinoza's principle, this ascription of properties would mean that affirming the death drive implies a negation, and hence leads back into nihilism. The major implication of this revision is that the death drive is now also associated with structures, and not simply with their dissolution.[68] In Lyotard's mature version of the libidinal economy, the libidinal intensity he privileges is no longer simply a function of the death drive as an unbinding or release of energy, but of necessary relations of force and structure. According to Lyotard every libidinal formation is necessarily a structure, and force must be expressed through structures. A force that is too disordered and unstructured loses its intensive potential. Likewise, Lyotard understands structures as more or less rigidly bound energetic formations, and structures that resist influxes of energy are bound to stagnancy. Given the ambiguity of the functions of Eros and the death drive, the maximization of intensity becomes a highly complex matter: releasing energy from a system might lead to either the intensification of energy (it allows the system to continue functioning at a high level of energy rather than blowing itself apart; the force released creates a new system or flows into and revitalizes an existing one) or disintensification of energy (the system loses too much energy and stagnates; the outflow of energy fails to create or connect with another system). The increased binding of energy might likewise lead to either vitalization or stagnation.

For Lyotard, this *duplicity* (rather than duality) of the two drives with respect to their functions is what ultimately prevents the libidinal economy from being a system of critical concepts that might straightforwardly be applied to phenomena through recognition, exclusively dividing the nihilistic from the affirmative (and thus reintroducing the bar of disjunction and nihilism). Furthermore, as we have seen, Lyotard asserts that all relatively stable structures and systems, whether they are theoretical, political, economic, or otherwise, can be described in terms of libidinal energy. In the libidinal economy, systems exploit libidinal intensities by channeling them into stable structures. Systems hide or *dissimulate* affects (libidinal intensities). And yet, these systems deny their own origins in intense and aleatory libidinal energy, taking themselves to be permanent and stable.[69] Lyotard thus describes structures, which have an oppositional relation to libidinal energy, as themselves consisting in transformations of libidinal energies. Since representational structures are associated with desire as wish, Lyotard also posits a continuity between desire as wish and the energetic desire of the libido, accounting for the former in terms of the latter. While structure opposes itself to libido, the libido can be said to have a *differential* relation to structure in the Deleuzean sense. Force and structure thus have a relationship of unilateral distinction in the libidinal economy. Lyotard refers to this relationship as *dissimulation*, and uses it to circumvent the logic of opposition and negation that are the insidious motors of theatricalization and nihilism. Bennington explains:

> [I]f there is an energetical continuity of Eros and Thanatos, and a further continuity between desire as libido and desire as *Wunsch*, then there can be no *opposition*...if the theatre is in fact a product of libidinal energy, then its apparent opposition to that energy is also part of the energy itself, one of its transformations.[70]

The principle of dissimulation involves a logic of difference that allows a circumvention of the logic of opposition and negation, and hence a way of positing an alternative to responding to nihilism through direct opposition.

Lyotard outlines a way of acting to put dissimulation to work that he characterizes as an "active passivity"; this active passivity describes the kinds of political acts that he takes to be efficacious responses to the problem of nihilism.[71] For Lyotard, the possibility of responding to nihilism amounts to the possibility of intensifying libidinal intensity in structures and systems. He argues that we do have a degree of agency that allows us to act in such a way as to promote the level of intensity in structures, but this agency involves a necessary dimension of passivity. This is because libidinal intensities, understood by Lyotard as events, are unpredictable and uncontrollable. Any attempt to consciously will specific outcomes and goals in terms of which affects and desires will be released in systems, and to what effect, is not only bound to fail, but reproduces the kinds of structures that dampen intensities, therefore reintroducing the problem of nihilism. The act of consciously willing a specific outcome is a function of the secondary psychical processes, already implying negation and theatricalization. Lyotard is aware of similar problems in responding to nihilism as is Heidegger: for the French philosopher, both the subject and the conscious, active will are structuring forces, which mean that any attempt to respond to nihilism through the willful conscious actions of subjects will in fact dampen intensity and deepen nihilism.

Lyotard's alternative to direct willful action combines the necessities of both activity and passivity. Active passivity does involve conscious willing, but what is willed is passivity with respect to the unconscious conduction of affects. This is a twofold process that, first, involves a conscious turn away from the attempt to actively overcome nihilism through those methods and strategies that are themselves implicated in nihilism: theory, subjective values, oppositional structures, alternative social institutions and political programmes. This first aspect of responding to nihilism also allows and requires a form of "critique," which is distinguished from the nihilistic critique Lyotard eschews because it does not depend on taking up an oppositional place. Hence the place of Lyotard's critical analyses of nihilistic structures and theories such as capitalism and semiotics. Such "critiques" identify the forms of life and thought that need to be avoided in order to avoid the reproduction of nihilism in its most extreme forms. Lyotard's critical analyses do not involve him in straightforward opposition and negation, however, for two reasons. Firstly, because the principle of dissimulation means that even those structures identified as nihilistic are seen as formations of desire, and hence are not absolutely negated, but accorded a degree of value. Secondly, because the aim and consequence of Lyotard's libidinal critiques is not to set up an alternative system of concepts, but to respond to nihilistic structures by maximizing the libidinal intensity that vitalizes them.

This maximization of libidinal intensity is enabled by the passive element of Lyotard's strategy. Consciously turning away from willing definite desires and outcomes, the libidinal economist seeks to passively and unconsciously "conduct" libidinal energies. This means working within existing structures to forge new connections between them and channel energy from one structure into another. This conduction of intensities loosens the repressive function of structures that bind and stabilize energies, allowing intensities to emerge in an unpredictable way. The general maximisation of the intensity of libidinal energies in systems means greater rates of change in systems, an increase of connectedness between systems, and an increased number of newly created systems.[72] Since libidinal energy never manifests directly but only through structures, the libidinal economist must act within structures in such a way as to introduce new desires and affects, but without seeking to control *which* desires and affects these will be, nor *how* they will affect the structure into which they are introduced. Since libidinal energies are unconscious processes, the passive conduction of intensities involves a necessary openness to these processes. This passive strategy allows a maximization of the affirmation and positivity Lyotard associates with the libido, and locates in the primary psychical processes.

Lyotard takes artistic composition as a practical model for active passivity and applies principles derived from such composition to show how dissimulation may be exploited in philosophy and politics. Taking Paul Cézanne and the tradition of modern art generally as examples, Lyotard argues that innovative artistic composition involves the two steps of active passivity: turning away from traditional methods and aesthetic principles, and creating in an experimental way that invites unconscious desires to take part in the process.[73] The experimental style of *Libidinal Economy* is an application of this model of artistic creation to academic theory. The book both theorizes and performs a response to nihilism, and by being attentive to both its form and content, we may see how Lyotard responds to the nihilism of dispassionate, representational theory. I turn now to an examination of the specific strategies of active passivity Lyotard recommends and enacts, beginning with those evident in *Libidinal Economy* itself.

As we have already seen, one of Lyotard's main targets in *Libidinal Economy* and *Des Dispositifs pulsionnels* is the nihilism of the semiotic sign, understood as the basic unit of meaning in representational structures. Lyotard's affirmative response to the semiotic sign is an alternative conception of the sign, which he calls the "tensor." The tensor is not a special kind of sign, but a way of viewing all signs from the perspective of the theory of dissimulation. While the semiotic sign functions purely in the realm of semantic meaning, manifesting an absence and deferral of the meaning it stands in for, the tensor is a theory of the sign that understands it as combining and dissimulating semantic meaning and libidinal energy. Considered as a tensor, a semiotic sign dissimulates desires and can impart a force or desire as well as convey a meaning. The tensor, for Lyotard, should be understood as a *tension* between these dimensions of signification and libidinal energy.[74] Moreover, since Lyotard understands libidinal intensities as events that can potentially give rise to a number of competing interpretations—that is, they can be dissimulated within incompossible structures—the tensor marks the meeting place of different structures and systems. Considered as a tensor, a sign can be inscribed into a number of different structures. What is important to Lyotard is not the different meanings the sign may have in these structures, but the different ways the energy of the tensor may be deployed to change those structures. The tensor, then, is an energetic sign that allows Lyotard to posit dissimulation as operational within linguistic systems of meaning.[75]

The principles of dissimulation and the tensor are put to work in the writing of *Libidinal Economy* through a number of identifiable techniques. Lyotard writes with the aim of releasing as much libidinal intensity in the text as possible, but without attempting to produce a book of "anti-theory," which would avoid representational effects entirely. The intensification of force within structure is accomplished by haphazardly juxtaposing genres of discourse, in particular the relatively static theoretical genre and the more dynamic, more intense genre of experimental fiction. The former *represents* the philosophy of libidinal economy in repeatable concepts, while the latter attempts to *perform* it through employing techniques that deliver an intense libidinal charge. Lyotard employs devices such as long sentences, lack of punctuation, swearing and emotive language in order to convey feelings and desires as directly and intensely as possible. The relatively sober theoretical passages that intersperse the whole text, however, supply a sophisticated semantic meaning. Such meaning forms the structure necessary for the force of the book to be expressed. The experimental style of *Libidinal Economy* is therefore a setting-to-work of dissimulation and the tensor that combines the dimensions of force and signification, maximising force within a signifying structure. The major book of Lyotard's libidinal philosophy constitutes a philosophical response to nihilism by showing how philosophy might proceed without stifling intensity through the hegemony of representational structures. More than just an example, however (which remains in the domain of representation), the book itself attempts to impart an affective charge to its readers, transmitting the libidinal energy that Lyotard understands as the affirmative expression of life itself.

In addition to the nihilism of representational thought and theory, Lyotard identifies capitalism and technoscience as dominant forms of nihilism. In chapter three, we saw how these forms of nihilism inform Lyotard's theory of postmodernity, and according to this theory constitute problems to which a response must be found in the contemporary situation. Following James Williams, I view Lyotard's libidinal philosophy as constituting a more effective response to nihilism than his later philosophy of the differend, and it is the resources for responding to nihilism available in the libidinal philosophy on which I am focusing here. However, Lyotard gives little consideration to technoscience in his libidinal writings, and I shall focus on his response to capitalism here. This focus finds some justification in the similarity of the analysis to which Lyotard subjects these two forms of nihilism. On Lyotard's analysis, technoscience contributes to the nihilism of postmodernity by dissolving traditional forms of the social bond, and by functioning together with capitalism to subject all dimensions of life to the criterion of performativity. It is this latter, reductive dimension of technoscience with which Lyotard is most concerned. The criterion of performativity functions in tandem with the law of value in capitalist political economy, enacting an overarching reduction. Given this similarity in the analysis of the nihilism of technoscience and capitalism, the response to the nihilism of capital proposed in the libidinal philosophy has import for the later analysis of technoscience as well.

In his libidinal philosophy, Lyotard responds to the nihilism of capitalism through a "politics of passivity" that engages with the traditional Marxist critique of capitalism, but turns this problematic toward different ends. The politics of the libidinal philosophy revolves around a nuanced reading of Marx and a duplicitous relation to capitalism. As we saw in the previous chapter, Lyotard presents the capitalist system as a conflict between two tendencies, one life-affirmative, one nihilistic. The affirmative tendency of capitalism lies in its drive to confer value on everything, and to seek out new desires and affects, new libidinal intensities, to incorporate into the system. In this way, capitalism acts as a system that encourages the development of new intensities. On the other hand, however, this tendency is qualified by the tendency to annul the very intensities sought and encouraged through the exploitation of these intensities within structures; their commodification and equalization in exchange value. This process of commodification and commensuration tends to take on absolute importance, annulling the singularity of the very intensities it seeks out.

Lyotard understands this ambiguity of the capitalist system on the model of dissimulation, and works towards a response to the nihilism of capitalism that puts this principle to work through the double strategy of "active passivity" outlined above. Firstly, Lyotard moves away from the Marxist tradition of critique, which he understands as *opposing* the capitalist system and setting up an ideal image of an unalienated society in its place. Lyotard argues that the idea of an unalienated society is nostalgic, in so far as it posits an impossible ideal that never really existed and which we can have no realistic expectation ever will exist. He expresses this argument through the claim that "[t]here are no primitive societies,"[76] by which he means that so-called "primitive" societies carry the same nihilistic traits as capitalism. For Lyotard, there is no society that is not subject to the desire to exploit and hoard libidinal energy in the way that the capitalist does. He explains:

> [O]f course, savages do not capitalize goods; but who considers that it is only the fully mercantile instance of the great Zero that sanctions and indeed demands the *scrupulous balancing of the inflows and outflows of affects* (in the form of relatives, words, beasts, lives, sexes), hanging over and maintaining these societies?[77]

Considered from a libidinal perspective, money is not the only way of stringently regulating the circulation of (and consequently dampening the intensity of) desire in society, and Lyotard argues that any social formation is therefore prone to the nihilism of the great Zero. This means that there is no utopian society free from exploitation, neither pre-capitalist nor post-revolutionary.

Secondly, Lyotard seeks to actively respond to the nihilism of capitalism through passive political acts. Lyotard's libidinal politics is not aimed at overthrowing capitalism (since he does not believe in the possibility of a non-nihilistic post-revolutionary society), but of working within it to release the libidinal energies dissimulated within its structures. This politics is micropolitical and marginal, not seeking to establish new institutions and governments, but rather attempting to work within existing political institutions in order to release as much libidinal intensity within and through them as possible. Lyotard's response to the nihilism of capitalism is therefore the same as his response to other nihilistic structures: "With respect to capitalism, same solution: to raise or maintain intensity at its highest level in order to obtain as strong (*Macht*) an energetic metamorphosis as possible."[78]

Following Lyotard's arguments outlined earlier, this maximization of libidinal intensities must be understood as a passive process: it must seek to introduce new feelings and desires in structures, but without determining in advance what these desires will be and what course the consequent metamorphoses of structures will take.

For Lyotard, capitalism is a particularly good economic system for the conduction of libidinal intensities, and the libidinal economist should exploit its tendencies to value everything without discrimination and to seek out new intensities. The political acts of "active passivity" should be understood as aimed at maximizing these positive opportunities for intensity and energetic transformation within capitalist societies at the expense of the nihilistic tendency of the law of value to dampen everything in the equalizing process of exchange. Libidinal economics works within the capitalist system to seize on and create singular intensive events that are not immediately annulled, and which produce changes or metamorphoses in the system. Such events, by definition, have no determinate form, and may consist in any occurrence where intensity is felt: a new product or market, an artwork, an activist demonstration, a caress. Lyotard's response to nihilism thus takes the form of a politics, but one that must be understood as a conspiracy or permanent revolution within the existing system rather than a decisive revolution that would overthrow the prevailing order and found a new one. The form of this politics is well summarised by Lyotard's exhortations in the concluding paragraphs of *Libidinal Economy*:

> We need not leave the place where we are, we need not be ashamed to speak in a "state-funded" university, write, get published, go commercial, love a woman, a man, and live together with them; there is no good place, the "private" universities are like the others, savage publications like civilized ones, and no love can prevail over jealousy... What would be interesting would be to stay put, but quietly seize every chance to function as good intensity-conducting bodies.[79]

In summary, Lyotard's response to nihilism seeks to deploy what he sees as the life-affirmative forces of feelings and desires against the nihilism of representational structures, which filter and dampen these desires. For Lyotard, life is devalued when libidinal energies are dampened, and affirmed when they are intensified. His reworking of the Freudian theory of the libido constitutes a sophisticated way of avoiding the impasse of oppositional negation by finding a principle of affirmation without negation in the primary psychical processes. This theory constitutes a form of the logic of difference in Lyotard's thought, which allows criteria for judgments concerning nihilism to be made without falling back into the nihilism of critique: nihilism consists in the dampening of libidinal intensities, and life affirmation consists in their maximization. However, there is no strict opposition between libidinal energies and the structures that dampen them. For Lyotard, there is an energetic continuity between intensity and structure. The maximization of intensity does not negate structure, but must work in and through it. Lyotard's "active passivity" is a kind of passive politics that allows a strategic response to nihilism, without attempting to oppose or overcome it, by maximizing intensity within structures. The principles of dissimulation and the tensor show how such a response to nihilism may be enacted, through a kind of conspiracy or permanent revolution, in theoretical writings and in the structures and institutions of the capitalist system.

Baudrillard: Seduction

Throughout his *oeuvre*, Baudrillard develops numerous concepts that he intends as affirmative counters to the nihilism of the postmodern world. Despite their differences in nuance, these concepts all express the same essential logic, and this allows an appreciation of the principal aspects of Baudrillard's response to nihilism through exclusive focus on a single concept. The concept I will focus on here is *seduction*, perhaps the most well-known of these affirmative terms. As we have seen, for Baudrillard nihilism is understood as the consequence of the attempt to impose a rational meaning on the world, first as the destruction of appearances by this rational meaning, and then as the self-destruction of rational meaning itself. Baudrillard understands the rational meaning he associates with nihilism on a structuralist model, where meaning is a function of the oppositional structure of the semiological sign. Seduction, like Baudrillard's other affirmative terms, attempts to articulate a form of meaning that is alternative to, and more existentially satisfying than, the rational order of meaning. Baudrillard understands rational meaning as based on a logic of opposition, and seduction is, in effect, a "logic of difference" that subverts opposition. We may therefore understand Baudrillard's response to nihilism as following, in its general contour, the path mapped out by Deleuze and taken by Lyotard.

The concept of seduction was briefly introduced in chapter two, where its logical relation to simulation was indicated. To reiterate, what Baudrillard calls seduction indicates the distance between representation and its simulated real. This distance is forever being crossed, calling forth the necessity for a new simulated real at a greater distance. Seduction is this movement within simulation; it is the "other" of, or the gap in, simulation that guarantees that there is always something left to simulate. In Baudrillard's theory of simulation and seduction, the real is always paradoxically both inside the system (since the real is simulated) and outside of it (since it functions as the other or limit to that system). We may see the relationship between simulation and seduction as following the "logic of difference" outlined above, and as incorporating a "unilateral distinction" between these two terms: Simulation *opposes* seduction, but seduction *differs* from simulation. Simulation functions according to a denial that there must be a distance between representation and reality, and constantly seeks to close this distance. This distance, however, *is* necessary for the functioning of representation. Seduction is the other side of simulation: it is what allows simulation to operate, revealing an elementary dynamic that is essential to simulation, but that simulation itself attempts to exclude. Simulation, with its model of meaning based on representation, deep structure, and stable oppositions between terms, opposes the dynamic force of seduction. Seduction, however, differs from simulation rather than opposing it by showing how the supposed identity of representation and real that simulation posits is dependent on a more fundamental difference between them.

This differential relationship between simulation and seduction allows Baudrillard to negotiate the aporia of the attempt to overcome nihilism. In his early works, Baudrillard arguably falls prey to the trap of *opposing* the nihilism of the semio-linguistic order of meaning by positing symbolic exchange as prior and external to the system of capitalist political economy. On Lyotard's analysis, Baudrillard sets up an impossible ideal that opposes and negates the current world, thereby devaluing life after the model of religious nihilism.[80] With the introduction of the terms "simulation" and "seduction" and the ambiguous relation between them, however, Baudrillard effectively replaces an oppositional hierarchy with a pair of unilaterally distinct terms.[81] This unilateral distinction and the logic of difference it embodies affords Baudrillard new conceptual possibilities for responding to nihilism beyond the aporia of a simple opposition. However, these possibilities are developed along lines distinctly different from those the logic of difference takes in Lyotard's work. For Baudrillard, the differential relation between nihilistic and affirmative terms leads to complex and ultimately undecidable possibilities with respect to the nihilism of the current situation. While Baudrillard sees simulation and seduction in a relation that is somehow complicit, he doesn't accord any value or necessity to simulation in the way that Lyotard does to libidinal *dispositifs*. Rather, Baudrillard sees simulation and seduction in conflict, and understands simulation's reliance on seduction—its ability to make seduction work for it - as a particularly pernicious aspect of the simulated system. Baudrillard's hope is for an eventual transformation of the system, which would bring seduction to the fore and effectively eliminate simulation. The path he proposes towards this end is the "exposure" of simulation *as* simulation (rather than merely accurate representation). As

Baudrillard argues, simulation rests on the "alibi" that what it represents is the real that pre-exists the system. By exposing the fact that simulated systems generate their own real, Baudrillard hopes, the whole system of simulation will collapse.

The role of seduction in this response to nihilism is explained by the fact that seduction is one name Baudrillard gives to the principle of *reversibility* which, he believes, underlies simulation. To reiterate, simulation is predicated on stable oppositions, anchored in a relationship to the real. Without this anchorage, oppositions become reversible since there is no independent measure that would allow one to judge whether one term or the other applies to a given object or situation. On Baudrillard's analysis, simulated systems are in fact reversible, and the revelation of this fact would be a mortal blow to the simulated systems themselves. Seduction is the principle of this reversibility, the dynamic by which simulated systems in fact operate. Baudrillard writes:

> Every *positive* form can accommodate itself to its negative form, but understands the challenge of the *reversible* form as mortal. Every structure can adapt to its subversion or inversion, but not to the reversion of its terms. Seduction is this reversible form.[82]

On this level, Baudrillard seeks a collapse of the nihilistic system, and to that extent remains a utopian who hopes for an eventual overcoming of nihilism.[83] The other side of the ambiguous relation between simulation and seduction, however, is the possibility that simulation will remain hegemonic, precisely because it hinges on seduction. As we saw in chapter two, Baudrillard rejects the possibility of overcoming nihilism through direct opposition because the reversibility of simulation means that it can incorporate any opposition: oppositions merely help to prop up the reality principle on which simulation operates. For Baudrillard, seduction is a more oblique response to the nihilism of simulation, which avoids the trap of straightforward opposition. Seduction itself, however, is a strategy with no guarantee of success. The possibility remains that seduction will simply perpetuate simulation insofar as it allows simulation to operate, and guarantees that there is always more to be simulated. As the principle of difference that allows and disrupts the identity of representation, seduction ensures that there will always be a differential element escaping representation, but this element can always be reclaimed by the system. Baudrillard concludes from the complicity of simulation and seduction that the fate of the social system with respect to nihilism is ultimately undecidable.

Despite this undecidability, Baudrillard develops the concept of seduction along the lines of a passive political strategy that aims at maximizing the potential of seduction to undermine simulation. In this way, seduction contributes to an affirmative response to nihilism through political acts. Baudrillard takes a particular, nineteenth century notion of seduction as a model and generalizes it to all forms of activity and interaction. Seduction, like Lyotard's "active passivity," is a passive strategy that is deployed against nihilism in the attempt to circumvent the aporia resulting from a direct confrontation. This theme is drawn out in Baudrillard's work through the association of seduction with passivity and weakness, and the argument that these qualities exhibit their own profound form of strength:[84]

> To seduce is to appear weak. To seduce is to render weak. We seduce with our weakness, never with strong signs or powers. In seduction we enact this weakness, and this is what gives seduction its strength.[85]

In emphasizing the weak character of seduction, Baudrillard differentiates it from a strategy of direct opposition that relies on brute strength. The seductive strategy is an indirect, oblique one: "it is not a matter of a frontal attack, but a diagonal seduction that glides like a (brush?) stroke..."[86]

Baudrillard explains the strategy of seduction as one of calculated risk, where the possibility of failure must be accepted in order to enter the game. Essentially, seduction is a game of one-upmanship between two parties in which each is trying to preempt the moves made by the other. Seduction is a reversible and uncertain game, since it is never certain who has the upper hand. One of the strategies that might be employed in seduction is to feign having the upper hand—or to feign *not* having it—in order to make the other incorrectly preempt one's next move. It is a passive game in that the goal is to make the other follow one's deceptive lead—one retreats, prompting one's opponent to fall into a trap. As Baudrillard understands seduction, one seduces with weakness, by a strategy of yielding to the other:

> [I]n a strategy (?) of seduction one draws the other into one's area of weakness, which is also his or her area of weakness. A calculated weakness, an incalculable weakness: one challenges the other to be taken in.[87]

Baudrillard gives a concrete example of the seductive strategy he has in mind through his reading of Søren Kierkegaard's "The Seducer's Diary."[88] In this story, the narrator, Johannes, attempts to seduce the young girl

Cordellia. Johannes does not approach her directly, with his intentions made explicit, but acts on behalf of a younger man who is courting her. Johannes is an unimpressive man, and does not seek to win Cordellia by selling her his own merits. Instead, he becomes a "mirror" in which she is reflected back to herself, and becomes conscious of herself. In this way, Johannes becomes indispensable to her, since he becomes the Other through which she comes to know herself. Cordellia breaks off her engagement to the young suitor, believing she wants Johannes. Having succeeded in the seduction, however, Johannes loses interest in the girl and spurns her. What interests Baudrillard in this story is the way seduction takes place as a game superior to and detached from sexual conquest; it is a game of appearances in which Johannes employs the passive strategy of "mirroring" Cordellia. Such a strategy is always a risk and always reversible, however, since Johannes can never be sure (at least not until the end) that he has correctly calculated Cordellia's intentions, or taken into account the possibility that she might be deploying a seductive strategy of her own. Johannes feigns indifference to Cordellia in order to seduce her, but she might just as easily have been feigning indifference to him.[89]

Baudrillard translates this nineteenth-century notion of seduction into a general theory of meaning that preserves the ambiguity, mystery, and challenge eliminated from the semio-linguistic theory of meaning. As a general theory of meaning, seduction is practically applied to the problem of nihilism in Baudrillard's own theoretical writings and in his treatment of contemporary politics. In his writings, seduction is translated into an approach to "doing theory." Baudrillard's texts both theorize and enact the way that seduction can be a strategy of writing and thinking. For Baudrillard, as we have seen, part of the impasse constitutive of the attempt to overcome nihilism consists in the fact that any attempt to analyze nihilism will remain within the order of representation, and hence of nihilism itself. Baudrillard sees the forms of thought that try to represent a real world, analyze its problems (such as nihilism), and propose solutions to them on the basis of this same principle of reality, as hopeless dead-ends. He argues that since the system that theory attempts to analyze has turned away from truth and reality, that is, has become simulated, then theory must change accordingly. He argues that theoretical discourse

> [...] must become excessive and sacrificial to speak about excess and sacrifice. It must become simulation if it speaks about simulation, and deploy the same strategy as its object. If it speaks about seduction,

theory must become seducer, and deploy the same stratagems. If it no longer aspires to a discourse of truth, theory must assume the form of a world from which truth has withdrawn. And thus it becomes its very object.[90]

Baudrillard's theory, therefore, does not seek to be a true representation of the real, and should not be assessed as such an attempt.[91] As an alternative strategy, Baudrillard takes the radical (and perhaps desperate) measure of playing a seductive game of one-upmanship with reality itself, attempting to seduce the world away from nihilism and back to the enchantment of appearances.

This seductive strategy of theory involves an ironic attempt to both capture the real in a representation, and at the same time foreground the necessary difference between representation and the real. Baudrillard describes this double strategy with the terms "doubling" and "shadowing"[92]: doubling represents or simulates the real, while shadowing accepts, accentuates, and makes obviously present in theory the differential element that must always be left out of any representation. It is this element that Baudrillard names "seduction," and the accentuation of this element in theory is what enables a strategic seduction. Baudrillard understands the objective world as seducing the subjects who try to understand it and capture it in theory through the fact that something must always be left out of theory.[93] This missing element is what drives the theorist on, to map every corner of the world, every infinitesimal part of existence.

With the idea of seductive theory, however, Baudrillard proposes that we turn this situation around and take on the seductive strategy ourselves. Theory then takes on the task of reproducing the world, but leaving something out, with the hope that the world will then change to meet the demands of theory. This "leaving something out" is precisely the making-present of the differential element of theory, since this differential element is nothing in itself—simply a difference between representation and the real. Baudrillard's theory attempts to "seduce" the world by "taking it in" or "leading it on"—it is a challenge to the world to meet its seductive demands. This theoretical strategy depends upon a radical rethinking of the usual presuppositions of theory, which assume an active thinking subject and a passive objective world. Baudrillard asserts that "the world thinks us," by which he means that there are aspects of the objective world that affect subjects in such a way that subjects cannot grasp the world in its entirety.[94] Although it may seem like a radical claim, the idea that "the world thinks us" accords with some widely accepted ideas: first, that our subjectivity is constituted by extra-subjective factors of which we may not be aware, and is therefore not self-transparent, and second, that objective reality forces us to take the world into account in ways that are not freely chosen by thinking subjects. Baudrillard effectively argues that, both in principle and in fact, thinking subjects cannot master the world with their thought. He takes Heisenberg's uncertainty principle as an example of this lack of mastery in physics, and suggests that this principle should be taken to apply equally to our attempts to understand any aspect of the world.[95] Considered in terms of mastery, the world "thinks" us just as surely as we think the world. For Baudrillard, then, thought is a *dual* relation between subjects and the objective world that may take the form of a seductive *duel*[96]: the world tries to master and change us, as we try to master and change the world.

Given his analysis of nihilism in terms of the system of simulation, Baudrillard's specific strategy is to continually "up the stakes" in the game of seduction with the system, trying to draw the system to the point where the reality principle can no longer be maintained. This strategy is enacted by proposing ever more unlikely or apparently untruthful hypotheses about the system, and challenging the system to respond. Baudrillard's writings attempt to show and foreground the way that theory produces its own (hyper) real, at the same time showing the element of seduction as essential to any representation. As such, theory partakes of and attempts to accelerate the logic of simulation to the point where it is no longer tenable. Baudrillard's aim is to show that there is no "real" in the sense implied by systems of representation, thus removing the alibi on which simulation rests.[97] His theories thus do not attempt to be accurate representations of the real in any traditional sense. At the same time, however, Baudrillard's writings attempt to seduce and provoke the "real" understood as that which exceeds theory. In order to be seductive of this "real," theory must represent or "mirror" the world: the similarities of Baudrillard's radical theory to the world (doubling) are just as essential as the ways in which it is different (shadowing). This strategy explains the apparent "untimeliness" of Baudrillard's theory, its simultaneous closeness to and difference from the world: like Nietzsche, he is attempting nothing less than a deflection of the world away from a nihilistic destiny.

On the performative level of Baudrillard's texts, seduction takes place through the gnomic and poetic nature of his prose, his penchant for undecidable hypotheses, and the resistance of his thought to being resolved into stable oppositional terms and meanings. His writings seem to be "about" the world we are familiar with, but present it in such a way that an element of ambiguity and mystery is introduced. Baudrillard asserts that his "concepts" are not concepts with a content to be proved or disproved, and nothing distinguishes them from mere assertions.[98] However, they are intended to have a performative function, to *enact* what they signify, and to constitute an event in the universe they describe.[99] Baudrillard gives to thought and theory a practical role, and the practice of theory itself is the primary dimension of his response to nihilism. The aim of such practices is to seduce the world away from or beyond simulation by showing the falsity of the reality principle, and the ineluctability of seduction as a deeper principle of meaning. Baudrillard gives radical thought a powerful role as a form of resistance to the attempted hegemony of the rational order of meaning:

> Thought must play a catastrophic role, must itself be an element of catastrophe, of provocation, in a world that wants absolutely to cleanse everything, to exterminate death and negativity.[100]

In chapter three, we saw that Baudrillard identifies technology (especially information technology and the mass media) and capitalism as two of the leading manifestations of nihilism in postmodernity. His analyses of technology and capitalism are not followed up with prescriptions for direct action in or on such systems, however, and we must understand Baudrillard as suggesting that radical thought and theory are the most efficacious ways of responding to all manifestations of nihilism in postmodernity. While we cannot, therefore, detail specific strategies for responding to these forms of nihilism, we may clarify the ways in which Baudrillard theorizes capitalism and technology, noting that such theorizations are directed towards accomplishing a reversal in the nihilistic tendencies of these cultural forms.

As we have seen, for Baudrillard, many contemporary developments in technology are manifestations of simulation. In *Seduction*, this simulation is presented as the eradication of seduction itself, and given expression in the well-known example of high fidelity stereophonic and quadraphonic music (an example also given in "The Year 2000 Will Not Take Place" and elsewhere[101]). In this example, Baudrillard shows how technology can function as a sophisticated means of representation, which is so refined that representation itself reaches a "vanishing point."[102] At this point, the thing represented—music, in this example—ceases to exist as such, and becomes hyperreal. In quadrophonics, Baudrillard claims, one no longer *hears* music, since the minimal distance required to constitute the charm of musical sound is abolished. With this abolition, sound no longer seduces us, and ceases to be music.[103]

Because of the necessary relation between simulation and seduction, however, technology is ambiguous. On the one hand, technology is a form of *reductive nihilism* contributing to the simulation of the world. On the other hand, there is a principle of reversibility in the essence of technology itself, whereby a critical reversal in simulation might be effectuated. In the context of Baudrillard's work on seduction, such a critical reversal would mean making explicit the necessary *distance* between representation and the real that simulation tries to abolish. In some of his later writings, Baudrillard explores the hypothesis that technological development might lead to an undermining of the reality principle and the collapse of simulation. This possibility is already indicated in *Seduction*, where Baudrillard alludes to "the brutal dis-simulation that would occur should the reality of a radical loss of meaning become too evident."[104] In perfecting representation, technology itself calls attention to the fact that what is represented is not in fact real, but illusory. This possibility is evident in the new technologies that seem to explicitly pass beyond the representation of the real to the construction of the hyperreal: virtual reality, computer graphics, and perhaps the quadraphonic sound of Baudrillard's previous example, which creates an experience of sound never possible in "reality." Baudrillard sees in this vision of the world as illusory the possibility of a new form of meaning with the potential to subvert the reductions of simulation, and to revive the qualities associated with symbolic exchange and seduction: ambiguity, reversibility, and challenge. Because of the ambivalent relation between simulation and seduction, however, Baudrillard believes the fate of technology is undecidable:

> At the stage we are at, we do not know whether technology, having reached a point of extreme sophistication, will liberate us from technology itself—the optimistic viewpoint—or whether in fact we are heading for catastrophe.[105]

The pessimistic hypothesis is well-illustrated in Baudrillard's brief reflections on the fate of seduction in the capitalist system. In *Seduction*, he sees a dis-intensified, "cold" or "ludic" seduction as the dynamic force that underlies capitalist exchange. He writes that

> [w]ith a vague collusion between supply and demand, *seduction becomes nothing more than an exchange value*, serving the circulation of

exchanges and the lubrication of social relations. What remains of the enchantment of that labyrinthine structure within which one could lose oneself?[106]

In effect, "cold" seduction is seduction reduced to that distance that is required for simulated systems to operate. Baudrillard understands this form of seduction as involving a maximal diffusion throughout the system and a minimal intensity of seductive effects. Cold seduction operates according to the same principle of reversibility and one-upmanship accorded to seduction in general, but is reduced to the function of lubricating the economic and social relations that ensure the smooth operation of the capitalist system. Baudrillard calls this form of seduction "ludic," since it is seduction reduced to the playfulness of the capitalist system in which nothing is really at stake (since all moves in the economic game consolidate the strength of the system of exchange itself). The form of seduction that Baudrillard privileges operates according to the same logic as the "cold" or "ludic" form, but differs in so far as there are real stakes, and the genuine possibility of the destabilization of existing relations. The two forms of seduction are not distinguished by type, then, but by intensity, and their relative relations to the capitalist system. Again, Baudrillard offers no prescriptions of direct intervention in the capitalist system in order to "up the stakes," but rather ends his discussion of capitalism and cold seduction (and ends the book *Seduction* itself) with undecidable hypotheses:

> Is this to be seduction's destiny? Or can we oppose this involutional fate, and lay a wager on *seduction as destiny*? Production as destiny, or seduction as destiny? Against the deep structures and their truth, appearances and their destiny? Be that as it may, we are living today in non-sense, and if simulation is its disenchanted form, seduction is its enchanted form.[107]

Despite this undecidability, the concept of seduction allows Baudrillard to advance a response to nihilism that avoids the impasse of the attempt to directly overcome it. Baudrillard recognizes this impasse in his understanding of the system of simulation as able to incorporate any direct opposition, and in his understanding of analyses of nihilism as themselves implicated in the problem they attempt to identify and confront. Seduction, with its "differential" relation to simulation, allows Baudrillard to posit a principle of existentially fulfilling meaning that is ineradicable by simulation, and which simulation in fact presupposes. The alternative to the nihilism of simulation is therefore not to be sought in opposition to the system, but in possibilities harbored by the system itself. Moreover, seduction provides a model of passive political action for a restoration of such meaning: passive, insofar as it offers a way to work in and through simulation (rather than actively opposing it), and political insofar as it works on the constitution of meaning in systems of communication, hence (in Lyotard's formulation) directly impinging on the social bond. While Baudrillard's strategies are confined to the realm of radical thought and writing, his reconfiguration of the relation between theory and the real gives theory a degree of agency to affect the real itself. Taking these points on board, we must conclude that Baudrillard is engaged in a far more positive project than most commentators are willing to allow. Nevertheless, his line of reasoning draws him to persistent equivocation about the possibility of an effective response to nihilism. In contrast to Lyotard, Baudrillard does not see the world as one in which nihilism and life-affirmation inevitably co-exist, and where the task of responding to nihilism consists in maximizing life-affirmative forces. Although he posits a similar duplicitous relation between simulation and seduction as Lyotard does between libidinal energies and *dispositifs*, for Baudrillard these opposing tendencies are locked in a battle for supremacy, the ultimate outcome of which is currently undecidable.

Vattimo: Verwindung

A version of the logic of difference is expressed in Vattimo's alternative to overcoming: *Verwindung*.[108] *Verwindung* acts as a criterion of discrimination that allows a negative assessment to be made of metaphysics, without opposing metaphysics entirely and without setting up an independent alternative. Rather, *Verwindung* suggests a difference *within* metaphysics, whereby metaphysics may be "twisted" towards an alternative mode of being that is free from its most negatively nihilistic aspects. For Vattimo, the *Verwindung* of metaphysics means to continue to think in metaphysical categories, but bereft of their ahistorical pretension to objective and universal truth. *Verwindung* functions to preserve ontological difference because it enables us to resist the temptation to oppose metaphysics with a new theory of Being, a move that Vattimo argues would inevitably construe Being metaphysically by thinking it as an entity (a new category, opposed to all the old metaphysical categories, but ultimately on the same ontological level). Instead of setting up a new theory of Being, *Verwindung* allows a thinking of Being nihilistically, as the groundlessness or foundationlessness *of metaphysics*.

Moreover, we may see a unilateral distinction between the categories of "metaphysics" and (positive) "nihilism"[109] in Vattimo's philosophy of weak thought: metaphysics opposes itself to nihilism, while nihilism differs from (in the sense of being a *Verwindung* of) metaphysics. Metaphysics opposes nihilism insofar as it attempts to be foundational; nihilism as Vattimo conceives it differs from but does not oppose metaphysics because it operates within metaphysical conceptual and linguistic structures, but undermines their foundational pretensions. Furthermore, *Verwindung* may be understood as a principle of difference in Vattimo's work insofar as it functions to preserve the *ontological difference*. It is this ontological form of difference—the difference between Being and beings—that metaphysics forgets. Vattimo's contention is that only the nihilistic understanding of Being as a foundationless nothingness allows the ontological difference to be preserved, since it clearly distinguishes Being from positively existing beings (entities). The *Verwindung* of metaphysics thus recalls the ontological difference within metaphysics by insisting on its non-foundational character. This lack of foundation in metaphysics is a way of thinking Being, and so responds to the problem of metaphysics as Heidegger frames it (that is, as the *forgetting* of Being). *Verwindung* may thus be seen as a "logic of difference" that enables Vattimo to negotiate the aporiae of trying to overcome (negative or metaphysical) nihilism, offering thought the possibility of a critical position *within* the metaphysical tradition, *differing* from it rather than *opposing* it.

The themes of weakness and passivity are apparent in Vattimo's response to metaphysics, as the term "weak thought" clearly suggests. The term "weak" (*debole*) in weak thought is linked to the recognition of the impossibility of overcoming metaphysics, and is an expression of the theme of "affirmative weakness" common to postmodern approaches to this problem. Giovanna Borradori explains that

> [...] the Italian speculation around the notion of "weakness" has an interesting specificity: its effort to make operative, in a constitutive function, the self-awareness of the impossibility of a "definitive farewell" to reason, of the impossibility of a radical overcoming of that nexus between rationality and hegemony upon which, following Nietzsche and perhaps Marx as well, the whole of western metaphysics is based.[110]

Weakness, then, is the attempt to "depotentiate" the metaphysical rationality of modernity. To think "weakly" means to weaken the claims of rationality to apodictic truth and secure foundation. In their preface to *Il pensiero debole*, Vattimo and Pier-Aldo Rovatti write that rationality must "shed its power, give ground, not be afraid to retreat to what is assumed to be a region of darkness, not remain paralyzed by the loss of the luminous, unique and stable Cartesian point of reference."[111] This retreat of rationality is the move that allows a "twisting free" from metaphysics, where metaphysics might be understood as "strong" thought insofar as it makes strong truth-claims and posits stable and enduring structures of Being.

Vattimo affirms weakness because he sees the weakening of metaphysical thought as the only alternative once it is recognized that a definitive step beyond metaphysics is impossible. Moreover, the strategy of *Verwindung* is affirmative in moving towards a positive conception of nihilism that responds to the political and ethical problems that Vattimo believes are associated with metaphysical thought. Vattimo's weak thought takes on an ethical and political character in the light of some of his statements on contemporary politics and on the ethics of interpretation. As we have seen, Vattimo asserts that a primary motivation of weak thought and the positive nihilism he advocates is the reduction of violence, where violence is understood as "the peremptory affirmation by an authority that forbids further interrogation, breaks down dialogue, and imposes silence."[112] For Vattimo, metaphysics is a violent form of thought because it recognizes as legitimate only those voices that refer their claims to what is considered to be a universal foundation for thought (whatever form this foundation takes). Voices that do not accept the same metaphysical premises, or whose claims cannot be seen to rest on the foundation metaphysical thought demands, are silenced. Weak thought responds to an ethical demand in that it reduces violence by reducing all truth-claims to the level of competing interpretations, and asserts the necessity of respecting all interlocutors who take part in the dialogical constitution of reality.

Weak thought can be understood as advocating a "politics of passivity" in so far as it is a political intervention that works towards the emancipation of society through a weakening of the violence of metaphysics. Emancipation, as Vattimo applies the term, refers to a free play of interpretations where no discourse has an overriding authority to silence other discourses. The politics of weak thought is passive insofar as the violence of metaphysics is not confronted directly with force, but undermined or weakened from within through the strategy of *Verwindung*. The interpretive philosophical activity of weak thought itself can be understood as politically efficacious insofar as it is directed towards a reduction of the violence of metaphysics. Vattimo's "weak" reconstruction of rationality, and the methods of textual interpretation he employs, can be understood as passive political engagements that contribute towards reconfiguring the horizons of the world. While Marx famously proclaimed that "[t]he philosophers have only *interpreted* the world, in various ways; the point is to *change* it,"[113] for Vattimo these activities are not necessarily distinct: interpretation can change the world, because the world is itself constituted by interpretations. Vattimo argues that in the era of nihilism, philosophy is intrinsically political, insofar as it 'is practiced as an interpretation of the epoch, a giving-form to widely felt sentiments about the meaning of being alive in a certain society and in a certain historical world.'[114] Moreover, Vattimo's more "traditional" political philosophy argues for a post-Marxist critique of capitalism and the adoption of democratic socialist principles as a way of weakening violence in postmodern societies. I will consider each of these strategies, which are Vattimo's "passive" ways of responding to the negative nihilism of metaphysics, in turn.

Unlike Lyotard and Baudrillard, Vattimo does not depart from a traditional academic style of writing. Rather, his attempt to weaken metaphysics employs a new style of argumentation that in turn rests on a new, "weaker" understanding of reason.[115] Weak thought does not attempt to latch onto ahistorical, objective structures of Being in order to determine the truth or falsity of its propositions according to whether or not they correspond with those structures. Instead, thinking gains its direction from its very positioning in the historical "thrownness," or "destining," in which it finds itself. Being is the historical transmission from the past of those thoughts and lived experiences that have shaped the horizons of the "opening" that constitutes the contemporary era. Rationality, for Vattimo, needs to be reconstructed in line with this "weak" ontology. Reason can no longer consist in deductive logic or other strong models of thought that consist in giving proofs or establishing facts. The concept of rationality today, Vattimo argues, can only be rigorously understood as *continuity*, a thinking that links itself with the past.

This weakened notion of rationality does not make argument obsolete, if we understand argument in a general sense as giving *publicly accessible reasons* for thinking or preferring one thing over another. The criteria used in interpreting and arguing for interpretations will not be an idea of their groundedness in fact, however, but the historical process of the transmission of messages that shows why it is currently more plausible to think one thing rather than another. An argument against belief in the existence of God, for example, might refer to the works of Nietzsche, Marx, and Darwin as providing alternative explanatory structures that weaken the reasons for believing in God, rather than analyzing the logical cogency of St. Anselm's ontological proof. Summarizing these points, Vattimo writes:

> Continuity seems to be the only meaning of rationality in the epoch of nihilism…For metaphysics it was a case of establishing itself on the ultimate and certain basis of primary foundations; for nihilistic hermeneutics it is a case of arguing in such a way that each new interpretation enters into dialogue with those that came before and does not constitute an incomprehensible dia-'logical' leap.[116]

Vattimo argues that since the historical opening that we find ourselves in is nihilistic—that is, we are in the age of the decline of Being—nihilism itself becomes the criterion by which we may make interpretive judgments and mount arguments. That is, the interpretation of the contemporary age as nihilistic gives us a point of reference for guiding the choice of interpretive positions. Broadly speaking, this means that one who follows Vattimo's thinking will privilege groundlessness and interpretation over strong metaphysical theses purporting to be well grounded and to establish objective truths.[117]

In Vattimo's work the *Verwindung* of metaphysics takes place through the *An-Denken* of the history of philosophy. As we have seen earlier, *An-Denken*—which may be roughly translated as "recollection"—is another term Vattimo takes from Heidegger and makes central to his own thought. It is a form of remembering that does not seek to preserve what is remembered in its original form, but seeks to understand it in terms of its meaning for the present.[118] As such, the *An-Denken* of philosophy recalls figures and ideas in the history of philosophy and seeks to understand their relevance in the context of the current situation. In addition to its indebtedness to Heidegger, Vattimo's strategy of recollection has roots in his work on the problem of historicism in Nietzsche. In several essays written in the 1960s, Vattimo charts the way that Nietzsche criticizes traditional philology for its excessively "static" conception of historical facts, in which such facts are taken to be objective and unchanging. Nietzsche argues that an excess of this kind of historical knowledge burdens the present, and undermines the creativity and health of current culture. In response to this "historical malady," Nietzsche argues that historical knowledge must been seen not as a matter of fact, but of interpretation, and that history should always be interpreted in relation to the needs of the living present.[119]

Vattimo's strategy of recollection may furthermore be understood as a corollary of his rejection of historical progress. Once philosophy relinquishes its ties to the modernist ideal of the "original" and understands itself as a thinking of Being, he argues, the form it should take is a thinking-through of the historical trans-mission of interpretations. Philosophy in the age of accomplished nihilism, then, has the task of recollecting and rethinking the history of philosophy. This recollection constitutes a *Verwindung* of metaphysics because it removes the most metaphysical aspect of philosophy: its tendency to make foundational claims in the form of positing permanent, ahistorical structures of existence. *An-Denken*, as a critical recollection of the history of philosophy, seeks to historicize and relativize metaphysical claims, but is saved from absolute historical relativism by granting our current perspective (that is, the nihilistic one) interpretive privilege.

Heidegger's studies of figures in the history of philosophy provide some practical examples of *An-Denken*, but Vattimo's conception of philosophy as recollection is best exemplified in his own writings. Vattimo often employs deliberate "distortions" of ideas, and interpretations of philosophical texts other than those explicitly endorsed by their authors, in the process of drawing out what he sees as relevant to contemporary contexts and problems. A prime example of this methodological distortion is Vattimo's "left" reading of Heidegger, a reading that enables him to position Heidegger *with* Nietzsche rather than against him and to develop a theory of the contemporary state of Being as an accomplished nihilism. Another clear example of distortion employed in the *An-Denken* of philosophy is in Vattimo's essay "Art and Oscillation," in which Heidegger's concept of "strife" and Walter Benjamin's concept of "shock" are deliberately conflated, producing Vattimo's own concept of "oscillation," which he presents as a theory of the current state of art and aesthetics.[120] For Vattimo, then, philosophy as *An-Denken* is an enactment of completed nihilism—an affirmative alternative to the "negative" nihilism of metaphysics—through a *Verwindung* of metaphysics by a "distorted" reading of the history of philosophy undertaken in order to illuminate the present. Weak thought thus attempts to find a way out of (negative, metaphysical) nihilism by turning back to the history of philosophy and thinking it through again, and in so doing weakening the claims of metaphysics by historicizing those claims. In effect, weak thought remains inside metaphysics by employing the same language and concepts, but reduces its violence by undermining its claims to foundational authority. The interpretive textual practices of weak thought can therefore be seen as political acts that respond "passively" to the nihilism of metaphysics, by developing a form of philosophical thinking that reduces the violence associated with the metaphysical tradition.

Vattimo's engagement with the political extends beyond the implications that may be drawn from the interpretive textual practices of weak thought, however, to more conventional engagements, both in his active career as a politician,[121] and in his writings on political philosophy. In his political writings, Vattimo draws out the implications of weak thought for the political realities of the current situation, and speculates on the ideal forms of government and the organization of society.[122] As we saw earlier, he identifies fundamentalism and capitalism ("supermarket culture") as the two main expressions of the violence of metaphysics in the contemporary world, and his political philosophy is directed towards a reduction of the violence of these two metaphysical trends. Vattimo's political philosophy may be broadly characterized as post-Marxist, insofar as he rejects many of the tenets of traditional Marxism, but insists on the continued necessity of a critical relation to capitalism and the ideology of the Right. One aspect of Marxist thought he rejects is violent revolution as a means to emancipation.[123] In answer to an interviewer's question, "[i]s it right to introduce a better order through force?" Vattimo alludes to "the horrors produced by the grand revolutionary movements, by armed and unarmed prophets," and asserts that "a respect for what lives and has lived is the only 'better' we recognize, and this excludes the use of force."[124]

Furthermore, Vattimo rejects the "traditional" Marxist critique of capital on the grounds that it posits "natural" categories and values that act as a foundation for this critique, thus remaining strongly metaphysical. As Jacques Derrida and others have noted, Marx's work relies on metaphysical categories such as "nature," "man," and "use value" and accords them an essential purity understood as prior to the alienation of man and the destruction of use value by exchange value with the inauguration of capitalism.[125] Rather, Vattimo argues that the ideas of nature and essence are themselves the characteristic features of ideology, and argues that "...the Left cannot leave aside the critique of ideology, which warns against the metaphysical foundations of duties and rights based on notions such as nature, essence, etc."[126] He further insists that the appeal to natural rights has become a characteristic of the political Right, and any appeal by the Left to such rights simply acts to reinforce the metaphysical ideology on which the Right, with its defense of capitalism, rests. Ideology critique, then, must find an alternative to the traditional Marxist form if it is to meet this demand.

Against the metaphysical categories implied by the discourse of *natural* rights, Vattimo argues for a conception of rights that is historically contingent and grounded only in the tradition of the ideas that have shaped the contemporary West. In light of this tradition, he argues that "we have more than enough reasons to take equality, which is unthinkable without solidarity and liberty, as an overriding value."[127] Vattimo expands on this by arguing that the ultimate source of equality is what he calls "projectuality," a right and duty every individual has to take control of their situation in the world through projects.[128] According to Vattimo, "there is no true equality unless all people have the chance to alter their own situations in the world through projects that will need consensus and collaboration if they are to be effectively realised."[129] Projectuality may be understood as a more practical, action-oriented conception of the right of all to take part in the dialogical constitution of reality that Vattimo argues for elsewhere. In Vattimo's political philosophy, then, projectuality and the right to have a voice are taken as the most basic rights of citizens in postmodern society. On this model, ideology critique is directed against metaphysical principles not because they conceal a pre-existing truth, or because they offend against some natural right, but because they do violence to the rights that individuals have been accorded in the Western tradition. While these rights are recognized as historically contingent, they are nevertheless upheld as valuable and defensible according to the criteria of weak thought.

Fundamentalisms, in particular religious fundamentalisms, are relatively unambiguous cases of social trends that display the violence of metaphysics: by insisting on a single framework for truth, they delegitimize the alternative voices and projects of individuals and groups. The politics of weak thought seeks to undermine fundamentalisms of all kinds by dissolving their claims to exclusive and universal truth, opening up the social arena to a multiplicity of legitimate voices and perspectives. Capitalism, however, is a more complex case of metaphysical violence. As we have seen, Vattimo argues that contemporary capitalism ("supermarket culture") is a nihilistic pluralism without the guiding thread of the reduction of violence.[130] Capitalism manifests the nihilistic disregard for anything essential or sacred (and hence assumed to be foundational) that Vattimo endorses, but displays its own metaphysical violence in subjecting everything to the capitalist doctrine of profit and development at any cost. Like Lyotard and Baudrillard, Vattimo acknowledges that the capitalist system of political economy has a certain positive value, but seeks to respond to its significant negative effects. In an essay entitled "Globalization and the Relevance of Socialism,"[131] these negative effects are identified as a globalised "colonization" of the political and social spheres by the economic sphere: the globalization of capitalist political economy is reducing all values to economic value. In the case of capitalism, we may understand economic value—or "development at any cost," as Vattimo says—as a foundational principle that does violence to alternative political and social values.

From this basic framework, consisting of a nihilistic ontology of the current situation, the idea of non-natural rights, and a critical stance towards the violence of fundamentalism and capitalism, Vattimo draws a variety of political implications. Leaving aside his specific policies on various social issues,[132] I will restrict my attention here to his prescriptions for large-scale political organization. As mentioned earlier, Vattimo is a democratic socialist, and advocates both democracy and socialism as forms of political organization that reduce violence. He further argues for a federated global system of governance to counter the violence of economic globalization. In so far as Vattimo's macropolitical prescriptions and engagements are primarily concerned with the reduction of violence rather than imposing a utopian social order through force, his macropolitics may also be considered to have a "passive" or "weak" character, and to compliment his philosophical concerns with weak ontology and thought. In the essay "Hermeneutics and Democracy," Vattimo links the two ideas announced in the title on the grounds that they share a common conception of the world as a conflict of interpretations. He writes that "hermeneutics most faithfully reflects the pluralism of modern society that is best expressed, in the political realm, through democracy."[133] For Vattimo, democracy is the form of political representation most consistent with his nihilistic ontology, since it does not base government on foundational values or a single perspective assumed to be an exclusive truth. In democracy—at least in its ideal form—government is the outcome of, and must take into account, the social fabric of multiple, competing interpretations.

Vattimo concedes, however, that anti-foundationalism and the view of the world as a conflict of interpretations are perfectly consistent with contemporary capitalism[134]; democracy alone is therefore not sufficient for reducing the violence entailed in capitalist development. The direction in which Vattimo believes a political resistance to capitalism should advance is most clearly developed in the afore-mentioned essay, "Globalization and the Relevance of Socialism." Here he argues that 'the realm of economics, of survival, is no more than a violent battlefield, unless there is mediation at a different level, the level of the political.'[135] The form of political organization he believes can accomplish this mediation, beyond simple democracy, is socialism. Vattimo develops a particular understanding of socialism that has its starting point in Hannah Arendt's affirmation of an "ethical" separation of politics from the sphere of private interests. He then extends this affirmation in an argument for the need to restore the independence of the political sphere from the economic. Restored to independent functioning, Vattimo argues, the relations between these three spheres (social, political, and economic) may be mediated in such a way as to ameliorate the violent imposition of the economic sphere on the other two. The function of the *political* sphere, for Vattimo, once it is set free from the influence of the *economic*, should be to uphold *social* interests and protect them from economic influences. This, he argues, is the central meaning of socialism today. He writes:

> [T]oday we are able to perceive the 'truth' of socialism, above all as a program for setting politics free of the laws of economics, especially the laws of the globalised economy, which, as we now see on every side, bring with them growing limits to freedom, to recognition, to the conditions for a 'good life.'[136]

For Vattimo, this sphere of social interests must be protected against the encroachment of economics by the State (the sphere of politics). On Vattimo's account, the State ought not have a homogenizing function, but rather it should function to protect individuals and communities from the potentially homogenizing effects of economics: "'socialism' in the sense in which I have used the term here has to mean a conception of the state as guarantor of the multiplicity of the communities that compose it..."[137] In addition to the anti-foundational and pluralist orientation of democracy, then, Vattimo advocates socialism, in this specific sense, as providing the "guiding thread of the reduction of violence" that is essential to his nihilistic philosophy. Together, democracy and socialism are forms of political organization that combat the violent tendencies of both fundamentalism and capitalism. As Vattimo's reflections concerning the conditions for the good life in the quote above suggest, his concern with responding to the negative, metaphysical nihilism prevalent in postmodernity is ultimately aimed at enriching the existential possibilities of life. As such, his political philosophy responds to the same demands announced in Nietzsche's theory of nihilism and engaged by all the thinkers we have examined here.

In summary, Vattimo responds to the "negative" nihilism of metaphysics by following a course marked out by the concept of *Verwindung*. Rather than opposing or seeking to overcome metaphysics—a move that mires us all the more firmly in metaphysics—the *Verwindung* of metaphysics allows a "twisting free" from the foundational claims of the metaphysical tradition. *Verwindung* is thus a version of the "logic of difference" that allows Vattimo to circumvent the aporia of seeking to overcome metaphysics through direct opposition. Vattimo's "weak thought" provides criteria for judgment; metaphysics is condemned as violent and "positive" nihilism is privileged. However, there is no strict separation and no opposition between these terms, and thus weak thought avoids the return of "negative, metaphysical" nihilism through oppositional negation. Weak thought also engages a number of passive political strategies against "metaphysical" nihilism: it undermines metaphysics through interpretive textual practices, and advocates democratic socialism as a form of political organization that reduces the violence of fundamentalism and capitalism. As such, although weak thought chooses positions and strategies that are "passive," it is actively engaged, on a number of levels, in the project of undermining "metaphysical" nihilism and completing "positive" nihilism in postmodernity.

We began this chapter by situating the postmodern approach in responding to nihilism as one that attempts to *overcome the desire to overcome* nihilism (Critchley's formulation), and which attempts to *find a way to live with* nihilism (Caygill's formulation), while nevertheless attempting to find *new forms of resistance* to nihilism. We have now seen how specific attempts to respond to nihilism in the works of Lyotard, Baudrillard, and Vattimo develop these themes. Despite their differences, the responses to nihilism offered by the three postmodernists considered here cohere in the direction of attempting to find an alternative to "overcoming." As distinct from attempts to overcome nihilism, I wish to suggest that these responses may be described as attempts to *negotiate* nihilism, in a double sense of this term. First, in the sense of negotiation as the avoidance of obstacles in navigating a terrain, these postmodern responses to nihilism negotiate around the aporia of the attempt to oppose and overcome the problem by developing concepts that embody a logic of difference and by enacting a politics of passivity. Second, in the sense of negotiation as an economic transaction, the postmodern responses attempt to intervene in the flows and exchanges of life-affirmative and nihilistic forces in contemporary culture. The attempt to negotiate nihilism, in this second sense, may be understood as a response to the postmodern situation, which refuses to passively accept meaninglessness despite the acknowledged impossibility and undesirability of instituting a new foundation for meaning that would eradicate nihilism once and for all. In this sense, negotiating nihilism means engaging in a political endeavor to *increase* ways of affirming the meaning and value of life, and to *decrease* the nihilistic cultural trends that devalue life.

The differences in the responses to nihilism outlined above may be understood, in part, as stemming from the fact that each postmodernist advocates different economic maneuvers in order to achieve a maximization of life-affirmation. In Lyotard's libidinal economy, there is no opposition between affirmation and nihilism, but a continuous scale of gradation between the affirmative expression of life and its nihilistic repression (between libidinal intensities and the great Zero). Lyotard's libidinal philosophy accepts an inevitable and necessary admixture of affirmation and nihilism, and attempts to maximize affirmation through allowing the intense expression of energy in and through structures. Baudrillard understands nihilism on a different economic model, proposing a dual antagonism between nihilism and the affirmative forms of meaning it attempts to destroy. While these antagonistic terms are, for Baudrillard, mutually implicated—and the nihilism of simulation and transfinitude therefore cannot simply be opposed—one term can take precedence over the other through an economy of "reversal." Baudrillard's response to the nihilism dominating the postmodern scene is therefore directed towards those subtle, seductive strategies that might bring about such a reversal. Vattimo employs a different economic maneuver yet again, attempting to decrease the violent traits of metaphysics by retaining its concepts and its general structures, but "ungrounding" them, metaphorically punching the bottom out of them from within.[138]

There are thus striking differences between each of the postmodern responses to nihilism discussed above, and the respective merits and demerits of each approach could certainly be compared and debated at length.[139] However, it is not my intention here to engage in such a debate. Rather, my aim is to outline and assess the general orientation of these postmodern responses to nihilism, understanding all as representative of a uniquely postmodern approach to the problem. Thus far, I have outlined the strategies these postmodern thinkers offer as positive responses to nihilism. In the final section of this chapter, I turn to the task of assessing the value of these strategies for responding to the problem of nihilism in postmodernity.

Facing the abyss: the problem of contingency

The task of assessing the merits of postmodern responses to nihilism is subject to certain methodological difficulties. These difficulties have already been discussed in the Introduction, but a brief reiteration will serve to clarify my approach here. The most significant of these difficulties is that an assessment of the postmodern responses cannot be made by treating them as "theories" that may or may not meet the demands of "reality": both postmodern theory and the discourse of nihilism question the independence of these categories. Such an approach would thus fail to understand the postmodern responses on their own terms, and render the assessment inaccurate.[140] In the Introduction, I indicated that I would attenuate this difficulty by following Vattimo's suggestion of viewing the discourse that *analyses* nihilism as itself a manifestation *of* nihilism. Continuing with this procedure, the postmodern responses to nihilism may be assessed according to the needs that the theories of nihilism themselves express—in other words, according to how well they answer the problems, and fulfill the tasks, they set for themselves.

Nihilism might be understood in Wittgensteinian terms as a "family resemblance" concept that displays a certain continuity through all the forms it has taken from Nietzsche onwards, but without these forms necessarily having a single dominant, common feature.[141] These changing theories of nihilism both develop the difficult logic of Nietzsche's formulation, and attempt to respond to changing cultural conditions and philosophical trends. In the preceding analysis, I have outlined the way in which the internal logic of nihilism makes the possibility of overcoming it highly problematic, how some of the early responses fall prey to this aporetic logic, and how postmodern responses to nihilism negotiate this aporia. In this respect, we may see the postmodern responses to nihilism succeeding where some earlier responses fail. I now wish to argue, however, that there are aspects of the problem of nihilism that are announced by Nietzsche, and taken up by later contributors to the discourse of nihilism—including the postmodernists themselves—which the postmodern responses outlined above do not adequately address.

These deficiencies in the postmodern responses can be discerned by recalling the distinction between "reductive" and "abyssal" nihilism outlined in the Introduction, and to which I have made intermittent reference throughout. To reiterate, "reductive nihilism" is the term I have used to indicate the negation of the value of existence that follows from processes of abstraction and rationalization. These processes reduce thought and practice to a point where they cease to constitute or connect with existentially meaningful forms of life. "Abyssal nihilism," on the other hand, indicates the collapse of structures of meaning and criteria of valuation that result in a debilitating loss of the ability to understand life in a meaningful context, or to choose meaningfully between various possibilities of existence. This second form of nihilism expresses the problem of the sheer *contingency* of existence, meaning that life appears to have no justification and is devoid of any necessity concerning reasons, values, or norms.

We have encountered forms of reductive nihilism in Heidegger's concept of *Ge-stell*, in the analysis of semiology/semiotics developed by both Lyotard and Baudrillard, and in Vattimo's interpretation of metaphysics as an essentially violent form of thought. We have encountered abyssal nihilism, on the other hand, in Nietzsche's analysis of the death of God, Sartre's theory of the radical contingency of existence, Heidegger's concern with the groundlessness that results from the oblivion of Being, and Baudrillard's theory of the viral dispersion of value in transfinite cultural forms. Although the postmodernists considered here develop theories of nihilism that take into account both reductive and abyssal forms, I wish to argue that their responses to nihilism are asymmetrically skewed towards undoing the tendencies of *reductive* nihilism in contemporary life and thought.

This emphasis on responding to reductive nihilism, I shall argue, is made at the expense of an adequate response to abyssal nihilism (the problem of contingency). This then indicates a significant deficiency in postmodern responses to nihilism, since the contingency associated with social fragmentation is arguably a key dimension of nihilism in postmodernity. The Nietzschean and Heideggerian analyses of social disintegration and loss of shared meanings have not been disputed by the theorists of postmodernity examined here. Rather, although the implications thinkers such as Vattimo and Lyotard draw from this theme have changed, the tendency to view contemporary society as marked by disintegration is an integral aspect of the theory of postmodernity. Indeed, the theme of the contingency of contemporary life stemming from social disintegration and disorientation may be considered part of the general postmodern "imaginary." This theme is expressed not only by the theorists I have concentrated on here, but also by various other leading theorists of postmodernity.[142]

Zygmunt Bauman and Fredric Jameson are two such prominent theorists of postmodernity; both emphasize a pervasive disorientation and sense of contingency in contemporary culture. According to Bauman, postmodernity is characterized by the collapse of faith in the modern rationalist interpretations of the world. This collapse leaves social subjects to face the contingency of existence without support or protection. Awakening from the modernist dream, the contemporary individual gains a feeling of radical freedom, an unsettling and vertiginous feeling that "anything goes." For Bauman, the postmodern condition "means the exhilarating freedom to pursue anything and the mind-boggling uncertainty as to what is worth pursuing and in the name of what one should pursue it."[143]

Jameson demonstrates a concern with the contingency of the postmodern condition in his account of the generalized disorientation that he believes is the product of developments in both the built environment and the virtual space of globalised communication networks. In his words:

> [P]ostmodern hyperspace...has finally succeeded in transcending the capacities of the individual human body to locate itself, to organize its immediate surroundings perceptually, and cognitively to map its position in a mappable external world. It may now be suggested that this alarming disjunction point between the body and its built environment—which is to the initial bewilderment of the older modernism as the velocities of spacecraft to those of the automobile—can itself stand as the symbol and analogon of that even sharper dilemma which is the incapacity of our minds, at least at present, to map the great global multinational and decentered communicational network in which we find ourselves caught as individual subjects.[144]

These spatial disorientations, Jameson argues, undermine individuals' abilities to locate themselves in a social world. This in turn undermines their capacity to act, since they are lacking the set of needs and demands that such a world provides, and which would function as a framework to guide meaningful choice and action.[145] For both Bauman and Jameson, the primary challenge of postmodernity is for disoriented social subjects to constitute and orient themselves in the face of an increasingly confusing world, in which every value and every choice appears to be absolutely contingent. Given this emphasis on the existential problem of contingency by a range of thinkers concerned with both nihilism and the postmodern condition, abyssal nihilism must be considered a key dimension of nihilism in postmodernity, to which an adequate response must be sought. The failure of the postmodernists who are the focus of this study to adequately respond to this issue can thus be regarded as a failure with respect to the internal demands of the discourse of postmodern nihilism.

The postmodernists considered here all recognize abyssal nihilism as a problem, yet focus their responses on reductive nihilism. The reasons for this focus are different: Baudrillard views reductive nihilism as the root cause of abyssal nihilism, and attempts to address abyssal nihilism by undermining this root cause. Lyotard and Vattimo, on the other hand, *affirm* the contingency that characterizes abyssal nihilism, seeing it as a means of undermining reductive nihilism. While these are contrary strategies, I shall argue that they both attempt to overcome *abyssal* nihilism indirectly by targeting *reductive* nihilism. This strategy may be seen as oriented by Nietzsche's project of an active overcoming of nihilism, in which nihilism will overcome itself if pushed far enough. As far as this is the case, this strategy fails to be an adequate response to abyssal nihilism because it implicitly relies on a progressive view of history, in which historical forces unfold predictably and lead to the establishment of a utopian state beyond nihilism. As such, it is incompatible with the postmodern themes of the "end of history" and the rejection of overcoming. I shall thus argue that there is a formal tension in the strategies that the postmodernists employ that prevent them from being effective responses to abyssal nihilism. Beyond this formal tension, I shall further argue, is the more serious problem that the strategy of responding directly only to reductive nihilism not only fails to mitigate abyssal nihilism, but in fact risks exacerbating it. I shall now outline the specific ways in which each of the postmodernists under consideration recognizes the problem of abyssal nihilism, yet responds directly only to reductive nihilism, before detailing the failings of this approach.

In Lyotard's formulation of the postmodern condition, the possibility of understanding this condition in terms of abyssal nihilism is implied through the link made between Nietzsche's theorization of the death of God and the postmodern loss of credulity toward metanarratives. I attempted to expand on this implication in the previous chapter through the suggestion that just as the category 'God' gives meaning to life with reference to a *transcendent* world, metanarratives give meaning to life with reference to a *future* world.

Both attempts to attribute meaning result in a devaluation of the *given* world. Lyotard recognizes the possibility of a crisis of meaning in postmodernity, writing in *The Postmodern Condition* that "[l]amenting the 'loss of meaning' in postmodernity boils down to mourning the fact that knowledge is no longer principally narrative."[146] Briefly, this loss of meaning accompanies the breakdown of metanarratives of legitimation and their replacement with scientific knowledge legitimated by the criterion of performativity (which also serves to legitimate capitalism). While the metanarratives operative in modernity provide some existential orientation (as indicated in the previous chapter), postmodernity replaces them with the criterion of performativity, which disables the connection between praxis and meaningful life. In *The Postmodern Condition* this crisis of meaning is quickly dismissed, however, with the claim that "[s]uch a reaction does not necessarily follow."[147] Indeed, Lyotard celebrates the fragmentation of contemporary culture and affirms the contingency resulting from the break-down of metanarratives because of the greater opportunity for justice he believes the postmodern condition affords. In the philosophy of Lyotard's "postmodern" period, instead of engaging with the problem of meaninglessness arising from the loss of credulity toward metanarratives, Lyotard focuses his attention on mitigating the reductive forces of the criterion of performativity, trying to reactivate ways of thinking and feeling that the criterion of performativity negates. While Lyotard admits the possibility of a problem of abyssal nihilism in postmodernity, he focuses almost exclusively on alleviating the influence of reductive nihilism.

Lyotard's libidinal philosophy likewise focuses on responding to reductive nihilism, while nevertheless recognizing abyssal nihilism as a potential problem. In the terms of this philosophy, reductive nihilism may be understood as the rigidity of structures or the excessive regulation of systems, since these economic configurations reduce the intensity of libidinal energies. Conversely, the dissolution of structures or excessive deregulation of systems may be associated with abyssal nihilism, since they lead to a "rootlessness" or "ungrounding" in which social traditions and institutions are disinvested, and can no longer provide life with a meaningful context. Lyotard's emphasis on the necessity of both force and structure, and the economic relations between them, indicates the dangers of both reductive and abyssal nihilism. In *Libidinal Economy*, Lyotard makes it clear that there is no pure expression of force, without structure. His frequent warnings against understanding him as a "liberator of desire" clearly mark this necessary relation of the two, which is the very meaning of dissimulation.[148] While libidinal force is privileged as the intense expression of life and meaning, there is an attendant valuation of structure as that within and against which force must be expressed.

This mutual necessity of force and structure suggests that an imbalance on either side may lead to nihilism. The possibility of such an imbalance may be understood in terms of the two instinctual drives, Eros and the death drive. While Lyotard complicates the functioning of these drives, so that there is no simple identity between structure and Eros, or force and the death drive,[149] we can nevertheless see that an *excess* of either Eros or the death drive leads to a nihilistic failure of the life-affirmative expression of force within structure. Excessive rigidity of structures brought about by the regulating influence of Eros results in reductive nihilism, while excessive instability of structures brought about by the deregulating influence of the death drive results in abyssal nihilism. In the attempt to affirm life, the libidinal economist therefore needs to strike a balance between these two extremes. James Williams explains:

> Under the impulse of the death drive, the system changes and in that sense dies. Under the impulse of Eros the system tends towards stasis and in that sense dies. The search for an active passivity in Lyotard (and Deleuze and Foucault) is a response to the consequent requirement to play off the two drives against one another—strategies for a life between two deaths.[150]

An excess of Eros in a system leads to ossification and stultification, whereas an excess of the death drive leads to the chaos of complete deregulation. Lyotard thus insists that force must be expressed through structure, and that an appropriate dynamic of regulation and deregulation must be in play in order for intense libidinal energy to be expressed within a system (where that system is understood as consisting in force-structure relations).

Despite this recognition of the dangers of both reductive and abyssal nihilism, Lyotard's libidinal tactics for responding to nihilism are principally concerned with breaking open or freeing-up structures in order to allow for the greater expression of libidinal force. This suggests that he is primarily concerned with responding to reductive, rather than abyssal, nihilism. In the libidinal philosophy, nihilism is predominantly understood as the great Zero; this "zero" can be seen as a reductive form of nihilism insofar as it filters and dampens libidinal energy, reducing its intensity and limiting its expression within structures. Moreover, Lyotard's view of society as modeled by the libidinal economy is one in which traditions and institutions are being dissolved by erosive forces such as capitalism, and the task of the libidinal economist is to hasten this dissolution in order to maximize the expression of libidinal intensities, while combating reductive tendencies such as the law of value. This is particularly evident in his valorization of the death drive in the essays preceding *Libidinal Economy*, where the liberation of desire is endorsed as a movement of active nihilism. In the following passage, Lyotard explains the strategy of these early essays:

> Here is a course of action: harden, worsen, accelerate decadence. Adopt the perspective of active nihilism, exceed the mere recognition—be it depressive or admiring—of the destruction of all values. Become more and more incredulous. Push decadence further still and accept, for instance, to destroy the belief in truth under all its forms.[151]

As I argued earlier, these essays are still animated by the hope of overcoming nihilism through the liberation of desire, where this liberatory force is associated with the death drive. Although the possibility of such a liberation is ruled out in *Libidinal Economy*, the techniques of active passivity this book develops for responding to nihilism retain an emphasis on freeing libidinal forces dissimulated within structures. While Lyotard's libidinal philosophy recognizes the necessity of both force and structure, then, he predominantly takes the side of force against structure. The problematic implications of this siding will be examined at the end of this chapter.

To a far greater extent than Lyotard and Vattimo, Baudrillard offers a vision of postmodernity that foregrounds the disappearance of meaning and the dissolution of the hopes and dreams of modernity. Baudrillard emphasizes the nihilism of contingency in his description of contemporary culture as a vast "orgy" in which coherent distinctions, and with them criteria for evaluation, have dissolved. The state of society in which simulation or transfinitude dominates is one in which the semio-linguistic form of meaning breaks down. For Baudrillard, the Enlightenment project that inaugurated this form of meaning has undermined itself, and postmodernity is characterized by a sense of meaninglessness associated with the pervasive confusion of cultural categories. In the name of the increased perfection of meaning in every cultural sphere, these spheres expand to include all others, effectively eroding their specific meanings. Contemporary society is therefore marked by a vast excrescence of meaning, where meaning is dispersed so far and wide that everything in effect becomes meaningless. This description of contemporary culture as suffering a loss of meaning because of a breakdown of traditional social categories and distinctions is reminiscent of the concerns of Nietzsche and Heidegger: Baudrillard therefore continues and accentuates the tradition of understanding nihilism as a loss of meaning stemming from a lack of social grounding and a confusion of cultural categories.

While Baudrillard describes the loss of meaning on a large scale, however, his analysis of the causes of this loss focuses on the smallest units of meaning. This is evident in his early semiological analysis of "the code" and his deconstruction of the sign, his analysis of simulation as the underlying logic of contemporary culture, and the later introduction of the "fractal" as that particle in the "microphysics of simulacra"[152] that explains the underlying logic of the orgy of transfinite systems. While Baudrillard gives a broad diagnosis of the contemporary state of culture, and examines the effects of particular social phenomena such as television, cinema, holograms, the Internet, and virtual reality, his arguments ultimately rest on his analyses of meaning on the micro-scale. For Baudrillard, the modernist conception of meaning is accurately modelled by the semiological sign and the presuppositions it embodies concerning the "ideal" sign, the "real" referent, and the supposed possibility of coincidence between the two. These presuppositions are evident in other forms of modernist epistemology, from the "depth model" of meaning espoused by psychoanalysis, to the pervasive conversion of the real into the hyperreal in the contemporary mass media. For Baudrillard, this model is highly reductive: it abstracts those elements of the real that can be signified and converted into a value that can be exchanged with other signs (or other "bits" of information). In particular, the semio-linguistic model of meaning reduces and negates ambiguity, reversibility, and challenge, those qualities that, on Baudrillard's analysis, allow the meaningful forms of social interaction that he theorizes as "symbolic exchange" and "seduction."

Baudrillard thus in effect sees the contingent or abyssal nihilism he diagnoses in contemporary culture as stemming from a form of reductive nihilism. The reduction of meaning to sign exchange value is what allows the proliferation and confusion of meanings by allowing units of meaning to be exchanged between different spheres of cultural value. For example, the sphere of aesthetics is liberated from a specific domain where aesthetic values are anchored in concrete social relations between artists and professional critics to the point where everyone is encouraged to make judgments concerning aesthetic value and any object can be conferred with such value. While this process takes place in the name of promoting and perfecting aesthetic values, the result is a loss of any coherent criteria for making aesthetic judgments.[153]

More technically, the reductive nihilism of the modernist theory of meaning gives rise to the nihilism of contingency because this model of meaning is inherently flawed: it posits the necessity of a simultaneous coincidence and separation between the sign and the real. As we have seen in Baudrillard's analysis of simulation, this contrary necessity causes the sign to posit its own referent, with the result that systems of meaning lose touch with the real. Since an anchorage in the real is the only thing grounding value-claims, such claims then become subject to a vulgar form of relativism: in a simulated system, there are no coherent criteria guiding the choice of one value over another. In these ways, the reductive nihilism of the modernist form of meaning leads to a nihilism of contingency where hierarchies of value collapse and a debilitating relativism ensues.

The greatest portion of Baudrillard's writings are given over to mapping the disappearance of meaning in contemporary culture. As I have argued, however, he is also concerned with the task of *responding* to contemporary nihilism. Arguably as a result of his views concerning the origin of abyssal nihilism in reductive nihilism, his responses are primarily directed towards countering this reduction. Concepts such as "symbolic exchange," "seduction," and "impossible exchange" attempt to demonstrate that the wholesale reductionism inherent in modern theories of meaning is ultimately unsuccessful. Baudrillard does not attempt to respond to abyssal nihilism directly, and argues that there is no more hope for meaning in the contemporary situation.[154] Rather, he directs his attention towards the underlying causes of meaninglessness and seeks to identify ways of reversing this situation by addressing these root causes. Since these causes are reductive in nature, Baudrillard's response to nihilism is primarily a response to reductive nihilism, despite the fact that he is also concerned with the nihilism of contingency. Moreover, this response is directed toward the "micro" level of the linguistic theory of meaning, where reductive nihilism is most clearly operative (the semio-linguistic model of the sign reduces ambiguity), rather than towards the "macro" level of social structures and institutions where abyssal nihilism manifests (cultural spheres become confused and lose meaning). A good indication of this focus is given in the following passage from *The Illusion of The End*, where Baudrillard suggests a possible counter to the nihilistic ramifications of "the end of history":

> Against this general movement, there remains the completely improbable and, no doubt, unverifiable hypothesis of a *poetic reversal*

of events, more or less the only evidence for which is the existence of the same possibility in language.[155]

As this passage indicates, Baudrillard's response to nihilism focuses on a "poetic reversal," where the meaninglessness of contemporary culture might find a new kind of meaning based on those principles that the modernist theory of meaning negates: reversibility and ambiguity. I will take up the implications of this Baudrillardian strategy for the possibility of effectively responding to nihilism towards the end of this chapter.

In contrast to Baudrillard, Vattimo views the social confusion and axiological contingency of postmodernity in a predominantly positive light. He celebrates the disorientation precipitated by exposure to multiple traditions, values, and perspectives in contemporary society.[156] Furthermore, Vattimo gives nihilism a thoroughly positive determination, celebrating the dissolution of strong structures of Being and the weakening of the powers of rationality in postmodernity. Arguably, the leading idea in Vattimo's work is that the nihilism of contingency should be positively affirmed for its ability to undermine the negative effects of reductive nihilism (as he understands it, metaphysics). Like Baudrillard, Vattimo acknowledges that abyssal nihilism arises from reductive nihilism (as, for example, with the reduction of all value to exchange value in capitalist political economy[157]), but views reduction itself as the primary cause for concern because of its association with the violence of metaphysics. Vattimo's solution to this problem is to push nihilism towards a completed state, where the reductive tendencies dissolve in the very contingency they have produced. In practice, Vattimo's central target is the reductive violence of metaphysics, which is undermined through the "ungrounding" effects of *Verwindung*. Like Lyotard, but arguably to an even greater degree, Vattimo celebrates the contingency of the postmodern scene, and responds critically primarily to reductive forms of nihilism.

Nevertheless, there are points in Vattimo's work at which he acknowledges the possible negative effects of this nihilism of contingency, and considers it as a problem in postmodernity that calls for a response. In the essay "The Wisdom of the Superman,"[158] Vattimo argues that the erosion of a stable and shared sense of reality in postmodernity means that everyone is today confronted with the need to interpret reality for themselves. In Nietzschean terms, Vattimo suggests, this means that we are all called upon to exhibit certain traits of the *Übermensch*: the ability to be inventors of our own visions of the world, and to make interpretive choices without the help of fixed norms passed down through tradition. However, the postmodern situation makes the task of being an original interpreter difficult, precisely because there are so many conflicting interpretations from which to choose, and from which to draw on in inventing a world-view of one's own. Moreover, this difficulty brings with it the danger that some people will not rise to the challenge that postmodernity presents: "Whoever does not succeed in becoming an autonomous 'interpreter,' in this sense, perishes, no longer lives like a person but like a number, a statistical item in the system of production and consumption."[159] In this manner, Vattimo acknowledges the danger that the abyssal nihilism of postmodernity represents with respect to existential meaning.

A second point at which Vattimo acknowledges the danger of abyssal nihilism is his analysis of capitalist "supermarket culture" as a nihilism that lacks the orienting task of reducing violence. Here he acknowledges that there is a kind of nihilism that does not escape the violence associated with metaphysics because, in the absence of argumentative criteria, brute force is recognised as the only means of asserting certain values over others. In capitalist society, the weak are then subject to the violence of the ideology of development at any cost, as the strong impose their self-interested values. In response, Vattimo argues that nihilism must be completed by taking the criterion of the reduction of violence as a guiding thread. This criterion draws its justification from historical, rather than deductive, premises: the nihilistic orientation in the history of philosophy, Vattimo argues, has been motivated by just such a reduction of violence. Adding a principle of the reduction of violence to nihilism can also be understood as "completing" nihilism by taking nihilism itself as a guiding value—that is, by recognizing all values as ungrounded or contingent. A completed nihilism allows no basis for coercion, and no rationale for the imposition of violence. In the case of capitalism, for example, a completed nihilism undermines the celebration of competition and the ideology of development at any cost, since these values are understood as purely contingent. In effect, Vattimo thus argues that there are problems associated with contingency understood as an "incomplete" form of nihilism, which might be attenuated by its completion.[160]

The postmodern theorists of nihilism examined here diverge strikingly in their treatments of abyssal nihilism (contingency): on the one hand, it is seen as a problem of meaninglessness in postmodernity (Baudrillard), and on the other, it is affirmed as a solution to the problem of reductive nihilism (Lyotard, Vattimo). Despite this divergence, however, for all three postmodernists, it is the reductive tendencies in postmodernity that must be addressed if nihilism is to be effectively confronted. This tendency of Lyotard, Baudrillard, and Vattimo to focus their responses to nihilism on its reductive form may be understood to be due to a number of related factors. Understanding these factors will allow an appreciation of the merits and limitations of this approach. First, in both France and Italy, Marxism and structuralist rationalism were leading trends in the academy in the nineteen-sixties, and it is through and against the "rational" view of society as economically, politically, or structurally determined that the theories of postmodernity examined here developed.[161] As such, postmodernists such as Lyotard and Vattimo concern themselves with loosening the bonds of a social system that appears over-determined, and embrace those contemporary social tendencies that move towards indeterminacy because they are seen as an opportunity for greater freedom.

Second, responding to a political exigency precipitated by Heidegger's infamous involvement with Nazism, both Lyotard and Vattimo desire to avoid the injustice of a politics that seeks the reimposition of a foundation, in whatever form. For both of these thinkers, a fragmented and pluralistic society offers greater opportunity for justice than an "autochthonous" society of shared meanings and a common dialect. While Lyotard and Vattimo might be willing to admit on occasion that such a society may give rise to problems of existential meaning, they focus on the political desirability of this social situation and therefore affirm contingency.

Finally, and most significantly, the postmodern focus on responding to reductive nihilism is arguably oriented by Nietzsche's project of an active destruction of nihilism, despite the postmodernists' explicit rejection of the *telos* of this project (a critical overcoming). While the postmodernists considered here have no *direct* strategies for responding to abyssal nihilism, their strategic focus on reductive nihilism may be understood to parallel Nietzsche's hope that nihilism, if pushed far enough, will overcome itself. Seen in this way, these strategies appear to focus on reductive nihilism in the *present* in the hope that they will, through a predictable historical process, have a decisive effect on abyssal nihilism in the *future*. This futural orientation, however, involves the postmodern responses to nihilism in a problematic tension of the same kind we saw at the end of chapter three, in which the "untimely" nature of the postmodern theories of nihilism conflicts with the postmodern theme of the "end of history." While the postmodern responses to nihilism may be considered coherent and effective responses to the *reductive* form of nihilism, then, when they are seen as attempts to respond to *abyssal* nihilism they run up against this problematic tension. This tension may be identified in both strategies taken by the postmodernists considered here with respect to contingency: Baudrillard's strategy of attempting to reverse it, and Lyotard and Vattimo's strategy of affirming it.

As we have seen, Baudrillard focuses on the attempt to undo the reductive nihilism embodied in the semiological sign and the "micro-particles" of simulation because he sees this reductive nihilism as the root cause of the abyssal nihilism prevalent in contemporary culture. The strategy he employs is similar to Nietzsche's strategy of active nihilism; where Nietzsche seeks to undermine the highest values hitherto posited, Baudrillard seeks to undermine the highest values of modernity: representation and the real. Despite his rejection of the project of a critical overcoming of nihilism, Baudrillard's response to nihilism is directed towards the future possibility of a "poetic reversal" in the order of things that would reinstitute the symbolic and seduction. While he is concerned to map the abyssal nihilism of the current state of culture, Baudrillard is less concerned to confront it directly than to undo the reductionism of modernist theories of meaning, hoping to thereby hasten this poetic reversal. Baudrillard thus stakes his hopes on a future reinstitution of meaning, a hope that seems at odds with his views on the end of history and his rejection of the theme of overcoming. While this critical reversal in the order of things remains an undecidable hypothesis for Baudrillard, it nevertheless governs his strategy for responding to the nihilism of the contemporary situation. To the extent that Baudrillard's thought both repeats the dynamic of Nietzsche's active overcoming of nihilism, and rejects the possibility of such an overcoming, it displays a problematic tension. Baudrillard thus fails to develop an adequate response to abyssal nihilism, since the strategy for such a response, which may be discerned from his works, runs up against the limit of this tension.

As I indicated earlier, both Lyotard and Vattimo affirm contingency, viewing it as a positive means of undermining reductive nihilism. For these thinkers, the reductive effects of cultural trends such as technological science, capitalism, and the process of secularization are the causes of contingency in contemporary culture, but may themselves be undermined by pushing this contingency to an extreme. These postmodernists thus follow Nietzsche in the project of an active destruction that involves nihilism in a self-overcoming, but resist the very moment of overcoming by affirming contingency rather than positing an end beyond it. Nevertheless, I wish to argue, if we understand this postmodern affirmation of contingency as

Negotiating Nihilism 235

a strategy that attempts to respond to abyssal nihilism, it retains a futural and utopian orientation, and falls prey to the tension indicated above. This utopian orientation is most clearly evident in Vattimo's work. Rather than attempt to explicate all the logical implications of nihilism in the present, Vattimo frequently indicates the provisional and preparatory nature of his analyses, emphasizing that we are only just beginning to comprehend the consequences of nihilism in the contemporary age.[162] Since Vattimo celebrates contingency, and does not offer any strategies for directly responding to the problem of existential meaning that may be associated with this contingency, if we are to find a response to abyssal nihilism in his work, then it is towards this future unfolding of nihilism that we should look.

Vattimo's most positive suggestion, with respect to the problem of abyssal nihilism, is his general suggestion that a completed or accomplished nihilism will enable an existentially meaningful form of existence. However, the details of how such an existence will be enabled is not filled out beyond the specification that completed nihilism will undermine the violent and reductive tendencies of metaphysics.[163] As we have seen, for Vattimo, the completion of nihilism involves taking nihilism itself as an orienting value that might act as a criterion for further valuation. In effect, this amounts to the same thing as affirming contingency. Affirmed as a value, contingency—or in Vattimo's terms, nihilism understood as *sfondamento*, "foundationlessness"—becomes a guiding thread for thought, which paradoxically saves this affirmation of contingency from *absolute* contingency (understood as a debilitating relativism). As we have seen, Vattimo argues that taking nihilism itself as a guiding value provides plenty of normative criteria, enough to satisfy people like Habermas.

It may be the case that a completed nihilism, which affirms contingency as a value, would provide the context for a meaningful world and the criteria for making existentially meaningful choices. However, Vattimo does not explore this thought, and it remains unclear how the completion of nihilism might effectively respond to the problem of abyssal nihilism. Interestingly, Vattimo's suggestion of taking nihilism as a value has a strong parallel with the suggestion with which Sartre closes *Being and Nothingness*. Using the term "freedom" to express the radical contingency of human reality, Sartre writes:

> [I]s it possible for freedom to take itself for a value, or must it necessarily be defined in relation to a transcendent value which haunts it? And in

case it could will itself as its own possible and its determining value, what would this mean?...And can one *live* this new aspect of being?... All these questions, which refer us to a pure and not an accessory reflection, can find their reply only on the ethical plane. We shall devote to them a future work.[164]

For Sartre, the possibility announced here would amount to a "radical conversion" that would allow the individual to overcome nihilism by seeing the desire to be God as futile and taking the radical freedom of human reality as the basis for a new fundamental project of being. In so far as Vattimo's affirmation of contingency depends upon the full development of the implications of nihilism at a future time, it may similarly be seen as a hope for the possibility of a "radical conversion," through which contingency will be adopted as a value, and after which the full implications of this adoption will be revealed. If we look to these future implications of a completed nihilism as providing a possible solution to abyssal nihilism, then Vattimo's strategy seems buttressed by faith in a future when "all will be revealed," and, as such, seems to rely on the kind of teleological history and utopianism he explicitly rejects.[165]

The strategies for responding to abyssal nihilism, which may be discerned from the postmodernists' works, can thus be understood as taking their lead from, and remaining within, Nietzsche's project of a critical overcoming of nihilism. Both the attempt to overcome abyssal nihilism through a "poetic reversal" (Baudrillard) and the affirmation of contingency itself as a value (Vattimo, Lyotard) implicitly rely on faith in a future utopia in which nihilism will overcome itself. As we have seen repeatedly argued, such a faith reiterates the logic of religious transcendence and therefore preserves nihilism. It is, of course, necessary that responses to nihilism have a futural orientation of a certain kind, in order that we not give up the hope that things might be otherwise (as Critchley says), and work towards mitigating nihilism in a future whose horizons are perceived to be open to historical change. However, the kind of futural orientation I have identified in the postmodern strategies for responding to abyssal nihilism is a *utopian* one that relies on a *progressive* notion of history: it looks forward to a future in which nihilism will have progressed historically to a point of self-overcoming. This progressive view of history is in conflict with the postmodern theme of the "end of history," and it retains the structure of religious nihilism possessed by modernist metanarratives: the present is devalued in relation to a non-nihilistic utopia. In so far as they are considered as attempts to respond to abyssal nihilism, the postmodern responses to nihilism thus remain within the purview of a philosophy of history and under the sign of a radical conversion.

The arguments we have considered so far point to a problematic tension in the postmodern responses to nihilism that indicate their failure to adequately address the existential problem of contingency in postmodernity. A more serious problem than the merely formal consideration of internal tension, however, is the danger that the strategy of responding directly only to reductive nihilism may in fact exacerbate abyssal nihilism. This point may most clearly be made in the context of Lyotard's work. In the terms of his libidinal philosophy, the strategy of freeing up structures for the greater expression of libidinal energy may lead to abyssal nihilism because structures may become too deregulated to express intensity. This danger may be made evident through a brief comparison of Lyotard's work with Gilles Deleuze and Félix Guattari's *Capitalism and Schizophrenia*.[166] Lyotard's *Libidinal Economy* is influenced by the first volume of this work, *Anti-Oedipus*, from which it borrows the term "line of flight" to describe the process of loosening structures and seeking out new intensities.[167] This use of the term remains faithful to the meaning Deleuze and Guattari give it in *Anti-Oedipus*, where it refers to processes of radical change and metamorphosis (in the terms of their work, "decoding" and "deterritorialization"). In *A Thousand Plateaus*, however, Deleuze and Guattari sound a note of caution, warning that the "line of flight" always stands in danger of becoming a "line of death." This occurs when the process of undoing existing structures becomes purely destructive, and fails to create new forms.[168] This danger is one we may also see in the terms of Lyotard's libidinal philosophy, although he does not foreground it: the process of seeking out new intensities may fail to go any further than the suicidal passion of destroying and deregulating existing structures, failing to create or connect with structures that are sufficiently regulated to allow the expression of intensity.

Moreover, I suggest, this danger is particularly prominent in postmodern society, where many existing structures and institutions are already significantly deregulated. While Lyotard's techniques of active passivity are aimed at creating new forms and structures, these creative acts implicitly rely on a background of existing structured investments. For example, the creation of new forms in modern art that Lyotard values so highly is set against the historical tradition of artistic invention, from which they arguably gain energy and within which their own energy is dissimulated. Furthermore, Lyotard's politics of active passivity takes the form of a conspiracy *within* existing social structures and traditions, and is marginal to, and parasitic upon, these structures and traditions. He moves away from the politics of parties and institutions in order to avoid setting up a new party or creed, which would simply repeat the nihilism that he sees as endemic to the position, rather than content, of such a politics. Libidinal intensities are expressed better, he argues, by passively working within existing institutions. However, this strategy of active passivity relies on these existing institutions as the minimal structures necessary for the expression of intensity. In libidinal terms, the postmodern society of plurality, fragmentation, and the confusion of categories may be understood as a society of deregulated systems and disinvested institutions. In the following passage, Lyotard explains that in the contemporary era, capitalism disinvests many of the "traditional" social structures and institutions:

> [E]nergy refuses to be harnessed, bound, and circulated in the "objects" of the system…(…here at the end of the twentieth century, bureaucratic capitalism seems likely to exhaust all the precapitalist institutions, such as religion, family, property, labour, decency)… the very forms through which energy is rendered circulable (the institutions, in the sense that I have given to the term) cease to be able to harness that energy—they become obsolete.[169]

In postmodern society, libidinal energy becomes deregulated because the existing institutions are no longer able to effectively channel the desires circulating in society. Arguably, although "lines of flight" become easier to take in this society of deregulated systems, since it is easier to escape existing structures that dampen intensity, they also stand in greater risk of becoming lines of death, because the requirement that force be expressed through structures with a minimal degree of regulation may not be met. By directly responding only to reductive nihilism, then, Lyotard and the other postmodernists considered here threaten to exacerbate the nihilism of contingency that already afflicts postmodern society.

As I have argued, the postmodern theorists examined here fail to meet the need of responding to existential contingency, a need expressed within the terms of their own understandings of the postmodern condition. The failure to meet this need, however, by no means invalidates the positive steps the postmodernists take in negotiating the aporia of the gesture of overcoming in responding to reductive nihilism. However, it does suggest that these responses to nihilism in postmodernity suffer from a significant deficiency and are in need of supplementation. While I have argued that the postmodern strategies, which respond effectively only to reductive nihilism, stand in danger of exacerbating abyssal nihilism, I suggest that this danger might be negotiated by employing new forms of imaginative resistance to abyssal nihilism. Such forms of resistance would aim directly at mitigating abyssal nihilism in the present, in the given world, rather than rely on a historical process to overcome it in some future world. While the postmodernists provide us with valuable strategies for resisting reductive nihilism, these new forms of resistance to abyssal nihilism remain to be imagined.

At the end of chapter three, I suggested that we may see the theories of nihilism in postmodernity as marked by two tensions: firstly, between the "untimely" nature of their analyses and the postmodern thesis of "the end of history," and secondly, between the desire to respond to nihilism and the rejection of the possibility of a decisive overcoming. The attempt to respond to abyssal nihilism by targeting reductive nihilism, I have suggested, accords with the first tension, which is problematic insofar as it clings to the Nietzschean thought of a self-overcoming of nihilism, at odds with the most distinctive features of the postmodern transformation of nihilism. In order to remove this problematic tension, I suggest that we should see the postmodern condition as a field of competing forces that must perpetually be negotiated. Rather than choose strategies that work towards a "poetic reversal" or a "radical conversion," we should employ strategies that meet both reductive and abyssal manifestations of nihilism on their own terms. Such a double strategy would aim to open spaces for the enhancement of the value of life against the encroachment of these dual nihilistic currents. Responding to nihilism would thus be a matter, as Williams says, of seeking out the possibilities for affirming life between two deaths. This approach would meet the needs announced by the second tension, and render it unproblematic: it would be a way of responding to nihilism beyond the hope of a definitive overcoming, and without deferring its mitigation to some distantly imagined future.

Conclusion

The contemporary *mise-en abŷme*

This study has elaborated the connection between nihilism and the postmodern, a connection often alluded to, but rarely explored in detail. An understanding of this connection is crucial to how we understand, and respond to, the current situation. The image of this situation that has emerged here is one that threatens us with a pervasive existential meaninglessness: we find ourselves bereft of the orienting goals and values of modernity as the *mise-en scene* of history plunges into the disorienting *mise-en abŷme* of a post-historical epoch. How we respond to this situation will depend on the attitudes we take towards a range of philosophical issues that are clarified and given expression by the concepts of nihilism and the postmodern. In the Introduction I suggested that the concept of nihilism gives a focused expression to feelings of meaninglessness which otherwise run the risk of remaining amorphous, and allows us to think through the problems and issues surrounding this felt meaninglessness in a philosophical manner. The concept of the postmodern, in a complimentary fashion, contributes to a thinking-through of this problem of meaninglessness by situating nihilism within a broad theory of the contemporary situation. My contention throughout has been that the status of nihilism has altered in accord with the "postmodern turn" in both culture and theory. Understanding the nature of this altered status of nihilism is essential, then, if we are to come to terms with the problem of meaning in the contemporary world. Having examined in detail the works of three major theorists of nihilism in postmodernity, we are now in a position to summarize and reflect on the nature of this altered status of nihilism, and the possibilities open to us for responding to the contemporary problem of meaninglessness.

The first aspect of the "postmodern turn" in the status of nihilism that we examined concerns a shift in the theoretical perspectives from which nihilism has been analyzed. These shifts are decisive for our understanding of the character of postmodern nihilism, and shape the possibilities for responding to nihilism in the current situation. In the early part of the twentieth century, nihilism was widely understood through the lens of existentialism, the Sartrean version of which emphasized the centrality of consciousness in the constitution of meaning and the necessity of an individual confrontation with meaninglessness. In the latter part of the twentieth century, the axiological disaffection associated with existentialism was displaced to postmodernism. As I have argued, the shift from existentialism to postmodernism broadly follows the "linguistic turn" in theory away from the conscious individual as arbiter of meaning towards extra-individual structures of meaning, analyzed in various ways by structuralists, post-structuralists, and hermeneutical philosophers. The focus on language and discourse ushered in by the linguistic turn is accompanied by an increasing *reflexivity* in the discourse of nihilism; postmodern analysts of nihilism are acutely aware that their own discourse is implicated within the nihilistic problematic and cannot hope to achieve full critical independence. Finally, changes in the theorization of nihilism under the influence of the postmodern turn have seen an increasing awareness of the aporetic nature of the attempt to overcome nihilism: following on from arguments proposed by Heidegger, the postmodernists considered here all reject the possibility of leaving nihilism behind in a decisive movement of overcoming.

These changes in theory, which accompany the broader "postmodern turn" in culture, have a number of decisive implications for how the problem of meaning in the current situation is to be understood. First, nihilism can no longer be thought solely in terms of the lone individual, as a problem to be confronted in the context of his or her private life (as exemplified by the protagonists of classic existentialist novels such as Sartre's *Nausea* and Camus' *The Outsider*[1]). Rather, the "linguistic turn" in theory means that the negotiation of nihilism in postmodernity gains a *political* exigency: questions of meaning pervade collective social arrangements and cultural conditions, and are political insofar as they impinge on our collective "being together." According to all of the postmodernists examined here, we do not make meaning for ourselves alone. Rather, meaning (and its lack) emerge within a complex of social relations and cultural conditions.

The sense of the political in question here is perhaps more primary than the politics of government, or even the politics of justice, since it concerns the capacity of the forms of life we embody and the projects we pursue to be imbued with a sense of meaning; it concerns that which makes the very project of life worthwhile. This politics responds to the demand that our lives be meaningful, valuable, and in some sense worthwhile, a demand that on Nietzsche's account emerges from the interpretive character of human existence. This demand calls on us to resist all those forces and pressures which devalue life and rob it of its worth, which reduce the meaningfulness of life to nothing and give "nihilism" its name.

The task of responding to nihilism in postmodernity thus appears as a political one: it is not simply a matter of making our individual lives more meaningful, but of intervening in wider social and cultural structures to increase the possibilities of meaning within collective life. Given this political determination, the possibilities open to us for responding to nihilism are shaped by the contours of the current social and historical context. Here, the themes of reflexivity in the discourse of nihilism and the arguments against overcoming converge with the social theories of the postmodern situation to place strict limitations on the possibilities for responding to nihilism. The theoretical considerations that point to an impasse in the attempt to overcome nihilism are confirmed on the cultural and historical plane by the social theories of postmodernity, which construe it as an epoch at "the end of history." These social theories of postmodernity, which point to recent decisive changes in the cultural climate of the world's most "developed" societies, indicate the second major aspect of the "postmodern turn" in the status of nihilism.

As we have seen, Lyotard, Baudrillard, and Vattimo employ different theoretical terms and images to encapsulate what is a shared understanding of the status of nihilism in postmodernity: nihilism in postmodernity consists in the decline of the goals and values that animated modernity. In Lyotard's work, this understanding is expressed through his influential formulation of the postmodern condition as that era in which metanarratives of legitimation have lost their cogency. A similar idea emerges in Baudrillard's thought with his proclamation that the stage of history, that *mise-en scene* in which events gain meaning with reference to a dominant teleology, is empty.[2] In Vattimo's work, the same theme is given by way of the image of the "Westering of Being," the decline or "sunset" of Being in the contemporary era.[3]

In modernity, nihilism may be conceived as the devaluation of life resulting from the secular project of the Enlightenment, which trades off the sense of meaning and value supplied by myth and religion for the gains of an increasingly rationalized world. The goals of modernity, however, take on the form and function of the religious categories of meaning and value by positing a future utopia, displacing the source of value from an afterlife to a distant future. In modernity, the religious eschatological narrative is replaced by a Grand narrative of the emancipation of Man, as the universal subject of history, from suffering. This Grand narrative supplies human existence with a sense of orientation and meaning in place of the old religious doctrines. The nihilism of postmodernity, however, is characterized by the bankruptcy of this Grand narrative of history, and the subsequent loss of the sense of meaning it supplied.

The theories of postmodern nihilism examined here all gesture towards a completion or becoming-complete of nihilism in postmodernity: the postmodernists see Nietzsche's predicted course of the development of nihilism as coming to fruition in the contemporary scene. In Nietzschean terms, such a completion of nihilism would involve a resolution of the problem of meaninglessness that beset modernity, and clear the ground for the creation of new values. As I have argued, however, these postmodern theories of nihilism display a degree of tension by insisting, firstly, that nihilism remains a crucial problem to be confronted – it has not quite yet achieved completion – and secondly, by rejecting the teleological theory of history which would seem necessary to posit the completion of nihilism at a future time. The story of nihilism becoming-complete—told in different ways by Lyotard, Baudrillard, and Vattimo, but converging in broad outline—suggests that nihilism has been driven towards completion by the forces of modernization (predominantly, capitalism and technological science) which have undermined not only premodern religious and mythical categories of valuation, but also the modern metanarratives of historical progress which previously gave them legitimation. In postmodernity, however, these forces of modernization have become autonomous forms of nihilism which reduce the value of life by imposing criteria of economic and technical efficiency on every area of life. Moreover, the undermining of both premodern and modern frameworks of valuation leaves us, in postmodernity, with the pervasive uncertainty of how to live, and why, in a culture substantially uprooted from its orienting traditions.

While this story of the "becoming-complete" of nihilism leaves meaninglessness as a problem in postmodernity which must be confronted, the postmodern theme of "the end of history" places clear limits on how we may understand this confrontation. As I have argued, this theme merges with the arguments against the possibility of overcoming nihilism, which originate with Heidegger and are refined by the postmodernists, to set the parameters of possible strategies for responding to nihilism in the contemporary era. As we have seen argued in a variety of ways, attempts to directly oppose and decisively overcome nihilism inevitably fail, because such attempts remain within the purview of the very nihilistic framework they attempt to escape. The postmodern theme of the end of history likewise problematizes the prospect of overcoming nihilism, since the historical process of overcoming is disallowed: if the idea of a unilinear history with a determinant teleology is bankrupt, we cannot place our hopes in a future, non-nihilistic utopia, toward which we presume the present to be moving. Moreover, as the postmodernists studied here have argued, the nostalgic desire for the return of what has been lost in the current situation is likewise embroiled in nihilism: it devalues the givenness of the present in favor of an idealized version of the past, and hopes for the restoration of this ideal in some distant future. The scene of nihilism at the end of history thus forbids both a restoration of the hopes of modernity or of premodern religion, and a transgression that would result in a historical overcoming of nihilism in a future utopia. The cultural psychoanalysis of postmodernity suggests a pervasive melancholy, beyond both nostalgia and mourning, in which the values of modernity cannot be relinquished in the name of a new beginning.

As I suggested in the opening paragraph of this conclusion, in postmodernity, the *mise-en scene* of historical progress gives way to a bewildering *mise-en abŷme*. This trope of the *mise-en abŷme*, suggested by Baudrillard,[4] is an apposite expression of the nature of the current situation revealed by the analyses of nihilism in postmodernity examined here. The vertigo of infinitely repeated images, suggesting the foundationlessness of a bottomless chasm, expresses the radical contingency of life in a fragmented, pluralistic society. Moreover, the fractal repetition of the *mise-en abŷme* recalls representation gone haywire in Baudrillard's fourth-order simulacra, where the stage of history is empty not because it is unoccupied, but because it has become inoperative, being occupied by too many ineffectual players. Moreover, the frame-within-frame of the *mise-en abŷme* recalls the position of the postmodern nihilist who tries to frame the problem of nihilism, only to realize that that he or she is enclosed in the same nihilistic frame, set on a larger scale.

Despite the apparently grim nature of the current situation suggested by the themes of melancholy and the disorienting *mise-en abŷme*, this situation is two-sided, ambiguous, like nihilism itself. Positively, it frees us from the nihilism of religion and history, in which life is devalued in the name of a transcendent or future ideal. Negatively, it places the possibilities for responding to nihilism in the current situation under strict limitations. Given this postmodern scene, a response to nihilism that speaks to the exigencies of the current situation must negotiate meaninglessness by increasing modes of thought and action that affirm the value of life without the hope that nihilism will ever be finally defeated. As I have argued, the postmodern thinkers examined here all positively contribute towards this task, moving beyond the aporia of the attempt to overcome nihilism by developing concepts and strategies that employ what I have called "the logic of difference" and "the politics of passivity." Lyotard's "dissimulation," Baudrillard's "seduction," and Vattimo's "*Verwindung*" each negotiate nihilism by avoiding the aporetic logic of direct opposition, providing non-oppositional criteria for evaluative judgments to be made concerning what negates and what affirms the value of life, and providing the basis for political strategies which work to decrease nihilism and increase life-affirmation.

As I have argued, nihilism may be understood to manifest at two "poles," which I have called *reductive* nihilism, on the one hand, and *abyssal* nihilism (or the nihilism of contingency) on the other. These two forms of nihilism frequently operate together, and we have seen that both are registered as integral dimensions of nihilism in postmodernity by the thinkers focused on here, as well as other theorists of the postmodern condition. The strategies of dissimulation, seduction, and *Verwindung* are novel and powerful ways of responding to *reductive* forms of nihilism in postmodernity, especially those forms on which each of the postmodernists examined here focus: academic theory, capitalism, and the technological and scientific developments that characterize the postmodern world. These forms of reductive nihilism have flourished in recent years, with the growth and pervasion of information technologies, the expansion of global capitalism, and the increasing pressure to reduce every aspect of life to performative efficiency. Responding to nihilism in postmodernity means resisting these pressures by opening up new spaces for forms of thought and action that affirm the value of life, against the forces of reduction. Such a response requires philosophical theories for understanding, and strategies for intervening in, these nihilistic phenomena. The strategies these postmodern thinkers employ indicate the direction in which the political task of responding to reductive nihilism must be taken up.

I have further argued, however, that the postmodernists considered here fail to adequately respond to the *abyssal* nihilism of postmodernity, which is the contemporary form of the contingency of existence acutely felt and addressed by the existentialists. The various strategies the postmodernists employ in attempting to respond to contingency, I have argued, remain beholden to the philosophy of historical overcoming that they reject. In different ways, Lyotard, Baudrillard, and Vattimo each point to a *future* resolution to the problem of contingency. Given the postmodern thesis of the end of history, however, I have argued that reductive and abyssal forms of nihilism must both be confronted directly, in the present, rather than hoping for some resolution (dialectical or otherwise) in a utopian future. Negotiating nihilism in postmodernity, I have suggested, requires a two-pronged strategy that attempts to activate and nourish the "life between two deaths" that James Williams finds as a central theme in the thought of the French post-structuralists.[5] The two deaths in question may be understood in the terms developed here as the reductive and abyssal forms of nihilism, and if the postmodernists provide useful resources for responding to the nihilism of reduction, then further imaginative forms of resistance are called for to combat the nihilism of contingency. Exploring the terrain of possible forms of such resistance is a task that lies beyond the scope of this book, and I must repeat Sartre's gesture of referring the reader to a future work.[6]

To conclude, I would like to indicate some implications of this study for wider debates concerning the postmodern, in particular debates involving the common accusation that postmodern theory is itself a form of nihilism which must be combated. Calls for a return to premodern forms of religion or philosophy, or for a re-invigoration of the Enlightenment project, are frequently accompanied by shallow characterizations of postmodern theory as nothing more than a symptomatic expression of the nihilism of our times. The image of postmodernism that has emerged from this study, however, is a far more positive one. As I have shown, the postmodern thinkers examined here take nihilism as a central issue of concern and develop new concepts and strategies for responding to the problem of meaninglessness. These strategies frequently cause the postmodernists to take antifoundationalist positions, and it is these positions—which call into question the traditionally assumed status of reason, knowledge, and even reality itself—which have provoked accusations of nihilism.

Postmodernists such as Vattimo are happy to concede that what they advocate is nihilism, if this means no more than antifoundationalism. However, critics of the postmodernists are quick to assert that from antifoundationalism, generalized axiological relativism and nihilism necessarily follow. Postmodern antifoundationalist philosophies, it is thought, cannot support any evaluative criteria, which are the minimal conditions necessary for an ethics, politics, or axiology which might respond to contemporary meaninglessness. Without engaging critics who espouse this position directly,[7] I have shown that all of the postmodernists considered here avoid foundationalist positions precisely because they associate such positions with nihilism, and develop evaluative criteria for responding to nihilism independently of foundationalist claims. While the epistemological issues surrounding the foundationalist/antifoundationalist debate are complex, and cannot be dealt with in any detail here, we may note the following strength of the postmodernist position. The postmodernists have the advantage of calibrating their theories to the pluralism and fragmentation of the postmodern scene, while the premodernists, modernists, and foundationalists all face the disadvantage of setting themselves against the grain of the current situation.[8]

Following Nietzsche, the postmodern approach to nihilism rests on the conviction that meaning is relative to historical and cultural conditions, and that thought must respond by attempting to calibrate itself to changes in these conditions. The connection between nihilism and the postmodern I have charted here allows us to face the contemporary situation in a way which is not simply defensive and reactionary, but which looks for the new possibilities of existence revealed by this situation as well as criticizing those aspects of contemporary life which tend towards meaninglessness. All in all, the postmodern gambit is that the embittered dreams of modernity are beyond the hope of restitution, but that these dreams are not the only stuff of which meaning is made. Such gambits are adventures in thought that must be taken if we are to come to terms with our current situation in a disenchanted, postmodern world.

Notes

1. *Postmodern Fables*, trans. Georges Van Den Abbeele (Minneapolis: University of Minnesota Press, 1997), p. vii.
2. *Simulacra and Simulation*, trans. Sheila Faria Glaser (Ann Arbor: University of Michigan Press, 1994), p. 159.
3. *The End of Modernity: Nihilism and Hermeneutics in Post-Modern Culture*, trans. John R. Snyder (Baltimore: John Hopkins University Press, 1988), p. 19.

Notes to Introduction

1. For two examples of these claims, see John Carroll, *Ego and Soul* (Pymble, N.S.W: Harper Collins, 1998) and the introduction to Donald A. Crosby's *The Specter of the Absurd: Sources and Criticisms of Modern Nihilism* (Albany: SUNY Press, 1988).
2. The link between suicide and social disintegration was influentially formulated by Émile Durkheim in his *Suicide: A Study in Sociology*, trans. John A. Spaulding and George Simpson; ed. G. Simpson (London: Routledge and Keegan, 1952) [orig. 1893].
3. Friedrich Nietzsche, *The Will To Power*, trans. Walter Kaufman and R.J. Hollingdale, ed. W. Kaufmann (New York: Vintage, 1968), 3.
4. Jean-François Lyotard, *The Postmodern Condition: A Report on Knowledge*, trans. Geoff Bennington and Brian Massumi (Minneapolis: University of Minnesota Press, 1984), 3.
5. See Richard Wolin, *Heidegger's Children* (Princeton; Oxford: Princeton University Press, 2001), 72–3. In the context of a discussion of Karl Löwith's analysis of the history of the discourse of nihilism, Wolin cites Goethe's 1825 letter to Zelter, Flaubert's *Bouvard and Pecuchet*, and Baudelaire's "The End of the World." For a more comprehensive study, see Arthur Herman, *The Idea of Decline in Western History* (New York: The Free Press, 1997).
6. Karen L. Carr, *The Banalization of Nihilism: Twentieth Century Responses to Meaninglessness* (Albany: SUNY Press, 1992), 10.
7. See for example Sylvère Lotringer and Sande Cohen (eds.), *French Theory in America* (New York: Routledge, 2000) and François Cusset, *French Theory: How Foucault, Derrida, Deleuze, & Co. Transformed the Intellectual Life of the United States* (Minneapolis: University of Minnesota Press, 2008).
8. David Michael Levin, *The Opening of Vision: Nihilism and the Postmodern Situation* (New York: Routledge and Kegan Paul, 1988); Keith Ansell-Pearson and Diane Morgan (eds.), *Nihilism Now! Monsters of Energy* (Houndmills, Basingstoke: Macmillan, 2000); Gary Banham and Charlie Blake (eds.), *Evil Spirits: Nihilism and the Fate of Modernity* (Manchester: Manchester University Press, 2000). (New York: Routledge and Kegan Paul, 1988).
9. Trans. Iain Hamilton Grant (London: Athlone, 1993).
10. James Williams, *Lyotard and the Political* (London: Routledge, 2000).
11. I have explored these themes in an earlier-published paper, "Was Baudrillard a Nihilist?" *The International Journal of Baudrillard Studies* 5.1 (January 2008).

12. For more detailed biographical information on Vattimo, see Jon R. Snyder's Introduction to Vattimo's *The End of Modernity: Nihilism and Hermeneutics in Post-Modern Culture*, trans. John R. Snyder (Baltimore: John Hopkins University Press, 1988) and Santiago Zabala's Introduction to *Weakening Philosophy: Essays in Honour of Gianni Vattimo*, ed. S. Zabala (Motreal & Kingston; London; Ithaca: McGill-Queens University Press, 2007).

13. For an outline of the general contours of this debate, see the section on Vattimo's nihilism in chapter two below.

14. "Current situation" is a term used by Vattimo to indicate the contemporary nature of existence in a way that places emphasis on the actuality of worldly conditions (as distinct from the metaphysical abstractions of "Being" and "essence"). See Vattimo's "Postmodernity, Technology, Ontology," in *Technology in the Western Political Tradition*, ed. A.M. Melzer, J. Weinberger, and M.R. Zinman (London; Ithaca: Cornell University Press, 1993), 215.

15. See Alan Pratt, *The Dark Side: Thoughts on the Futility of Life from the Ancient Greeks to the Present* (New York: Citadel, 1994).

16. The history of the term and its various uses can be traced back to the twelfth century. See J. Ritter and K. Gründer (eds.), "Nihilismus" in *Historisches Wörterbuch der Philosophie* [Historical Dictionary of Philosophy], vol. 6 (Basel/Stuttgart: Schwabe & Company, 1971–), 846–54.

17. Friedrich Heinrich Jacobi, "Open Letter to Fichte," trans. D.I. Behler in *Philosophy of German Idealism*, ed. E. Behler (New York: Continuum, 1987).

18. See Johann Gottlieb Fichte's *Foundations of the Entire Science of Knowledge* in *The Science of Knowledge*, trans. and ed. Peter Heath and John Lachs (Cambridge: Cambridge University Press, 1982).

19. Jacobi, *op. cit.* p. 135. Quoted by Simon Critchley in *Very Little…Almost Nothing: Death, Philosophy, Literature* (London: Routledge, 1997), 4.

20. Keiji Nishitani, *The Self-Overcoming of Nihilism* trans. Graham Parkes with Setsuko Aihara (Albany: SUNY Press, 1990), xx.

21. Michael Allen Gillespie, *Nihilism Before Nietzsche* (Chicago; London: University of Chicago Press, 1995); Connor Cunningham, *Genealogy of Nihilism* (London; New York: Routledge, 2002); Karl Löwith, *Martin Heidegger and European Nihilism*, ed. R. Wolin (New York: Columbia University Press, 1995). Gillespie's *Nihilism Before Nietzsche* is particularly noteworthy since he presents a genealogy that threatens to undermine the legitimacy of theorisations of nihilism that take Nietzsche as canonical. Gillespie presents an original interpretation of the history of nihilism, focusing on the period that extends from scholastic philosophy, through Romanticism, to Nietzsche. Gillespie contends that Nietzsche misunderstood the concept, and argues that the appropriate response to nihilism is not an affirmation of the will (which he understands Nietzsche as advocating), but a stepping-back from it.

22. See, for example, Crosby, *The Specter of the Absurd*, and Carr, *The Banalization of Nihilism*.

23. For a survey and analysis of the metaphor of the abyss in the works of various existentialist philosophers, see David K. Coe, *Angst and the Abyss: The Hermeneutics of Nothingness* (New York: Oxford University Press, 1985).

24. Critchley, *op. cit.*, 10.
25. Fredric Jameson, *Postmodernism, or, The Cultural Logic of Late Capitalism* (London; New York: Verso, 1991), xxii.
26. For example, see John Frow, *What Was Postmodernism?* (Sydney: Local Consumption Publications, 1991).
27. See Robert B. Pippin's discussion of the difficulty of characterising modernity and the modern in *Modernism as a Philosophical Problem* (Oxford: Blackwell, 1999), 3–4.
28. See Jürgen Habermas, "Modernity – An Incomplete Project" in Patricia Waugh (ed.), *Postmodernism: A Reader* (London: Edward Arnold, 1992), 160. Habermas is relying here on the research of Hans Robert Jauss.
29. The periodisation suggested here follows a distinction Lyotard makes in *The Postmodern Condition*: 'Our working hypothesis is that the status of knowledge is altered as societies enter what is known as the postindustrial age and cultures enter what is known as the postmodern age. This transition has been under way since at least the end of the 1950s…' (3). Foucault also marks the 1950s as the end of modernity and posits a new historical period (without using the term "postmodernity"). See Michel Foucault, *Foucault Live*, trans. John Johnson, ed. Sylvère Lotringer (New York: Semiotext(e), 1989), 30. Quoted in Steven Best and Douglas Kellner, *Postmodern Theory: Critical Interrogations* (London: Macmillan, 1991), 37.
30. A well-known alternative, however, is Charles Jencks' very specific dating of the beginning of the postmodern period with the demolition of the Pruitt-Igore housing development in St. Louis, Missouri, at 3:32 pm on 15 July 1972. See *The Language of Post-Modern Architecture*, 6th ed. (London: Academy Editions, 1991), 23.
31. Alex Callinicos, *Against Postmodernism: A Marxist Critique* (Cambridge: Polity, 1989), 2–3.
32. The concept of post-industrial society was originated by Daniel Bell, and received an influential treatment by Alain Touraine. Daniel Bell, *The Coming of Post-Industrial Society* (London: Heinemann, 1974). Alain Touraine, *The Post-Industrial Society*, trans. Leonard Mayhew (London: Wildwood House, 1974).
33. Manfred Frank, "Two Centuries of Philosophical Critique of Reason and Its "Postmodern" Radicalisation," in Dieter Freundlieb and Wayne Hudson (eds.), *Reason and Its Other* (Providence/Oxford: Berg, 1993), 69.
34. This link was made by Ihab Hassan, and received a highly influential treatment by Fredric Jameson. Ihab Hassan, *The Dismemberment of Orpheus: Toward a Postmodern Literature* (New York: Oxford University Press, 1982); Fredric Jameson, "Postmodernism, or, The Cultural Logic of Late Capitalism," *New Left Review* 146 (1984): 53–93.
35. This focus depends upon it being granted that Baudrillard is a philosopher. While the disciplinary positioning of Baudrillard's work is by no means straightforward, my approach here is to read his work in line with philosophers whose concerns he shares, extracting and focusing on the philosophical claims in his texts. Baudrillard may be considered a philosopher in the same vein as Nietzsche or Georges Bataille, thinkers who were not philosophers by profession, but whose works have philosophical value.
36. Vincent Descombes, *Modern French Philosophy*, trans. L. Scott-Fox and J.M. Harding (Cambridge: Cambridge University Press, 1980), 1.

37. Frank, *op. cit.*, 67.
38. For some early criticisms of the Enlightenment focus on reason, see Isaiah Berlin, *Three Critics of the Enlightenment: Vico, Hamann, Herder*, ed. Henry Hardy (Princeton: Princeton University Press, 2000).
39. Giovanna Borradori, "'Weak Thought' and Postmodernism: The Italian Departure from Deconstruction," *Social Text* 18 (1987–8), 39 and 40.
40. Descombes, *op. cit.*, 76.
41. Under the aspect or species (or "from the point of view") of eternity. The phrase is Benedict de Spinoza's. See his *Ethics*, trans. and ed. Edwin Curley (London: Penguin, 1996) II/126 Cor. 2, 60. In other words, the modernist epistemic subject is thought to have access to knowledge that is universally true since it occupies a universal perspective *outside* the world that transcends the particularities and contingencies associated with any position *in* the world.
42. The term is Thomas Nagel's. *The View from Nowhere* (New York: Oxford University Press, 1986).
43. Michel Foucault, *The Order of Things* (New York: Vintage, 1970), 386–7.
44. Gianni Vattimo, "The End of (Hi)Story," *Chicago Review* 35.4 (1986), 20.
45. For an early version of this way of thinking, see Nietzsche's "On Truth and Lie in a Nonmoral Sense" in *Philosophy of Truth*, trans. Daniel Breazeale (Highlands, N.J.: Humanities Press, 1979). For its most significant development, see Gilles Deleuze, *Difference and Repetition*, trans. Paul Patton (New York: Columbia University Press, 1994).
46. The earliest use of the term "postmodern" seems to have been by the English painter John Watkins Chapman in 1870. See Steven Best and Douglas Kellner, *Postmodern Theory: Critical Interrogations* (New York: Guilford, 1991), 5. On the origins of the postmodern, see also Hans Bertens, *The Idea of the Postmodern: A History* (London; New York: Routledge, 1995) and Perry Anderson, *The Origins of Postmodernity* (London; New York: Verso, 1998).
47. Cited in Best and Kellner, *op. cit.*, 6.
48. Cited in Best and Kellner, *op. cit.*, 6. It was in fact D.C. Sommerville who, in a summary of the first six volumes of Toynbee's *A Study of History*, suggested the term postmodern for the contemporary age. Toynbee subsequently used it himself in volumes VIII and IX.
49. (New York: Oxford University Press). Cited in Best and Kellner, 8; Anderson, 12–13.
50. In *Decline of the New* (New York: Horizon). Cited in Best and Kellner, 10; Anderson, 13.
51. In *The Collected Essays of Leslie Fiedler*, vol. II (New York: Stein and Day, 1971). Cited in Best and Kellner, 10–11; Anderson 13–14.
52. *New Literary History*, 3.1 (1971): 5–30.
53. *Postmodern Theory*, 14.
54. See Stanley Rosen, *Hermeneutics As Politics* 2nd. ed. (New Haven; London: Yale University Press, 1987); Alex Callinicos, *op. cit.*; Jürgen Habermas, *The Philosophical Discourse of Modernity*, trans. Frederick Lawrence (Cambridge: Polity Press, 1990); Christopher Norris, *What's Wrong With Postmodernism: Critical Theory and the Ends*

of *Philosophy* (New York; London: Harvester Wheatshaft, 1990); Norris, *Uncritical Theory: Postmodernism, Intellectuals, and the Gulf War* (London: Lawrence and Wishart, 1992); Norris, *The Truth About Postmodernism* (Oxford; Cambridge: Blackwell, 1993); and Terry Eagleton, *The Illusions of Postmodernism* (Oxford; Cambridge: Blackwell, 1996).

55. For a discussion of this question-begging tendency in Baudrillard scholarship, see Rex Butler, *Jean Baudrillard: The Defence of the Real* (London; Thousand Oaks; New Delhi: Sage, 1999), 13–14.

56. Jean-François Lyotard, *Peregrinations: Law, Form, Event* (New York: Columbia University Press, 1988), 13.

57. Jean Baudrillard, "The Year 2000 Will Not Take Place" trans. Paul Foss and Paul Patton in *Futur*Fall: Excursions into Post-modernity*, ed. E.A. Grosz (Sydney: Power Institute of Fine Arts, 1986), 19.

58. Gianni Vattimo, "Postmodernity, Technology, Ontology," 218.

59. Jeff Malpas, "Gadamer, Davidson, and the Ground of Understanding" in *Gadamer's Century: Essays in Honor of Hans-Georg Gadamer*, ed. Jeff Malpas, Ulrich Arnswald and Jens Kertscher (Cambridge, Mass.: MIT Press, 2002), 195–6.

Notes to Chapter 1, The Advent of Nihilism

1. *The Will To Power*, trans. Walter Kaufman and R.J. Hollingdale, ed. W. Kaufmann (New York: Vintage, 1968), Preface § 2, 3. [In this and subsequent Nietzsche references, section numbers are followed by page numbers.]
2. *The Will to Power*, § 2, 9.
3. Albert Camus, *The Rebel*, trans. Anthony Bower (London: Penguin, 1971), 57.
4. *The Will to Power*, § 1, 7.
5. Gilles Deleuze, *Nietzsche and Philosophy*, trans. Hugh Tomlinson (New York: Columbia University Press, 1983), 147.
6. *The Will to Power*, § 1, 7.
7. According to Nietzsche, the manifestations of social distress in European culture of the late nineteenth century included such things as "vice–the addiction to vice; sickness–sickliness; crime–criminality; celibacy–sterility; hystericism–weakness of the will; alcoholism; pessimism; anarchism; libertinism (also of the spirit). The slanderers, underminers, doubters, destroyers." *The Will to Power*, § 42, 26.
8. *The Will to Power*, Preface § 2, 3.
9. *Ibid.*
10. Alan White, "Nietzschean Nihilism: A Typology," *International Studies in Philosophy* 14.2 (1987): 29–44.
11. "…[Mankind's] problem, however, was *not* suffering itself, but rather the absence of an answer to his questioning cry: *Why* do I suffer?" Nietzsche, *On the Genealogy of Morals*, trans. Douglas Smith (Oxford: Oxford University Press, 1996), 136.
12. *The Will to Power*, § 247, 143.
13. See *On the Genealogy of Morals*.
14. *The Will to Power*, § 12, 12–3.
15. *Ibid.* § 12(A), 12.

16. *Ibid.*
17. *On the Genealogy of Morals*, 92.
18. "In which case, the case of an ascetic life, life functions as a bridge to that other existence. The ascetic treats life as a wrong track along which one must retrace one's steps to the point at which it begins; or as a mistake which one rectifies through action—indeed, which one *should* rectify..." *On the Genealogy of Morals*, 96.
19. Vincent Descombes, *Modern French Philosophy*, trans. L. Scott-Fox and J.M. Harding (Cambridge: Cambridge University Press, 1980), 180.
20. *On the Genealogy of Morals*, 127.
21. "Strictly speaking, there is absolutely no science 'without presuppositions,' the very idea is inconceivable, paralogical: a philosophy, a 'belief' must always exist first in order for science to derive from it a direction, a meaning, a limit, a method, a *right* to existence." *On the Genealogy of Morals*, 127. See also *The Will to Power*, § 481, 267.
22. See the first essay, "'Good and Evil,' 'Good and Bad'" in *On the Genealogy of Morals*.
23. "While all noble morality grows from a triumphant affirmation of itself, slave morality from the outset says no to an 'outside,' to an 'other,' to a 'non-self': and *this* no is its creative act." *On the Genealogy of Morals*, 22.
24. *On the Genealogy of Morals*, 22.
25. Nietzsche, *Twilight of the Idols*, "Expeditions of an Untimely Man," § 5 in *Twilight of the Idols / The Anti-Christ*, trans. R.J. Hollingdale (London: Penguin, 1990), 80.
26. Nietzsche, *Human, All-Too-Human*. Quoted in Steven Best and Douglas Kellner, *The Postmodern Turn* (New York; London: Guilford, 1997), 57.
27. *The Will to Power*, § 12(A), 13.
28. Nietzsche, *The Gay Science*, trans. Walter Kaufmann (New York: Vintage, 1974), § 125, 181.
29. *The Will to Power*, § 585(A), 318.
30. *Ibid.*, § 22, 17.
31. *Ibid.*, § 24, 18.
32. *Ibid.*
33. *The Gay Science*, § 124, 180–1.
34. *Being and Nothingness*, trans. Hazel E. Barnes (New York: Washington Square Press, 1956), 140.
35. Moreover, a common reception of Sartre situates him as a principle theorist of nihilism. For example, see Robert C. Olson, "Nihilism" in *The Encyclopedia of Philosophy*, Vol. 5, ed. Paul Edwards (New York: Macmillan, 1967) and Donald A. Crosby, "Nihilism" in *The Routledge Encyclopedia of Philosophy*, Vol. 7, ed. Edward Craig (London; New York: Routledge, 1998).
36. Sartre, "Existentialism is a Humanism" in *Existentialism from Dostoevsky to Sartre*, ed. Walter Kaufmann (New York: Meridian, 1975), 369.
37. Sartre's term "human reality" is a rough translation of Heidegger's term *Dasein* (see the section on Heidegger later in this chapter), and is meant to indicate the specifically existential aspects of the human being. That is, "human reality" signifies those aspects of the human being and its lived experience which are relevant to an analysis of its mode of being and which specify its way of existing as different from

other existents. Existential considerations may be distinguished from empirico-scientific facts about human beings. For example, it is existentially relevant (and therefore part of the analysis of human reality) that human beings are embodied, but not that iron is required to form red blood cells.
38. Sartre, "Existentialism is a Humanism," 349.
39. There are two main forms of reduction in Husserl's phenomenology: the eidetic reduction (the focus on essences) and the transcendental reduction or *epochē* (bracketing of the natural attitude). It is generally accepted that Sartre employs the eidetic reduction. However, it is common for critics to assert that Sartre did not adopt the transcendental reduction from Husserl, and that his phenomenological descriptions take place entirely on the level of the "natural attitude" (see, for example, Dermot Moran, *Introduction to Phenomenology* (London; New York: Routledge, 2000), p. 359; Christopher Macann, *Four Phenomenological Philosophers: Husserl, Heidegger, Sartre, Merleau-Ponty* (London; New York: Routledge, 1993), p. 204). However, Thomas W. Busch has convincingly argued (with much textual support) that a certain conception of the *epochē* is not only present in Sartre's work, but crucial to its intelligibility. I follow Busch's interpretation of this aspect of Sartre's work here. See Busch, "Sartre's Use of the Reduction: *Being and Nothingness* Reconsidered" in *Jean-Paul Sartre: Contemporary Approaches to his Philosophy*, ed. Hugh J. Silverman and Frederick A. Elliston (Pittsburgh: Duquesne University Press, 1980). In what follows, the term "reduction" refers to Sartre's version of the transcendental reduction (*epochē*).
40. Edmund Husserl, *Ideas: General Introduction to Pure Phenomenology*, trans. W. R. Boyce Gibson (New York: Collier, 1962), 93–96.
41. Sartre's "ontological proof" of the existence of the external world in *Being and Nothingness* is the argument that if consciousness is always intentional, i.e. always consciousness *of* something, (as Husserl himself holds) then it must be *of* something which is *not* consciousness. Otherwise, consciousness would *be* its objects, not be *of* its objects. Sartre concludes that being is *transphenomenal*; it cannot be reduced to its appearances to consciousness. See *Being and Nothingness*, 21–4.
42. Sartre, *The Psychology of Imagination*, trans. Bernard Frechtman (New York: Washington Square Press, 1966), 233. Cited by Busch, *op. cit.*, 22.
43. *Factum sur la contingence*. See Dermot Moran, *op. cit.*, 365.
44. Sartre, *Nausea*, trans. Robert Baldick (Harmondsworth: Penguin, 1965), 185–6.
45. Sartre, *The Transcendence of the Ego: An Existentialist Theory of Consciousness*, trans. Forest Williams and Robert Kirkpatrick (New York: Hill and Wang, 1960).
46. See *The Transcendence of the Ego*, 37–40. Sartre concludes: "the phenomenological conception of consciousness renders the unifying and individualising role of the *I* totally useless. It is consciousness, on the contrary, which makes possible the unity and the personality of my *I*. The transcendental *I*, therefore, has no *raison d'être*" (40).
47. *The Transcendence of the Ego*, 98–9.
48. *Being and Nothingness*, 725; "Existentialism is a Humanism," 348 (the translation here reads, "*existence* comes before *essence*").
49. "Existentialism is a Humanism," 353.
50. Sartre draws a distinction between phenomenological ontology and metaphysics: phenomenological ontology is content to describe the structures of existence as they

appear to us, whereas metaphysics speculates about what lies behind appearances. For a discussion of this distinction, see Thomas W. Busch, *The Power of Consciousness and the Force of Circumstances in Sartre's Philosophy* (Bloomington; Indianapolis: Indiana University Press, 1990), 28.

51. Sartre often abbreviates "being-for-itself" to "for-itself" and "being-in-itself" to "in-itself."
52. Sartre, *Being and Nothingness*, 134.
53. *Ibid.*
54. *Ibid.*, 133–46.
55. *Ibid.*, 136.
56. *Ibid.*, 140.
57. *Ibid.*, 140.
58. *Ibid.*, 797.
59. In *Being and Nothingness*, Sartre intermittently indicates that an ethics which would overcome the nihilism of human reality is possible, but is beyond the scope of the book (see Busch, *op. cit.*, for citations). In concluding, he promises a future work on this subject, but this work was never finished. The notes towards this book on ethics, written between 1947 and '48, were published in 1983, and translated as *Notebooks for an Ethics*, trans. D. Pellauer (Chicago: University of Chicago Press, 1992).
60. *Being and Nothingness*, 796.
61. Christopher Macann argues that Sartre's phenomenological descriptions in *Being and Nothingness* remain on the level of the natural attitude, while Busch argues the similar point that these descriptions refer to consciousness not engaged in the reduction. Macann, *Four Phenomenological Philosophers*, 207; Busch, "Sartre's Use of the Reduction," 25.
62. *Notebooks for an Ethics*, 11.
63. *Being and Nothingness*, 712–734.
64. Sartre gives bad faith a complex description in the well-known chapter devoted to it in *Being and Nothingness* (86–116). There is another side to bad faith, which involves affirming our transcendence too strongly, and denying our "facticity"—the essence of our past selves we create through our concrete actions, and the effects these actions have in the world.
65. *Being and Nothingness*, 534.
66. *Ibid.*, 798.
67. *Ibid.*, 797.
68. *Ibid.*, 116, note 9.
69. *Ibid.*, 729–30.
70. *Ibid.*, 797. Sartre's biographies on figures such as Jean Genet and Gustave Flaubert are studies in existential psychoanalysis, which both attempt such an analysis on their subjects, and present examples of people who have analysed themselves. See Sartre's *Saint Genet: Actor and Martyr*, trans. Bernard Frechtman (New York: Braziller, 1963) and *The Family Idiot: Gustave Flaubert, 1821–1857*, trans. Carol Cosman (Chicago: University of Chicago Press, 1981).
71. *Ibid.*, 76.

72. "Existentialism is a Humanism," 367–8.
73. Heidegger, "Nihilism as Determined by the History of Being" in *Nietzsche Vol. IV: Nihilism*, trans. David Farrell Krell, (San Francisco: Harper & Row, 1987), 211.
74. On the global significance of nihilism Heidegger writes that "Nihilism, at first merely European...appears in its planetary tendency...the movement of nihilism in the many forms of its inexorable and planetary character that eats away at and consumes everything has become more evident. No one of any insight would today wish to deny that nihilism in its most diverse and hidden forms is the 'normal condition' of humankind." Heidegger, "On the Question of Being," trans. William McNeill in *Pathmarks*, ed. William McNeill (Cambridge: Cambridge University Press, 1998), 294 and 296.
75. In reference to Nietzsche's analysis of nihilism, Heidegger writes that "this 'idealistic' and moralistic interpretation of nihilism remains provisional, in spite of its importance...nihilism must be grasped more fundamentally as the essential consequence of the abandonment of being." See Heidegger, *Contributions to Philosophy (from Enowning)*, trans. Parvis Emad and Kenneth Maly (Bloomington, Ind.: Indiana University Press, 1999), § 72 "Nihilism," 96.
76. Beistegui, *The New Heidegger*, 14. Beistegui cites Heidegger's 1925 "Kassel Lectures," published in the *Dilthey-Jahrbuch* 8 (1992–3).
77. Michael E. Zimmerman has shown that Heidegger's thought concerning the nihilism of modernity was significantly shaped by German thinkers such as Otto Spengler and Ernst Jünger, themselves influenced by Nietzsche's rhetoric of nihilism, prior to his explicit engagement with Nietzsche's work. See Zimmerman, *Heidegger's Confrontation with Modernity: Technology, Politics, Art* (Bloomington; Indianapolis: Indiana University Press, 1990).
78. Heidegger, *Discourse on Thinking*, trans. John M. Anderson and E. Hans Freund (New York: Harper & Row, 1969), 48.
79. *Ibid.*, 48–9.
80. Heidegger, *Nietzsche, Vol. 1: The Will to Power as Art*, trans. David Farrell Krell (London; Henley: Routledge and Kegan Paul, 1981), 157. Quoted by Hubert L. Dreyfus, "Heidegger on the Connection between Nihilism, Art, Technology, and Politics" in *The Cambridge Companion to Heidegger*, ed. Charles Guignon (Cambridge; New York: Cambridge University Press, 1993), 290–1.
81. As Michael Inwood notes, Heidegger's use of the term "world" (*Welt*) varies between different texts. However, for our purposes we need not venture beyond a general sense of the (complex) meaning of this term as it is developed in *Being and Time*, where *Dasein*'s Being-in-the-world implies involvement in a world rich with significance, where every being encountered is related to other beings in light of projected possibilities, and the world appears as a totality of involvements and significance. This conception of the world is contrasted with the world as simply a collection of entities, and with Descartes' view of the world as *res extensa*. See Inwood, *A Heideger Dictionary* (Oxford; Malden, Massachusetts: Blackwell, 1999), "world and beings as a whole," 245–8, and Heidegger, *Being and Time*, trans. John Macquarrie and Edward Robinson (Oxford: Blackwell, 1962), chapter III (especially § 18, "Involvement and significance: the worldhood of the world").

82. Heidegger, "Only A God Can Save Us" in *The Heidegger Controversy: A Critical Reader*, ed. Richard Wolin (Cambridge, Mass.: MIT Press, 1993), 106.
83. Heidegger, "Nihilism as Determined by the History of Being," 229.
84. For a thorough analysis of the complex and changing meanings Heidegger gives to the term essence, see Alfons Grieder, "What did Heidegger mean by 'Essence'?" in *Martin Heidegger: Critical Assessments*, Vol. 1, ed. Christopher Macann (London; New York: Routledge, 1992).
85. These points paraphrase Inwood, *op. cit.*, 47–8.
86. Trans. John Macquarrie and Edward Robinson (Oxford: Blackwell, 1962).
87. This "turn" is often called the *Kehre*, although Heidegger scholars are increasingly seeking to disengage this term—one which he uses in a technical sense to describe the dynamic of Being—from the shift in his thought. See for example Thomas Sheehan, "A Paradigm Shift in Heidegger Research," *Continental Philosophy Review* 34 (2001), 195–6; and Daniela Vallega-Neu, *Heidegger's* Contributions to Philosophy: *An Introduction* (Bloomington; Indianapolis: Indiana University Press, 2003), 5, note 7.
88. Human being in its special relation to Being, as that being for which existence itself is an issue, which can ask about the meaning of Being, and to whom Being discloses itself.
89. In *Being and Time*, Heidegger defines meaning as follows: "*Meaning is the 'upon-which' of a projection in terms of which something becomes intelligible as something…*" (193). Dasein is what projects here, and what it projects are possibilities. For Heidegger this projection of possibilities is an essential constituent of understanding, and a necessary condition for things to show up as intelligible (see 184–5). Thus, he concludes that '[m]eaning is an *existentiale* of Dasein, not a property attaching to entities…*Hence only Dasein can be meaningful [sinnvoll] or meaningless [sinnlos]*. That is to say, its own Being and the entities disclosed with its Being can be appropriated in understanding, or can remain relegated to non-understanding" (193).
90. Beistegui, *The New Heidegger*, 60. Heidegger gives a brief exposition of this argument in the Introduction to *Being and Time*, 47–8.
91. Heidegger, *An Introduction to Metaphysics*, trans. Ralph Manheim (London; New Haven: Yale University Press, 1959), 161. For a detailed exposition, see Heidegger, "On the Essence and Concept of Φύσις in Aristotle's *Physics* B, I" in *Pathmarks*.
92. *Beiträge zur Philosophie (Vom Ereignis)* [*Contributions to Philosophy*], Gesamtausgabe Band 65 (Frankfurt am Main: Vittorio Klostermann, 1989), 338f. Quoted in Michael Inwood, *A Heidegger Dictionary*, 14.
93. See "aletheia and truth" in Inwood, *op. cit.*, 13–14.
94. See "On the Essence of Truth" in *Martin Heidegger: Basic Writings*, ed. David Farrell Krell (New York: Harper Collins, 1993).
95. See Richard Polt, "The Event of Enthinking the Event" in *Companion to Heidegger's* Contributions to Philosophy, ed. Charles E. Scott, Susan M. Schoenbohm, Daniela Vallega-Neu, and Alejandro Vallega (Bloomington and Indianapolis: Indiana University Press, 2001), 93–4.
96. This term has been variously translated as "event," "appropriation," "befitting," and "enowning." For a discussion of the merits and demerits of these various translations, which defends "enowning," see the section on "*Ereignis* and Related

Words" in the "Translator's Foreword" to Heidegger's *Contributions to Philosophy*, xix–xxii. For a vigorous criticism of this translation as "enowning," see Sheehan, "A Paradigm Shift in Heidegger Research."

97. Heidegger, *Contributions to Philosophy*, 5–6.
98. *Contributions to Philosophy*, 330: "Be-ing is en-owning."
99. See Polt, "The Event of Enthinking the Event," 93–4.
100. According to Heidegger, the Latin *subiectum* is a translation of the Greek *hypokeimenon*, which has the meaning given here. See "The Age of the World Picture," in *The Question Concerning Technology and Other Essays*, trans. William Lovitt (New York: Harper & Row, 1977), 128.
101. "The Age of the World Picture," 137.
102. See "The Question Concerning Technology," trans. William Lovitt (slightly altered by David Farrell Krell) in *Martin Heidegger: Basic Writings*, ed. David Farrell Krell (New York: Harper Collins, 1993), 324.
103. As evidence for this disclosure of human beings as *Bestand* Heidegger cites the current talk of "human resources" and the "supply" of patients for a clinic. See "The Question Concerning Technology," 323.
104. Heidegger, "The Word of Nietzsche: God is Dead" in *The Question Concerning Technology*, 104.
105. Heidegger, "Nihilism as Determined by the History of Being," 211.
106. See "Nihilism as Determined by the History of Being," 219.
107. The unity of authentic and inauthentic nihilism rests on the fact that authentic nihilism—the ontological concealing of Being—has taken place historically through the development of metaphysical thinking, which is a form of inauthentic nihilism. Thus Heidegger writes that "Precisely in the way it takes place, the authenticity of nihilism *is not* something authentic. To what extent? Nihilism takes place as metaphysics in its own inauthenticity." And further: "The authenticity of nihilism historically takes the form of inauthenticity, which accomplishes the omission of the default by omitting this very omission." ("Nihilism as Determined by the History of Being," 220.)
108. Heidegger's engagement with Nietzsche is found in the four volumes of his lectures on Nietzsche [*Nietzsche*, trans. David Farrell Krell] and in several essays. I shall focus here on the essay "The Word of Nietzsche: God is Dead" [in *The Question Concerning Technology*] which presents a summary of the lecture series. Heidegger's engagement with Sartre is found in the "Letter on Humanism," trans. Frank A. Capuzzi in collaboration with J. Glenn Gray in *Martin Heidegger: Basic Writings*.
109. In the final aphorism of *The Will to Power*, Nietzsche gives the following vivid description of his ontological vision: "This world: a monster of energy, without beginning, without end; a firm, iron magnitude of force that does not grow bigger or smaller, that does not expend itself but only transforms itself; as a whole, of unalterable size, a household without expenses or losses, but likewise without increase or income…a play of forces and waves of forces, at the same time one and many, increasing here and at the same time decreasing there; a sea of forces flowing and rushing together, eternally changing, eternally flooding back, with tremendous years of recurrence, with an ebb and a flood of its forms…*this world is the will to power—and nothing besides!*" (*The Will to Power*, § 1067, 550.)

110. See *The Will to Power*, §§ 1062, 1063, and 1064, 546–7.
111. "The Word of Nietzsche," 81–2.
112. While the characterisation of Nietzsche's doctrines as metaphysical tends to dominate his interpretations, Heidegger does sometimes think through ideas such as the eternal recurrence of the same in a way which indicates that they contain something which resists the metaphysical tradition, and which remains unthought in metaphysics. Heidegger thus positions Nietzsche as ambiguously situated at the end of metaphysics as both its culmination, and as a transition to a new beginning.
113. "The Word of Nietzsche," 71. Italics Heidegger's.
114. *Ibid.*, 71–2.
115. *Ibid.*, 74.
116. *Ibid.*
117. Heidegger writes: "The grounding principle of the metaphysics of the will to power is a value-principle." "The Word of Nietzsche," 86.
118. "Letter on Humanism," 251.
119. *Ibid.*, 251.
120. "The Age of the World Picture," 142.
121. *Ibid.*, 251.
122. "Letter on Humanism" in *Matin Heidegger: Basic Writings*, 232.
123. Quoted by Heidegger, "Letter on Humanism," 237.
124. *Ibid.*
125. Heidegger writes that "[e]very humanism is either grounded in a metaphysics or is itself made to be the ground of one. Every determination of the essence of man that already presupposes an interpretation of beings without asking about the truth of Being, whether knowingly or not, is metaphysical…Accordingly, every humanism remains metaphysical." ("Letter on Humanism," 225–6.)
126. Heidegger, "On the Question of Being," trans. William McNeill in *Pathmarks*, ed. William McNeill (Cambridge: Cambridge University Press, 1998).
127. *Ibid.*, 314.
128. "Nihilism as Determined by the History of Being," 224.
129. The necessity of thinking Being in its oblivion is also articulated in *Contributions to Philosophy*, where Heidegger associates a "knowing awareness" of the history of Being with the overcoming of nihilism: "Because this knowing awareness thinks nihilism still more originarily into the abandonment of being, this knowing is the actual overcoming of nihilism…" Heidegger, *Contributions to Philosophy*, 123.
130. *Destruktion*, sometimes translated as "deconstruction," does not have the usual negative connotations of the English term in Heidegger's thought, and is aimed at the positive task of retrieving a more originary way of thinking Being. See *Being and Time*, "Introduction," Section 6, "The task of Destroying the history of ontology," 41–49.
131. Heidegger writes: "If releasement toward things and openness to the mystery awaken within us, then we should arrive at a path that will lead to a new ground and foundation. In that ground the creativity which produces lasting works could strike new roots" (*Discourse on Thinking*, 56–7).
132. See Beistegui, *The New Heidegger*, 86.

133. Gregory Bruce Smith, *Nietzsche, Heidegger, and the Transition to Postmodernity* (Chicago: University of Chicago Press, 1996), 273. Text in square brackets mine.
134. For example, see Allan D. Schrift, *Nietzsche and the Question of Interpretation: Between Hermeneutics and Deconstruction* (New York: Routledge, 1990).

Notes to Chapter 2, Postmodern Nihilism

1. Jean-François Lyotard, *Signé Malraux* (Paris: Grasset, 1996), 99. Quoted and translated by James Williams, *Lyotard and the Political* (London: Routledge, 2000), 6.
2. Lyotard, *Libidinal Economy*, trans. Iain Hamilton Grant (London: Athlone, 1993). 49.
3. James Williams is the only Lyotard scholar who pays sustained attention to this theme. See his *Lyotard and the Political* and "The Last Refuge from Nihilism," *International Journal of Philosophical Studies* 8.1 (2000): 115-24.
4. Lyotard, *Signed, Malraux*, trans. Robert Harvey (Minneapolis: University of Minnesota Press, 1999). Lyotard, *Soundproof Room: Malraux's Anti-Aesthetics*, trans. Robert Harvey (Stanford, Calif.: Stanford University Press, 2001). Lyotard, *The Postmodern Condition: A Report on Knowledge*, trans. Geoff Bennington and Brian Massumi (Manchester: Manchester University Press, 1984); Lyotard, *The Differend: Phrases in Dispute*, Trans. Georges Van Den Abbeele (Manchester: Manchester University Press, 1988).
5. These essays are collected in *Dérive à partir de Marx et Freud* (Paris: Union Général d'Editions, 1973) and *Des Dispositifs pulsionnels* (Paris: Union Général d'Editions, 1973).
6. Lyotard, "Notes on the Return and Kapital," trans. Roger McKeon, *Semiotexte* 3.1 (1978), 48.
7. Lyotard, *Peregrinations* (New York: Columbia University Press, 1988), 13–4.
8. Williams, *Lyotard and the Political*, 34–38.
9. Simon Malpas suggests a distinction between the "Nietzschean" reading of Lyotard given by James Williams and his own "Kantian" reading. These differing perspectives perhaps help explain their respective preferences for the earlier and later periods of Lyotard's thought. Malpas, *Jean-François Lyotard* (New York: Routledge, 2002), 143.
10. Williams, *Lyotard and the Political*, 135–6.
11. See Geoffrey Bennington, *Lyotard: Writing the Event* (Manchester: Manchester University Press, 1988); Bill Readings, *Introducing Lyotard: Art and Politics* (London: Routledge, 1991); James Williams, *Lyotard: Towards a Postmodern Philosophy* (Cambridge: Polity Press, 1998).
12. Peter Dews, *Logics of Disintegration: Post-structuralist Thought and the Claims of Critical Theory* (London; New York: Verso, 1987), 112.
13. Lyotard, *Phenomenology*, trans. Brian Beakley (Albany: SUNY Press, 1991).
14. Dews argues that Jacques Derrida is such a thinker.
15. Lyotard, *Discours, figure* (Paris: Klincksieck, 1971).
16. Lyotard writes: 'Theatre places us right in the heart of what is religious-political: in the heart of absence, in negativity, in nihilism as Nietzsche would say…' "The

Tooth, The Palm," trans. Anne Knap and Michel Benamou, *Sub-Stance* 15 (1976), 105.

17. Lyotard's most concise statement of the basic dynamic of representational nihilism is in "The Tooth, The Palm": "Take two places A and B; a move from A to B means two positions and a displacement; now declare that B comes from A; you are no longer taking B's position positively, affirmatively, but in relation to A, subordinated to A, itself absent (gone by, hidden). B is turned into nothingness; as an illusion of presence, its being is in A; and A is affirmed as truth, that is to say absence. Such is the apparatus of nihilism" (105).

18. Lyotard, *Libidinal Economy*, 49.

19. These points are derived from *Libidinal Economy*, 43.

20. *Libidinal Economy*, 44.

21. Paul Ricoeur, "Phenomenology and Hermeneutics," in *From Text to Action: Essays in Hermeneutics II*, trans. Kathleen Blamey and John B. Thompson (Illinois: Northwestern University Press, 1991), 40.

22. *Libidinal Economy*, 43.

23. *Ibid.*

24. *Ibid.*

25. More precisely, according to Saussure it is the two constituent elements of the sign—signifieds and signifiers—which gain their value from their differences with other signifieds and signifiers (respectively).

26. *Libidinal Economy*, 44.

27. In *Libidinal Economy* Lyotard refers to specifically religious semiotic systems, such as those of Augustine or the Victorins of the twelfth century, in which the world is understood as a series of signs, God is the absent great signifier to which all signs ultimately refer and from whom they gain their meaning, and we are in a situation such that we will never be in full possession of the code. On the Victorins, see page 49.

28. *Libidinal Economy*, 47.

29. *Ibid.*, 49.

30. Lyotard, "March 23" in *Jean-François Lyotard: Political Writings*, trans. Bill Readings and Kevin Paul (Minneapolis: University of Minnesota Press, 1993), 64.

31. For Lyotard's discussion of the two senses of desire in Freud, see his essay "On a Figure of Discourse," trans. Mark S. Roberts in *Toward the Postmodern*, ed. Robert Harvey and Mark S. Roberts (New Jersey: Humanities Press, 1993).

32. *Libidinal Economy*, 26.

33. See Lyotard, "Acinema," trans. Paisley N. Livingston in collaboration with the author, *Wide Angle* 2.3 (1978): 52–59.

34. See Lyotard, "March 23."

35. Lyotard takes this term, meaning "not possible together," from Gottfried Wilhelm Leibniz.

36. *Libidinal Economy*, 5.

37. Lyotard writes: "Marx said in 1844 that socialism doesn't need atheism because the *question* of atheism is *positionally* that of religion; it remains a critique. What is important in the question is not its negativity, but its position (the position of the problem)." "Energumen Capitalism," trans. James Leigh, *Semiotexte* 2.3 (1977), 11.

38. The role of negation and opposition in the problem of overcoming nihilism is given an extended discussion in chapter four.
39. *Libidinal Economy*, quoted in translator's introduction, xxvii.
40. *Ibid.*, 6.
41. *Ibid.*, 42.
42. *Ibid.*, 50.
43. Lyotard combines the meanings of both the terms "dissimulate" and "dissimilate" in this concept.
44. *Libidinal Economy*, 11–12.
45. The following passage from the writings of John Cage, one of Lyotard's favourite composers, sums up this aspect of the libidinal economy well: "Structure without life is dead. But Life without structure is unseen. Pure life expresses itself within and through structure." John Cage, "Lecture on Nothing" in *Silence* (Middletown, Connecticut: Wesleyan University Press, 1961), 113.
46. This *contra* Dews, who argues that there is a loss of all critical distinctions and criteria for judgement in *Libidinal Economy*. See *The Logics of Disintegration*, chapter four.
47. *Libidinal Economy*, 242.
48. Further discussion of the experimental techniques Lyotard uses in *Libidinal Economy* is given in chapter four.
49. *Libidinal Economy*, 52.
50. *Simulacra and Simulation*, trans. Sheila Faria Glaser (Ann Arbor: University of Michigan Press, 1994), 160 and 162.
51. See, for example, Douglas Kellner, *Jean Baudrillard: From Marxism to Postmodernism and Beyond* (Cambridge: Polity, 1989) and Anthony King, "Baudrillard's Nihilism and the End of Theory," *Telos* 112 (1998): 89–106.
52. This interpretation is given definitive expression in Paul Foss' "Despero Ergo Sum" in *Seduced and Abandoned: The Baudrillard Scene*, ed. André Frankovits (Glebe: Stonemoss Services, 1984). Foss compares Baudrillard's supposed passive or "negative" nihilism unfavourably with Nietzsche's active nihilism, arguing that "whereas Nietzsche goes beyond the (apparent) last stage [of nihilism], namely, the engulfment of the world by pure negativity, this is precisely where Baudrillard collapses, "melancholy and fascinated'" (14–5). Douglas Kellner offers a similar perspective, writing that 'Baudrillard completely divests himself of any Nietzschean vitalism or celebration of life and the body. Nietzsche's "gay science" and moods of joy also dissipate in the Baudrillardian atmosphere of melancholy.' *Op. cit.*, 120.
53. For example, Kellner, *op. cit.* and King, *op. cit.*
54. Butler in fact argues for the need for a combination of "internal" and "external" readings of Baudrilard in order to attain an adequate critical perspective on his work. See Butler, *Jean Baudrillard: The Defence of the Real* (London; Thousand Oaks; New Delhi: Sage, 1999).
55. Gary Genosko, *Baudrillard and Signs: Signification Ablaze* (London and New York: Routledge, 1994). Mike Gane, *Jean Baudrillard: In Radical Uncertainty* (London: Pluto, 2000).
56. Baudrillard, "On Nihilism," in *Simulacra and Simulation*.

57. "On Nihilism," 159.
58. Jean Baudrillard, *The Ecstasy of Communication*, trans. Bernard and Caroline Schutze, ed. Sylvère Lotringer (New York: Semiotext(e), 1988), 79. Translation slightly altered.
59. While Lyotard writes on "semiotics," Baudrillard positions his work in relation to "semiology." Semiotics refers to the tradition of the study of signs stemming from Charles Sanders Pierce, and semiology refers to the study of signs inspired by Ferdinand de Saussure. While in the nineteen-seventies a distinction was made between these two traditions, they have largely converged and the study of signs in general is now simply referred to as semiotics. For my purposes, there is no substantial difference between these traditions as understood by Lyotard and by Baudrillard.
60. See Baudrillard, *The System of Objects*, trans. James Benedict (London; New York: Verso, 1996) and Baudrillard, *The Consumer Society: Myths and Structures* (London: SAGE Publications, 1998). "The code" will be given further consideration in chapter three.
61. Baudrillard's concept of the symbolic is radically distinguished from both Jacques Lacan's and Claude Lévi-Stauss' use of the term. See Baudrillard, *Symbolic Exchange and Death*, trans Iain Hamilton Grant (London: Sage, 1993), 133 and 188, note 10.
62. Baudrillard, *For a Critique of the Political Economy of the Sign*, trans. Charles Levin (St. Louis: Telos, 1981).
63. *Ibid.*, 146.
64. *Ibid.*, 155, note 9. The semiologist quoted is J.-M. Lefebvre.
65. *Ibid.*, 155–6, note 9.
66. Gary Genosko is the only commentator who pays serious attention to the semiological dimension of simulation. See his *Baudrillard and Signs*, chapter 2.
67. Excerpt from *Simulacra and Simulation* in *Jean Baudrillard: Selected Writings*, ed. Mark Poster (Cambridge: Polity Press, 1988), 167.
68. Plato, "Cratylus," *The Dialogues of Plato*, Vol. II (Oxford: The Clarendon Press, 1875), 257. Quoted by Rex Butler, "Jean Baudrillard's Defence of the Real: Reading *In the Shadows of the Silent Majorities* as an Allegory of Representation" in *Jean Baudrillard, Art and Artefact*, ed. Nicholas Zurbrugg (Brisbane: Institute of Modern Art, 1997), 51.
69. Baudrillard, "The Precession of Simulacra," in *Simulacra and Simulation*, 6.
70. Baudrillard, "On Nihilism," 159.
71. Baudrillard writes: "…nothing separates one pole from another anymore, the beginning from the end; there is a kind of contraction of one over the other, a fantastic telescoping, a collapse of the two traditional poles into each other: *implosion* – an absorption of the radiating mode of causality, of the differential mode of determination, with its positive and negative charge – an implosion of meaning. *That is where simulation begins.*" "The Precession of Simulacra," 31.
72. See Baudrillard, *Symbolic Exchange and Death*, 133 and 188, note 9, respectively.
73. Baudrillard, "The Precession of Simulacra," in *Simulacra and Simulation*.
74. "The Precession of Simulacra," 19.
75. "On Nihilism," 162–3.

76. See the epigraph to this section.
77. "On Nihilism," 163.
78. In Baudrillard's early works, including *For A Critique of the Political Economy of the Sign*, he understands the symbolic order of meaning as a *transgression* of the system of political economy which might contribute to a revolutionary overthrow of this system. In *The Ecstasy of Communication* he retrospectively indicates his move away from this position: "...after *Symbolic Exchange and Death* and with *Seduction* the dream of a transgression, of a possible subversion of codes, and the nostalgia for a symbolic order of any kind, born out of the deep of primitive societies, or out of historical alienation, have been lost. With *Seduction*, there is no longer any symbolic referent to the challenge of signs, no more lost object, no more recovered object, no more original desire" (79–80). In *Libidinal Economy*, Lyotard gives an extensive criticism of what he sees as the nostalgia of Baudrillard's idea of symbolic exchange. While he has never admitted as much, one might conjecture that Baudrillard's change of position was influenced by this critique. See Lyotard, *Libidinal Economy*, 103–127.
79. Butler, *Jean Baudrillard: The Defence of the Real*, 72.
80. Baudrillard, "On Nihilism," 164.
81. *The End of Modernity: Nihilism and Hermeneutics in Post-Modern Culture*, trans. John R. Snyder (Baltimore: John Hopkins University Press, 1988), 19; 20.
82. *Ibid.*, 12.
83. Vattimo, *Nihilism and Emancipation: Ethics, Politics, and Law*, trans. William McCuaig, ed. Santiago Zabala (New York: Columbia University Press, 2004), 30. One place where Vattimo does explicitly focus on these existential problems is his discussion of the "art of living" in the essay "The Wisdom of the Superman" in *Dialogue with Nietzsche*, trans. William McCuaig (New York: Columbia University Press, 2006).
84. This positive revaluation of nihilism poses potential problems of terminological clarity, since throughout this work I am in general concerned with the meaning of nihilism as an existential problem, as it is construed by all other thinkers under consideration. Henceforth, where the meaning of the term "nihilism" is not clearly established by the context in which it is used, I shall use the term "negative nihilism" to designate nihilism as an existential problem, and "positive nihilism" to designate Vattimo's revaluation of nihilism as a solution to the problem of metaphysics.
85. Vattimo, "Le deboli certezze," *Alfabeta* 67 (1984), 8. Cited by Jon R. Snyder in Vattimo, *The End of Modernity*, xi.
86. Emanuele Severino, "Riturno a Parmenide" [To Return to Parmenides] in *Essenza del nichilismo* (Milan: Adelphi, 1982).
87. Vattimo and Pier Aldo Rovatti (eds.), *Il pensero debole* (Milan: Feltrinelli, 1983).
88. Giovanna Borradori, in her introduction to *Recoding Metaphysics: The New Italian Philosophy*, ed. G. Borradori (Evanston, IL: Northwestern University Press, 1988) suggests that the provincialism of Italian philosophy is due in part to the country's nationalism and traditionalism, severely exacerbated by two decades of fascism.
89. See Jon R. Snyder's introduction to *The End of Modernity* and Giovanna Borradori's introduction to *Recoding Metaphysics* for fuller expositions of the background to, and nature of, the contemporary Italian philosophical scene.

90. Marta Frascati-Lochhead, *Kenosis and Feminist Theology: The Challenge of Gianni Vattimo* (Albany: SUNY Press, 1998), 37.
91. Vattimo employs this expression, coined by Michel Foucault, in "Postmodernity, Technology, Ontology," in *Technology in the Western Political Tradition*, ed. A.M. Melzer, J. Weinberger, and M.R. Zinman (London; Ithaca: Cornell University Press, 1993), 214.
92. Vattimo, "Nietzsche and Heidegger," trans. Thomas Harrison, *Stanford Italian Review* 6.1–2 (1986), 20.
93. *Ibid.*, 28.
94. See "Nietzsche and Heidegger" and Vattimo, *Nietzsche: An Introduction*, trans. Nicholas Martin (Stanford, California: Stanford University Press, 2001), 1–7.
95. Dilthey's interpretation of Nietzsche can be found in his book *The Essence of Philosophy*, trans. Stephen A. Emery and William T. Emery (Chapel Hill: University of North Carolina Press, 1954).
96. Vattimo writes that "Nietzsche's works are commonly divided into three periods: a) the early works; b) the genealogical and deconstructive thought from *Human, All-Too-Human* to *The Gay Science*; c) the philosophy of eternal recurrence that begins with *Zarathustra*." Vattimo, *Nietzsche: An Introduction*, 87.
97. Nietzsche, *Untimely Meditations*, ed. Daniel Breazeale, trans. R.J. Hollingdale (Cambridge; New York: Cambridge University Press, 1997). Nietzsche, *The Gay Science*, trans. Walter Kaufmann (New York: Vintage, 1974).
98. *Nietzsche: An Introduction*, 43.
99. Friedrich Nietzsche, *Human, All-Too-Human*, trans. Marion Faber and Stephen Lehmann (London: Penguin, 1984), § 1, 13–14.
100. In Vattimo's words, "[t]he belief in the superiority of truth over non-truth or error is a belief which arises in specific vital situations (insecurity, *bellum omnium contra omnes* in the more primitive phases of history, etc.)." *The End of Modernity*, 167.
101. This argument is given in Nietzsche's essay "On Truth and Lie in a Nonmoral Sense" in *Philosophy of Truth*, trans. Daniel Breazeale (Highlands, N.J.: Humanities Press, 1979). Vattimo briefly summarises it as follows: "This series goes from the thing to the mental image, from the image to the word which expresses the individual's state of mind, from this to the word which social conventions determine to be the 'right' one, and then once again from this canonical word to the thing, which we now see only in terms of the traits which may most easily be metaphorized in the vocabulary that we have inherited…" *The End of Modernity*, 167.
102. Nietzsche, *Human, All Too Human*, § 638, pp. 266–7. (In the Penguin edition, the phrase is translated as 'the *philosophy of the forenoon*').
103. *The End of Modernity*, 169.
104. *Human, All-Too-Human*, § 20, as quoted by Vattimo in *Nietzsche: An Introduction*, 81–2.
105. Vattimo, *The Adventure of Difference: Philosophy after Nietzsche and Heidegger*, trans. Cyprian Blamires with Thomas Harrison (Baltimore: Johns Hopkins University Press, 1993), 164.
106. See "How the 'Real World' at last Became a Myth" in Friedrich Nietzsche, *Twilight of the Idols / The Anti-Christ*, trans. R.J. Hollingdale (London: Penguin,

1990), and Nietzsche, *The Will to Power*, trans. Walter Kaufman and R.J. Hollingdale, ed. W. Kaufmann (New York: Vintage, 1968), §12, 12–14.

107. "Against positivism, which halts at phenomena—"There are only *facts*"—I would say: No, facts is precisely what there is not, only interpretations." Nietzsche, *The Will to Power*, trans. Walter Kaufman and R.J. Hollingdale, ed. W. Kaufmann (New York: Vintage, 1968), §481, 267.

108. See Vattimo, *Beyond Interpretation: The Meaning of Hermeneutics for Philosophy*, trans. David Webb (Stanford: Stanford University Press, 1997), 13. Although these two readings may bear some political affinities, Vattimo does not explicitly relate them to the political Right or Left.

109. The textual evidence Vattimo refers to most in emphasising the interpretation of Heidegger as a foundationless thinker are the opening of *On Time and Being* and the end of "On the Essence of Ground." Heidegger, *On Time and Being*, trans. Joan Stambaugh (New York: Harper & Row, 1972). Heidegger, "On the Essence of Ground" in *Pathmarks*, ed. William McNeill (Cambridge: Cambridge University Press, 1998). Vattimo develops this reading of Heidegger most fully in his paper "*An-Denken*. Thinking and the Foundation" in *The Adventure of Difference*.

110. *Beyond Interpretation*, 13.

111. "*An-Denken*: Thinking and the Foundation," 114.

112. Vattimo, "Dialectics, Difference, and Weak Thought," *Graduate Faculty Philosophy Journal* 10 (1984), 156.

113. See Vattimo's "Hermeneutics and Nihilism: An Apology for Aesthetic Consciousness," in *Hermeneutics and Modern Philosophy*, ed. B. Wachterhauser (New York: SUNY Press, 1986).

114. Hans-Georg Gadamer, *Truth and Method*, 2nd ed., trans. Joel Weinsheimer and Donald Marshall (New York: Continuum, 1989), 475.

115. For a concise statement of Vattimo's interpretation of Gadamer, see his essay "Gadamer and the Problem of Ontology" in *Gadamer's Century: Essays in Honor of Hans-Georg Gadamer*, ed. Jeff Malpas, Ulrich Arnswald, and Jens Kertscher (Cambridge, Mass.: MIT Press, 2002).

116. A term Vattimo employs, suggested by Jürgen Habermas' remark that Gadamer "urbanised the Heideggerian province." See *Beyond Interpretation*, 3.

117. "Dialectics, Difference, and Weak Thought," 157.

118. For Vattimo's understanding of truth in relation to Heidegger and others, see his essay "The Truth of Hermeneutics" in *Beyond Interpretation*.

119. See Vattimo, "Toward an Ontology of Decline," trans. B. Spakman in *Recoding Metaphysics*.

120. See Vattimo, "Metaphysics, Violence, Secularisation" trans. B. Spakman in *Recoding Metaphysics*, and *Beyond Interpretation*, chapter 3 (especially 30–31 and 115, note 3).

121. Vattimo, "Hermeneutics and Democracy," *Philosophy and Social Criticism* 23.4 (1997), 5.

122. By contrast, Vattimo explains that the form of thought he advocates "…sets out on the way towards thinking Being as temporality, as living life (and therefore also as passion, *eros*, need and welcome), as growing old and decline. In such a way

it includes in Being, as the essential way it is given, all those features excluded from it by the metaphysical tradition in its quest for assurance and so for force (and the violence bound up with the imposition of presence)." "Dialectics and Difference" in *The Adventure of Difference*, 184.
123. "Nietzsche and Heidegger," 28.
124. *The End of Modernity*, 173.
125. Most importantly for Vattimo, in the first essay of Heidegger's *Identity and Difference*, trans. Joan Stambaugh (New York: Harper and Row, 1974). Heidegger also uses the term in the context of a discussion of nihilism in "The Question of Being" in *Pathmarks*, ed. William McNeill (Cambridge: Cambridge University Press, 1998).
126. It is with regard to this inflection of meaning that Vattimo draws a connection between Heidegger's notion of *Verwindung* and Nietzsche's use of the idea of convalescence, in particular in the Preface from the second edition of *The Gay Science* [trans. Walter Kaufmann (New York: Vintage, 1974), 32–38] and "The Convalescent" in Part Three of *Thus Spoke Zarathustra* [trans. R.J. Hollingdale (London: Penguin, 1961), 232–238]. See Vattimo, *Dialogue with Nietzsche*, 151 and 179.
127. Vattimo's most thorough analysis of the term *Verwindung*, on which I have drawn here, is in *The End of Modernity*, 172–3.
128. See *Beyond Interpretation*, 121, note 16.
129. *Impossible Exchange*, trans. Chris Turner (London; New York: Verso, 2001), 73.
130. See Lyotard, "A Success of Sartre's," foreword in Denis Hollier, *The Politics of Prose: Essay on Sartre* (Minneapolis: University of Minnesota Press, 1986). Baudrillard's opposition to Sartrean existentialism is not so explicitly stated, but may be inferred from comments such as the epigraph to this chapter section, and the statement that his focus on the object was an attempt to break with the problematic of the subject. See Baudrillard, *Passwords*, trans. Chris Turner (London; New York: Verso, 2003), 3. (Baudrillard's relation to Sartre is complicated, however, by the fact that in the same place he cites the famous tree root in Sartre's *Nausea* as the inspiration for his interest in the object.)
131. Vattimo writes that "[t]oday's philosophical climate shows little interest in [the existentialist] subject and is in general unreceptive to the themes of 'classic' existentialism, such as the individual, freedom to choose, responsibility, death, and *Angst*..." "The Decline of the Subject and the Problem of Testimony" in *The Adventure of Difference*, 40–41. For a succinct reiteration of Nietzsche's and Heidegger's arguments concerning the subject, see also Vattimo's "The Crisis of the Notion of Value from Nietzsche until Today" in *The Search for Absolute Values* (New York: ICF Press, 1976). For a more extended treatment of the theme of the subject in Nietzsche's work, see Vattimo's *Il soggetto e la maschera: Nietzsche e il problema della liberazione* (Milan: Bompiani, 1999).
132. The radicality of Sartre's "deconstruction" of the subject is increasing being recognized. For a recent treatment of this issue, see Nik Farrell Fox, *The New Sartre: Explorations in Postmodernism* (New York; London: Continuum, 2003), chapter 1.
133. See Heidegger, "On the Question of Being" in *Pathmarks*, ed. William McNeill (Cambridge: Cambridge University Press, 1998).

134. Baudrillard, "On Nihilism" in *Simulacra and Simulation*, 161.
135. Butler argues that this is a necessary implication of Baudrillard's thought which he himself indicates, but which he does not always keep in mind. For a discussion of this issue, see the Conclusion to Butler's *Jean Baudrillard: The Defence of the Real* (London; Thousand Oaks; New Delhi: Sage, 1999).

Chapter 3, Postmodernity and Nihilism

1. Jean-François Lyotard, *The Postmodern Condition: A Report on Knowledge*, trans. Geoff Bennington and Brian Massumi (Manchester: Manchester University Press, 1984).
2. Lyotard, *The Differend: Phrases in Dispute*, Trans. Georges Van Den Abbeele (Manchester: Manchester University Press, 1988).
3. The continuity between these two phases of Lyotard's work is emphasised by his insistence that "*Le Différend* remedies the shortcomings of *Economie libidinale*; it is an attempt to say the same things but without unloading problems so important as justice." Dick Veerman and Willem van Reijen, "An Interview with Jean-François Lyotard," *Theory, Culture, and Society* 5 (1988), 300–1. Quoted by Iain Hamilton Grant in his introduction to Lyotard's *Libidinal Economy*, xxiv–xxv. Moreover, James Williams construes the primary difference between the libidinal and postmodern phases of Lyotard's work as consisting in different interpretations of how the end of defending the event against the tendency of structure to negate it is to be achieved (the maximisation of libidinal intensities vs. testifying to the differend). According to Williams, the means (experimentation), central field (events), and end result (difference affirmed at the expense of illegitimate systematisation) remain consistent between these two major phases of Lyotard's thought. See Williams' *Lyotard and the Political* (London: Routledge, 2000), 92.
4. Lyotard gives a concise description of society in terms of libidinal economy in the section "The System and the Event" in the essay "March 23." See *Jean-François Lyotard: Political Writings*, trans. Bill Readings and Kevin Paul (Minneapolis: University of Minnesota Press, 1993), 63–66.
5. These essays are collected in *The Inhuman: Reflections on Time*, trans. Geoffrey Bennington and Rachel Bowlby (Cambridge: Polity Press, 1991) and *Postmodern Fables*, trans. Georges Van Den Abbeele (Minneapolis: University of Minnesota Press, 1997).
6. For an interpretation of the postmodern in relation to art, see Lyotard's "Answering the Question: What is Postmodernism?" in *The Postmodern Condition*. For a definition of the postmodern which combines narrative structure in writing and the temporal organisation of history, see "A Postmodern Fable" in *Postmodern Fables*.
7. Lyotard here means the most technologically advanced societies, in which knowledge has become the primary means of production. He references Daniel Bell, *The Coming of Post-Industrial Society* (New York: Basic Books, 1973) and Alain Touraine, *The Post-Industrial Society* (London: Wildwood House, 1974).
8. Lyotard is somewhat equivocal about this periodization, also stating that the social and cultural changes to which he is referring have been underway since the turn of the century. See *The Postmodern Condition*, 3 and xxiii.

9. *The Postmodern Condition*, xxiv.
10. Lyotard, *The Postmodern Explained to Children: Correspondence 1982–1985*, trans. Julian Pefanis and Morgan Thomas (Sydney: Power Publications, 1992), 36.
11. *Postmodern Fables*, 97.
12. *The Postmodern Explained to Children*, 40.
13. See, for example, Madan Sarup, *An Introductory Guide to Post-structuralism and Postmodernism* (New York; London: Harvester Wheatsheaf, 1993), Karl-Otto Apel, "What is Philosophy?: The Philosophical Point of View After the End of Dogmatic Metaphysics" in *What is Philosophy?*, ed. C.P. Ragland and Sarah Heidt (New Haven: Yale University Press, 2001), and Gianni Vattimo, "The End of (Hi)Story," *Chicago Review* 35. 4 (1986): 20–30.
14. See *The Postmodern Condition*, 38–39.
15. Nietzsche, *The Will to Power*, trans. Walter Kaufman and R.J. Hollingdale, ed. W. Kaufmann (New York: Vintage, 1968), §2, 9.
16. Wittgenstein's "language game" is a multi-faceted concept. Arguably, however, the primary significance of this concept for Wittgenstein is to express the idea that semantic meaning is given in rule-governed and purposive uses of language as concretely expressed in forms of life, and cannot be uncovered solely by logical analysis. Lyotard appropriates this idea because it suggests that there is no meta-discourse (such as logical analysis) which governs all meaningful discourse: uses of language are heterogenous, and often incommensurable. The analysis of discourses in terms of language games allows him to show that there are limits to rational, representational schemas, thus allowing space for events. For Wittgenstein on language games, see *The Wittgensten Reader*, ed. Anthony Kenny (Oxford: Blackwell, 1994), 46–49. For concise statements of Lyotard's reading of Wittgenstein and language games, see *The Postmodern Condition*, 9–11, and "Wittgenstein, After" in *Jean-François Lyotard: Political Writings*, trans. Bill Readings and Kevin Paul (Minneapolis: University of Minnesota Press, 1993).
17. Lyotard, *The Postmodern Condition*, 37.
18. *Ibid.*, 39–40.
19. *Ibid.*, 40.
20. See David Hume, *A Treatise of Human Nature*, ed. David Fate Norton and Mary J. Norton (Oxford: Oxford University Press, 2000), Book III, Part I, Section I. Lyotard expands on the is/ought gap in *Just Gaming*, trans. Wlad Godzich (Manchester: Manchester University Press, 1985), 17. Simon Malpas discusses the significance of this theme in Lyotard's work in *Jean-François Lyotard* (New York: Routledge, 2002), 53–4.
21. *The Postmodern Condition*, 45.
22. Lyotard, *The Postmodern Condition*, 37. Despite Lyotard's criticisms of Critical Theory in general (see *The Postmodern Condition*, 11–14) and Adorno in particular (see "Adorno as the Devil," trans. Robert Hurley, *Telos* 19 (1974): 127–137), Lyotard's closeness here to the critique of instrumental reason in Adorno and Horkheimer's *Dialectic of Enlightenment* (trans. trans. John Cumming (New York; London: Verso, 1997)) is striking.
23. See Lyotard, "New Technologies" in *Jean-François Lyotard: Political Writings*, trans. Bill Readings and Kevin Paul (Minneapolis: University of Minnesota Press, 1993), 15–16.

24. Lyotard writes that "it is fair to say that for the last forty years the 'leading' sciences and technologies have had to do with language: phonology and theories of linguistics, problems of communication and cybernetics, modern theories of algebra and informatics, computers and their languages, problems of translation and the search for areas of compatibility among computer languages, problems of information storage and data banks, telematics and the perfection of intelligent terminals, paradoxology." *The Postmodern Condition*, 3–4.
25. Lyotard, "New Technologies," 17.
26. Lyotard, *The Inhuman*, 50.
27. *The Postmodern Condition*, 40.
28. *Ibid.* 15.
29. This analysis is given in the "Missive on Universal History" in *The Postmodern Explained to Children*, 35–39.
30. Lyotard, *Peregrinations: Law, Form, Event* (New York: Columbia University Press, 1988), 72.
31. Lyotard writes: "Kapital…is *metamorphosis* without end or purpose. Such a metamorphosis operates on the one hand as a dissolution of *old* pre-capitalist institutions and on the other hand as a self-dissolution of its own institutions, constantly undone and redone." "Notes on the Return and Kapital," trans. Roger McKeon, *Semiotexte* 3.1 (1978), 47.
32. *Ibid.*, 51.
33. *Ibid.*, 47.
34. "The *only* untouchable axiom bears on the condition of metamorphosis and transfer: exchange value….The only axiom of this system entirely made up of indifference and equivalence…, the law of value, is as well the only *limit*, an impassable limit if you wish, always displaceable and displaced, keeping capitalism from being carried off by the meandering flood of molecular energetics." Lyotard, "Energumen Capitalism," trans. James Leigh, *Semiotexte* 2.3 (1977), 20–1.
35. *Ibid.*, 24.
36. In *Libidinal Economy*, Lyotard in fact analyses capital in terms of two "zero"s, the concentratory zero and the zero of conquest. This analysis is too detailed to go into here. See *Libidinal Economy*, chapter 5.
37. "Notes on the Return and Kapital," 48.
38. See, for example, *Baudrillard Live*, ed. Mike Gane (London; New York: Routledge, 1993), 21–3.
39. Nicholas Zurbrugg, "Baudrillard, Modernism, and Postmodernism" in *Baudrillard: A Critical Reader*, ed. Douglas Kellner (Oxford; Cambridge: Blackwell, 1994), 227.
40. Best and Kellner write that "Baudrillard's acolytes praise him as the 'talisman' of the new postmodern universe, as *the* commotion who theoretically energises the postmodern scene, as *the* supertheorist of a new postmodernity." *Postmodern Theory: Critical Interrogations* (London: Macmillan, 1991), 11. See also Arthur Kroker and Charles Levin, "Baudrillard's Challenge," *Canadian Journal of Political and Social Theory* VIII.1–2 (1984): 5–16.
41. Baudrillard, "On Nihilism" in *Simulacra and Simulation*, trans. Sheila Faria Glaser (Ann Arbor: University of Michigan Press, 1994).

42. Adapted from "On Nihilism," 159–160.
43. The meaning Baudrillard gives to the term "interpretation" must be distinguished from the meaning it has for many other theorists, including Nietzsche and Vattimo. For Nietzsche, Vattimo and others, interpretation is exactly what we do when we *don't* seek to go beyond appearances, when we don't assume we have access to an objective truth.
44. Paul Ricoeur famously identifies Marx, Freud and Nietzsche as the three "masters" of this hermeneutics of suspicion. See his *Freud and Philosophy: An Essay on Interpretation*, trans. Denis Savage (New Haven: Yale University Press, 1970), 32.
45. "On Nihilism," 160.
46. *Ibid.*, 161
47. *Ibid.*, 159 and 160.
48. Mike Gane alludes to this theme in noting the similarity between Baudrillard's "The Precession of Simulacra" and Nietzsche's "How the 'True World' At Last Became a Fable." *Jean Baudrillard: In Radical Uncertainty* (London: Pluto, 2000), 15.
49. Baudrillard, *In the Shadow of the Silent Majorities*, trans. Paul Foss, Paul Patton, and John Johnston (New York: Semiotext(e), 1983).
50. *Ibid.*, 104.
51. *Ibid.*, 65.
52. The parallel between Baudrillard's theory of the masses and his theory of simulation is argued by Rex Butler in both "Jean Baudrillard's Defence of the Real: Reading *In the Shadows of the Silent Majorities* as an Allegory of Representation" in *Jean Baudrillard, Art and Artefact*, ed. Nicholas Zurbrugg (Brisbane: Institute of Modern Art, 1997) and *Jean Baudrillard: The Defence of the Real* (London; Thousand Oaks; New Delhi: Sage, 1999), 58–63.
53. *In the Shadow of the Silent Majorities*, 78.
54. Butler, "Jean Baudrillard's Defence of the Real," 57.
55. *Ibid.*, 58.
56. *In the Shadow of the Silent Majorities*, 30.
57. See *Ibid.*, 89, note 5.
58. "The masses are not an external, contingent limit to the social, but an *internal*, necessary limit." Butler, "Jean Baudrillard's Defence of the Real," 57.
59. *In the Shadow of the Silent Majorities*, 31. This passage is significant because it evokes an image of postmodern society in contrast to which Lyotard develops his own theory of postmodernity. With reference to Baudrillard's *In the Shadow of the Silent Majorities*, Lyotard writes: "This breaking up of the grand Narratives (…) leads to what some authors analyse in terms of the dissolution of the social bond and the disintegration of social aggregates into a mass of individual atoms thrown into the absurdity of Brownian motion. Nothing of the kind is happening: this point of view, it seems to me, is haunted by the paradisaic representation of a lost 'organic' society." *The Postmodern Condition*, 15.
60. *In the Shadow of the Silent Majorities*, 100.
61. See Marshall McLuhan, *Understanding Media: The Extensions of Man* (London: Sphere Books, 1967).
62. Baudrillard, "The Ecstasy of Communication" in *The Anti-Aesthetic: Essays on Postmodern Culture*, ed. Hal Foster (Port Townsend, Washington: Bay Press, 1983), 131.

63. *Ibid.*
64. Baudrillard, *Symbolic Exchange and Death*, trans. Iain Hamilton Grant (London: Sage, 1993).
65. Baudrillard's model for his first study of sign value and the system of consumption, *The System of Objects* (trans. James Benedict (London; New York: Verso, 1996)) was Roland Barthes' *The Fashion System* (trans. Matthew Ward and Richard Howard (London: Cape, 1985)).
66. Gary Genosko, *Baudrillard and Signs: Signification Ablaze* (London; New York: Routledge, 1994), 36.
67. *Ibid.*
68. *Ibid.*, 135.
69. Baudrillard, *The Transparency of Evil: Essays on Extreme Phenomena*, trans. James Benedict (London; New York: Verso, 1993).
70. *Ibid.*, 10.
71. The transfinite is a concept originating in set theory, and was developed for linguistics by Julia Kristeva. Mike Gane explains that the transfinite "indicates that which has passed beyond the finite, which is thus 'more than' a finite figure, but is not infinite." *Baudrillard's Bestiary: Baudrillard and Culture* (London; New York: Routledge, 1991), 126–7.
72. *The Transparency of Evil*, 3.
73. *Ibid.*, 5–6.
74. Baudrillard, *The Illusion of the End*, trans. Chris Turner (Cambridge: Polity, 1994), 7.
75. *Ibid.*
76. *The Illusion of the End*, 11.
77. Jean Baudrillard, "The Year 2000 Will Not Take Place," trans. Paul Foss and Paul Patton, in *Futur*Fall: Excursions into Post-modernity*, ed. E.A. Grosz (Sydney: Power Institute of Fine Arts, 1986).
78. *Ibid.*, 19.
79. *Ibid.*, 20.
80. In his meditation on the meaning of September 11, "The Spirit of Terrorism," Baudrillard suggests that the terrorist attack in America was the first event since the "strike of events" in the nineteen-nineties. He is hesitant, however, to conclude from this that history has somehow re-begun. This is an issue for Baudrillard's theory of the contemporary situation which deserves attention, but which lies beyond the scope of the present study. See Baudrillard, *The Spirit of Terrorism and Other Essays*, trans. Chris Turner (London; New York: Verso, 2003).
81. Baudrillard, "Game With Vestiges," in *Baudrillard Live*, 95.
82. Baudrillard calls this reversal poetic because the only evidence for its possibility exists in language (see the passage quoted on page 255 of the present text). Having drawn an analogy between the formalistic structures of language and capital, Baudrillard is in effect hoping for the possibility that the poetic, reversible effects found in language might also be found in capitalism and in contemporary society generally. On this point, see also chapter four, note 155.
83. Baudrillard, *Impossible Exchange*, trans. Chris Turner (London; New York: Verso, 2001).

84. Baudrillard, *Fatal Strategies*, trans. Philip Beitchman and W.G.J. Niesluchowski (London: Pluto Press, 1990).
85. *Impossible Exchange*, 3.
86. This accordance is suggested by a comparison of the following representative passages. In *The Transparency of Evil*, Baudrillard writes: "The law that is imposed on us is a law of the confusion of categories. Everything is sexual. Everything is political. Everything is aesthetic. All at once" (9). In *Impossible Exchange* he writes: "The economic sphere, the sphere of all exchange, taken overall, cannot be exchanged for anything…indeterminacy induces a fluctuation of equations and postulates at the very heart of the economic sphere and leads, in the end, to that sphere lurching off into speculation, its criteria and elements all interacting madly…The other spheres—politics, law and aesthetics—are characterised by this same non-equivalence, and hence the same eccentricity. Literally, they have no meaning outside themselves and cannot be exchanged for anything…this impossible equivalence finds expression in the increasing undecidability of its categories, discourses, strategies and issues" (3–4).
87. *Ibid.*, 4. The systems Baudrillard mentions here are economics, politics, law, and aesthetics.
88. *Ibid.*, 7.
89. Baudrillard, *Impossible Exchange*, 8. This is hardly a radical claim, since the Latin word *ex-sistere*, from which "existence" is derived, means "to stand out from nothing." For details of this etymology, see John Macquarrie, *Existentialism* (Harmondsworth: Penguin, 1972), 62.
90. In an interview Baudrillard explains: "I found the idea of the 'nothing' in Macedonio Fernandez, an Argentine author who is very little known in France, even though two of his books have been translated! He wrote a very remarkable book on the continuation of the nothing." This book is *Papiers de Nouveauvenu et continuation du Rien* (Paris: José Corti, 1997). See Baudrillard, *Fragments: Conversations with François L'Yvonnet*, trans. Chris Turner (London; New York: Routledge, 2004), 38 and 115, note 6.
91. Martin Heidegger, "What is Metaphysics?" in *Martin Heidegger: Basic Writings* ed. David Farrell Krell (New York: Harper Collins, 1993).
92. For example, Baudrillard writes: "[T]he world hides behind the radical illusion of technology…the mystery (of the continuation of the Nothing) conceals itself beneath the universal banality of information. Heidegger: 'When we look into the ambiguous essence of technology, we behold the constellation, the stellar course of the mystery.'" Baudrillard, *The Perfect Crime*, trans. Chris Turner (London; New York: Verso, 1996), 72–73. See also *Impossible Exchange*, 23.
93. Gianni Vattimo, *The Transparent Society*, trans. David Webb (Baltimore: Johns Hopkins University Press, 1992), 1–2.
94. Vattimo, *The End of Modernity: Nihilism and Hermeneutics in Post-Modern Culture*, trans. John R. Snyder (Baltimore: John Hopkins University Press, 1988), 2.
95. Vattimo cites Walter Benjamin's "Theses on the Philosophy of History" as particularly influential in this regard. This essay is collected in Benjamin, *Illuminations*, trans. Harry Zorn, ed. Hannah Arendt (London: Pimlico, 1999).

96. Vattimo, "Dialectics, Difference, and Weak Thought," trans. Thomas Harrison, *Graduate Faculty Philosophy Journal* 10 (1984), 154.
97. Theodor W. Adorno and Max Horkheimer, *Dialectic of Enlightenment*, trans. John Cumming (London; New York: Verso, 1997), 120–67.
98. Vattimo, *The Transparent Society*, 7.
99. Vattimo elaborates this point in *Dialogue with Nietzsche*, where he argues that Nietzsche's work reveals "…the increased power acquired by myth thanks to the instruments of mass communication' (61). Vattimo argues that '[p]rint, radio, cinema, television, and the culture industry in general amount to so many channels of diffusion and sites of fabrication of new myths (*ibid.*)…we all know that television lies and that the media do not in the least supply disinterested and objective representations of the world." Vattimo, *Dialogue with Nietzsche*, trans. William McCuaig (New York: Columbia University Press, 2006), 128.
100. Arnold Gehlen, "Die Säkularisierung des Fortschritts" in *Einblicke*, Vol. VII, ed. K.S. Rehberg (Frankfurt: Klostermann, 1978).
101. Vattimo, *The End of Modernity*, 8.
102. Fredric Jameson, *Postmodernism, or, The Cultural Logic of Late Capitalism* (London; New York: Verso, 1991), ix.
103. See Gianni Vattimo, "The End of (Hi)Story," *Chicago Review* 35.4 (1986): 20–30.
104. *Ibid.*, 25.
105. *The End of Modernity*, 2–3.
106. "The End of (Hi)Story," 28–29.
107. The charge of performative contradiction, I would argue, is only a valid one when the performance contradicts the theory in ways not anticipated and acknowledged by the theory itself. This does not necessarily mean that theories which consciously involve a tension with their performances are not problematic on this count, but indications of problems must take a more specific form than the general charge of performative contradiction.
108. Heidegger, *Identity and Difference*, trans. Joan Stambaugh (New York: Harper and Row, 1969).
109. *Ibid.*, 36–7. To Stambaugh's translation, I have added Heidegger's key German terms—now well-known by Anglophone Heidegger scholars—in square brackets.
110. *Ibid.*, 38. Translation modified to restore German terms.
111. *Ibid.*, 37.
112. Vattimo's most detailed discussion of *Ge-Stell* can be found in the paper "Dialectic and Difference" in *The Adventure of Difference: Philosophy after Nietzsche and Heidegger*, trans. Cyprian Blamires with Thomas Harrison (Baltimore: Johns Hopkins University Press, 1993).
113. *The End of Modernity*, 26.
114. *Ibid.*, 21.
115. *Ibid.*, 21–22.
116. *Dialogue with Nietzsche*, 128.
117. On this issue see Vattimo's essay "Ethics of Communication or Ethics of Interpretation?" in *The Transparent Society*.
118. For this claim, see "The Postmodern: A Transparent Society?" in *The Transparent Society*.

119. See Vattimo, "Hermeneutics and Democracy," *Philosophy and Social Criticism* 23.4 (1997): 1–7.

120. This argument is given in the essay "Disenchantment and Dissolution" in *The Transparent Society*, where Vattimo writes that "…a rejection of violence and oppression…requires that equality, as the meaning of disenchantment, be accompanied by an explicit commitment to the 'weakening' of being, that is, for a thought that openly attempts to locate itself outside the logic of the struggle for survival, or the liberal vision of the affirmation of rights in competition with each other" (102).

121. A term Vattimo prefers to "utopia," since it better reflects the social pluralism he valorises. See his essay "Utopia or Heterotopia?" in *The Transparent Society*.

122. For Vattimo's engagement with Deleuze and Derrida, see the title essay in *The Adventure of Difference*. Vattimo's confrontations with Severino—a major Italian philosopher who calls for a return to Parmenides—are more oblique, but are clearly evident in his comments which link Parmenides to the atom bomb (*The End of Modernity*, 5). In championing becoming over Being, Vattimo's work can be understood as standing in opposition to Severino's body of thought.

123. See "Hermeneutics and Democracy." French philosopher Alain Badiou characterises these same traits, fundamentalism and capitalism, as a "disjunctive synthesis" of two nihilisms which characterise the contemporary era. This agreement reinforces my contention that Vattimo is concerned with contemporary problems that other philosophers term nihilism, but because of his positive revaluation of this term, he uses other terms (such as metaphysics or violence) to express these problems. See Badiou, *Infinite Thought*, trans. and ed. Oliver Feltham and Justin Clemens (London; New York: Continuum, 2003), 158–62.

124. Vattimo's views on religious fundamentalism in particular are strongly manifest in his reaction to the Ayatollah Khomeini's *fatwah* against Salman Rushdie: "the… sentence of Khomeini against Rushdie…is not the voice of a different kind of culture, it is merely the expression of a backwardness which we can reasonably hope to overcome by means of a correct work of secularisation." "Our Savage Brother," *La Stampa*, 18 February 1989. Quoted by Dario Antiseri, *The Weak Thought and its Strength* (Aldershot: Avebury, 1996), 69.

125. "Hermeneutics and Democracy," 5. Vattimo's critical analysis of capitalism is given further discussion in chapter four.

126. *Ibid.*

127. *The Illusion of the End*, 8.

128. Julian Young, *The Death of God and the Meaning of Life* (London; New York: Routledge, 2003), 3.

129. Proponents of such a view include early theorists of postmodernity such as Rudolf Pannwitz, Arnold Toynbee, and C. Wright Mills, discussed in the Introduction.

130. Karen L. Carr, *The Banalization of Nihilism: Twentieth Century Responses to Meaninglessness* (Albany: SUNY Press, 1992), 5.

131. *Ibid.*, 7.

132. The concept of the untimely (*Unzeitgemässe*) is owed to Nietzsche, who most famously defines it as "acting counter to our time and thereby acting on our time and, let us hope, for the benefit of a time to come." Nietzsche, *Untimely Meditations*, trans.

R.J. Hollindale (Cambridge: Cambridge University Press, 1997), 60. For a fuller discussion of the several meanings this term has for Nietzsche, see pages xlv–xlvii of the same volume.
133. Vattimo, *The End of Modernity*, 19–20.
134. *The Postmodern Condition*, 17.
135. Baudrillard, *The Perfect Crime*, trans. Chris Turner (London; New York: Verso, 1996), 64–5.
136. Vattimo, "Postmodernity, Technology, Ontology," in *Technology in the Western Political Tradition*, ed. A.M. Melzer, J. Weinberger, and M.R. Zinman (London; Ithaca: Cornell University Press, 1993), 220. To meet the demands of Lyotard's thought on this issue, Vattimo's "interpretive" must be asserted as preferable to his "descriptive" here. Lyotard rails against the attempt to deduce prescriptive (i.e. normative) implications from correct descriptions of society, identifying it as characteristic of the "modern" forms of social theory he wishes to reject. See Lyotard, *Just Gaming*, trans. Wlad Godzich (Manchester: Manchester University Press, 1985), 19–26. In the same text, Lyotard suggests that a preferable social theory would take the form of an Idea in Kant's sense. That is, it would move beyond the sensible and the possibility of demonstration to a supersensible ideal which has regulatory value. The key point of Lyotard's argument is that social theory should not be considered theoretical knowledge with a demonstrable truth value. To simplify a complex issue, Vattimo's theory of postmodernity, insofar as it is presented as an *interpretation*, does not seek to be descriptive in a purely "factual" sense.
137. *The Differend*, 135–6.
138. Heidegger develops this idea in a complex way through the notion of the "Other Beginning." See his *Contributions to Philosophy (from Enowning)*, trans. Parvis Emad and Kenneth Maly (Bloomington, Ind.: Indiana University Press, 1999), especially Part III: Playing-Forth, 119–157.
139. See the reference in chapter one, note 68.
140. See Baudrillard, "On Nihilism," and Lyotard, "A Postmodern Fable."
141. *The Illusion of the End*, 120.
142. *On Metapsychology*, trans. James Strachey, ed. Angela Richards (London: Penguin, 1984), 251–268.
143. *Ibid.*, 266–7.
144. *Beyond Hermeneutics*, 13.

Notes to Chapter 4, Negotiating Nihilism

1. *Very Little...Almost Nothing: Death, Philosophy, Literature* (London: Routledge, 1997), 12.
2. See the "Preamble" in Critchley, *Very Little...Almost Nothing*.
3. Critchley, *op. cit.*, 10.
4. Pope John Paul II, *Restoring Faith in Reason: A New Translation of the Encyclical Letter FAITH AND REASON of Pope John Paul II*, ed. Laurence Hemming and Susan Frank Parsons (Notre Dame: University of Notre Dame Press, 2003). For a discussion of this Encyclical Letter in relation to Nietzsche and nihilism, see Howard

Caygill, "The Survival of Nihilism" in *Nihilism Now!: Monsters of Energy*, ed. Keith Ansell Pearson and Diane Morgan (Houndmills, Basingstoke: Macmillan, 2000).
5. Critchley, *op. cit.*, 11.
6. For an examination of nihilistic tendencies within contemporary analytic philosophy, see Bruce Wilshire, *Fashionable Nihilism: A Critique of Analytic Philosophy* (Albany: SUNY Press, 2002). Needless to say, the tradition of analytic philosophy is vastly diverse and cannot be reduced to those tendencies identified by either Critchley or Wilshire.
7. Critchley, *op. cit.*, 11.
8. Critchley, *op. cit.*, 11-12.
9. Martin Heidegger, *An Introduction to Metaphysics*, trans. Ralph Manheim (New Haven; London: Yale University Press, 1959), 199.
10. Critchley, *op. cit.*, 12.
11. See the epigraph to this chapter.
12. Critchley, *op. cit.*, 12.
13. The course I follow here, although varying somewhat in detail, takes its bearings from James Williams' treatment of the problem of nihilism in Lyotard's work. In chapters three and four of *Lyotard and the Political* (London: Routledge, 2000), Williams shows how a logic of difference and a politics of passivity are the keys to Lyotard's response to nihilism. Here I chart similar terrain, drawing on Williams in my treatment of Lyotard, but extending my analysis to show that these themes are also evident in the works of Baudrillard and Vattimo, and drawing on the works of other commentators which support this line of interpretation. The context of Williams' analysis of nihilism is a study of the political in Lyotard's work, and his analysis is limited by this focus on Lyotard and the role that nihilism plays in his political thought. My own analysis, focused on the problem of nihilism itself for postmodern thinkers, broadens the analysis of nihilism and differs on some issues. Like Williams', my analysis of nihilism in postmodern thinkers involves comparisons with Heidegger and Deleuze on this issue, but extends these comparisons beyond the limits of Williams' brief engagements. A marked point of difference between my analysis and Williams' involves the relationship of Deleuze to the postmodernists in question here on the issue of nihilism. While acknowledging their stylistic differences, Williams focuses on the thematic continuities between Deleuze's *Nietzsche and Philosophy* and Lyotard's *Libidinal Economy*, arguing that "*Libidinal Economy* could be *Nietzsche and Philosophy* brought to life and drawn away from the dangers of a status as definitive theory" (*Lyotard and the Political*, 50). While I agree that the approach to the problem of nihilism found in the works of Lyotard, Baudrillard, and Vattimo is well-articulated by Deleuze's "logic of difference," unlike Williams I underline the significant disagreement between Deleuze and the postmodernists over the issue of whether or not nihilism may be overcome.
14. Judith Norman argues that Heidegger, Derrida, Paul de Man, Maurice Blanchot and Vincent Descombes all follow some form of this line of reasoning in their treatments of Nietzsche. See Norman, "Nietzsche contra *contra*: Difference and opposition," *Continental Philosophy Review* 33.2 (2000): 189–206.

15. See Norman, *op. cit.*, Williams, *op. cit.*, and Michael Hardt, *Gilles Deleuze: An Apprenticeship in Philosophy* (Minneapolis: University of Minnesota Press, 1993).
16. Gilles Deleuze, *Nietzsche and Philosophy*, trans. Hugh Tomlinson (New York: Columbia University Press, 1983).
17. Heidegger, "The Word of Nietzsche: God is Dead" in *The Question Concerning Technology and Other Essays*, trans. William Lovitt (New York: Harper & Row, 1977), 61. Quoted in Williams, *Lyotard and the Political*, 54. In "Who is Nietzsche's Zarathustra?" Heidegger explains: "Metaphysical thinking rests on the distinction between what truly is and what, measured against this, constitutes all that is not truly in being. However, what is decisive for the *essence* of metaphysics is by no means the fact that the designated distinction is formulated as the opposition of the suprasensuous to the sensuous realm, but the fact that this distinction—in the sense of a yawning gulf between the realms—remains primary and all-sustaining. The distinction persists even when the Platonic hierarchy of suprasensuous and sensuous is inverted and the sensuous realm is experienced more essentially and more thoroughly...." "Who is Nietzsche's Zarathustra?" in *Nietzsche, Vol. II: The Eternal Recurrence of the Same*, trans. David Farrell Krell (London and Henley: Routledge and Kegan Paul, 1984), 230.
18. In *Contributions to Philosophy*, Heidegger states that any "opposition" to metaphysics puts metaphysics back in place anew. *Contributions to Philosophy (from Enowning)*, trans. Parvis Emad and Kenneth Maly (Bloomington, Ind.: Indiana University Press, 1999), 121. See also pages 122 and 127.
19. Heidegger, *Martin Heidegger: Basic Writings*, ed. David Farrell Krell (New York: Harper Collins, 1993), 232. This principle is abstract and general, but is given concrete illustration by Heidegger in his analyses of the ways that both Nietzsche and Sartre attempt to overcome nihilism through a reversal of metaphysics. These specific arguments, concerning topics such as the creation of values, subjectivity, and the will, were outlined in chapter one.
20. "The Survival of Nihilism," 191.
21. Nietzsche writes: "I do not want to accuse; I do not even want to accuse those who accuse. *Looking away* shall be my only negation. And all in all and on the whole: some day I wish to be only a Yes-sayer." Nietzsche, *The Gay Science*, trans. Walter Kaufmann (New York: Vintage, 1974), § 276, 223.
22. For an overview of these various commentators, see Norman, *op. cit.*
23. Benedict de Spinoza, Letter 50 (to Jarig Jelles) in *Spinoza: The Letters*, trans. Samuel Shirley (Indianapolis/Cambridge: Hackett, 1995).
24. Caygill, *op. cit.*, 196.
25. Caygill writes: "The argument in terms of 'life' frees the concept from its associations with the 'higher values' of Christianity, but only to convert them into another higher value. Christianity is condemned for 'negating life' for 'shifting the centre of gravity out of life' for 'poisoning life' but all in the name of the new higher value of 'life.' The details of the affirmation of instinct and the body merely conceal that a new highest value has been insinuated, one that began in the negation of Christian higher values... [y]et the negation of this negation in the name of life does not achieve the *Aufhebung* of nihilism, but only its confirmation and survival." *Op. cit.*, 194.

26. For a treatment of nihilism which differs somewhat in the details of its argument, but arrives at the same conclusion concerning this double bind, see Maurice Blanchot, "Nihilism: The Limits of Experience," in *The New Nietzsche*, ed. David B. Allison (Cambridge, Mass.: MIT Press, 1985). For an analysis of Blanchot's argument, see my article "The Obscure: Blanchot at the Limits of Nihilism," *Janus Head* 12.1 (forthcoming – 2010).

27. See *The Logic of Hegel*, trans. William Wallace (London: Oxford University Press, 1931), 215-229, and *Hegel's Science of Logic*, vol. 2, trans. W.H. Johnston and L.G. Struthers (London: George Allen and Unwin, 1951), 43–58.

28. Hegel writes: "The Positive is the identical self-relation in such a way as not to be the Negative, and the Negative is the different by itself so as not to be the Positive. Thus either has an existence of its own in proportion as it is not the other. The one is made visible in the other, and is only in so far as that other is. Essential difference is therefore Opposition; according to which the different is not confronted by *any* other but by *its* other. That is, either of these two (Positive and Negative) is stamped with a characteristic of its own only in its relation to the other: the one is only reflected into itself as it is reflected into the other. And so with the other. Either in this way is the other's *own* other." *The Logic of Hegel*, 220.

29. Gilles Deleuze, *Difference and Repetition*, trans. Paul Patton (New York: Columbia University Press, 1994).

30. I follow Judith Norman's account of Deleuze's theory of difference here (see Norman, *op. cit.*) An account of the role of negation in Deleuze's thought which seemingly contrasts with Norman's account is given by Michael Hardt (*op. cit.*, xii and 37-38). Hardt argues that Deleuze employs a concept of negation that is *more* negative than Hegel's oppositional negation: while in Hegel's philosophy both opposing terms are preserved in an *Aufhebung*, Deleuze insists on the complete destruction of that which denies or opposes difference. This contrast between the interpretations offered by Norman and Hardt can be understood as a case of each emphasising a different aspect of Deleuze's theory: Norman emphasises the initial moment of affirmation, while Hardt emphasises the resulting negation (see below in the text for an explanation of these two moments). I follow Norman here because her emphasis best explains the logic of difference employed by the postmodern theorists under consideration. (This is arguably the case despite the fact that Norman's conclusion – that Deleuze's logic of difference succeeds in overcoming nihilism – is at odds with the conclusions of the postmodernists discussed here. For a discussion of the different conclusions reached by Deleuze, on the one hand, and Lyotard, Baudrillard, and Vattimo, on the other, see pages 199-201 below.) Moreover, Hardt's emphasis seems to miss the point with respect to the issue of nihilism: it is not the preservation implied in the synthesis of opposites which constitutes the nihilism of Hegel's dialectic, but rather the fact that it is predicated on a metaphysics of negation, in which life is understood as a constantly self-negating movement. On the issue of Hegel and nihilism, see Michael Allen Gillespie, *Nihilism Before Nietzsche* (Chicago; London: University of Chicago Press, 1995), 115-121.

31. Deleuze writes: "Oppositions are roughly cut from a delicate milieu of overlapping perspectives, of communicating distances, divergences and disparities,

of heterogenous potentials and intensities." *Difference and Repetition*, 50. For Nietzsche's critique of oppositional thinking, see *Beyond Good And Evil*, trans. R.J. Hollingdale (London: Penguin, 1990), section 2, 33-34, and Norman's discussion of this, *op. cit.*, 193-194.

32. *Difference and Repetition*, 28.
33. *Ibid.*, 128.
34. Norman, *op. cit.*, 195.
35. *Nietzsche and Philosophy*, 119-122.
36. Nietzsche, *On the Genealogy of Morals*, trans. Douglas Smith (Oxford: Oxford University Press, 1996), essay I, § 10, 22.
37. *Nietzsche and Philosophy*, 122.
38. See Nietzsche, *Thus Spoke Zarathustra*, trans. R.J. Hollingdale (London: Penguin, 1961), "The Awakening," 319-322. See also Norman's discussion on this issue in *op. cit.*, 198.
39. On this point, see also Vattimo's argument that saying "No" is not, in itself, an essential trait of reactive or passive nihilism. *Dialogue with Nietzsche*, trans. William McCuaig (New York: Columbia University Press, 2006), 134-135.
40. *Nietzsche and Philosophy*, 188.
41. *Difference and Repetition*, 54.
42. Norman, *op. cit.* This claim is most clearly made in footnote 24, page 204.
43. *Nietzsche and Philosophy*, 198.
44. For a concise treatment of these themes by Deleuze, see his essay "Nietzsche" in *Pure Immanence: Essays on A Life*, trans. Anne Boyman (New York: Zone Books, 2001). For more detailed treatments, see *Nietzsche and Philosophy* and *Difference and Repetition*.
45. The criticisms of Deleuze that Lyotard, Baudrillard and Vattimo make are too nuanced and varied to cover adequately here. For Baudrillard's criticisms, see *Seduction*, trans. Brian Singer (New York: St. Martin's Press, 1990), 144-9 and *Forget Foucault* (New York: Semiotext(e), 1987), *passim*. For Vattimo's criticisms, see the title essay in *The Adventure of Difference: Philosophy after Nietzsche and Heidegger*, trans. Cyprian Blamires with Thomas Harrison (Baltimore: Johns Hopkins University Press, 1993), and *Dialogue with Nietzsche*, trans. William McCuaig (New York: Columbia University Press, 2006), 24 and 137.
46. Jean-François Lyotard, *Libidinal Economy*, trans. Iain Hamilton Grant (London: Athlone, 1993), 42.
47. For a more adequate treatment of the differences between Deleuze and Lyotard on the issue of whether nihilism can be overcome, only briefly glossed here, see my essay "Eternal Return in Dispute: Deleuze and Lyotard on Nihilism," *Proceedings of the Australasian Society for Continental Philosophy*, 2003.
48. Keiji Nishitani, *The Self-Overcoming of Nihilism*, trans. Graham Parkes with Setsuko Aihara (Albany SUNY Press, 1990), 1.
49. Caygill, "The Survival of Nihilism," 196.
50. Lyotard, "On a Figure of Discourse" in *Toward The Postmodern*, ed. Robert Harvey and Mark S. Roberts (New Jersey: Humanities Press, 1993), 12.
51. Heidegger, "Nihilism as Determined by the History of Being" in *Nietzsche Vol. IV: Nihilism*, trans. David Farrell Krell (San Francisco: Harper & Row, 1987), 223; 224.

52. Gary Genosko discusses this theme with respect to the works of Lyotard, Baudrillard, and Vattimo. See *Baudrillard and Signs: Signification Ablaze* (London; New York: Routledge, 1994), 72-81.
53. *Nietzsche and Philosophy*, 102.
54. *Libidinal Economy*, 14.
55. Geoffrey Bennington, *Lyotard: Writing the Event* (Manchester: Manchester University Press, 1988), 15.
56. Lyotard glosses the way desire as wish gives rise to representation, theatricalisation, and hence nihilism, as follows: "The quanta of energy (which is the same as desire, insofar as it is force) that cannot be discharged in a specific action with respect to reality become represented on a scene opened up within the psychical apparatus (or is it within the subject?)—a scene opened by this impossibility, by this very lack." Lyotard, "On A Figure of Discourse," 13.
57. Lyotard writes: "The word *desire* has two meanings in Freud's work: there is the sense of wish (*Wunsch*) and that of force or energy (Nietzsche's *Wille*)." *Ibid*.
58. Sigmund Freud, *On Metapsychology*, trans. James Strachey, ed. Angela Richards (London: Penguin, 1984), 190.
59. "Cathexis" and "investment" are alternative translations of Freud's *Besetzung*. In his translation of *Libidinal Economy*, Iain Hamilton Grant uses the English "investment" to translate Lyotard's *investissement*, the standard French version of this Freudian term. See *Libidinal Economy*, xi, for an explanation of this translation.
60. Freud, *loc. cit.*
61. "On A Figure of Discourse," 15. As Bennington notes, Lyotard consequently revises Freud by denying his claim that desire as wish is also at the heart of the unconscious. See Bennington, 16 and Freud, "The Unconscious" in *On Metapsychology*, 190: "The nucleus of the *Ucs.* consists of instinctual representatives which seek to discharge their cathexis; that is to say, it consists of wishful impulses." Lyotard advances an argument against Freud's positing of wish and representation in the unconscious in the context of his example of the boy's *fort-da* game in "Beyond the Pleasure Principle." See *Libidinal Economy*, 22–25.
62. On this point, Lyotard cautions that "[t]o take the side of the primary process is still a consequence of secondary processes." Baudrillard quotes this passage in *Seduction*, 145.
63. Sigmund Freud, "Beyond the Pleasure Principle" in *The Essentials of Psycho-Analysis*, trans. James Strachey, ed. Anna Freud (London: Penguin, 1986), 250, 258, and 266, footnote.
64. Lyotard explains the structuring force of Eros according to a repetition of the same (which institutes principles of identity and opposition): "Repetition, the principle of not only the metric but even of the rhythmic, if taken in the narrow sense as the repetition of the same (same colour, line, angle, chord), is the work of Eros and Apollo disciplining the movements, disciplining them to the movements, limiting them to the norms of tolerance characteristic of the system or whole in consideration." "Acinema," trans. Paisley N. Livingston in collaboration with the author, *Wide Angle* 2.3 (1978), 55.

65. "'Death instinct': not at all because it seeks death, but insofar as it is a partial, singular affirmation and a subversion of apparent totalities (the Ego, Society) in its very assertion. Any high *emotion* is a death effect, a dissolution of the completed, of the historical." Lyotard, "Notes on the Return and Kapital," trans. Roger McKeon, *Semiotexte* 3.1 (1978), 51.

66. In "Energumen Capitalism," Lyotard writes: "[C]apitalism will never croak from bad conscience, it will not die of a lack or of a failure to render unto the exploited what is owed them. If it disappears, it is by excess, because its energetics unceasingly displace its limits…it is thus in this viscosity that all revolutionary potential lies" (trans. James Leigh, *Semiotexte* 2.3 (1977), 17 and 26). Lyotard's privileging of art and of marginal groups (hippies, the mad, etc.) in these early essays is similarly aligned with this affirmation of the death drive as unbinding, liberating energy. See James Williams, *Lyotard and the Political* (London: Routledge, 2000), 66, for a discussion of the problematic nature of this privileging.

67. *Libidinal Economy*, 29.

68. "[I]t is just as much the death drives whose deregulation or deregulating, when its effect is the fixation of impulses, produces quite as many configurations, stases, economic rigidities which will pass (in silence…) for formal structures." *Libidinal Economy*, 26.

69. Lyotard writes: "[T]he structuralist …[is] incapable of hearing, in the silence, the crackling masses of flux which circulate in the system, and which are, however, the 'final cause' of their operativity." *Libidinal Economy*, 26.

70. Bennington, *Lyotard: Writing the Event*, 25.

71. Here I follow Williams' commentary on active passivity. See *Lyotard and the Political*, chapter four.

72. Williams writes that "[a]n increase in power becomes a difficult trade-off between an increase in the intensity of flows, an increase in their connectedness and an increase in their number." *Lyotard and the Political*, 63.

73. See Lyotard, "La peinture comme dispositif libidinal" in *Des Dispositifs pulsionnels* (Paris: Union Général d'Editions, 1973), and Williams' discussion of this article in *Lyotard and the Political*, 67-71.

74. In Lyotard's words, the tensor is "[a]t the same time a sign which produces meaning through difference and opposition, and a sign producing intensity through force [puissance] and singularity." *Libidinal Economy*, 54.

75. For Lyotard's discussion of the tensor, see *Libidinal Economy* chapter II, especially pages 50–60.

76. See *Libidinal Economy*, 122–7. Lyotard's prime target here is Baudrillard's concept of "symbolic exchange."

77. *Libidinal Economy*, 109.

78. "Notes on the Return and Kapital," 49.

79. *Libidinal Economy*, 262.

80. See Lyotard's critique in *Libidinal Economy*, chapter III.

81. See chapter two, note 78 for Baudrillard's avowal of this shift in his work.

82. Baudrillard, *Seduction*, trans. Brian Singer (New York: St. Martin's Press, 1990), 21.

83. Baudrillard writes: "It is perhaps utopian to claim to pass beyond value, but it is an operative utopia, an attempt to conceive a more radical functioning of things." *Passwords*, trans. Chris Turner (London; New York: Verso, 2003), 11.

84. With seduction, we are entering into one of the most controversial areas of Baudrillard's thought, and it is worth briefly noting the nature of this controversy in order to acknowledge, and perhaps attenuate, possible problems associated with this concept. Baudrillard's work on seduction has been widely criticised by feminists because he associates seduction and weakness with women and femininity, thus reinforcing conceptual categories which have frequently been understood as contributing to the subjugation of women. See for example Luce Irigaray's review of *Seduction*, *Histoires d'Elles* 21 (1980), Jane Gallop, "French Theory and the Seduction of Feminism" in *Men in Feminism*, ed. Alice Jardine and Paul Smith (New York: Methuen, 1987), and Sadie Plant, *The Most Radical Gesture: The Situationist International in a Post-Modern Age* (London: Routledge, 1992). To some degree at least, these criticisms involve mistaken interpretations of Baudrillard's thought. In *Passswords*, Baudrillard responds to these criticisms as follows: "It is true that it seemed to me that historically, women had a privileged position in the field of seduction. But some have taken the view that to link women and seduction was to consign them to the realm of appearances—and hence to frivolity. This is a total misunderstanding: the seduction I was referring to is really the symbolic mastery of forms, whereas the other is merely the material mastery of power by way of a stratagem." (23). For a defence of Baudrillard and his concept of seduction from a feminist perspective, see Victoria Grace, *Baudrillard's Challenge: A Feminist Reading* (London: Routledge, 2000), especially pages 158-164.

85. *Seduction*, 83.

86. *Ibid.*, 102.

87. *Ibid.*, 83.

88. "The Seducer's Diary" is a part of Kierkegaard's *Either/Or*, trans. Alastair Hannay (London: Penguin, 1992). Baudrilard's analysis is found in *Seduction*, 98–118.

89. This gloss draws on Rex Butler's analysis. See Butler, *Jean Baudrillard: The Defence of the Real* (London; Thousand Oaks; New Delhi: Sage, 1999), 107-11.

90. Baudrillard, *The Ecstasy of Communication*, trans. Bernard and Caroline Schutze, ed. Sylvère Lotringer (New York: Semiotext(e), 1988), 98.

91. This is a point which many of Baudrillard's commentators fail to appreciate. See, for example, Chris Rojek and Bryan S. Turner's claim that Baudrillard is wrong more often than he is right, and hence "fails the validity test." "Introduction: Regret Baudrillard?" in Chris Rojek and Bryan S. Turner (eds.), *Forget Baudrillard?* (London; New York: Routledge, 1993), xv.

92. See Butler, *Jean Baudrillard: The Defence of the Real*, back cover.

93. Baudrillard explores the notion of the ironic strategies of objects in *Fatal Strategies*, trans. Philip Beitchman and W.G.J. Niesluchowski (London: Pluto Press, 1990).

94. For Baudrillard's clearest explanation of this difficult idea, see *Passwords*, 85–7.

95. Baudrillard writes: "The uncertainty principle, which states that it is impossible to calculate the speed of a particle and its position simultaneously, is not confined

to physics. It applies also to the impossibility of evaluating both the reality and the meaning of an event as it appears in the information media, the impossibility of distinguishing causes and effects in a particular complex process—of distinguishing the terrorist from the hostage (in the Stockholm syndrome), the virus from the cell (in viral pathology). This is just as impossible as isolating subject from object in experiments in sub-atomic physics." *Impossible Exchange*, trans. Chris Turner (London; New York: Verso, 2001), 19. Baudrillard's appropriation of Heisenberg's uncertainty principle is rather free and potentially quite contentious. With all his usages of scientific terms, however, we should not suppose that the value of the insights he uses them to express depends upon the accuracy of his usage as judged according to the scientific genre. Inspired by Alfred Jarry's "pataphysics," Baudrillard adapts scientific terms and concepts creatively in order to interpret culture, and we should judge such adaptations according to how successful they are in this task. While he does occasionally seem to be making claims about science (for example, complex systems and viral pathology in the preceding quote), such claims may arguably be interpreted as a rhetorical device: the point to be made is always cultural or philosophical, not scientific. For Werner Heisenberg's statement of the uncertainty principle, see "The Copenhagen Interpretation of Quantum Theory" in *The World Treasury of Physics, Astronomy, and Mathematics*, ed. Timothy Ferris (Boston: Little, Brown and Company, 1991). On pataphysics, see Alfred Jarry, *Selected Works of Alfred Jarry*, ed. Roger Shattuck and Simon Watson Taylor (New York: Grove Press, 1965).

96. The French word *duel* has the senses of both the English words "duel" and "dual," and Baudrillard plays on this double meaning. See the translator's note, page 42, in *Seduction*.

97. Given this, those commentators who accuse Baudrillard of a pessimistic quietism are profoundly mistaken. On the contrary, his entire *oeuvre* can be seen as an ambitious attempt to change the world in deep and lasting ways.

98. *The Ecstasy of Communication*, 101.

99. Baudrillard explains that "[t]he enunciation of the fatal is also fatal, or it is not at all" (*The Ecstasy of Communication*, 101). As such, Baudrillard's concepts might be thought of as performatives in J.L Austin's sense: performatives do what they say they do in the act of utterance, and are not to be considered in terms of truth and falsity (e.g. the utterance "I promise" is a performative one). See Austin, *How To Do Things With Words* (Oxford; New York: Oxford University Press, 1962), 4-11.

100. Baudrillard, *Passwords*, 92. Baudrillard provides a qualification to the form of radical thought he advocates: "This type of thought is clearly an *agent provocateur*, managing illusion by illusion. I do not claim that it applies everywhere. Perhaps we have to accept two levels of thought: a causal, rational thought, corresponding to the Newtonian world in which we live; and another, much more radical level of thought which could be said to be part of this secret destining of the world, of which it might be a kind of fatal strategy." *Ibid.*, 87.

101. "The Year 2000 Will Not Take Place," trans. Paul Foss and Paul Patton in *Futur*Fall: Excursions into Post-modernity*, ed. E.A. Grosz (Sydney: Power Institute of Fine Arts, 1986), 21.

102. *Ibid.*
103. *Seduction*, 30.
104. *Ibid.*, 163.
105. Baudrillard, *Passwords*, 42. The undecidability of hypotheses concerning our fate is clearly expressed in *The Perfect Crime*: "We are faced, ultimately, with two irreconcilable hypotheses: that of the extermination of all the world's illusion by technology and the virtual, or that of an ironic destiny of all science and all knowledge in which the world—and the illusion of the world—would survive. The hypothesis of a 'transcendental' irony of technology being by definition unverifiable, we have to hold to these two irreconcilable and simultaneously 'true' perspectives. There is nothing which allows us to decide between them." (trans. Chris Turner (London; New York: Verso, 1996), 74.
106. Baudrillard, *Seduction*, 176.
107. *Ibid.*, 180.
108. It should be noted that Vattimo explicitly criticizes the French "philosophies of difference" represented by thinkers such as Derrida and Deleuze (see the title essay of *The Adventure of Difference: Philosophy after Nietzsche and Heidegger*, trans. Cyprian Blamires with Thomas Harrison (Baltimore: Johns Hopkins University Press, 1993). Vattimo's criticism of the French post-structuralists is that they think difference as a metaphysics—that is, as a permanent structure of the world. Unsurprisingly, Vattimo asserts that the most important sense of difference is that of the *ontological* difference emphasised by Heidegger; it is precisely this sense of difference, he claims, that the French miss. Regardless of whether or not Vattimo is correct, I believe that the logical structure of the ideas of difference developed by Vattimo and the post-structuralists is significantly similar (in the sense outlined above), and this logic allows a way beyond the impasse of nihilism in both the French and Italian strands of thought.
109. It is essential to note again that for Vattimo, "nihilism" is here understood in a positive sense—it holds the place of the "positive" category in this distinction, while "metaphysics" holds the place of the "negative" category (labelled "nihilism" by other philosophers).
110. Giovanna Borradori, "'Weak Thought' and Postmodernism: The Italian Departure from Deconstruction," *Social Text* 18 (1987–8), 39.
111. Vattimo and Rovatti, "Premessa" in *Il pensiero debole* (Milan: Feltrinelli, 1983), 10. Quoted and translated by Dario Antiseri, *The Weak Thought and its Strength* (Aldershot: Avebury, 1996), 4.
112. Vattimo, "Hermeneutics and Democracy," *Philosophy and Social Criticism* 23.4 (1997), 5.
113. Karl Marx, *Writings of the Young Marx on Philosophy and Society*, trans. and ed. Loyd D. Easton and Kurt H. Guddat (New York: Anchor, 1967), 423.
114. Vattimo, *Nihilism and Emancipation: Ethics, Politics, and Law*, trans. William McCuaig, ed. Santiago Zabala (New York: Columbia University Press, 2004), 87–8.
115. For a concise statement of Vattimo's views on weak thought and rationality (on which this exposition draws), see his essay "The Reconstruction of Rationality" appended to *Beyond Interpretation*.

116. *Beyond Interpretation*, 116, footnote 18.
117. Vattimo in fact asserts that his nihilistic, postmodern philosophy "involves plenty of normative content, which can provide the basis for satisfying the reasonable preoccupations of people like Habermas." "The End of (Hi)Story," *Chicago Review* 35.4 (1986), 30.
118. Vattimo's most extended discussion of this concept is the essay "An-Denken. Thinking and Foundation" in *The Adventure of Difference*. The text Vattimo most frequently cites as the source of his understanding of this concept is Heidegger's *What is Called Thinking?*, trans. J. Glenn Gray and F. Wieck (New York; London: Harper and Row, 1972).
119. See Vattimo, "The Problem of Historical Knowledge and the Formation of the Nietzschean Idea of Truth" in *Dialogue with Nietzsche*. On the problem of historicism in Nietzsche, see also "Nihilism and the Problem of Temporality" and "Nietzsche's Vision of the World," both also in *Dialogue with Nietzsche*.
120. This article appears as a chapter in Vattimo's *The Transparent Society*, trans. David Webb (Baltimore: Johns Hopkins University Press, 1992).
121. Vattimo represented the Democratic Left in the European Parliament from 1999 to 2004, where he served on the Commission of Freedom and Citizen's Rights, Justice, and Home Affairs; the Commission for Culture, Youth, Education, the Media, and Sport, and the delegation for relations with South Africa.
122. A selection of Vattimo's essays on political philosophy are collected in *Nihilism and Emancipation*. These essays are brief, schematic, and not entirely consistent in their detail. This perhaps suggests that he has not finished thinking through the problem of drawing out the political implications of his nihilist ontology, the difficulty of which he acknowledges (*Nihilism and Emancipation*, 89). In what follows, I draw selectively from several different essays to outline the most prominent contours of his political thought.
123. The issue of Marxist revolution is explored in some detail in Vattimo's work in the early nineteen-seventies. In the 1973 essay "Nietzsche, the Superman, and the Spirit of the Avant-garde" (collected in *Dialogue with Nietzsche*) and the 1974 book *Il soggeto e la maschera. Nietzsche e il problema della liberazione* (Milan: Bompiani), Vattimo explores the possible contribution of Nietzsche's thought to the Marxist revolutionary project, in particular the notion of the *Übermensch* as the dissolution of bourgeoise subjectivity and the realisation of a nonalienated subject. However, he later moves away from this position and away from the revolutionary project, at least as conceived in a "traditional" Marxist sense, as grounded in a dialectical conception of history. He explains this move as follows: "[I]n *Il soggetto e la maschera* there was still an overriding effort to think the possibility, beyond the decline of the subject, of a substantially 'reconciled' humanity, on the model of dialectic. I now believe that this aspect of my interpretation requires revision, having come to a more radical recognition of the nexus between the overman and the dissolution of the subject..." (*Dialogue with Nietzsche*, 229, note 9). Moreover, Vattimo has since given more general reasons for being dissatisfied with the dialectical conception of history, reasons related to the problem of nihilism and the understanding of modernity in terms of a "new

beginning." See his "Dialectics, Difference, and Weak Thought," trans. Thomas Harrison, *Graduate Faculty Philosophy Journal* 10 (1984): 165-77. In this move away from the Marxist project of liberation through revolution, Vattimo's thought can been seen as charting a path parallel to that of Lyotard and Baudrilard with respect to this political problem.

124. Vattimo, "Bottles, Nets, Revolution, and the Tasks of Philosophy," trans. Iain Chambers, *Cultural Studies* 2.2 (1988), 144.

125. Derrida identifies Marx's 1844 *Economic and Philosophical Manuscripts*, in which the theory of alienation is developed, as bearing the stamp of metaphysical humanism. See "The Ends of Man" in *Margins of Philosophy*, trans. Alan Bass (Chicago: University of Chicago Press, 1982), 117. The 1844 *Manuscripts* can be found in *Writings of the Young Marx on Philosophy and Society*.

126. "Hermeneutics and Democracy," 4.

127. *Nihilism and Emancipation*, 103.

128. Vattimo doesn't supply a clear definition of projectuality, but we may venture some clarification by suggesting that he is drawing here on Heidegger's notion of *Dasein*'s "projection" in *Being and Time*. For Heidegger, projection (*Entwurf*) refers to the way in which Dasein is always more than it factually is, because it understands itself in terms of possibilities. Daesin "*is* existentially that which, in its potentiality-for-being, it is *not yet*" (*Being and Time*, trans. John Macquarrie and Edward Robinson (Oxford: Blackwell, 1962), 185-6). We may understand Vattimo as suggesting that every citizen, as a projecting *Dasein*, has a right to develop these possibilities. For Heidegger's understanding of this term, see *Being and Time*, 185-6, especially the translators' explanation in note 1, page 185.

129. *Nihilism and Emancipation*, 103.

130. *Ibid.*, 5.

131. In *Nihilism and Emancipation*, 120–129.

132. For Vattimo's views on domestic issues in Italy such as abortion, education, dental care, and the minimum wage, see the essay "A Project For the Left" in *Nihilism and Emancipation*, 102–13.

133. "Hermeneutics and Democracy," 1.

134. *Ibid.*, 2.

135. "Globalisation and the Relevance of Socialism" in *Nihilism and Emancipation*, 121.

136. *Ibid.*, 129.

137. *Ibid.*

138. See the explanation of Vattimo's term *sfondamento* in chapter two.

139. The contours of such a debate are indicated by the occasional criticisms these thinkers have for each other's works, sometimes no more than in passing: Lyotard criticises Baudrillard (*Libidinal Economy*, 103—27) and Vattimo (*Postmodern Fables*, trans. Georges Van Den Abbeele (Minneapolis: University of Minnesota Press, 1997), 237), Baudrillard criticises Lyotard (*Forget Foucault* (New York: Semiotext(e), 1987), 17–18 and 39) and Vattimo (*Cool Memories II: 1987–1990*, trans. Chris Turner (Durham: Duke University Press, 1996), 61), and Vattimo criticises Lyotard ("The End of (Hi)story," 23–4).

140. This is the same problem encountered above in the context of Baudrillard's work, where—as Rex Butler points out—most commentators fail to understand Baudrillard on his own terms, and produce criticisms which are simply question-begging. See Butler, *Jean Baudrillard: The Defence of the Real*, 13–14.

141. Wittgenstein explains the idea of family resemblance as follows: "...we see a complicated network of similarities overlapping and criss-crossing: sometimes overall similarities, sometimes similarities of detail. I can think of no better expression to characterise these similarities than 'family resemblances'; for the various resemblances between members of a family: build, features, colour of eyes, gait, temperament, etc. etc. overlap and criss-cross in the same way." *The Wittgenstein Reader*, ed. Anthony Kenny (Oxford: Blackwell, 1994), 49.

142. In addition to the discussion of Zygmunt Bauman and Fredric Jameson which follows, see the discussion of the history of theories of the postmodern in the Introduction.

143. Zygmunt Bauman, *Intimations of Postmodernity* (London; New York: Routledge, 1992), vii.

144. Fredric Jameson, *Postmodernism, or, The Cultural Logic of Late Capitalism* (London; New York: Verso, 1991), 44.

145. See Jameson's discussion of these themes in *op. cit.*, 44–54. For a critical overview of these same themes, see Steven Best and Douglas Kellner, *Postmodern Theory: Critical Interrogations* (London: Macmillan, 1991), 188–92.

146. Lyotard, *The Postmodern Condition: A Report on Knowledge*, trans. Geoff Bennington and Brian Massumi, (Manchester: Manchester University Press, 1984), 26.

147. *Ibid.*

148. "We do not speak as the liberators of desire: idiots with their little fraternities, their Fourieresque fantasies, their policy-holder's expectations over the libido." *Libidinal Economy*, 42.

149. Because, as noted earlier, Lyotard asserts that structures might be stabilised by deregulations and destabilised by regulations, rather than simply the *vice versa* operations that Freud assumes.

150. Williams, *Lyotard and the Political*, 68.

151. Lyotard, *Driftworks*, ed. Roger McKeon (New York: Semiotext(e), 1984), back cover.

152. Baudrillard, *The Transparency of Evil: Essays on Extreme Phenomena*, trans. James Benedict (London; New York: Verso, 1993), 5.

153. For Baudrillard's discussion of the "disappearance of art" through its very proliferation, see "Transaesthetics" in *Ibid*.

154. See Baudrillard, *Simulacra and Simulation*, trans. Sheila Faria Glaser (Ann Arbor: University of Michigan Press, 1994), 164.

155. Baudrillard, *The Illusion of the End*, trans. Chris Turner (Cambridge: Polity Press, 1994), 120. Baudrillard's clearest indication of the existence of this "poetical reversal" in language is his analysis of Saussure's theory of the anagram in *Symbolic Exchange and Death*, trans. Iain Hamilton Grant (London: Sage, 1993). For Baudrillard, the anagram manifests those qualities of ambiguity and reversibility that Saussure's general linguistics reduces out of language, and he argues for a

privileging of the Swiss linguist's work on anagrams over his more well known "structural" theories.

156. For Vattimo's argument for the value of such a disorientation, see "The Postmodern – A Transparent Society?" in *The Transparent Society*.

157. See Vattimo, *The End of Modernity: Nihilism and Hermeneutics in Post-Modern Culture*, trans. John R. Snyder (Baltimore: John Hopkins University Press, 1988), 21 and 26.

158. In *Dialogue with Nietzsche*.

159. *Ibid.*, 130.

160. For Vattimo's treatment of these themes, see "Hermeneutics and Democracy" and the essay "Disenchantment and Dissolution" in *The Transparent Society*.

161. Lyotard, for example, explains that *Libidinal Economy* was in part a purgative which sought to rid political reflection of both Lacanian Hegelianism and Althusserian Marxism. See *Just Gaming*, trans. Wlad Godzich (Manchester: Manchester University Press, 1985), 89.

162. See for example *The End of Modernity*, 180.

163. A good indication of Vattimo's suggestions in this respect is the following passage in *Nihilism and Emancipation*: "To realise everyone's entitlement to a meaningful existence, or, if you like, their right to 'happiness,' is the goal that philosophy is striving to attain by finding the meaning of history not in quantitative development but in a generalised intensification of the meaning of existence, implying solidarity rather than competition and the reduction of all forms of violence rather than the affirmation of metaphysical principles or the endorsement of scientific models of society" (36).

164. Jean-Paul Sartre, *Being and Nothingness*, trans. Hazel E. Barnes (New York: Washington Square Press, 1956), 798.

165. Some of the criticisms I have made of Vattimo here are neatly summarised in a passage he writes about Nietzsche, which seems equally true of his own work: "[W]ithin his oeuvre there is a prophetic tension that never seems to reach its climax in a description of structures, an outline of specific tasks, or the assertion and denial of clear-cut positions." *Dialogue with Nietzsche*, 157.

166. Two volumes: *Anti-Oedipus*, trans. Robert Hurley, Mark Seem, and Helen R. Lane (Minneapolis: University of Minnesota Press, 1983); *A Thousand Plateaus*, trans. Brian Massumi (Minneapolis: University of Minnesota Press, 1987).

167. *Libidinal Economy*, 42.

168. Deleuze and Guattari warn that lines of flight "themselves emanate a strange despair, like an odour of death and immolation, a state of war from which one returns broken: they have their own dangers…Why is the line of flight a war one risks coming back from defeated, destroyed, after having destroyed everything one could? This, precisely, is the fourth danger: the line of flight crossing the wall, getting out of the black holes, but instead of connecting with other lines and each time augmenting its valence, *turning to destruction, abolition pure and simple, the passion of abolition*…like suicide, double suicide, a way out that turns the line of flight into a line of death." *A Thousand Plateaus*, 229.

169. "March 23," in *Jean-François Lyotard: Political Writings*, trans. Bill Readings and Kevin Paul (Minneapolis: University of Minnesota Press, 1993), 65.

Notes to Conclusion

1. *Nausea*, trans. Robert Baldick (Harmondsworth: Penguin, 1965); *The Outsider*, trans. Joseph Laredo (Harmondsworth: Penguin, 1982).
2. Baudrillard writes: "The dialectic stage, the critical stage is empty…There is no longer a stage, not even the minimal illusion that makes events capable of adopting the force of reality…" "On Nihilism" in *Simulacra and Simulation*, trans. Sheila Faria Glaser (Ann Arbor: University of Michigan Press, 1994), 161 and 164.
3. Vattimo writes that "[a]ccording to a well-known thesis of Heidegger, the name 'Occident,' *Abendland*, not only designates our civilisation's place in a geographical sense but names it ontologically as well insofar as *Abendland* is the land of the setting sun, of the sunset of Being." "Toward an Ontology of Decline," trans. B. Spakman in *Recoding Metaphysics: The New Italian Philosophy*, ed. Giovanna Borradori (Evanston, IL: Northwestern University Press, 1988), 63.
4. See for example *Baudrillard Live*, ed. Mike Gane (London; New York: Routledge, 1993), 83-4.
5. See the discussion of this point in chapter four.
6. Jean-Paul Sartre, *Being and Nothingness*, trans. Hazel E. Barnes (New York: Washington Square Press, 1956), 798. See the discussion of this point in the previous chapter.
7. For examples of such critics, see the Introduction, note 54.
8. Here I follow Paul Patton, who develops a similar argument in his article "Deleuze and Guattari: Ethics and Post-modernity," *Leftwright Intervention* 20 (1986): 24-32. In this article Patton contrasts the neo-Aristotelean ethics advocated by Alasdair MacIntyre with the ethics developed in Gilles Deleuze and Félix Guattari's *A Thousand Plateaus*. He argues for the superiority of Deleuze and Guattari's approach because, while MacIntyre's ethics set themselves against the pluralistic and fragmented character of contemporary social and individual life, Deleuze and Guattari's ethics acknowledge and work within this fragmented condition.

Bibliography

Adorno, Theodor W. and Horkheimer, Max, *Dialectic of Enlightenment*, trans. John Cumming (London; New York: Verso, 1997).

Anderson, Perry, *The Origins of Postmodernity* (London; New York: Verso, 1998).

Ansell-Pearson, Keith and Diane Morgan (eds.), *Nihilism Now! Monsters of Energy* (Houndmills, Basingstoke: Macmillan, 2000).

Antiseri, Dario, *The Weak Thought and its Strength* (Aldershot: Avebury, 1996).

Apel, Karl-Otto, "What is Philosophy?: The Philosophical Point of View After the End of Dogmatic Metaphysics" in *What is Philosophy?*, ed. C.P. Ragland and Sarah Heidt (New Haven: Yale University Press, 2001).

Austin, J.L. *How To Do Things With Words* (Oxford; New York: Oxford University Press, 1962).

Badiou, Alain, *Infinite Thought*, trans. and ed. Oliver Feltham and Justin Clemens (London; New York: Continuum, 2003).

Banham, Gary and Charlie Blake (eds.), *Evil Spirits: Nihilism and the Fate of Modernity* (Manchester: Manchester University Press, 2000).

Baracchi, Claudia, Review of Gianni Vattimo, *The Adventure of Difference*, *The Review of Metaphysics* 48 (1995): 681-3.

Barthes, Roland, *The Fashion System*, trans. Matthew Ward and Richard Howard (London: Cape, 1985).

Baudrillard, Jean, *For a Critique of the Political Economy of the Sign*, trans. Charles Levin (St. Louis: Telos, 1981).

———, *Simulations*, trans. Paul Foss, Paul Patton and Philip Beitchman (New York; Brooklyn: Semiotext(e), 1983).

———, "The Ecstasy of Communication" in *The Anti-Aesthetic: Essays on Postmodern Culture*, ed. Hal Foster (Port Townsend, Washington: Bay Press, 1983).

———, *In the Shadow of the Silent Majorities*, trans. Paul Foss, Paul Patton, and John Johnston (New York: Semiotext(e), 1983).

———, "The Year 2000 Will Not Take Place" trans. Paul Foss and Paul Patton in *Futur*Fall: Excursions into Post-modernity*, ed. E.A. Grosz (Sydney: Power Institute of Fine Arts, 1986).

———, *Forget Foucault* (New York: Semiotext(e), 1987).

———, *Jean Baudrillard: Selected Writings*, ed. Mark Poster (Cambridge: Polity Press, 1988).

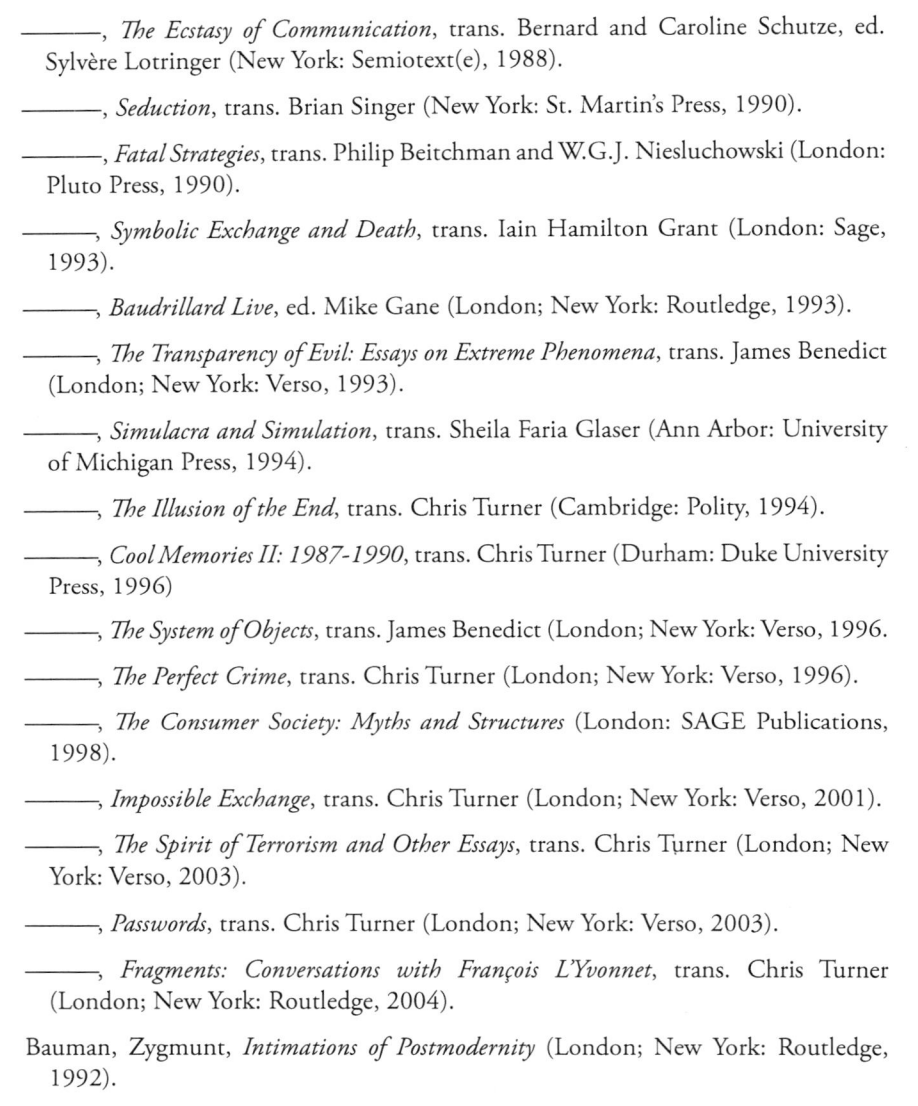

———, *The Ecstasy of Communication*, trans. Bernard and Caroline Schutze, ed. Sylvère Lotringer (New York: Semiotext(e), 1988).

———, *Seduction*, trans. Brian Singer (New York: St. Martin's Press, 1990).

———, *Fatal Strategies*, trans. Philip Beitchman and W.G.J. Niesluchowski (London: Pluto Press, 1990).

———, *Symbolic Exchange and Death*, trans. Iain Hamilton Grant (London: Sage, 1993).

———, *Baudrillard Live*, ed. Mike Gane (London; New York: Routledge, 1993).

———, *The Transparency of Evil: Essays on Extreme Phenomena*, trans. James Benedict (London; New York: Verso, 1993).

———, *Simulacra and Simulation*, trans. Sheila Faria Glaser (Ann Arbor: University of Michigan Press, 1994).

———, *The Illusion of the End*, trans. Chris Turner (Cambridge: Polity, 1994).

———, *Cool Memories II: 1987-1990*, trans. Chris Turner (Durham: Duke University Press, 1996)

———, *The System of Objects*, trans. James Benedict (London; New York: Verso, 1996.

———, *The Perfect Crime*, trans. Chris Turner (London; New York: Verso, 1996).

———, *The Consumer Society: Myths and Structures* (London: SAGE Publications, 1998).

———, *Impossible Exchange*, trans. Chris Turner (London; New York: Verso, 2001).

———, *The Spirit of Terrorism and Other Essays*, trans. Chris Turner (London; New York: Verso, 2003).

———, *Passwords*, trans. Chris Turner (London; New York: Verso, 2003).

———, *Fragments: Conversations with François L'Yvonnet*, trans. Chris Turner (London; New York: Routledge, 2004).

Bauman, Zygmunt, *Intimations of Postmodernity* (London; New York: Routledge, 1992).

Bell, Daniel, *The Coming of Post-Industrial Society* (London: Heinemann, 1974).

Benjamin, Walter, *Illuminations*, trans. Harry Zorn, ed. Hannah Arendt (London: Pimlico, 1999).

Bennington, Geoffrey, *Lyotard: Writing the Event* (Manchester: Manchester University Press, 1988).

Berlin, Isaiah, *Three Critics of the Enlightenment: Vico, Hamann, Herder*, ed. Henry Hardy (Princeton: Princeton University Press, 2000).

Bertens, Hans, *The Idea of the Postmodern: A History* (London; New York: Routledge, 1995).

Best, Steven and Douglas Kellner, *Postmodern Theory: Critical Interrogations* (London: Macmillan, 1991).

———, *The Postmodern Turn* (London; New York: Guilford, 1997).

Blanchot, Maurice, "Nihilism: The Limits of Experience," in *The New Nietzsche*, ed. David B. Allison (Cambridge, Mass.: MIT Press, 1985).

Borradori, Giovanna, "'Weak Thought' and Postmodernism: The Italian Departure from Deconstruction," *Social Text* 18 (1987-8): 39-49

———, (ed.), *Recoding Metaphysics: The New Italian Philosophy* (Evanston: Northwestern University Press, 1988).

Busch, Thomas W. "Sartre's Use of the Reduction: *Being and Nothingness* Reconsidered" in *Jean-Paul Sartre: Contemporary Approaches to his Philosophy*, ed. Hugh J. Silverman and Frederick A. Elliston (Pittsburgh: Duquesne University Press, 1980).

———, *The Power of Consciousness and the Force of Circumstances in Sartre's Philosophy* (Bloomington; Indianapolis: Indiana University Press, 1990).

Butler, Rex, "Jean Baudrillard's Defence of the Real: Reading *In the Shadows of the Silent Majorities* as an Allegory of Representation" in *Jean Baudrillard, Art and Artefact*, ed. Nicholas Zurbrugg (Brisbane: Institute of Modern Art, 1997).

———, *Jean Baudrillard: The Defence of the Real* (London; Thousand Oaks; New Delhi: Sage, 1999).

Cage, John, *Silence* (Middletown, Connecticut: Wesleyan University Press, 1961).

Callinicos, Alex, *Against Postmodernism: A Marxist Critique* (Cambridge: Polity, 1989).

Camus, Albert, *The Rebel*, trans. Anthony Bower (London: Penguin, 1971).

———, *The Outsider*, trans. Joseph Laredo (Harmondsworth: Penguin, 1982).

———, *The Myth of Sisyphus*, trans. Justin O'Brien (London: Penguin, 2000).

Carr, Karen L. *The Banalization of Nihilism: Twentieth Century Responses to Meaninglessness* (Albany: SUNY, 1992).

Carravetta, Peter, *Prefaces to the Diaphora: Rhetorics, Allegory, and the Interpretation of Postmodernity* (West Lafayette, Indiana: Purdue University Press, 1991).

Carroll, David, *Paraesthetics: Foucault, Lyotard, Derrida* (New York: Methuen, 1987).

Carroll, John, *Ego and Soul* (Pymble, N.S.W: Harper Collins, 1998).

Caygill, Howard, "The Survival of Nihilism" in *Nihilism Now!: Monsters of Energy*, ed. Keith Ansell Pearson and Diane Morgan (Houndmills, Basingstoke: Macmillan, 2000).

Coe, David K., *Angst and the Abyss: The Hermeneutics of Nothingness* (New York: Oxford University Press, 1985).

Critchley, Simon, *Very Little...Almost Nothing: Death, Philosophy, Literature* (London: Routledge, 1997).

Connor, Steven, *Postmodernist Culture*, 2nd ed. (Oxford; Cambridge: Blackwell, 1997).

Crosby, Donald A. *The Specter of the Absurd: Sources and Criticisms of Modern Nihilism* (Albany: SUNY, 1988).

———, "Nihilism" in *The Routledge Encyclopedia of Philosophy* Vol. 7, ed. Edward Craig (London; New York: Routledge, 1998).

Crownfield, David, "The Last God" in *Companion to Heidegger's* Contributions to Philosophy, ed. Charles E. Scott, Susan M. Schoenbohm, Daniela Vallega-Neu, and Alejandro Vallega (Bloomington and Indianapolis: Indiana University Press, 2001).

Cunningham, Connor, *Genealogy of Nihilism* (London; New York: Routledge, 2002).

Cusset, François, *French Theory: How Foucault, Derrida, Deleuze, & Co. Transformed the Intellectual Life of the United States* (Minneapolis: University of Minnesota Press, 2008).

Darby, Tom, Bela Egyed, and Ben Jones (eds.), *Nietzsche and the Rhetoric of Nihilism* (Ottawa: Carleton University Press, 1989).

De Beistegui, Miguel, *The New Heidegger* (London; New York: Continuum, 2005).

Deleuze, Gilles, *Nietzsche and Philosophy*, trans. Hugh Tomlinson (New York: Columbia University Press, 1983).

———, *Difference and Repetition*, trans. Paul Patton (New York: Columbia University Press, 1994).

———, *Pure Immanence: Essays on A Life*, trans. Anne Boyman (New York: Zone Books, 2001).

Deleuze, Gilles and Félix Guattari, *Anti-Oedipus*, trans. Robert Hurley, Mark Seem, and Helen R. Lane (Minneapolis: University of Minnesota Press, 1983).

———, *A Thousand Plateaus*, trans. Brian Massumi (Minneapolis: University of Minnesota Press, 1987).

Derrida, Jacques, *Margins of Philosophy*, trans. Alan Bass (Chicago: University of Chicago Press, 1982).

Descartes, Rene, *Descartes: Philosophical Writings*, trans. and ed. Elizabeth Anscombe and Peter Thomas Geach (Middlesex: Open University Press, 1954).

Descombes, Vincent, *Modern French Philosophy*, trans. L. Scott-Fox and J.M. Harding (Cambridge: Cambridge University Press, 1980).

Devaney, M.J. *'Since at least Plato…' and Other Postmodernist Myths* (London; New York: Macmillan/St. Martin's, 1997).

Dews, Peter, *Logics of Disintegration: Post-structuralist Thought and the Claims of Critical Theory* (London; New York: Verso, 1987).

Dilthey, Wilhelm, *The Essence of Philosophy*, trans. Stephen A. Emery and William T. Emery (Chapel Hill: University of North Carolina Press, 1954).

Dreyfus, Hubert L., "Heidegger on the Connection between Nihilism, Art, Technology, and Politics" in *The Cambridge Companion to Heidegger*, ed. Charles Guignon (Cambridge; New York: Cambridge University Press, 1993).

Durkheim, Émile, *Suicide: A Study in Sociology*, trans. John A. Spaulding and George Simpson; ed. G. Simpson (London: Routledge and Keegan, 1952).

Eagleton, Terry, *The Illusions of Postmodernism* (Oxford; Cambridge: Blackwell, 1996).

Evans, Fred J. *Psychology and Nihilism: A Genealogical Critique of the Computational Model of Mind* (Albany, NY: SUNY Press, 1993).

Fernandez, Macedonio, *Papiers de Nouveauvenu et continuation du Rien* (Paris: José Corti, 1997).

Fichte, Johann Gottlieb, *Foundations of the Entire Science of Knowledge* in *The Science of Knowledge*, trans. and ed. Peter Heath and John Lachs (Cambridge: Cambridge University Press, 1982).

Fiedler, Leslie, "The New Mutants" in *The Collected Essays of Leslie Fiedler*, vol. II (New York: Stein and Day, 1971).

Foss, Paul, "Despero Ergo Sum" in *Seduced and Abandoned: The Baudrillard Scene*, ed. André Frankovits (Glebe: Stonemoss Services, 1984).

Foucault, Michel, *The Order of Things* (New York: Vintage, 1970).

———, *Foucault Live*, trans. John Johnson, ed. Sylvère Lotringer (New York: Semiotext(e), 1989).

Fox, Nik Farrell, *The New Sartre: Explorations in Postmodernism* (London; New York: Continuum, 2003).

Frank, Manfred, "Two Centuries of Philosophical Critique of Reason and Its 'Postmodern' Radicalisation," in *Reason and Its Other*, ed. Dieter Freundlieb and Wayne Hudson (Providence/Oxford: Berg, 1993).

Frankovits, André (ed.), *Seduced and Abandoned: The Baudrillard Scene* (Glebe, N.S.W.: Stonemoss Services, 1984).

Frascati-Lochhead, Marta, *Kenosis and Feminist Theology: The Challenge of Gianni Vattimo* (Albany: SUNY Press, 1998).

Freud, Sigmund, *On Metapsychology*, trans. James Strachey, ed. Angela Richards (London: Penguin, 1984).

———, *The Essentials of Psycho-Analysis*, trans. James Strachey, ed. Anna Freud (London: Penguin, 1986).

Frow, John, *What Was Postmodernism?* (Sydney: Local Consumption Publications, 1991).

Gadamer, Hans-Georg, *Truth and Method*, 2nd ed., trans. Joel Weinsheimer and Donald Marshall (New York: Continuum, 1989).

Gallop, Jane, "French Theory and the Seduction of Feminism" in *Men in Feminism*, ed. Alice Jardine and Paul Smith (New York: Methuen, 1987).

Gane, Mike, *Baudrillard: Critical and Fatal Theory* (London; New York: Routledge, 1991).

———, *Baudrillard's Bestiary: Baudrillard and Culture* (London; New York: Routledge, 1991).

———, *Jean Baudrillard: In Radical Uncertainty* (London: Pluto, 2000).

Gehlen, Arnold, "Die Säkularisierung des Fortschritts" in *Einblicke*, Vol. VII, ed. K.S. Rehberg (Frankfurt: Klostermann, 1978).

Genosko, Gary, *Baudrillard and Signs: Signification Ablaze* (London; New York: Routledge, 1994).

Gillespie, Michael Allen, *Nihilism Before Nietzsche* (Chicago; London: University of Chicago Press, 1995).

Goudsblom, Joseph, *Nihilism and Culture* (Totowa, New Jersey: Rowman and Littlefield, 1980).

Grace, Victoria, *Baudrillard's Challenge: A Feminist Reading* (London: Routledge, 2000).

Grieder, Alfons, "What did Heidegger mean by 'Essence'?" in *Martin Heidegger: Critical Assessments*, Vol. 1, ed. Christopher Macann (London; New York: Routledge, 1992).

Habermas, Jürgen, *The Philosophical Discourse of Modernity*, trans. Frederick Lawrence (Cambridge: Polity Press, 1990).

———, "Modernity – An Incomplete Project" in *Postmodernism: A Reader*, ed. Patricia Waugh (London: Edward Arnold, 1992).

Hardt, Michael, *Gilles Deleuze: An Apprenticeship in Philosophy* (Minneapolis: University of Minnesota Press, 1993).

Harvey, David, *The Condition of Postmodernity* (Oxford: Blackwell, 1989).

Hassan, Ihab, "POSTmodernISM: A Paracritical Bibliography," *New Literary History*, 3.1 (1971): 5-30.

———, *The Dismemberment of Orpheus: Toward a Postmodern Literature* (New York: Oxford University Press, 1982).

Hegarty, Paul, *Jean Baudrillard: Live Theory* (London; New York: Continuum, 2004).

Hegel, G.W.F., *The Logic of Hegel*, trans. William Wallace (London: Oxford University Press, 1931).

———, *Hegel's Science of Logic*, vol. 2, trans. W.H. Johnston and L.G. Struthers (London: George Allen and Unwin, 1951).

Heidegger, Martin, *An Introduction to Metaphysics*, trans. Ralph Manheim (London; New Haven: Yale University Press, 1959).

———, *Being and Time*, trans. John Macquarrie and Edward Robinson (Oxford: Blackwell, 1962).

———, *Discourse on Thinking*, trans. John M. Anderson and E. Hans Freund (New York: Harper & Row, 1969).

———, *Identity and Difference*, trans. Joan Stambaugh (New York: Harper and Row, 1969).

———, *What is Called Thinking?*, trans. J. Glenn Gray and F. Wieck (New York; London: Harper and Row, 1972).

———, *On Time and Being*, trans. Joan Stambaugh (New York: Harper & Row, 1972).

———, *The Question Concerning Technology and Other Essays*, trans. William Lovitt (New York: Harper & Row, 1977).

———, *Nietzsche, Vol. I: The Will to Power as Art*, trans. David Farrell Krell (London and Henley: Routledge and Kegan Paul, 1981).

———, *Nietzsche, Vol. II: The Eternal Recurrence of the Same*, trans. David Farrell Krell (London and Henley: Routledge and Kegan Paul, 1984).

———, *Nietzsche, Vol. IV: Nihilism*, trans. David Farrell Krell (San Francisco: Harper & Row, 1987).

———, *Beiträge zur Philosophie (Vom Ereignis)*, Gesamtausgabe Band 65 (Frankfurt am Main: Vittorio Klostermann, 1989).

———, *Martin Heidegger: Basic Writings*, ed. David Farrell Krell (New York: Harper Collins, 1993).

———, "Only A God Can Save Us" in *The Heidegger Controversy: A Critical Reader*, ed. Richard Wolin (Cambridge, Mass.: MIT Press, 1993).

———, *Pathmarks*, ed. William McNeill (Cambridge: Cambridge University Press, 1998).

———, *Die Geschichte des Seyns*, Gesamtausgabe Band 69 (Frankfurt am Main: Vittorio Klostermann, 1998).

———, *Contributions to Philosophy (from Enowning)*, trans. Parvis Emad and Kenneth Maly (Bloomington, Ind.: Indiana University Press, 1999).

———, "My Way to Phenomenology," trans. John Macquarrie and Edward Robinson in *The Phenomenology Reader*, ed. Dermot Moran and Timothy Mooney (London; New York: Routledge, 2002).

Heisenberg, Werner, "The Copenhagen Interpretation of Quantum Theory" in *The World Treasury of Physics, Astronomy, and Mathematics*, ed. Timothy Ferris (Boston: Little, Brown and Company, 1991).

Herman, Arthur, *The Idea of Decline in Western History* (New York: The Free Press, 1997).

Howe, Irving, "Mass Society and Postmodern Fiction" in *Decline of the New* (New York: Horizon, 1970).

Hume, David, *A Treatise of Human Nature*, ed. David Fate Norton, Mary J. Norton (Oxford: Oxford University Press, 2000).

Husserl, Edmund, *Ideas: General Introduction to Pure Phenomenology*, trans. W. R. Boyce Gibson (New York: Collier, 1962).

Inwood, Michael, *A Heidegger Dictionary* (Oxford; Malden, Massachusetts: Blackwell, 1999).

Irigaray, Luce, Review of Jean Baudrillard, *Seduction*, *Histoires d'Elles* 21 (1980).

Jacobi, Friedrich Heinrich, "Open Letter to Fichte," trans. D.I. Behler in *Philosophy of German Idealism*, ed. E. Behler (New York: Continuum, 1987).

Jameson, Fredric, "Postmodernism and Consumer Society" in *The Anti-Aesthetic: Essays on Postmodern Culture*, ed. Hal Foster (Port Townsend, Washington: Bay Press, 1983).

———, "Postmodernism, or, The Cultural Logic of Late Capitalism," *New Left Review* 146 (1984): 53-93.

———, *Postmodernism, or, The Cultural Logic of Late Capitalism* (London; New York: Verso, 1991).

Jarry, Alfred, *Selected Works of Alfred Jarry*, ed. Roger Shattuck and Simon Watson Taylor (New York: Grove Press, 1965).

Jencks, Charles, *The Language of Post-Modern Architecture*, 6th ed. (London: Academy Editions, 1991).

Kaufmann, Walter (ed.), *Existentialism from Dostoevsky to Sartre* (New York: Meridian, 1975).

Kellner, Douglas, *Jean Baudrillard: From Marxism to Postmodernism and Beyond* (Cambridge: Polity, 1989).

Kierkegaard, Søren, *Either/Or*, trans. Alastair Hannay (London: Penguin, 1992).

King, Anthony, "Baudrillard's Nihilism and the End of Theory," *Telos* 112 (1998): 89-106.

Kroker, Arthur and Charles Levin, "Baudrillard's Challenge," *Canadian Journal of Political and Social Theory* VIII.1-2 (1984): 5-16.

Lane, Richard J. *Jean Baudrillard* (London: Routledge, 2000).

Levin, Charles, *Jean Baudrillard: A Study in Cultural Metaphysics* (London: Prentice Hall, 1996).

Levin, David Michael, *The Opening of Vision: Nihilism and the Postmodern Situation* (New York: Routledge and Kegan Paul, 1988).

Lotringer, Sylvère and Sande Cohen (eds.), *French Theory in America* (New York: Routledge, 2000).

Löwith, Karl, *Martin Heidegger and European Nihilism*, ed. R. Wolin (New York: Columbia University Press, 1995).

Lyotard, Jean-François, *Discours, figure* (Paris: Klincksieck, 1971).

———, *Dérive à partir de Marx et Freud* (Paris: Union Général d'Editions, 1973).

———, *Des Dispositifs pulsionnels* (Paris: Union Général d'Editions, 1973).

———, "Adorno as the Devil," trans. Robert Hurley, *Telos* 19 (1974): 127-137.

———, "The Tooth, The Palm," trans. Anne Knap and Michel Benamou, *Sub-Stance* 15 (1976): 105-110.

———, "Energumen Capitalism," trans. James Leigh, *Semiotexte* 2.3 (1977): 11-26.

———, "Acinema," trans. Paisley N. Livingston in collaboration with the author, *Wide Angle* 2.3 (1978): 52-59.

———, "Notes on the Return and Kapital," trans. Roger McKeon, *Semiotexte* 3.1 (1978): 44-53.

———, *The Postmodern Condition: A Report on Knowledge*, trans. Geoff Bennington and Brian Massumi (Manchester: Manchester University Press, 1984).

———, *Driftworks*, ed. Roger McKeon (New York: Semiotext(e), 1984).

———, *Just Gaming*, trans. Wlad Godzich (Manchester: Manchester University Press, 1985).

———, "A Success of Sartre's," foreword in Denis Hollier, *The Politics of Prose: Essay on Sartre* (Minneapolis: University of Minnesota Press, 1986).

———, *The Differend: Phrases in Dispute*, Trans. Georges Van Den Abbeele (Manchester: Manchester University Press, 1988).

———, *Peregrinations: Law, Form, Event* (New York: Columbia University Press, 1988).

———, *Phenomenology*, trans. Brian Beakley (Albany: SUNY Press, 1991).

———, *The Inhuman: Reflections on Time*, trans. G. Bennington and Rachel Bowlby (Cambridge: Polity Press, 1991).

———, *The Postmodern Explained to Children: Correspondence 1982-1985*, trans. Julian Pefanis and Morgan Thomas (Sydney: Power Publications, 1992).

———, *Libidinal Economy*, trans. Iain Hamilton Grant (London: Athlone, 1993).

———, *Jean-François Lyotard: Political Writings*, trans. Bill Readings and Kevin Paul (Minneapolis: University of Minnesota Press, 1993).

———, *Toward the Postmodern*, ed. Robert Harvey and Mark S. Roberts (New Jersey: Humanities Press, 1993).

———, *Postmodern Fables*, trans. Georges Van Den Abbeele (Minneapolis: University of Minnesota Press, 1997).

———, *Signé Malraux* (Paris: Grasset, 1996).

———, *Signed, Malraux*, trans. Robert Harvey (Minneapolis: University of Minnesota Press, 1999).

———, *Soundproof Room: Malraux's Anti-Aesthetics*, trans. Robert Harvey (Stanford: Stanford University Press, 2001).

Marcel, Gabriel, *The Philosophy of Existence*, trans. Manya Harari (London: Harvill Press, 1948).

Macann, Christopher, *Four Phenomenological Philosophers: Husserl, Heidegger, Sartre, Merleau-Ponty* (London; New York: Routledge, 1993).

Macquarrie, John, *Existentialism* (Harmondsworth: Penguin, 1972).

Malpas, Jeff, "Gadamer, Davidson, and the Ground of Understanding" in *Gadamer's Century: Essays in Honor of Hans-Georg Gadamer*, ed. Jeff Malpas, Ulrich Arnswald and Jens Kertscher (Cambridge, Mass.: MIT Press, 2002).

Malpas, Simon, *Jean-François Lyotard* (New York: Routledge, 2002).

Marx, Karl, *Writings of the Young Marx on Philosophy and Society*, trans. and ed. Loyd D. Easton and Kurt H. Guddat (New York: Anchor, 1967).

Mautner, Thomas (ed.), *The Penguin Dictionary of Philosophy* (London: Penguin, 1996).

McLuhan, Marshall, *Understanding Media: The Extensions of Man* (London: Sphere Books, 1967).

Moran, Dermot, *Introduction to Phenomenology* (London; New York: Routledge, 2000).

Mills, C. Wright, *The Sociological Imagination* (New York: Oxford University Press, 1959).

Nagel, Thomas, *The View from Nowhere* (New York: Oxford University Press, 1986).

Nietzsche, Friedrich, *Thus Spoke Zarathustra*, trans. R.J. Hollingdale (London: Penguin, 1961).

———, *The Will To Power*, trans. Walter Kaufman and R.J. Hollingdale, ed. W. Kaufmann (New York: Vintage, 1968).

———, *The Gay Science*, trans. Walter Kaufmann (New York: Vintage, 1974).

———, "On Truth and Lie in a Nonmoral Sense" in *Philosophy of Truth*, trans. Daniel Breazeale (Highlands, N.J.: Humanities Press, 1979).

———, *Human, All-Too-Human*, trans. Marion Faber and Stephen Lehmann (London: Penguin, 1984).

———, *Beyond Good And Evil*, trans. R.J. Hollingdale (London: Penguin, 1990).

———, *Twilight of the Idols / The Anti-Christ*, trans. R.J. Hollingdale (London: Penguin, 1990).

———, *On the Genealogy of Morals*, trans. Douglas Smith (Oxford: Oxford University Press, 1996).

———, *Untimely Meditations*, trans. R.J. Hollingdale, ed. Daniel Breazeale (Cambridge: Cambridge University Press, 1997).

Nishitani, Keiji, *The Self-Overcoming of Nihilism*, trans. Graham Parkes with Setsuko Aihara (Albany SUNY Press, 1990).

Norman, Judith, "Nietzsche contra *contra*: Difference and opposition," *Continental Philosophy Review* 33.2 (2000): 189-206.

Norris, Christopher, "Lost in the Funhouse: Baudrillard and the Politics of Postmodernism," *Textual Practice* 8.3 (1990): 360-87.

———, *What's Wrong With Postmodernism: Critical Theory and the Ends of Philosophy* (New York; London: Harvester Wheatshaft, 1990).

———, *Uncritical Theory: Postmodernism, Intellectuals, and the Gulf War* (London: Lawrence and Wishart, 1992)

———, *The Truth About Postmodernism* (Oxford; Cambridge: Blackwell, 1993).

Novak, Michael, *The Experience of Nothingness* (New York: Harper and Row, 1970).

Olson, Robert C., "Nihilism" in *The Encyclopedia of Philosophy*, Vol. 5, ed. Paul Edwards (New York: Macmillan, 1967).

Patton, Paul, "Deleuze and Guattari: Ethics and Post-modernity," *Leftwright Intervention* 20 (1986): 24-32.

Pefanis, Julian, *Heterology and the Postmodern: Bataille, Baudrillard, and Lyotard* (Durham: Duke University Press, 1991).

Pippin, Robert B., *Modernism as a Philosophical Problem* (Oxford: Blackwell, 1999).

Plant, Sadie, *The Most Radical Gesture: The Situationist International in a Post-Modern Age* (London: Routledge, 1992).

Plato, *The Dialogues of Plato*, Vol. II (Oxford: The Clarendon Press, 1875).

Polt, Richard, "The Event of Enthinking the Event" in *Companion to Heidegger's Contributions to Philosophy*, ed. Charles E. Scott, Susan M. Schoenbohm, Daniela Vallega-Neu, and Alejandro Vallega (Bloomington and Indianapolis: Indiana University Press, 2001).

Pope John Paul II, *Restoring Faith in Reason: A New Translation of the Encyclical Letter FAITH AND REASON of Pope John Paul II*, ed. Laurence Hemming and Susan Frank Parsons (Notre Dame: University of Notre Dame Press, 2003).

Pratt, Alan, *The Dark Side: Thoughts on the Futility of Life from the Ancient Greeks to the Present* (New York: Citadel, 1994).

———, "Nihilism" in *The Internet Encyclopedia of Philosophy*, ed. James Fieser and Bradley Dowden http://www.iep.utm.edu/n/nihilism.htm, 29/6/2005

Readings, Bill, *Introducing Lyotard: Art and Politics* (London: Routledge, 1991).

Ricoeur, Paul, *Freud and Philosophy: An Essay on Interpretation*, trans. Denis Savage (New Haven: Yale University Press, 1970).

———, *From Text to Action: Essays in Hermeneutics II*, trans. Kathleen Blamey and John B. Thompson (Illinois: Northwestern University Press, 1991).

Ritter, J. and K. Gründer (eds.), "Nihilismus" in *Historisches Wörterbuch der Philosophie* [Historical Dictionary of Philosophy], vol. 6 (Basel/Stuttgart: Schwabe & Company, 1971-).

Rojek, Chris and Bryan S. Turner (eds.), *Forget Baudrillard?* (London; New York: Routledge, 1993).

Rose, Gillian, *Dialectic of Nihilism* (Oxford: Blackwell, 1984).

Rosen, Stanley, *Nihilism: A Philosophical Essay* (New Haven; London: Yale University Press, 1969).

———, "Thinking About Nothing" in *Heidegger and Modern Philosophy: Critical Essays*, ed. Michael Murray (New Haven: Yale University Press, 1978).

———, *Hermeneutics As Politics*, 2nd. ed. (New Haven; London: Yale University Press, 1987).

Sartre, Jean-Paul, *Being and Nothingness*, trans. Hazel E. Barnes (New York: Washington Square Press, 1956).

———, *The Transcendence of the Ego: An Existentialist Theory of Consciousness*, trans. Forrest Williams and Robert Kirkpatrick (New York: Hill and Wang, 1960).

———, *Saint Genet: Actor and Martyr*, trans. Bernard Frechtman (New York: Braziller, 1963).

———, *Nausea*, trans. Robert Baldick (Harmondsworth: Penguin, 1965).

———, *The Psychology of Imagination*, trans. Bernard Frechtman (New York: Washington Square Press, 1966).

———, "Existentialism Is A Humanism" in *Existentialism from Doestoevsky to Sartre*, ed. Walter Kaufmann (New York: Meridian, 1975).

———, *The Family Idiot: Gustave Flaubert, 1821-1857*, trans. Carol Cosman (Chicago: University of Chicago Press, 1981).

———, *Notebooks for an Ethics*, trans. David Pellauer (Chicago: University of Chicago Press, 1992).

———, "Intentionality: A Fundamental Idea of Husserl's Phenomenology," trans. Joseph P. Fell in *The Phenomenology Reader*, ed. Dermot Moran and Timothy Mooney (New York; London: Routldege, 2002).

Sarup, Madan, *An Introductory Guide to Post-structuralism and Postmodernism* (New York; London: Harvester Wheatsheaf, 1993).

Schacht, Richard, "Nietzsche and Nihilism," *Journal of the History of Philosophy* 11.1 (1973): 65-90.

Schrift, Allan D. *Nietzsche and the Question of Interpretation: Between Hermeneutics and Deconstruction* (New York: Routledge, 1990).

———, "The Becoming-Postmodern of Philosophy" in *After the Future: Postmodern Times and Places*, ed. Gary Shapiro (Albany: SUNY Press, 1990).

———, *Nietzsche's French Legacy: A Genealogy of Post-structuralism* (New York: Routledge, 1995).

Scott, Charles E., Susan M. Schoenbohm, Daniela Vallega-Neu, and Alejandro Vallega (eds.), *Companion to Heidegger's* Contributions to Philosophy (Bloomington and Indianapolis: Indiana University Press, 2001).

Severino, Emanuele, *Essenza del nichilismo* (Milan: Adelphi, 1982).

Sheehan, Thomas, "A Paradigm Shift in Heidegger Research," *Continental Philosophy Review* 34 (2001): 183-202.

———, "Nihilism and It's Discontents" in *Heidegger and Practical Philosophy*, ed. François Raffoul and David Pettigrew (Albany: SUNY Press, 2002).

Sim, Stuart, *Jean-François Lyotard* (New York: Prentice Hall / Harvester Wheatsheaf, 1996).

Smith, Gregory Bruce, *Nietzsche, Heidegger, and the Transition to Postmodernity* (Chicago: University of Chicago Press, 1996).

Spinoza, Benedict de, *Spinoza: The Letters*, trans. Samuel Shirley (Indianapolis; Cambridge: Hackett, 1995).

———, *Ethics*, trans. and ed. Edwin Curley (London: Penguin, 1996).

Touraine, Alain, *The Post-Industrial Society*, trans. Leonard Mayhew (London: Wildwood House, 1974).

Turim, Maureen, "Desire in Art and Politics: The Theories of Jean-François Lyotard," *Camera Obscura* 12 (1984): 91-125.

Van der Will, Wilfried, "Nietzsche and Postmodernism" in *The Fate of the New Nietzsche*, ed. Keith Ansell-Pearson and Howard Caygill (Aldershot, England: Avebury, 1993).

Van Reijen, Willem and Dick Veerman, "An Interview with Jean-François Lyotard," *Theory, Culture, and Society* 5 (1988): 300–1.

Vattimo, Gianni, "The Crisis of the Notion of Value from Nietzsche until Today" in *The Search for Absolute Values* (New York: ICF Press, 1976).

———, "Dialectics, Difference, and Weak Thought," trans. Thomas Harrison, *Graduate Faculty Philosophy Journal* 10 (1984): 165–177.

———, "Le deboli certezze," *Alfabeta* 67 (1984).

———, "Myth and the Destiny of Secularization," *Social Research* 52.2 (1985): 347–362.

———, "The End of (Hi)Story," *Chicago Review* 35.4 (1986): 20–30.

———, "Nietzsche and Heidegger," trans. Thomas Harrison, *Stanford Italian Review* 6.1-2 (1986): 1929.

———, "Nietzsche and Contemporary Hermeneutics" in *Nietzsche as Affirmative Thinker*, ed. Y. Yovel (Dordrecht: Nijhoff, 1986).

———, "Hermeneutics and Nihilism: An Apology for Aesthetic Consciousness" in *Hermeneutics and Modern Philosophy*, ed. B. Wachterhauser (Albany: SUNY Press, 1986).

———, "Bottles, Nets, Revolution, and the Tasks of Philosophy," trans. Iain Chambers, *Cultural Studies* 2.2 (1988): 143–151.

———, "Metaphysics, Violence, Secularisation" trans. B. Spakman in *Recoding Metaphysics: The New Italian Philosophy*, ed. Giovanna Borradori (Evanston: Northwestern University Press, 1988).

———, "Toward an Ontology of Decline," trans. B. Spakman in *Recoding Metaphysics: The New Italian Philosophy*, ed. Giovanna Borradori (Evanston: Northwestern University Press, 1988).

———, *The End of Modernity: Nihilism and Hermeneutics in Post-Modern Culture*, trans. John R. Snyder (Baltimore: John Hopkins University Press, 1988).

———, "Nihilism: Reactive and Active" in *Nietzsche and the Rhetoric of Nihilism*, ed.

Tom Darby, Bela Egyed, and Ben Jones (Ottawa: Carleton University Press, 1989).

———, "Postmodern Criticism: Postmodern Critique" in *Writing the Future*, ed. David Wood (London: Routledge, 1990).

———, *The Transparent Society*, trans. David Webb (Baltimore: Johns Hopkins University Press, 1992).

———, *The Adventure of Difference: Philosophy after Nietzsche and Heidegger*, trans. Cyprian Blamires with Thomas Harrison (Baltimore: Johns Hopkins University Press, 1993).

———, "Postmodernity, Technology, Ontology," in *Technology in the Western Political Tradition*, ed. A.M. Melzer, J. Weinberger, and M.R. Zinman (London; Ithaca: Cornell University Press, 1993).

———, *Beyond Interpretation: The Meaning of Hermeneutics for Philosophy*, trans. David Webb (Stanford: Stanford University Press, 1997).

———, "Hermeneutics and Democracy," *Philosophy and Social Criticism* 23.4 (1997): 1–7.

———, *Belief*, trans. Luca D'Isanto and David Webb (Cambridge: Polity, 1999).

———, *Il soggetto e la maschera: Nietzsche e il problema della liberazione* (Milan: Bompiani, 1999).

———, *Nietzsche: An Introduction*, trans. Nicholas Martin (Stanford, California: Stanford University Press, 2001).

———, "Gadamer and the Problem of Ontology" in *Gadamer's Century: Essays in Honor of Hans-Georg Gadamer*, ed. Jeff Malpas, Ulrich Arnswald, and Jens Kertscher (Cambridge, Mass.: MIT Press, 2002).

———, *Nihilism and Emancipation: Ethics, Politics, and Law*, trans. William McCuaig, ed. Santiago Zabala (New York: Columbia University Press, 2004).

———, *Dialogue with Nietzsche*, trans. William McCuaig (New York: Columbia University Press, 2006).

Vattimo, Gianni, and Pier Aldo Rovatti (eds.), *Il pensiero debole* (Milan: Feltrinelli, 1983).

Vallega-Neu, Daniela, *Heidegger's* Contributions to Philosophy*: An Introduction* (Bloomington; Indianapolis: Indiana University Press, 2003).

Weiss, Martin, *Gianni Vattimo. Einführung. Mit einem Interview mit Gianni Vattimo* (Wien: Passagen Verlag, 2003).

White, Alan, "Nietzschean Nihilism: A Typology," *International Studies in Philosophy* 14.2 (1987): 29-44.

Williams, James, *Lyotard: Towards a Postmodern Philosophy* (Cambridge: Polity Press, 1998).

———, "Jean-François Lyotard" in *Encyclopedia of Aesthetics*, ed. Michael Kelly (New York: Oxford University Press, 1998).

———, *Lyotard and the Political* (London: Routledge, 2000).

———, "The Last Refuge from Nihilism," *International Journal of Philosophical Studies* 8.1 (2000): 115-24.

———, *Gilles Deleuze's* Difference and Repetition: *a Critical Introduction and Guide* (Edinburgh: Edinburgh University Press, 2003).

Wilshire, Bruce, *Fashionable Nihilism: A Critique of Analytic Philosophy* (Albany: SUNY Press, 2002).

Wittgenstein, Ludwig, *The Wittgenstein Reader*, ed. Anthony Kenny (Oxford: Blackwell, 1994).

Wolin, Richard (ed.), *The Heidegger Controversy: A Critical Reader* (Cambridge, Mass.: MIT Press, 1993).

———, *Heidegger's Children* (Princeton; Oxford: Princeton University Press, 2001).

Woodward, Ashley, "Nihilism and the Postmodern in Vattimo's Nietzsche," *Minerva – An Internet Journal of Philosophy* 6 (2002): 51–67. http://www.ul.ie/~philos/vol6/nihilism.html

———, "Eternal Return in Dispute: Deleuze and Lyotard on Nihilism," *Proceedings of the Australasian Society for Continental Philosophy*, 2003.

———, "Jean-François Lyotard" in *The Internet Encyclopedia of Philosophy*, ed. James Fieser and Bradley Dowden. http://www.iep.utm.edu/l/Lyotard.htm

———, "Was Baudrillard a Nihilist?" *The International Journal of Baudrillard Studies* 5.1 (January 2008). http://www.ubishops.ca/BaudrillardStudies/vol5_1/v5-1-article12-woodward.html

———, "The *Verwindung* of Capital: On the Philosophy and Politics of Gianni Vattimo," *Symposium: The Canadian Journal of Continental Philosophy* 13.1 (2009): 73–99.

———, "The Obscure: Blanchot at the Limits of Nihilism," *Janus Head* 12.1 (forthcoming – 2010).

Young, Julian, *The Death of God and the Meaning of Life* (London; New York: Routledge, 2003).

Zabala, Santiago, (ed.), *Weakening Philosophy: Essays in Honour of Gianni Vattimo*, (Motreal & Kingston; London; Ithaca: McGill-Queens University Press, 2007).

Zimmerman, Michael E. *Heidegger's Confrontation with Modernity: Technology, Politics, Art* (Bloomington; Indianapolis: Indiana University Press, 1990).

Zurbrugg, Nicholas, "Baudrillard, Modernism, and Postmodernism" in *Baudrillard: A Critical Reader*, ed. Douglas Kellner (Oxford; Cambridge: Blackwell, 1994).

Index

abstraction 11, 12, 91, 143, 223
absurd(ity) 44, 117, 134, 171
abyss 11, 59, 222, 250n. 23
abyssal nihilism (*see* nihilism, abyssal)
action(s) 11, 12, 45, 46, 53, 185–7, 194, 207, 210, 217, 224, 246, 256n. 64
active passivity 187, 193, 194–5, 197, 198, 199, 203, 227, 228, 237, 238, 283n. 71
Adorno, Theodor W. 12, 111, 152, 172, 270n. 22, 275n. 97
affect(s) 28, 81, 83, 85, 88, 185, 188, 193–8
affirmation, pure 176–7, 179, 180, 182 (*see also* life-affirmation)
affirmative weakness 173, 187, 211
agency 193, 210
aim(s) 30, 32–3, 34, 37, 46, 65, 66, 128, 130
alētheia 59
alibi 92–5, 99, 120, 138, 202, 206
ambiguity 91, 101, 119, 147, 204, 207, 208, 229–31, 289n. 155
analyst / analysand 53
analytic philosophy (and nihilism) 278n. 6
An-Denken 113, 214–15
anguish 39, 45, 52, 118, 135, 136
antifoundationalism 26, 103, 108, 218, 247
anti-humanism 16, 18
anti-theory 85, 196
aporia(e) 28, 30, 70, 74, 115, 120, 167, 169, 172–74, 182, 187, 201, 203, 211, 220, 222, 238, 246
appearances 134, 135, 136, 147, 204, 205, 209, 255n. 41, 256n. 50, 272n. 43, 284n. 84
destruction of 134, 135, 147, 200
architecture 21, 251n. 30
Aristotle 57, 58, 105, 258n. 91

art(s) 13, 14, 15, 20, 67, 77, 123, 135, 144, 150, 171, 173, 195, 199, 215, 229, 237, 269n. 6, 283n. 66, 289n. 153
artistic composition 195
ascetic ideal 32–6
asymptote 145
atheism 42, 84, 132, 262n. 37
Aufklärung 126
Auschwitz 124, 125
authenticity 52–3, 64, 71, 72, 115, 186, 259n. 107

bad conscience 32, 35
bad faith 52–3, 115, 256n. 64
bar of disjunction / disjunctive bar 189–90, 192
Baudrillard, Jean 3, 4, 5, 6, 10, 13, 15, 23, 24, 25, 26, 27, 28, 29, 75, 81, 88–102, 115, 116, 117, 118, 119, 120, 121, 133–49, 150, 151, 158, 159, 160, 161, 162, 163, 164, 166, 167, 169, 171, 172, 173, 174, 181, 182, 183, 184, 185, 187, 200–10, 213, 218, 220, 221, 223, 225, 228, 229, 230, 231, 232, 233, 234, 236, 243, 244, 245, 246, 247, 249n. 11, 251n. 35, 253n. 55, 263n 52, 54, 264n. 59, 61, 71, 265n. 78, 268n. 130, 269n. 135, 271n. 40, 272nn. 43, 48, 52, 58, 59, 273nn. 65, 80, 82, 274nn. 86, 90, 92, 278n. 13, 280n. 30, 281n. 45, 282n. 52, 282n. 62, 283n. 76, 283n. 81, 284nn. 83, 91, 93, 95, 285nn. 95 cont., 96, 97, 99, 100, 105, 288n. 139, 289nn. 140, 153, 155, 291n. 2
beginning
 first 72
 other 72, 277n. 138
Being 37, 41, 45–52, 54–73, 104, 108, 109, 110, 111, 112, 113, 114,

117, 118, 119, 149, 150, 154, 155, 156, 157, 158, 159, 160, 163, 164, 166, 167, 175, 180, 181, 186, 210, 211, 212, 213, 214, 215, 223, 231, 235, 236, 243, 250n. 14, 255n. 41, 257nn. 75, 81, 258nn. 87, 88, 89, 259n. 107, 260nn. 125, 129, 130, 262n. 17, 267–8n. 122, 276nn. 120, 122, 279n. 17, 288n. 128, 291n. 3
  and language 110–11
  as a text 117
  as event 60, 65, 109, 111, 118
  as presence 58
  as value 66, 67
  concealing of 64
  decline of 150, 153, 155, 158, 214, 243, 291n. 3
  default of 71, 72
  destiny of 105, 112, 157, 158
  disclosure of 59
  forgetting of 61, 62, 63, 64, 72, 109, 111, 211
  history of 56, 58, 59, 63, 71, 72, 73, 109, 111, 113, 154, 158, 159
  meaning of 56, 57, 59, 150, 213
  oblivion of 12, 54, 70, 72, 104, 109, 112, 155, 156, 160, 223
  opening of 111, 114
  problem of 58
  question of 57, 58, 63, 66, 68, 73
  return of 108, 109
  selective 180
  self-recovery of 52
  truth of 58, 59, 69
  turning in 71, 72
  weakening of 109, 111, 113
being-for-itself / for-itself 46–9, 51, 52, 256n. 51
being-in-itself / in-itself 46–9, 51, 256n. 51
being-in-itself-for-itself 48, 49, 51
Bell, Daniel 128, 251n. 32, 269n. 7
Bennington, Geoffery 189, 193, 282n. 61

Benveniste, Emile 93
Best, Steven 21, 271n. 40
black hole 139
Borradori, Giovanna 17, 211, 265nn. 88, 89
Busch, Thomas W. 50, 255n. 39, 256nn. 50, 61
Butler, Rex 89, 95, 96, 100, 138, 253n. 55, 263n. 54, 269n. 135, 272nn. 52, 58, 284n. 89, 289n. 140

Cage, John 263n. 45
Callinicos, Alex 14, 22
Camus, Albert 8, 30, 242
capitalism 27, 36, 99, 122, 123, 131–2, 134, 140, 141–3, 150, 152, 154, 155, 157, 159, 162, 194, 196, 197–8, 207, 209, 213, 216–18, 219, 220, 226, 227, 232, 234, 237, 238, 244, 246, 271n. 34, 273n. 82, 276nn. 123, 125, 238n. 66
capitalist system 91, 132, 133, 142, 143, 157, 184, 191, 197, 199, 200, 208, 209, 218
cathexis / cathexes 166–7, 190, 282nn. 59, 61
Caygill, Howard 175–6, 185, 220, 277–8n. 4, 279n. 25
Cézanne, Paul 195
chaos theory 133
christ 32
Christianity 32, 35, 124, 153, 175, 279n. 25
Christian-moral interpretation 32–4, 36, 39, 65, 78, 83, 84, 126
code 79, 80, 90, 91, 142, 143, 229, 262n. 27, 264n. 60, 265n. 78
colonialism 152
commodity 92, 133, 141, 142
  exchange 91
  fetishism 132
communication 36, 55, 79, 80, 128, 129, 141, 142, 152, 210, 224, 271n. 24, 275n. 99

condensation 190
consciousness 41–53, 67, 69, 88, 117, 165, 183, 189, 242, 255nn. 41, 46, 256n. 61
   impure reflective (ancillary) 50, 73, 165
   pre-reflective (unreflective) 50, 73, 165
   pure reflective 50, 51, 73
   self- 17, 49
   transcendental 43
conspiracy 199–200, 237
consumption / consumer 90, 91, 131, 157, 232, 273n. 65
contingency 11, 42, 43–5, 47, 51, 222–39, 245–7
Copernican revolution 37
copy 96, 101
critique
   as nihilistic 26, 84–5, 88
   of reason 16–17
   of religion 84–5
   of the subject 17–18
Critchley, Simon 12, 27, 169–72, 220, 236, 278n. 6
Critical Theory 6, 89, 270n. 22

dada 134, 135
dandyism 134
Darwin, Charles 37, 214
death drive 190–3, 227–8, 283nn. 66, 68
deconstruction 5, 94, 95, 99, 102, 105, 106, 150, 172, 229, 260n. 130, 266n. 96, 268n. 132
deconstructive method 92
deferral 34, 80, 83, 86, 188, 189, 195
Deleuze, Gilles 15, 27, 31, 81, 159, 174, 177–82, 188, 193, 200, 227, 237, 252n. 45, 276n. 122, 278n. 13, 280nn. 30, 31, 281nn. 44, 45, 47, 286n. 108, 290n. 168, 291n. 8
deliverance 52–3
democracy 36, 158, 186, 218–19
depth-models 136

Derrida, Jacques 5, 15, 81, 92, 159, 162, 216, 261n. 14, 276n. 122, 278n. 14, 286n. 108, 288n. 125
Descartes, René 15, 17, 257n. 81
Descombes, Vincent 16–7, 34, 278n. 14
desire
   as libido 81, 82, 85, 188, 189, 190, 193, 195, 199, 289n. 148
   as wish (Wunsch) 81, 189, 193, 282nn. 56, 57, 61
Dews, Peter 77, 261n. 14, 263n. 46
dialectical reason 135
difference 19
   logic of 27, 173, 174–82, 183, 187, 188, 193, 199, 200, 201, 210, 211, 220, 246, 278n. 13, 280n. 30
   ontological 57, 109, 210, 211, 286n. 108
Dilthey, Wilhelm 105
disappearance, mode of 88 (see also meaning, disappearance of)
discourse(s) 11, 23, 86, 87, 99, 117, 119, 143, 184, 185, 204, 205, 212, 217, 242, 270n. 16, 274n. 86
   genres of 130, 196
   of nihilism 1, 13, 15, 16, 22, 23, 24, 25, 26, 27, 30, 55, 75, 76, 99, 102, 118, 128, 222, 225, 242, 243, 249n. 5
   of the postmodern/ postmodernism / postmodernity 2, 3, 13, 14, 19–20, 21, 22, 25, 122, 123, 133, 154, 225
   representational 24
   second-level 126–7
disenchantment 134–5, 276n. 120
disjunction, exclusive 178
Disneyland 98
displacement 190, 262n. 17
dispositif(s) 82–3, 201, 210
dissimulation 85–7, 182, 188–200, 226, 246

drives 144, 190, 191, 192, 227, 283n. 68
　duplicity of 190, 192
Eagleton, Terry 22
economic liberalism 125
efficiency 127, 128, 130, 244, 246
emancipation 15, 16, 20, 102, 115, 123, 124, 127, 129, 137, 139, 150, 151, 158, 160, 212, 216, 244
Enlightenment 12, 14, 15, 16, 18, 20, 21, 27, 37, 123, 124, 134, 135, 139, 150, 151, 152, 160, 167, 170, 228, 243, 247, 252n. 38
ens causa sui 49
epochē (*see* reduction, transcendental)
Ereignis 60, 72, 155, 156, 258n. 96
eros 190, 191, 192, 193, 227, 267n. 122, 282n. 64
eschatology 145, 150, 160, 164
essence 34, 42, 43, 45, 46, 47, 48, 54, 56, 58, 59, 61, 62, 63, 64, 66, 69, 70, 71, 72, 106, 155, 157, 175, 179, 180, 186, 208, 216, 250n. 14, 255nn. 39, 48, 256n. 64, 358n. 84, 260n. 125, 274n. 92, 279n. 17
eternal return / eternal recurrence of the same 40, 66, 260n. 112, 266n. 96
　as selective being 180, 181
ethics 19, 21, 52, 173, 181, 212, 247, 256n. 59, 291n. 8
ethos 158
event(s) 19, 33, 37, 59, 60, 65, 66, 77, 78, 79, 81, 82, 86, 87, 107, 109, 111, 113, 117, 118, 122, 123, 124, 125, 131, 132, 133, 145, 146, 151, 152, 153, 155, 188, 193, 195, 199, 207, 230, 243, 258n. 96, 269n. 3, 270n. 16, 273n. 80, 284–5n. 95, 291n. 2
evolution 37
existence 1, 8, 10, 11, 12, 23, 27, 32, 33, 34, 35, 37, 38, 39, 40, 42, 43, 44, 45, 46, 47, 49, 51, 52, 53, 56, 60, 64, 66, 68, 69, 85, 95, 112, 115, 121, 136, 148, 152, 161, 176, 178, 188, 205, 215, 223, 224, 230, 235, 243, 244, 246, 248, 250n. 14, 254n. 18, 254n. 21, 255nn. 48, 50, 258n. 88, 274n. 89, 280n. 28, 290n. 163
existentialism 6, 10, 29, 42, 53, 69, 70, 115, 116, 242, 268nn. 130, 131
existentialist(s) 5, 8, 29, 117, 183, 246, 250n. 23
existential project(s) 46, 47, 48, 51
existential psychoanalysis 51–2, 256n. 70
existing, the 47–8
experimentation 4, 36, 40, 269n. 3

facticity 54, 256n. 64
facts 34, 43, 107, 108, 145, 213, 214, 254–5n. 37, 267n. 107
fall / fallen 50–1, 165
fascination 136, 137
fascism 103, 265n. 88
feelings 26, 81, 84, 188, 196, 198, 199
Fiedler, Leslie 20–1
Fichte, Johann Gottlieb 7, 171
figure(s) 82, 83, 85
figuring negation 176
force(s) 65, 67, 80, 81, 83, 87, 99, 101, 105, 117, 132, 133, 144, 158, 180, 181, 184, 187, 188, 189, 191, 192, 193, 194, 195, 196, 196, 199, 201, 206, 208, 210, 212, 216, 218, 221, 226, 227, 228, 232, 238, 239, 243, 244, 246, 259n. 109, 282n. 56, 282nn. 57, 64, 283n. 74
for-itself (*see* being-for-itself)
forms, world of the 79
Foucault, Michel 15, 18, 227, 251n. 29, 266n. 91
foundation 11, 16, 17, 18, 34, 42, 43, 45, 46, 48, 49, 57, 61, 71, 103, 105, 106, 107, 108, 109, 111, 112, 113, 114, 115, 150, 151, 157,

Index

211, 212, 214, 216, 217, 221, 233, 260n. 131
Frank, Manfred 15–16
Frascati-Lochhead, Marta 104
freedom 8, 10, 20, 36, 39, 40, 45, 46, 48, 51, 52, 53, 112, 115, 219, 224, 233, 235, 236, 268n. 131
Freud, Sigmund / Freudian 4, 10, 26, 53, 76, 80, 81, 82, 85, 122, 166, 188, 189, 190, 191, 199, 262n. 31, 272n. 44, 282nn. 57, 59, 61, 289n. 149
fundamental attitude 52
fundamentalism(s) 159, 162, 170, 216, 217, 218, 219, 220, 276nn. 123, 124

Gadamer, Hans-Georg 5, 110, 267nn. 115, 116
Gehlen, Arnold 152
genealogy 9, 32, 35, 134, 136, 137, 160, 179, 250n. 21
Genosko, Gary 89, 142, 187, 264n. 66, 282n. 52
genres of discourse 130, 196
Ge-schick 110
Ge-stell 62–5, 70, 72, 149, 155, 156, 223, 275n. 112
gift 91
goal(s) 15, 33, 37, 51, 56, 106, 107, 123, 128, 145, 151, 154, 175, 186, 193, 203, 241, 243, 290n. 163
God 11, 18, 33, 36, 37, 42, 45, 46, 49, 51, 57, 83, 97, 124, 130, 132, 160, 214, 225, 262n. 27
　death of 30, 37–8, 41, 42, 53, 90, 97, 104, 107, 132, 135, 156, 173, 223, 225
　desire to be 49, 50–2, 165, 236
grand narratives (*see* metanarratives)
great Zero 79, 83, 84, 86, 87, 119, 131, 133, 188, 198, 221, 227

Habermas, Jürgen 13, 235, 251n. 28, 267n. 116, 287n. 117

Hassan, Ihab 21, 251n. 34
Heidegger, Martin 5, 6, 8, 9, 10, 12, 15, 16, 25, 26, 27, 28, 29, 30, 41, 54–74, 75, 84, 99, 102–5, 108–20, 128–30, 145, 149, 150, 154, 155, 156, 157, 158, 161, 164, 165, 170, 171, 172, 174, 175, 183, 186, 187, 194, 211, 214, 215, 223, 228, 233, 242, 244, 254n. 37, 257–261nn., 267nn. 109, 116, 118, 268nn. 125, 126, 131, 274n. 92, 277n. 138, 278nn. 13, 14, 279nn. 17, 18, 19, 286n. 108, 287n. 118, 288n. 128, 291n. 3
Hegel, G.W.F. 15, 16, 126, 152, 160, 177, 280nn. 28, 30
Hegelian 6, 8, 18
Hegelianism 125, 290n. 161
hermeneutics 5, 6, 104, 186, 214, 218
　of suspicion 134, 272n. 44
hermeneutic ontology 10, 75, 104, 110, 115, 116, 117, 183
heterotopia 159, 276n. 121
history 14, 18, 19, 31, 51, 56, 105, 107, 110, 113, 123, 125, 129, 134, 135, 145, 146, 150, 151, 152, 153, 154, 169, 215, 225, 236, 241, 243, 244, 245, 266n. 100, 269n. 6, 273n. 80, 287n. 123, 290n. 163
　end of 16, 18–19, 27, 120, 122, 145, 151, 152, 153, 154, 159–67, 225, 230, 233, 236, 239, 243, 244, 245, 247
　philosophy of 19, 123, 124, 125, 149, 153, 170, 236
　teleological 145, 151, 152, 236
Holocaust 125, 129, 153
holograms 133, 229
Horkheimer, Max 12, 152, 270n. 22
Howe, Irving 20, 21
humanism 18, 19, 20, 69, 70, 74, 260n. 125, 288n. 125
human reality 41–54, 69, 73, 165, 235, 236, 254–5n. 37, 256n. 59

Hume, David 127
Husserl, Edmund 43, 44, 255nn. 39, 41
hyperreal / hyperreality 90, 96, 97, 98, 119, 133–49, 160, 162, 164, 207, 208, 229
Ideas
  (Platonic) 80, 175
  (Kantian) 277n. 136
  (Hegelian) 123
identity, principle of 19
ideology 82, 129, 152, 159, 216, 217, 232
  critique of 99, 105, 216, 217
il pensiero debole (see weak thought)
imaginary 98, 120, 223
immanent world 33, 79, 175
imperialism 152
implosion 137, 138, 140, 143, 145, 146, 264n. 71
impossible exchange 90, 147–8, 230
individual 10, 19, 31, 33, 35, 36, 38–42, 48, 51, 52, 53, 60, 73, 88, 112, 117, 118, 131, 135, 173, 183, 184, 186, 187, 217, 219, 224, 236, 242, 243, 266n. 101, 268n. 131, 291n. 8
Industrial Revolution 127, 128
information 4, 15, 79, 80, 128, 129, 139, 140, 141, 146, 152, 207, 229, 246, 271n. 24, 274n. 92, 284–5n. 95
in-itself (see Being-in-itself)
injustice 125, 129, 130, 152, 158, 233
innovation 127, 128, 133, 152, 153
intensities 22, 81, 83–7, 131, 132, 185, 193, 194, 195, 197, 198, 199, 221, 228, 237, 269n. 3, 280–1n. 31
intensity 82, 83, 131, 132, 191, 192, 193, 194, 196, 198–200, 226, 227, 237, 238, 283nn. 72, 74
  dampening of 83, 84, 86, 133, 194, 198, 238

interpretation 10, 34, 104, 108, 110, 112, 114, 134, 135, 158, 159, 212, 213, 214, 215, 218, 267n. 107, 272n. 43
  bounds of 117
is/ought gap 127, 270n. 20
Italian philosophy 5, 6, 103, 265n. 88
Jameson, Fredric 13, 121, 153, 224, 251n. 34, 289n. 142
Jaspers, Karl 8
Jacobi, Friedrich Heinrich 7–8
Jacobson, Roman 97
Jencks, Charles 21, 251n. 30
Jünger, Ernst 8, 70, 171, 257n. 77
justice 76, 122, 129, 133, 226, 233, 242, 269n. 3
justification 32, 34, 40, 43, 46, 68, 107, 197, 223, 232

Kant, Immanuel 7, 15, 122, 261n. 9, 277n. 136
Kapital 132, 271n. 31
Kellner, Douglas 21, 133, 263n. 52, 271n. 40
Kierkegaard, Søren 8, 11, 183, 203
knowledge 7, 11, 15, 16, 17, 18, 19, 61, 97, 106, 114, 123, 126, 127, 128, 130, 138, 150, 152, 158, 160, 214, 226, 247, 251n. 29, 252n. 41, 269n. 7, 277n. 136, 286n. 105
Kroker, Arthur 133, 134

Lacan, Jacques 15, 80, 264n. 61, 290n. 161
lack 51, 75, 78, 79, 80, 85, 86, 124, 165, 189, 190, 282n. 56, 283n. 66
  of being 47–9, 51, 165
lacked, the 47–9
lacking, the 47–8
language 77, 93, 97, 110, 111, 117, 118, 122, 126, 128, 130, 141, 142, 170, 183, 184, 185, 190, 230, 242, 271n. 24, 273n. 82, 289n. 155
language game(s) 126, 127, 129, 130, 131, 163, 164, 184, 270n. 16

law of excluded middle 189
law of noncontradiction 189
law of value 91, 132, 133, 197, 199, 228, 271n. 34
  commodity 133, 141, 142
  structural 141
Levinas, Emmanuel 112
libidinal energies 82, 83, 84, 85, 86, 131, 132, 188, 189, 191, 193, 194, 195, 198, 199, 210, 226
libidinal investment(s) 132, 166, 190
libidinal philosophy 4, 76, 78, 79, 81, 86, 131, 185, 196, 197, 221, 226, 227, 228, 237
libido (*see* desire, as libido)
life 1, 4, 7–12, 16, 20–2, 28–42, 45–7, 49, 51–4, 60, 61, 64, 66, 67, 73, 75, 77, 82–4, 88, 105, 107, 112, 115, 124, 128, 131, 142, 152, 153, 161, 162, 170, 171, 173, 175, 176, 178, 181–4, 187, 188, 191, 194, 196, 197, 199, 201, 219, 221, 223, 225–7, 239, 242–8, 254n. 18, 263nn. 45, 52, 267n. 122, 270n. 16, 279n. 25, 280n. 30, 291n. 8
life-affirmation 10, 32, 33, 35, 36, 40, 41, 77, 87, 100, 102, 176, 182, 188, 191, 197, 199, 210, 221, 227, 246
linguistic turn 27, 116–18, 183, 184, 242
literature 20, 21, 123, 172
logic 27, 31, 39, 130, 142, 154, 160, 162, 171, 172, 200, 209, 222, 229, 236, 276n. 120, 286n. 108
  Aristotelean 189
  Baudrillard's 89, 137
  deductive 114, 213
  of difference 27, 173, 174–83, 187, 188, 193, 199, 200, 201, 210, 211, 220, 246, 278n. 13, 280n. 30
  of negation and opposition 174–82, 193

  of opposition 200, 246
  of political economy 92, 119
  of self-decomposition 126
  of simulation 95, 96, 206
  of the commodity 92
  of the Saussurean sign 92
  of the signifier 81
Löwith, Karl 5, 8, 249n. 5
Lyotard, Jean-François 2–6, 10, 13–15, 22–9, 75–88, 91, 92, 94, 101, 102, 115–20, 121, 122–33, 136, 145, 147, 150, 151, 153, 154, 157–67, 169, 171, 172, 173, 174, 181, 182, 183, 184, 185, 187, 188–200, 201, 203, 210, 213, 218, 220, 221, 223, 225, 226, 227, 228, 231, 232, 233, 234, 236, 237, 238, 243, 244, 246, 247, 251n. 29, 261–3nn., 264n. 59, 265n. 78, 268n. 130, 269–71nn., 272n. 59, 277n. 136, 278n. 13, 280n. 30, 281nn. 45, 47, 282n. 52, 282–3nn., 287–8n. 123, 288n. 139, 289n. 149, 290n. 161

macropolitics 185, 218
Malpas, Jeff 25
Malpas, Simon 261n. 9, 270n. 20
Malraux, André 76
Marcel, Gabriel 8, 183
Marx, Karl 12, 15, 84, 92, 122, 132, 141, 142, 143, 156, 157, 158, 160, 197, 211, 213, 214, 216, 262n. 37, 272n. 44, 288n. 125
Marxism 4, 6, 18, 20, 22, 76, 78, 89, 91, 123, 124, 125, 134, 136, 171, 185, 197, 213, 216, 217, 233, 287–8n. 123
  Althusserian 290n. 161
  Gramscian 103
masses, the 137–40, 145–6, 272nn. 52, 58
Mauss, Marcel 91
mauvaise foi (*see* bad faith)
May '68 4, 82

meaning 1, 6, 10, 11, 12, 17, 22, 23, 26, 28, 29, 30, 31, 32, 33, 34, 37, 38, 39, 40, 41, 42, 43, 44, 45, 46, 49, 50, 51, 52, 53, 54, 55, 56, 58, 60, 61, 64, 67, 68, 69, 70, 73, 78, 79, 80, 81, 82, 83, 84, 88, 91, 92, 93, 94, 98, 99, 101, 102, 108, 115, 117, 118, 121, 122, 123, 124, 129, 130, 133, 134, 135, 136, 137, 139, 140, 141, 143, 145, 146, 147, 158, 160, 161, 164, 165, 166, 170, 183, 184, 189, 195, 196, 200, 201, 207, 208, 209, 210, 221, 223, 225, 226, 228, 229, 230, 231, 233, 234, 235, 241, 242, 243, 244, 248, 254n. 21, 258n. 89, 265n. 78, 283n. 74, 290n. 163
   cultural 91, 158
   destruction of 101, 134, 135, 136, 141, 143, 147, 160
   disappearance of 88, 99, 136, 16, 228, 230
   discursive 87
   existential 11, 30, 54, 61, 71, 91, 103, 116, 119, 122, 135, 142, 149, 184, 209, 223, 232, 233, 235, 290n. 163
   freezing over of 118
   hypertelos of 136, 137
   implosion of 137, 140, 145, 264n. 71
   post-structuralist theories of 81, 88, 101
   semantic 119, 184, 196, 270n. 16
   semio-linguistic theory of 91, 94, 97, 100, 101, 119, 148, 184, 204, 229
   theories of 75, 77, 79, 84, 97, 116, 117, 118, 139, 204, 230, 231, 234
   (*See also* Being, meaning of)
meaninglessness 3, 4, 6, 9, 28, 32, 38, 39, 53, 73, 119, 121, 122, 161, 162, 169, 171, 183–5, 221, 226, 228, 230–2, 241, 242, 244, 246–8

media 4, 98, 128, 137, 140, 141, 145, 146, 275n. 99, 284–5n. 95
   mass 55, 56, 140, 146, 150, 152, 207, 229
metanarrative(s) 122–33, 150, 153, 160, 161, 162, 163, 165, 225, 226, 236, 243, 244
metaphysics 28, 33, 54, 56, 57, 59, 61, 62, 63, 64, 65, 66, 68, 69, 71, 72, 79, 103, 105, 107, 108, 109, 111, 112, 113, 114, 115, 118, 119, 120, 154, 155, 156, 157, 159, 162, 164, 169, 175, 181, 187, 210, 211, 212, 213, 214, 215, 216, 217, 220, 221, 223, 231, 232, 235, 255–6n. 50, 259n. 107, 260nn. 112, 117, 125, 265n. 84, 276n. 123, 279nn. 17, 18, 19, 280n. 30, 286nn. 108, 109
   critique of 74, 112
   deconstruction of 105, 106
   end of 105
   errors of 106
   history of 58, 68, 72, 108, 111, 113
   ladder of 106–7
   of difference 181
   overcoming of 66, 69, 103, 106, 107, 108, 109, 112, 115, 154, 211, 220
   (*See also* Verwindung; violence; and metaphysics)
McLuhan, Marshall 140
Melancholia / melancholy 80, 99, 166, 167, 245, 263n. 52
metarécit (*See also* metanarrative(s))
micropolitics 185
Mills, C. Wright 20, 21
mode of existence 51, 178
modern philosophy 14, 15, 16, 61, 67, 68, 76
modernism 13, 16, 224
modernity 2, 12–15, 18, 21, 27, 29, 30, 31, 32, 34–8, 40, 41, 54, 55, 56, 61, 63, 64, 68, 72, 73, 100,

Index

102, 120–7, 129, 130, 131, 134, 135, 136, 139, 143–7, 150–4, 157, 160, 161, 162, 164–7, 170, 171, 185, 212, 226, 228, 234, 241, 243, 244, 245, 248, 251n. 27, 29, 257n. 77, 287n. 123

morality 33, 36, 181
  herd 35, 36
  master / noble 35–6, 40, 178, 254n. 23
  slave 35–6, 41, 178, 254n. 23
mourning 164, 166, 226, 245
mystery 63, 71, 149, 204, 207, 260n. 131, 274n. 92

narrative(s) 19, 82, 123, 124, 125, 126, 127, 129, 165, 226, 243, 244, 269n. 6, 272n. 59
  (*See also* metanarrative(s))
natural attitude 43, 50, 52, 255n. 39, 256n. 61
negation 7, 32, 34, 49, 80, 84, 173, 174–82, 188, 189, 190, 192, 193, 194, 199, 220, 263n. 38, 279nn. 21, 25, 280n. 30
  (*See also* logic, of negation and opposition)
neo-nihilism 75, 76, 133
Nietzsche, Friedrich 1, 4, 5, 6, 7, 8, 9, 10, 11, 15, 20, 22, 25, 26, 27, 28, 29, 30–41, 42, 53, 54, 55, 57, 63, 65–70, 73, 74, 76, 78, 80, 84, 87, 88, 90, 97, 100, 102–9, 112–7, 119, 120, 122, 123, 124, 125, 126, 129, 130, 131, 135, 136, 145, 150, 154, 156, 157, 158, 160, 161, 162, 164, 165, 170, 171, 172, 174, 175, 176, 177, 178, 179, 180, 181, 184, 186, 188, 190, 206, 211, 214, 215, 220, 222, 223, 225, 228, 231, 233, 234, 236, 239, 243, 244, 248, 250n. 21, 251n. 35, 252n. 45, 253–4nn., 257nn. 75, 77, 259nn. 108, 109, 260n. 112, 261nn. 9, 16, 263n. 52, 266nn.

95, 96, 101, 266–7n. 106, 267n. 107, 268nn. 126, 131, 272n. 43, 272n. 48, 275n. 99, 276–7n. 132, 277–8n. 4, 278n. 14, 279nn. 19, 21, 280–1n. 31, 282n. 57, 287n. 119, 287n. 123, 290n. 165

nihilism 1–6, 7–12, 13, 15, 16, 19–22, 23, 24, 25, 26, 27, 28, 29, 30, 31, 34, 35, 36, 40, 41, 42, 47, 50, 53, 54, 55, 61, 65, 66, 67, 68, 69, 70, 71, 75, 76, 77, 78, 79, 80, 83, 84, 85, 86, 87, 88, 89, 90, 91, 92, 94, 95, 97, 99, 100, 101, 102, 103, 104, 105, 106, 107, 108, 112, 113, 114, 116, 117, 118, 119, 120, 121, 122, 123, 124, 125, 126, 129, 130, 131, 132, 133, 134, 135, 136, 137, 143, 145, 147, 148, 149, 150, 154, 156, 157, 158, 159, 160, 161, 162, 163, 164, 165, 166, 167, 169, 170, 171, 172, 174, 175, 176, 177, 178, 179, 180, 183, 184, 185, 187, 188, 189, 191, 192, 193, 194, 196, 197, 198, 199, 200, 201, 202, 204, 205, 206, 207, 209, 210, 211, 212, 213, 214, 216, 220, 221, 222, 223, 224, 225, 227, 228, 229, 230, 231, 232, 233, 234, 235, 236, 237, 238, 239, 241, 242, 243, 244, 245, 246, 247, 248, 250nn. 13, 21, 254n. 35, 257nn. 74, 75, 77, 261n. 16, 262n. 17, 265n. 84, 268n. 125, 276n. 123, 277n. 4, 278n. 13, 279n. 25, 280nn. 26, 30, 282n. 56, 286nn. 108, 109, 287n. 123
  abyssal 11, 12, 28, 41, 222–39, 246
  accomplished 102, 107, 108, 112, 113, 115, 155, 158, 163, 215, 235
  active 31, 38, 39, 131, 169, 171, 228, 234, 263n. 52
  actual 56, 63
  advent of 29–74, 107, 130

aesthetic 134
and the postmodern 19–22, 104, 241
authentic 64, 259n. 107
banalization of 161–2
complete(d) 31, 39, 40, 107, 108, 112, 115, 158, 215, 232, 235
completion of 108, 122, 130, 158, 159, 160, 161, 163, 166, 232, 235, 244
discourse of 1, 13, 16, 23, 24, 26, 30, 55, 75, 76, 99, 102, 118, 128, 222, 242, 243, 249n. 5
epistemological 97
epoch / era of 213, 214
essence of 61, 63, 64, 71, 72
essential 56, 58, 63
European 126
existential 22, 49, 50, 52, 115, 118, 162
genealogy of 134, 137, 160
history of 3, 72, 75, 250n. 21
inauthentic 64, 72, 259n. 107
logic of 171
modern 165
melancholic 147
metaphysical 211, 215, 219, 220
negative 115, 119, 120, 162, 211, 213, 215, 219, 220, 263n. 52, 265n. 84
negotiation of 169–239, 242, 246, 247
of postmodernity 147, 149, 164, 166, 170, 197, 232, 244, 246
of transparency 88–102, 135, 136, 142
of value 148
ontological 118, 155
overcoming of 26, 27, 28, 39, 41, 51, 52, 53, 61, 65, 69, 70, 71, 72, 73, 74, 99, 100, 101, 103, 108, 109, 115, 119–20, 122, 167, 169, 171, 172, 173, 174, 175, 176, 180, 181, 182, 185, 186, 194, 201, 202, 204, 220, 225, 228, 234, 236, 242, 243, 245, 246, 256n. 59, 260n. 129, 263n. 38, 278n. 13, 279n. 19, 280n. 30, 281n. 47
passive 31, 38, 39, 169, 171, 183, 263n. 52, 281n. 39
political 134
positive 102–15, 211, 212, 220, 265n. 84, 286n. 109
postmodern 24, 29, 75–120, 162, 165, 186, 225, 241, 244
psychology of 35
radical 31, 37, 38, 39
reductive 11, 12, 41, 64, 84, 97, 131, 208, 223, 225, 226, 227, 229, 230, 231, 232, 233, 234, 237, 238, 239, 246
religious 31, 32, 33, 34, 35, 36, 39, 40, 41, 65, 78, 79, 80, 81, 83, 84, 87, 100, 124, 129, 130, 131, 133, 160, 161, 162, 165, 170, 175, 188, 201, 236
resistance to 169, 172, 220
response(s) to 5, 6, 7, 25, 27, 28, 30, 53, 65, 68, 70, 76, 77, 85, 87, 90, 99, 115, 120, 122, 162, 169, 170, 171, 173, 174, 182, 183, 184, 185, 187, 188, 193, 194, 195, 196, 198, 199, 200, 202, 203, 207, 209, 210, 220, 221, 222, 223, 227, 228, 230, 231, 232, 233, 234, 236, 238, 239, 243, 245, 250n. 21
return of 179
rhetoric of 4
stages of (Baudrillard) 134–6
survival of 176, 279n. 25
(*See also* neo-nihilism)
Nishitani, Keiji 8, 183
noble (*see* morality, master)
Norman, Judith 177, 180, 278n. 14, 280n. 30
Norris, Christopher 22
nostalgia 94, 150, 164, 165, 166, 245, 265n. 78

nothing 7, 39, 63, 86, 109, 111, 147–9, 156, 274nn. 89, 90, 92
nothingness 46, 101, 211, 262n. 17

object(s) 16, 24, 43, 45, 47, 50, 61, 62, 67, 68, 70, 71, 77, 83, 84, 90, 91, 92, 94, 95, 110, 113, 118, 140, 141, 142, 156, 157, 165, 166, 167, 186, 202, 204, 205, 229, 238, 255n. 41, 265n. 78, 268n. 130, 284n. 93, 284–5n. 95
ontological difference (*see* difference, ontological)
ontological proof
    St. Anselm's 214
    Sartre's 255n. 41
ontology 19, 23, 49, 65, 66, 68, 104, 109, 110, 158, 184, 213
    fundamental 57–8
    nihilistic 110, 218, 287n. 122
    of decline 111
    phenomenological 46, 68, 255n. 50
    (*See also* hermeneutic ontology)
ontologie de l'actualité 104
opposition(s) 34, 35, 99, 100, 102, 139, 140, 142, 143, 145, 149, 174–82, 188, 189, 191, 193, 194, 199, 200, 201, 202, 203, 209, 210, 220, 221, 246, 263n. 38, 279nn. 17, 18, 280nn. 28, 31, 282n. 64, 283n. 74
    binary 86, 92, 97, 98, 101
    (*See also* logic, of opposition; logic, of opposition and negation)
orgy 144, 228, 229
origin(s) 106, 107, 150
original(s) 95, 96, 101, 215
original project of being 51

Pannwitz, Rudolf 20, 21, 276n. 129
Parmenides 103, 276n. 122
pensiero debole, il (*see* weak thought)
performativity, criterion of 127, 128, 130, 131, 133, 162, 164, 197, 226

phenomenology 43, 44, 75, 77, 115, 116, 255n. 39
Plato 32, 95, 175
Platonism 35, 65, 79, 80, 175, 279n. 17
poetic reversal 147, 148, 162, 230, 231, 234, 236, 239
polis 185
political, the 184, 185, 216, 219, 242, 278n. 13
political action 185, 210
    Heidegger's problematisation of 186
political economy 90, 91, 92, 97, 119, 127, 141, 143, 156, 197, 201, 218, 231, 265n. 78
politics 15, 19, 21, 77, 87, 98, 159, 173, 181, 195, 197, 198, 199, 204, 212, 217, 219, 233, 237, 242, 247, 274nn. 86, 87
    of passivity 27, 173, 174, 183–88, 197, 212, 220, 246, 278n. 13
    post-Marxian 76
Pope John-Paul II 170
post-history 146, 152
post-industrial society 2, 14, 123, 128, 129, 251n. 32
postmodern, the 3, 4, 5, 6, 7, 13–22, 23, 25, 26, 28, 76, 104, 123, 153, 164, 241, 247, 248, 252n. 46, 269n. 6, 289n. 142
    (*See also* discourse, of the postmodern)
postmodernism 3, 6, 12, 13, 14, 15, 20, 21, 22, 102, 104, 116, 133, 170, 242, 247
postmodernity 2, 3, 4, 5, 6, 9, 12, 13, 14, 18, 21, 22, 23, 24, 25, 26, 27, 28, 88, 90, 102, 104, 120, 121–67, 169, 170, 171, 173, 183, 184, 185, 186, 188, 196, 197, 207, 219, 220, 222, 223, 224, 225, 226, 228, 231, 232, 233, 236, 238, 239, 241, 242, 243, 244, 245, 246, 247, 251n. 29, 271n. 40, 272n. 59, 276n. 129, 277n. 136

post-structuralism 4, 6, 14, 15, 16, 75, 103, 116, 117, 174, 183
power 38, 39, 106, 184, 185, 187, 283n. 72, 284n. 84
praxis 12, 127, 130, 226
prescription / prescriptive statements 127, 277n. 136
primary psychical processes 189–90, 195, 199, 282n. 62
primitive societies 91, 198, 265n. 78
production 14, 88, 90, 128, 137, 142, 144, 209, 232, 269n. 7
progress 15, 18, 19, 20, 21, 36, 60, 127, 147, 150–4, 157, 158, 160, 162, 215, 225, 236, 244, 245
psychoanalysis 6, 76, 134, 136, 192, 229
   cultural 245
   existential 51, 52, 53, 256n. 70

question-begging 89, 253n. 55, 289n. 140

radical conversion 52, 119, 165, 236, 239
real, the 22, 94, 95, 96, 97, 98, 120, 136, 137, 138, 139, 140, 143, 145, 146, 148, 163, 164, 200, 202, 205, 206, 208, 210, 229, 230, 234
reality 17, 23, 24, 25, 34, 46, 59, 73, 77, 93, 94, 95, 96, 98, 103, 106, 135, 137, 138, 139, 140, 146, 149, 152, 159, 163, 181, 184, 201, 202, 204, 205, 206, 207, 208, 212, 217, 222, 231, 247, 282n. 56, 284–5n. 95, 291n. 2
redemption 32, 34, 123, 164
reduction (phenomenology)
   eidetic 255n. 39
   phenomenological 51, 52, 165
   transcendental (epochē) 43, 51, 255n. 39
repetition 132, 282n. 64
repression (psychoanalysis) 190

reference / referent 23, 33, 80, 81, 93, 94, 95, 96, 97, 98, 114, 126, 137, 138, 139, 140, 141, 144, 212, 229, 230, 265n. 78
reflexivity 153, 154
   in the discourse of nihilism 23, 27, 99, 118–19, 242, 243
relativism 20, 49, 97, 215, 230, 235, 247
representation 7, 22, 23, 24, 25, 26, 77, 78, 79, 80, 81, 83, 84, 85, 86, 87, 95, 96, 97, 99, 101, 119, 122, 131, 135, 136, 137, 138, 139, 140, 148, 162, 188, 189, 190, 191, 193, 195, 196, 199, 200, 201, 202, 204, 205, 206, 207, 208, 218, 234, 245, 262n. 17, 270n. 16, 275n. 99, 282n. 56, 282n. 61
   paradox of 100
ressentiment 32, 35, 84, 85
reversibility 90, 91, 98, 99, 101–02, 119, 132, 147, 149, 202, 208, 209, 229, 231, 289n. 155
reversion 96, 102, 149, 164, 202
revolution 37, 98, 135, 141, 142, 143, 171, 172, 173, 185, 191, 216, 265n. 78, 283n. 66, 287–8n. 123
   permanent 199, 200
   (See also Industrial Revolution)
Ricoeur, Paul 79
romanticism 134, 164, 250n. 21
Roquentin, Antoine 44, 117
Rorty, Richard 16, 162
Rovatti, Pier Aldo 103, 212

salvation 52, 53, 107, 150, 153
Sartre, Jean-Paul 8, 9, 11, 25, 26, 28, 29, 30, 41–54, 65, 68–70, 73, 75, 88, 116, 117, 119, 165, 175, 183, 186, 223, 235, 236, 242, 247, 254–6nn., 259n. 108, 268nn. 130, 132, 279n. 19
Saussure, Ferdinand de 92, 93, 117, 264n. 59, 289n. 155
Saussurean linguistics 80, 91, 262n. 25

Index

science 14, 34, 61, 67, 75, 79, 126, 127, 128, 150, 152
  positive 126, 170
  technological 27, 122, 154, 162, 234, 244, 254n. 21, 263n. 52, 271n. 24, 284–5n. 95, 286n. 105
  (*See also* technoscience)
secondary psychical processes 189, 193, 282n. 62
secularisation 149–59, 276n. 124
security 48, 51, 106
seduction 28, 90, 100, 101, 147, 148, 149, 182, 200–10, 229, 230, 234, 246, 284n. 84
self 7, 32, 35, 45, 48, 98, 171, 183
  fragmentation of 129
semiology 91, 94, 223, 264n. 59
semiotics 4, 10, 75, 76, 78, 79, 80, 81, 84, 88, 94, 103, 117, 118, 162, 194, 223, 264n. 59
sense 53, 78, 79, 80, 81, 83
Severino, Emanuele 103, 159, 276n. 122
sfondamento 114, 235, 288n. 138
sign(s) 31, 38, 73, 79, 80, 81, 90, 92–7, 101, 117, 118, 136–8, 140, 142, 143, 148, 149, 189, 195, 196, 200, 203, 229, 230, 234, 262n. 25, 27, 264n. 59, 265n. 78, 283n. 74
  deconstruction of 92–4
  value 91, 96, 143, 273n. 65
signals 142
significance(s) 10, 43, 44, 46, 54, 55, 56, 60, 64, 65, 67, 68, 71, 75, 257n. 81
signification 10, 80, 83, 87, 91–4, 140, 142, 195, 196
signified 80, 92, 93, 96, 140, 189, 262n. 25
signifier 80, 81, 92, 93, 94, 140, 143, 189, 262nn. 25, 27
silencing 112, 212, 129
simulacrum / simulacra 90, 94, 97, 163, 118, 229, 245

simulation 23, 28, 90, 91, 92, 94, 95, 96, 97, 98, 99, 100, 101, 102, 119, 120, 135, 136, 137, 138, 139, 143, 144, 148, 149, 200, 201, 202, 203, 204, 206, 207, 208, 209, 210, 221, 228, 229, 230, 234, 264nn. 66, 71, 272n. 52
singularity 132, 197, 283n. 74
social, the 137, 138, 139, 140, 142, 146, 163, 184, 272n. 58
social bond 91, 128, 197, 210, 272n. 59
socialism 36, 186, 218, 219, 220, 262n. 37
society 4, 13, 14, 15, 16, 20, 24, 31, 36, 60, 67, 77, 78, 88, 90, 101, 103, 112, 121, 122, 123, 125, 128, 129, 130, 133, 134, 136, 137, 138, 139, 140, 142, 143, 151, 152, 156, 157, 158, 159, 161, 163, 164, 171, 183, 184, 186, 198, 212, 213, 216, 217, 218, 223, 227, 228, 231, 232, 233, 237, 238, 245, 269n. 4, 272n. 59, 273n. 82, 277n. 136, 283n. 65, 290n. 163
  consumer 131
  unalienated 197
  utopian 198
  (*See also* post-industrial society)
sociology 4, 14, 137–9
soteriology 150
Socrates 95
  and the Sophists 177
Spinoza, Benedict de 176
Spinoza's principle 176, 179, 190, 192
spirit of seriousness, the 50, 52
stake(s) 77, 99, 129, 135, 143, 184, 206, 209
statements 126, 152
  denotative 126, 127
  prescriptive (*see* prescription / prescriptive statements)
strategy 225, 228, 231, 233, 234, 236, 237, 239, 247, 285n. 100

of deterrence 98
of recollection 214, 215
of the real 98
of seduction 202–6, 221
of Verwindung 212
strategies 3, 5, 28, 87, 115, 120, 173, 188, 194, 207, 210, 213, 220, 221, 222, 225, 227, 233, 235, 236, 238, 239, 244, 246, 247, 274n. 86, 284n. 93
of active passivity 195, 197, 203, 238
weak 187
structure(s) 11, 12, 17, 26, 28, 34, 42, 43, 44, 45, 46, 47, 48, 49, 50, 51, 54, 57, 59, 60, 73, 77, 78, 81, 82, 83, 84, 85, 86, 87, 88, 89, 91, 92, 93, 95, 97, 98, 99, 101, 102, 103, 107, 108, 110, 111, 112, 117, 118, 122, 131, 133, 134, 135, 138, 139, 142, 152, 158, 161, 175, 180, 183, 185, 188, 189, 190, 191, 192, 193, 194, 195, 196, 197, 198, 199, 200, 201, 202, 209, 211, 212, 213, 214, 215, 221, 223, 226, 227, 228, 230, 231, 236, 237, 238, 242, 243, 255n. 50, 263n. 45, 269nn. 3, 6, 273n. 82, 283n. 68, 286n. 108, 289n. 149, 290n. 165
structuralism 4, 6, 76, 77, 78, 80, 81, 83, 84, 88, 103, 115, 116, 117, 118, 162, 183
style(s) 14, 22, 23, 87, 119, 122, 195, 196, 213
subject, the 17, 19, 24, 50, 61, 62, 65, 67, 68, 69, 70, 71, 74, 110, 117, 124, 129, 156, 157, 183, 184, 186, 194, 205, 206, 224, 252n. 41, 268nn. 130, 131, 132, 279n. 19, 282n. 56, 284–5n. 95, 287n. 123
and existentialism 10, 268n. 131
centrality of 14, 116
critique of (*see* critique, of the subject)
of history 18, 129, 244

surrealism 134
symbolic exchange 90, 91, 101, 147, 201, 208, 229, 230, 265n. 78, 283n. 76
synthetic totality (consciousness as) 45

technology 55, 56, 61, 62, 63, 64, 65, 68, 127, 128, 140, 141, 146, 149, 150, 152, 155, 156, 157, 158, 207, 208, 274n. 92, 286n. 105
technologies, new 123, 128, 133, 208
technoscience 27, 127, 128, 130, 131, 133, 155, 196, 197
tensor 195–6, 200, 283nn. 74, 75
terrorism 134, 171
  theoretical 100
Thanatos (*see* death drive)
theory 1, 2, 4, 10, 11, 13, 20, 21, 23, 24, 25, 26, 31, 37, 41, 42, 45, 63, 66, 69, 75, 76, 77, 78, 79, 80, 81, 83, 84, 85, 87, 88, 89, 90, 91, 94, 95, 97, 100, 101, 104, 111, 115–20, 122, 123, 125, 126, 127, 128, 129, 130, 131, 133, 134, 135, 136, 137, 139, 140, 141, 143, 148, 149, 150, 151, 153, 154, 158, 159, 161, 162, 165, 166, 180, 184, 189, 190, 191, 194, 195, 196, 199, 200, 204, 205, 206, 207, 210, 211, 215, 220, 222, 223, 229, 230, 231, 241, 242, 244, 246, 247, 272nn. 52, 59, 273nn. 71, 80, 275n. 107, 277n. 136, 278n. 13, 280n. 30, 288n. 125, 289n. 155
etymological root 78
postmodern 12, 14, 22, 28, 75, 115–20, 121, 247
rational 78, 135, 189
representational 26, 78, 79, 85, 195
theatre of representation 84
theatrical volume 85, 86
theology 132

Index

time 60, 66, 72, 123, 124, 145, 146, 150, 151, 159, 166, 236, 244
  as meaning of Being 57, 58
time-space 58, 60
Touraine, Alain 128, 251n. 32
Toynbee, Arnold 20, 21, 252n. 48
tradition(s) / traditional values 1, 11, 12, 20, 21, 28, 39, 54, 55, 56, 60, 61, 104, 128–33, 139, 144, 170, 226, 227, 228, 231, 237, 238, 244, 265n. 88
transcendence 35, 45, 48, 78, 87, 94, 95, 149, 189, 236, 256n. 64
transcendental ego 44, 45, 53
transcendental field (consciousness as) 45
transcendental reduction (*see* reduction, transcendental)
transfinite 90, 143–5, 147, 148, 149, 221, 223, 228, 229, 273n. 71
true world 33, 34, 37, 65, 108, 124, 160, 165, 175
truth 16, 17, 18, 32, 33, 34, 35, 37, 38, 58, 59, 69, 98, 100, 103, 106, 111, 114, 126, 127, 130, 134, 136, 170, 175, 204, 205, 209, 210, 212, 213, 214, 217, 218, 219, 228, 260n. 125, 262n. 17, 266n. 100, 267n. 118, 272n. 43, 277n. 136, 285n. 99
truthfulness 37
tyranny 129–30

Ueber-lieferung 110
Übermensch 40, 231, 287n. 123
Überwindung 113
uncertainty 88, 224, 244
unconscious, the 189–90, 282n. 61
undecidability 149, 162, 201, 202, 203, 206, 208, 209, 210, 234, 274n. 86, 286n. 105
unity 32, 33, 34, 37, 130, 175
unilateral distinction 177–9, 182, 193, 200, 201, 211
untimely, the 163, 164, 166, 233, 239, 276–7n. 132

valuation 8, 32, 36, 38, 39, 40, 41, 67, 68, 145, 157, 160, 170, 182, 223, 226, 235, 244
value 6, 7, 8, 9, 10, 11, 12, 22, 29, 30, 31, 32, 33, 34, 37, 38, 39, 40, 41, 42, 44, 45, 46, 47, 48, 49, 51, 52, 53, 65, 68, 79, 86, 115, 127, 131, 132, 133, 142, 143, 144, 148, 150, 151, 153, 156, 157, 160, 161, 176, 178, 182, 186, 194, 197, 201, 217, 218, 221, 223, 224, 229, 230, 231, 232, 235, 236, 239, 243, 244, 246, 260n. 117, 262n. 25, 279n. 25, 284n. 83
  exchange 92, 132, 141, 142, 143, 156, 157, 159, 197, 208, 216, 229, 231, 271n. 34
  fractal, viral, radiant 144
  Heidegger's critique of 66–8
  law of 91, 132, 133, 141, 142, 197, 199, 228, 271n. 34
  ontological structure of 48–9
  structural revolution of 141, 143
  surplus- 127
  use 92, 141, 156, 157, 216
  (*See also* sign(s), value)
values 11, 12, 15, 22, 27, 28, 31, 35, 36, 37, 39, 40, 41, 42, 43, 46, 48, 50, 53, 54, 66–8, 69, 73, 99, 108, 128, 129, 142, 144, 151, 170, 176, 179, 183, 186, 187, 194, 216, 218, 223, 228, 229, 231, 232, 241, 243, 244, 245, 279n. 25
  creation of 36, 40, 42, 52, 53, 54, 173, 186, 279n. 19
  highest 27, 30, 31, 32, 33, 34, 36, 37, 38, 39, 40, 41, 78, 83, 100, 106, 107, 126, 136, 160, 161, 170, 175, 234
  revaluation of 40, 41, 68, 176, 185
  transcendent 38, 39, 124, 175
  (*See also* sign(s), value)
Vattimo, Gianni 3–6, 10, 13, 14, 16, 18, 23–9, 75, 102–15,

116–20, 121, 125, 149–59, 160–4, 167, 169, 171, 172, 173, 174, 181, 182, 183, 184, 185, 187, 210–22, 223, 225, 228, 231, 232, 233, 234, 235, 236, 243, 244, 246, 247, 250nn. 12, 13, 14, 265–8nn., 272n. 43, 274–6nn., 277n. 136, 278n. 13, 280n. 30, 281nn. 39, 45, 282n. 52, 286nn. 108, 109, 286–8nn., 290nn. 156, 160, 163, 165, 291n. 3
Verwindung 28, 113, 114, 154, 159, 164, 167, 182, 210–22, 231, 246, 268nn. 126, 127
violence 92, 100, 112, 135, 151, 159, 212, 217, 218, 276nn. 120, 123
 and metaphysics 111, 112, 181, 212, 213, 216, 217, 231, 232, 267–8n. 122
 reduction of 158, 159, 186, 212, 213, 215–16, 216, 217, 218, 219, 220, 232, 290n. 163
virtual reality 133, 208, 229

Watergate 98
weak thought (il pensiero debole) 5, 16, 17, 103, 114, 154, 159, 211, 212, 213, 215, 216, 217, 220, 286n. 115
Webb, David 114
West 2, 75, 217
Westerners 152
Western civilization 1
Western culture 15, 21, 31, 35, 38, 39, 41, 54, 55, 63, 73, 136, 158, 160
Western metaphysics 72, 187, 211
Western philosophy 66, 104, 107
Western society 60, 152, 171
Western thought 7, 31, 32, 54, 63
Western world 15
White, Alan 31
Williams, James 4, 76, 196, 227, 239, 247, 261nn. 3, 9, 269n. 3, 278n. 13, 283nn. 66, 71, 72, 73

will to power 40, 65–8, 105, 175, 190, 260n. 117
Wittgenstein, Ludwig 122, 126, 222, 270n. 16, 289n. 141
World War, Second 14, 42, 123, 128

Yea-saying Ass 179
Yes and No 179
Young, Julian 160

Zurbrugg, Nicholas 133–4

Made in the USA
Lexington, KY
16 August 2010